LUTHER
ALIVE

Martin Luther and the Making of the Reformation

EDITH SIMON

HODDER AND STOUGHTON

Reproduced from the U.S. edition by arrangement with
Doubleday & Company, Inc., New York.

Printed in Great Britain for Hodder and Stoughton Limited, St. Paul's
House, Warwick Lane, London, E.C.4 by Compton Printing Ltd.

886852

270.6   12/1/69

POLAND

Frankfurt-
on-Oder

Torgau

Oder

ENBURG

AUSTRIA
Marburg

HUNGARY

Karlstadt

miles
0   50   100   150

N

LUTHER ALIVE

Books by Edith Simon

THE PIEBALD STANDARD

THE MAKING OF FREDERICK THE GREAT

THE CHOSEN

BITING THE BLUE FINGER

WINGS DECEIVE

THE OTHER PASSION

THE GOLDEN HAND

THE HOUSE OF STRANGERS

THE TWELVE PICTURES

THE SABLE COAT

THE GREAT FORGERY

THE PAST MASTERS

WALTER SIMON
in loving memory

I

THE BEGETTING

✳

II

PARTURITION

✳

III

THE WORD MADE FLESH

✳

CONTENTS

I. THE BEGETTING

✳

II. PARTURITION

✳

III. THE WORD MADE FLESH

❄

I

THE BEGETTING

*

1. Sensation, 1521

Doctor Martin Luther was a monk, a Black Friar of the Augustinian Hermits to be exact, articled professor of Biblical studies at the small-town University of Wittenberg in deepest Germany, and for the first thirty-five out of his thirty-seven years quite unknown outside that place except to a handful of specialists.

In the week beginning Monday 5 May 1521 the news broke that he was missing, presumed dead since having been kidnapped on the Sunday by a posse of raging horsemen, in transit through the wilds of the Thuringian Forest. The resulting uproar now boosted his name to truly international resonance.

"We are rid of him," a special agent of the Archbishop of Mainz wrote to his master, "but the people are in such a state about it we shall be lucky to escape with our lives if we don't look for him with lighted candles and bring him back."

"There will be a revolution," the Roman legate to the German Imperial Assembly predicted. "The people kiss his pictures and in the streets put their hands to their swords and gnash their teeth at me. I hope the Pope will give me plenary indulgence and look after my brothers and sisters if anything happens to me." There was a small, wry joke in this remark, not likely to cause much amusement at the Holy See, however. The subject of indulgence was a sore one: the pebble that had started the landslide.

"They speak of him as crucified," another high-placed commentator jested, hardly more felicitously. "I fear the chances are he will rise on the third day."

The pessimist was right, save in his time estimate. It was in fact three months before the vanishing professor gave unmistakable signs of life, and ten months until he was finally resurrected in the flesh to the public scene.

During that interval there lived with the garrison of a celebrated Thuringian mountain fortress a rough-and-ready knight just like his hosts Hans von Berlepsch and Burckhard Hund Herr von Altenstein, though named less picturesquely plain Squire George, black-bearded, bushy-haired, sturdy and swashbuckling, whom his own mother did not recognize for the pale, emaciated, tonsured cleric who had disappeared.

During that period, too, a civil war was avoided, a death sentence rendered infeasible; a novel national consciousness became cemented, a novel curb was placed upon imperial governance and novel bargaining factors became employable vis-à-vis the Holy See; thoughts were made facts, certain treatises were converted into blueprints, and preaching was turned into practice. Cloisters emptied, churches filled with unknown activity, forbidden books became established bestsellers for years to come, women shed the stigma of intrinsic unholiness that had adhered to them throughout the Middle Ages, the class divisions of society attained a different character and power politics got a different slant. The constant drain of gold from central and northern Europe across the Alps slowed down. The fishing trade, on which much mercantile power had been built up, received an ominous blow. Hard work and industry, from earthly blights specifically attaching to the underprivileged, were put in the way of acquiring sacred virtue; and princes saw their chance of a hitherto impossible autonomy. An idea materialized as an ideology. A movement forged far ahead of its leader on whom therefore henceforth inescapable pressures would be brought to bear—while at the same time that leader, hidden in abeyance, was forced to co-ordinate his thinking and to acquire both the habit of quick decisions and the capacity of standing by them if they turned out wrong. He made the personal acquaintance of the Devil and learned to equate periodical depressions with personal attack by the Devil— as good an antidote as any to melancholy—and to fight back, if all argument failed, with a good sound Christian fart. "That I may not be idle," meanwhile, he laid the foundations of a language and a literature, and made an opening for unheard-of developments of music in the future (though all he did for the visual arts was to sit for his improbable portrait).

For better or worse, an absolute reality whether one would approve or deplore it, the reformation of the Church, which had been canvassed throughout the West for close on two centuries, was finally set in motion at that juncture. In taking shape, it would emerge with rather a different look and different semantic sound to it from the expected: and that difference also was determined between May 1521 and March 1522. History is hindsight, clearing the wood that cannot be seen for trees, of the live and chaotic present.

What, then, did Doctor Martin Luther stand for at the moment of his abduction and rumoured assassination? To the papacy he stood for cosmic lèse majesté, treason against the Holy Universal Church, subversion of the kingdom of Christ and the apostolic monarchy, and a very serious threat to its temporal economy. To the Emperor—the Spaniard Holy Roman Emperor of the German Nation—he stood for all these too and on top of that for frustration and anarchy. Some of the three-hundred-odd sovereign units of the Empire shared that view; to the rest he stood for divinely authorized independence. To a rising middle class he stood for freedom from foreign interference and inroads. To a landless petty nobility he stood for reorganization of the state, with proper function restored to themselves; to the landless peasantry he stood for enfranchisement and equity. To orthodox theologians he stood for neo-primitive barbarism, to those of a progressive cast for dazzling revelation, to liberals in the middle for a tragic disappointment. To champions of education he was either a prophet of the millennium or the last word in philistinism, to pious hearts a fifth evangelist and second St. Paul or a hound of hell. To spiritual ennui, lassitude, and confusion he had brought a general revival of ardour and meaning. To friend and foe he had the glamour— fair or foul—of a hero. He was designated a bumptious alcoholic, a crabbed intellectual, a slimy hedonist, a monster resulting from the adulterous union of his mother with a demon, a reincarnation of St. John the Divine or alternatively of Hercules: "miracle-man," "pestilent boil," "tool of God," "tool of political intrigue," and so on and so forth.

In brief, the professor's basic propositions which formed the root of it all were these: one, that man is saved by faith alone; two, that faith is by divine grace only, merit an unearned boon; three, that every baptized Christian has access to God without intermediaries; four, that the papacy was not instituted by Jesus as claimed but a comparatively modern fiction; five, that if ecclesiastical authority refused to rectify flagrant ecclesiastical anomalies and abuses, the secular authorities had not only the right but the duty to see to this; six—and first and last and always—that the Bible comprised the sole, definitive record of God's purpose and commandments, in which everybody should be thoroughly instructed, while the man-made code of canon law was an obstructive, cancerous excrescence which spelt death unless it were cut away.

On these propositions Western Christendom was to be torn apart and wren hed into a new era, which retrospectively settled the preceding thousand years as a "Middle" Age between antiquity and modern times.

And only three weeks before the yet unrecognized turning point, any of it had been barely on the cards.

*

2. Vir Heroicus

Not three weeks before, on Tuesday 16 April, the man had entered the city of Worms—Town of the Dragon, Mother of Diets—in a two-wheeled cart and under no illusions.

The cart was equipped with a modest canopy and had been furnished free of charge by a member of the goldsmith's guild of Wittenberg, to which moreover the town council had added the loan of three horses and the university twenty gulden journey money. Never had he travelled in such style.

With him were a senior professor, a student of noble extraction, a fellow-friar acting as his obligatory travelling companion, and last but not least the imperial herald, burnished, plumed, infallibly beguiling in his ceremonial tabard with the great red eagle. Doctor Martinus was perfectly aware that the remarkable turn-out of gaping men, women, and children even at the most godforsaken villages en route was due to that element of pageantry. For at the townships where he halted and where those who came to meet him actually knew what it was all about, everyone was full of misgivings and monotonously intoned, "Remember Hus!"

The reminder was unnecessary.

All the world remembered Johann Hus, also a university professor, also in his time a traveller under safe-conduct from the Emperor, also hailed in his day as a man of God and national redress, also officially designated Arch-heretic—whose name now was disgraced by the scars of countless communities in Germany, a name to frighten naughty children with and send shivers of loathing down their elders.

Hus at the end of even such a journey as this had gone to the stake with the shameful paper crown on his head and had been burnt to ashes. That was a hundred years ago, but the repercussions were still loud and obnoxious.

There was one difference. Hus had been summoned to give an account of himself to a General Council of the Church, Doctor Martinus was scheduled to do so at the Diet or general assembly of secular government. But as he would be interrogated by a committee of theological experts, the difference was, to risk a pun, academic; and neither Luther nor anybody else fully appreciated it at that point.

Of course he was afraid, but not so much as he had been on lesser occasions in the past. There comes a point when custom dulls suspense, when the game of cat and mouse, drawn out too long, may become almost boring to the destined victim. He had got used to his apparent destiny, had come to terms with it, and knew his part. For he was by no means modest. Humble, yes: but being humble applied only in respect of the Deity and in abnegation of any personal merit or independence.

He knew himself the instrument of God, and he called this humility, while others gave it quite a different name. Of course he feared death like any creature, and like any person of imagination feared a hideously painful, hideously degrading death. But he was now ready for that as he had not been, at heart, on the way to Augsburg three years earlier. He had not been so sure then that he was right; they had made him sure since, beginning with their "silliness"—his word—at Augsburg. This time there was not going to be any silliness; with fifty doctors brought on against him under the management of two special papal nuncios they were likely to make sure of him this time.

The great thing was to make the most of martyrdom, to be heard and make a splash as he went under, to make the most godalmighty reek as he burnt. It was the inscrutable way of God to win his victories more often by the deaths of martyrs than by the agency of champions who lived out their span. Luther's own patron saint, St. Martin of Tours, was one of a very few exceptions to that rule.

The auspices for perishing to some purpose were distinctly good. Everybody who was anybody in the Empire would be at Worms, and the eyes of all the outer world were keenly focussed on the first Diet of the new reign. The young Emperor was on the spot—Charles V, beloved grandson of the shining Maximilian, whom Luther's hopes prefigured as the latest addition to the ranks of historic "god's-tools" like Cyrus, Themistokles, Alexander, David, Augustus, Constantine, Charlemagne, and possibly the present lord of Saxony, Elector Frederick III, surnamed the Wise. Though doubtless they would not meet face to face, the Emperor would hear what Luther had to say, directly and not at a long remove, cooled, over-condensed, and devitalized by distance. Whatever happened to him, it would be enacted within reach of the Emperor's immediate consciousness, not in some vague, hearsay zone of such a mighty monarch's uncomprehended dominions. The impression would, with any luck, be fresh and strong and fruitful.

It is one thing to expect the worst but quite another to see the expectation materialize.

Half-way between Wittenberg and Worms Luther and his friends were thrown into a state of panic as it was brought to their notice that, the imperial safe-conduct notwithstanding, the Emperor had already published a "mandate of sequestration" to impound Luther's books and have them burnt—the usual prelude to burning the author, usually at no great interval. Imperial couriers were everywhere, posting copies of the proclamation in all the towns.

They had it in black and white now, that the worst was coming.

"The Devil saw clearly the mood I was in when I went to Worms. Had I known as many devils would set upon me there as there were tiles on the roofs, I should have leapt among them with joy. I was undismayed and trembled at nothing—so foolish can God make a man!" But, in reminiscent vein such as men will adopt after some major surgical operation, Luther did himself less than justice. True valour is in overcoming tremulous dismay. For all the excellent tone of his spirit, his treacherous insides punctually played him up once again.

He fell ill with stomach cramps and dysentery, so severely that his fellow-travellers seriously feared for his life. They need not have worried; the man himself was certain even in his prostration that his hour would not strike so prematurely. Having enquired whether Luther suffered from syphilis—always the first, pertinent question in face of sickness except when it was caused by obvious injuries—the local medico prescribed bleeding and physick; Luther got some sleep, and kept going. The enforced rest, short as it was, had given him time to think, and as ever allowed collapse of morale around him to restore his own nerve: "Eigensinnissimus (stubbornissimus)," he rightly said, should have been his middle name. There was no cordial so potent to his system as other people's faintheartedness—unless it were other people's disapproval and antagonism.

He began to wonder whether the entire object of the precipitate "mandate" were not in fact *to* frighten him. It was not in the nature of great affairs, or of a new Emperor feeling his way in a strange country, to move with such abrupt decision. The Diet had been sitting since January, and the idea of bringing Luther to Worms for examination had been mooted as long ago as the previous November. Thus it had taken something like five months altogether for the order to be so much as formulated—he had heard about the Emperor's vacillation in the matter, and that the princes of the Empire in their conferences on it had all but come physically to blows on the floor of the Diet. (The Electors of Saxony and Brandenburg, admittedly traditional opponents, had had to be forcibly separated by the Archbishop of Salzburg, and the normally soft-spoken Elector Palatine had "bellowed like a bull," according to witnesses.) It showed that things were going in the right direction, at least insofar as increasing importance had accrued to his case.

The main programme of the Diet was a) to vote subsidies for the Emperor's projected journey to his coronation by the Pope in Rome, b) to review and revise the governance of the realm in the absence of the Emperor—who was King of Spain, King of Sicily, Archduke of Austria, Duke of Burgundy, to name only the foremost of his long string of suzerain titles, and therefore would spend very little of his time on visitations to the Empire, and c) to reorganize the imperial judicature so that justice might come to function again as over the last few decades it had pretty well ceased to do. A detail of supposedly abstract ecclesiastical moment, such as the teachings of one friar at a provincial university, normally was quite outside the business of the supreme legislative body of the realm: and here it had not only got a place on the agenda but was prolonging the session which had virtually completed its programme otherwise.

Luther's information came principally from his good friend Spalatin who was at Worms in his capacity of secretary to the senior Elector, Frederick the Wise of Saxony (or "Uncle Fred" to the Emperor and princes). From this and other sources, too, all sorts of warnings had come to him, to guard against poison, kidnapping, and diversion if he wished to reach Worms—not to mention mimic messages like the presentation to him of a picture of Savonarola, the Florentine Dominican who in living memory had been burnt for heresy like Hus, or the suspicious invitation to meet the Emperor's confessor secretly at, of all unlikely places, the fortress of Ebernburg which was the seat of the Emperor's biggest headache, the radical knighthood. What with the counsel of despair reaching Luther from the old Vicar-general of his Order, furthermore, and the reported chagrin (not less illogical) of the papal legate to the Diet that Luther had accepted the lure to his prospective undoing at Worms—a vaguely familiar pattern seemed to emerge.

It was the pattern of the fairytale: obstacles and trials sown by infernal machinations across the path of the poor but honest and pure-hearted hero, who as sure as fate would overcome, one way or another—the Teutonic folk mythology which was real and alive in every hill and dale, every stick and stone, bred in the marrow of every man brought up amongst its ubiquitous appearances. Could it be that the mandate of sequestration, publicized with such unusual efficiency, was part and parcel of an underhand campaign to keep Luther out of Worms? It could, indeed. Perhaps his sudden illness, even, had been the result of attempted poisoning: nothing more.

That was enough to put new heart into anybody.

If the opposition wanted so badly to put him off, they must be afraid of him; if they were afraid of him, the situation was more hopeful than he would have dared estimate.

"I am coming, my Spalatin!" he exulted, never able to keep his fingers off the pen for very long. "Charles' mandate I am sure was only meant to intimidate me. But Christ lives and we will enter Worms even be it through the gates of hell and against all the demons of the air. Please arrange a lodging for me."

The imperial herald wrote by the same post to the same effect, and the papal legate passed the news to Rome: "We are thunderstruck to hear that Martinus is coming after all, and that his journey appears to resemble a triumphal march." As foreign correspondents will, the legate was exaggerating; but he went on, "We are going to have the scoundrel slipped into the town as quietly as possible. I had hoped to get him confined incommunicado in the bishop's palace where I am staying with the Emperor, and to have only one overall question put to him—i.e. whether he is willing to recant. The Emperor and his confessor had agreed to this, but now I hear that the heretic is to be put up at the Augustinian monastery, under close surveillance to be sure, but required only to recant his theological errors without any reference to his attacks on the papacy. The Emperor is however sanguine that everything will go according to plan. I only hope he is right."

Luther had guessed correctly. Still he was taken aback to be met early in the morning on the last stretch of the journey by a cavalcade of some hundred cheering knights, come from Worms to bring him in. His feelings were mixed: such a welcome and the protection it afforded were an agreeable enough surprise, but he had not done his utmost all these months to dissociate himself from active political entanglement, especially with the rampageous petty nobility, to let himself become a detonator of civil disturbance now.

As the cavalcade with the eagle-decked herald in front approached the outer walls of the city, the watchman on the look-out tower blew his trumpet, without orders, in the signal reserved for the arrival of distinguished visitors. Worms was inured to fanfares, the town was bursting with distinguished personages, but the rumour had got about that the Saxon contingent of the Estates was expecting the Wittenberg monk to arrive today. It was 10 A.M., the hour of the mid-day meal, when the Imperial Council had reckoned the inhabitants would be deeply engrossed indoors. So they were, but the trumpet blast on this occasion proved capable of interrupting dinner. Everyone rushed out into the streets. There was no question of smuggling the heretic through unnoticed. There was no question of quietly securing him in the bishop's palace or the Augustinian cloister.

Eight of the blatant horsemen escorted him into town, the rest stayed outside—which could be interpreted as one liked. Even so had they and their kind camped outside Frankfurt during the imperial election, in tacit menace to ensure election of their favoured candidate. On the other hand, there really was no room inside; all available accommodation was already overcrowded. The town possessed two inns among its serried, corbelled, timbered houses, and everywhere was crammed with the German representatives and their retinues, up to the attics.

A space had been made for Doctor Martinus at the hospice of the Knights of St. John, where some of the overflow of Elector Frederick's suite in the Swan Inn next door were lodged and could let him share their chamber, already sleeping two. Such was the press in the streets that it took the two-wheeled cart an hour or more to get there.

By the count of an agent of the papal legate Girolamo Aleandro, at least two thousand people surged about the cart, out of a total population of at most seven thousand. There was no mistaking the excitement—even by the centre of attraction—for being caused by either herald or horsemen such as were two a penny here the while the Emperor was in residence.

"Martinus has of course spoilt everything by his coming," Aleandro wrote off the same day—the day on which the period of Luther's safe-conduct to Worms would have expired. "When he alighted, a priest threw his arms round him, touched his garments three times with his hand, and went away exulting as if he had handled a relic of the greatest of saints. I expect it will soon be said he works miracles!"

The papal legate and agents did not understand German, or they would have known that the people here were calling Luther "wonder-man" already, and "holy doctor"; they would have realized that to the tune of unexceptionable chanting the words of a blasphemous, popular *German Litany* went:

"Christ hear the Germans. Christ hear the Germans. From evil counsellors deliver Charles, O Lord. From poison on the way to Worms deliver Martin Luther, O Lord. Suffer not thyself, Lord, to be crucified afresh. Purge Aleander, O Lord. The nuncios working against Luther at Worms, smite from heaven. O Lord Christ, hear your Germans."

No linguistic accomplishments were required to comprehend the drift of "very wagonloads" of pamphlets, tracts, broadsheets—illustrated with cartoons that showed the Pope as an ass playing the bagpipes or Luther with a halo and a dove above his head, among a spate of kindred graphic felicities—which sold out no sooner than the ink was dry. Nobody knew where were the underground presses from which these productions poured right under the noses of supreme authority, and which preserved their clandestine elusiveness forever. ("Printing," said Martin Luther, "is God's latest and best work.") Booksellers continued to risk life and limb and salvation, constantly replenishing the market with the works of Luther, in the teeth of the imperial mandate of sequestration.

"The other day a Spaniard tore up [a Lutheran publication] and trampled it in the mire. Then a chaplain of the Emperor and two Spaniards set upon a man with sixty copies of *The Babylonian Captivity*

[Luther's climactic attack on sacerdotalism in Catholic teaching].
The people came to the rescue and the assailants had to take to their
heels. Another time a mounted Spaniard chased one of our people,
who just managed to escape through a doorway, forcing the Spaniard
to pull up so suddenly that he fell off his horse and could not get up
again till a German lifted him."

For the Romanists the scene was a classic nightmare, even though
Worms was teeming with the Emperor's Spanish guards "galloping on
their mules across the market place so that everybody has to scramble
out of the way: such is our freedom!"

Aleandro complained that anti-Lutheran publications had no sale
at all. To be sure, few of these were in the German language, which
Luther used concurrently with the Latin to which orthodox literati
mostly still confined themselves.

The atmosphere at Worms was not calculated to deter the representatives of the Estates from their novel attention to public opinion
which had so scandalized the lamented, glamorous Emperor Max before
his death.

"So this Luther as he stepped from the wagon," Aleandro pursued,
"looked about him with demoniacal eyes and said, 'God will be with
me!'" The Beast (as they called him in Rome).

Among the heaving crowd voices were heard asking for his blessing,
extolling the happiness of the mother who had borne such a son,
opining that he looked too young and much too thin, the sainted
doctor. The Beast and sainted doctor was nearing forty, an age when
many a man had grandchildren, and they should have seen him last
year! when he was "entirely skin and bone" whereas now his friends
were relieved to note him on the way to a more "becoming plumpness."

Luther might set little store by crowd reactions in general and repose
small trust in their constancy; but flesh and blood could not fend off
some answering elation. "My Palm Sunday!" he was careful to curb it.

"Then after dinner all the world ran in to see him," Aleandro
finished bitterly. A stream of callers flowed through the dining room
of the St. John's hospice, but again it was not so bad as all that:
there was hardly anybody above the rank of count apart from the
Duke of Brunswick and the sixteen-year-old Landgrave of Hesse—the
latter prematurely eager to discuss a passage from *The Babylonian
Captivity* concerning the possibility of divorce on the grounds of the

husband's impotence. Though Luther did not let this fascinating conversation prosper, the noble youth on leaving shook hands with him as man to man and boldly wished him luck—an encounter so loaded with prophetic signposts that only life, not fiction, could have let them stand.

Luther possessed a rich diversity of gifts and insights, but political acumen was not among them. He had entered politics, but he did not recognize the fact, except in that his good cause obviously had become intertwined with various strands of current affairs, unworthy as well as worthy ones. He saw himself as doggedly pursuing the single track of religious regeneration, which of course did impinge on all aspects of earthly life; he did not clearly appreciate that this had brought him into the thick of finite actuality. He knew it, and he knew it not, that he was laying down principles right and left which entailed immediate, particular, revolutionary application. For he yet had nothing to do with such application; he was yet merely asserting and defending the principles. It did not escape his intelligence that all kinds of material self-interest were culling encouragement from his spiritual message, just as a contrary self-interest combatted the message tooth and nail. But to his mind the whole issue was a matter of ultimate, transcendent self-interest—namely, the salvation of mankind in the victory of God; and if God chose to bait his divine hook with worldly appetizers, fine. The human, practical approach had proved Luther's own forte ever since he had experienced revelation; God was properly the master technician in the field.

He was quite aware that the German Estates wanted liberation from Rome: that the princes wanted integrity of power and revenue, the merchants and manufacturers influx, rather than perpetual outflow, of money into the country; that the German knighthood wanted to cease being a living anachronism. He was himself one of the people, which was crying out for internal peace and effective judicial administration; he was one of the scholars who strove to free thought from speculative verbiage, one of the paladins of education, one of the writers awake to the potentialities of the live and spoken language as against the petrified conventions of a dead and dusty; he was not behind in the nation-wide clamour for national recognition. But all these cravings happened to square with the correct Gospel Truth, with liberty of conscience, and with godly conduct. So?

So he did not give too much thought to the intricacies of diplomatic process in which he was being tossed up and down, as he did not feel himself tossed and what you do not know can't shake you. No more than he took credit for himself did he give credit to any force but God for his survival even so far. And no more than anybody else, including the highest, mightiest, and best-equipped with news facilities, did he have any accurate idea what was really going on behind the scenes of any given moment—nor very often afterwards, for that matter. At the best of times, which in point of communications his time was not, panoramic perspectives take a good while to develop.

Luther's position as he saw it was plain. He had framed certain propositions on the basis of which the Holy Roman Catholic or Universal Church of which he was a devout member should reform itself as long since proposed and agreed. Some of his propositions had been conceded, others declared unacceptable. He for his part conceded the human element of ever-latent error and from the first had declared himself most willing to yield to proof that he was wrong. The vested interests of his Church however would not have it so and demanded that he acknowledge himself in error without argument: that the Pope said Luther was wrong *was* proof.

He must recant.

He would be glad to recant if only the authorities would tell him where he was wrong.

Never mind about that; he must recant.

He would be very glad to. . . .

Although from a scarcely perceptible puff the thing had grown into a howling storm, the drift of it was unchanged. Recant. Prove to me that I am wrong.

The Church was a gigantic institution with infinite concrete resources, he was alone and had only his conscience. Yet, having found it necessary to go into general mobilization against one small conscience, the only proof the Church had produced was that it had cast him out. Before he could be liquidated, however, excommunication from the spiritual community had to be complemented by the secular ban. To accomplish this technicality, which had unexpectedly hung fire, was the purpose of bringing him to Worms.

All Luther knew about the unremitting tug of war in the Imperial Council as to precisely how his case should be finally handled, was that even yet the parties were hard at it. All he knew about those parties was that one was roughly for and one roughly against giving him a genuine hearing. There were extremists, moderates, and aspiring coalitionists on both sides; he had no inkling of their motivations other than the broad assumption that God and the Devil were respectively working in them. He who could differentiate with lofty ease the most subtle shades of the philosophical spectrum, found the political distinctions between Romanists, papalists, imperialists, et cetera, unprofitably esoteric. What had been good enough for Christ was good enough for him: he that is not for me is against me.

Blessedly simple, but not so good when all at once it came to the point.

Having had the sacred satisfaction and distraction of ministering to a dying knight (who could have sent for someone else from the present superabundance in Worms of unimpeachable priests, instead of an excommunicate heretic), Luther before dinner next morning was suddenly notified to make himself ready to appear before the Emperor and Estates at four o'clock.

So much for his hopes of a closed committee of impartial experts.

He was on no account to attempt discussion but must strictly confine himself to answering the questions put to him.

So much for his hopes.

Materially, there was nothing further he could do to prepare for the daunting occasion than having his tonsure freshly clipped and enlarged to the limit of baldness. This did not kill much of the six hours' waiting time.

The streets were no emptier than yesterday. They were more impassable, as the waiting crowds were not in movement. To attempt forging through them would make him late. He was taken by a roundabout way to the bishop's palace where the Emperor and papal emissaries lodged and the Diet met. Here, in company with his escort of imperial marshall, imperial herald, several Electoral-Saxon councillors and his accustomed legal counsel Professor Schurpff, not to mention a breezy to and fro of idling foot soldiers, he was left to kick his heels for two more hours. At last he was called and ushered into a low-ceilinged chamber too small for admittance without "most rudely" jostling the caucus of princes, clerics, and foreign dignitaries who filled it to capacity.

Curiosity veiled with dignity, they watched his entry and obeisance, in deep silence. Again his large, dark, sinisterly flashing eyes were much remarked on, as they swept round the assembly, trying to locate his own, prudent sovereign and perhaps another familiar face or two before his gaze must settle on the sacrosanct lord of them all, and his concentration battle against the awkward posture—one knee lightly bent—prescribed for the duration of the interview. He tried to look pleasant and confident.

"The idiot," Aleandro recounted, "entered laughing, and while he stood before the Emperor constantly moved his head about. . . . The Emperor said immediately he saw him, 'That one will never make a heretic of me!' . . . It is clear that he is too uncouth and uncultivated to have written the books ascribed to him. . . ."

This was a thoughtless slip on Aleandro's part, as the case against Luther rested on his books, a pile of which formed the corpus delicti in front of his official interrogator, Dr. Ecken of Trier. Dr. Ecken opened the proceedings by asking, first in Latin, then in German, whether Luther owned to having written these, and secondly whether he were ready to renounce them or part of them. Professor Schurpff alertly vindicated his electoral retaining fee, with a shout from the defendant's side, for a detailed description of the exhibit. About twenty titles were read, and the grinning idiot of Aleandro's report acknowledged them his works. But his voice for all its long training failed him. He was hardly audible at first, almost "as if he were frightened or awed," the delegate of the city of Frankfurt noted with obtuse wonder at the "German Hercules," whose compelling oratory was a byword.

Perhaps in that low, packed courtroom the acoustics were poor. A brazen heretic or second Elijah, either one, surely would not be abashed by the pale, youthful, hieratic figure on the throne above him; the fabulous aura of Caesarian glory, Habsburg race, and Spanish pride surrounding the heir to it all, surely could not impress him, a low-born mendicant friar, who thought nobody was great but Jesus Christ; the Spanish grandees and halberdiers, the stern-visaged and resplendently attired cardinals, and the hulking German nobles of whom Luther himself had said they would gobble up a peasant for breakfast any day of the week—none of these would tie the tongue of Martin Luther, surely.

Well, they did not tie his tongue; he answered, did he not—only not very audibly. At all events he kept his wits about him well enough to see, not only that the second question might be regarded either as a trap or as an eleventh-hour loophole, but also that it offered him a chance to state his views, after all.

He said, "This touches God and his Word. This affects the salvation of souls. In this sort of context Christ said, 'He who denies me before men, him will I deny before my father.' To say too little or too much would be equally dangerous. I beg you, give me time to think about it."

The request plus the comments of the German representatives and Italian advisers had to be translated for the Emperor, who spoke only French and Flemish, and the Emperor's comments had to be translated into Latin and German for the benefit of the assembly. With a rider expressing astonishment that a doctor of theology should require further time to think over what he had expressly come all the way here to do, the request was granted. But Luther was to have one day only, and would not be allowed to read his answer from written notes.

The last condition was a shrewd thrust. Luther to the end of his life felt unhappy without a manuscript to hold on to—even if in the event his speech as actually delivered radically diverged from the written draft. It was a staple anxiety dream of his that he stood in the pulpit without copy. But at least, now that he knew what was wanted of him and was beginning to form an idea how he might exploit it, he would be able to sit down and compose his statement with due care, even if he must thereafter leave it at home.

The acoustics on Thursday 18 April were much better. They were marvellous, by all accounts.

Word had got round of the second hearing in good time, so that there was no resisting the pressure of the Estates for a plenary session. The second hearing therefore was held in the great hall of the bishop's palace, which was so thronged that hardly anyone besides the Emperor could sit, many having queued up since morning to make sure of getting in at all. Princes contended for standing room, and Luther with his counsellors was forced against all protocol to stand among the noble lords. People stood up on the stone benches along the walls. "It was very warm," Luther would remember, "on account of the crowd, and the torches," for, again summoned for four o'clock, he had been kept waiting until darkness fell and artificial light was needed.

The torches wedged flaring and smoking in their iron brackets, the throne was brought in, and the Emperor followed with his confessor and his chief minister and former tutor who still had to sleep in the same room as he at night; the guards amid subdued glint and chime of metal took up their stations by the door. The exalted audience, cased in hairy, becoming plumpness and layers of substantial finery, began to perspire and chafe already under the heat.

Dr. Ecken—a big, imposing man—stepped forward and repeated the unanswered question of the day before: was Luther ready to renounce all or any of the books which he had confessed to be his?

Luther was in excellent voice. He answered that his books were not all of one sort but fell into three classes: first, the purely theological ones, which had never been officially condemned—he could not retract them; second, his writings on "the evil lies and incredible tyranny" of the papacy, especially as perpetrated against the German nation— he could not retract these either, without opening the door to worse; third, his attacks on individual opponents—these he would admit to have been unbecomingly violent sometimes, and he was sorry for the manner but could not retract the matter.

There were murmurs and ejaculations, of various tenor; the Emperor's consummate deportment broke down at one point, as he jumped up and shouted, "No!" at the interpreter.

Luther had herewith created his opportunity to turn his stipulated yea-or-nay of an answer into a speech. Everybody wanted to hear what would come next. Straight as an arrow and as swift he went to the crux of the long struggle.

"When Christ stood before Annas, he said, 'Produce witnesses.' If our Lord, who could not err, made this demand, why may not a worm like me ask to be convicted of error by proof from the prophets and the Gospels? I will accept the proof from a simple child, only let it be given. If I am shown my error, I will be the first to throw my books into the fire. There has been talk of the dissensions which my teaching has brought. I can answer only in the words of the Lord, 'I came not to bring peace but a sword.' If our God be so stern, let us beware lest we bring down on ourselves a deluge of wars and catastrophes—lest the reign of this noble youth, Charles, be doomed by an inauspicious start. Take warning from the examples of Pharaoh, the King of Babylon, the kings of Israel!" Commotion. "I do not say this because I think that great lords like yourselves need me to instruct you, but because I dare not shirk my duty to this country. I must walk in the fear of the Lord, for me there is no other way."

Dr. Ecken, ignoring the intimation of fire and brimstone: "Ah, Martin, you have not described your works sufficiently. Let me do it

for you: the earlier were bad and the later ones worse. Your plea to
rest on Scriptural authority alone is the one always made by heretics.
You do nothing but parrot the fallacies of Wyclif and Hus. How will
the Jews, how will the Turks rejoice to hear of the Christians discussing whether they have been wrong all these centuries! Martin, how
can you believe that you are the only one to understand the meaning of
the Bible? Would you put your judgment above that of so many famous
men and claim that you know more than they all? You have no right
to call in question the most holy orthodox faith, instituted by Christ
the perfect lawgiver, proclaimed throughout the world by the apostles,
sealed by the red blood of the martyrs, confirmed by the sacred Councils,
defined by the Church which all our fathers believed in unto death
and handed on to us as an inheritance, and which nowadays we are
forbidden to discuss lest there be no end of wrangling. So cease from
trying to turn this into a disputation on articles of faith to which you
are committed unconditionally. For the last time I ask you, Martin—
will you now make a plain answer, without hidden horns or quibbles:
do you or do you not repudiate your books and the errors they contain?"

It was the finish. At least he had tried. Luther took breath. "Very
well, your Majesty and Highnesses, since that is what you wish, I will
give a simple answer, without horns, or teeth either. Unless I am proved
to be wrong by the testimony of the Scriptures or by incontrovertible
reasoning—for I cannot bow merely to the authority of either popes or
Councils, since it is known that they have often erred and contradicted
one another—until this be done my conscience is prisoner to the Word
of God. I cannot and will not recant, for to go against conscience is
neither right nor healthy. Here I stand, I cannot do otherwise."

The sweat was visibly running down his face—on account of the
crowd, and the torches, to be sure. Someone cried out, "You have done
enough, monk, you have done well!" for each time he had spoken
first in German and then repeated his address in Latin; but he did so
again now nonetheless. Concluding, as he was wont to end his sermons
at home, "God help me. Amen," he raised his arms with hands out-
spread in the traditional gesture of the winner at a tournament, and
then stood silent.

For a moment there was no sound. Uproar followed.

They admired courage above anything—as who does not—these
fire-eaters and gobblers of peasants for breakfast, these arrogant and
honour-ridden, noble braves in velvet clothing, and their sedentary

opposite numbers from the strapping Free Towns; the great prelates, too, with their self-same blue-blooded origins and itching fists, their ambivalent tastes, divided loyalties, and twinned cynicism and relig-iosity—insofar as they were of German nation and language.

The Spaniards and Italians were only pained and irritated by the want of style and breeding of the "mangy monk" come to spout stale redundancies in these august precincts. They hissed the performance and called out, "Al fuego! into the fire with him!"

But the Germans, milling numbers of them, delightedly took up the gesture of victorious chivalry, and stamped round cheering, which presently they interspersed with threatening growls and rattling of swords as they misinterpreted the Emperor's sign of dismissal, thinking Luther was to be placed under arrest. Luther shouted, "Peace! I am only being escorted!" But they came with him all the same, an avalanche of enthusiastic tumult rushing him on into the other crowds outside who followed suit and saw him safely if dishevelled back to the House of the Knights of St. John. To his anxious friends there—who, not being covered by safe-conducts, were under orders to lie low—he "stretched out his hands and exclaimed with a beaming face, 'I am through! I have got through!'" as one of them wrote to Nuremberg on the instant: in a letter dated only nine o'clock that evening.

Yes, that was Thursday. But tomorrow was another day. Elector Frederick the Wise, Luther's lord and patron, retiring without éclat to his tavern, damped Spalatin's euphoria with the pedestrian observation, "Martinus spoke wonderfully well: in Latin and in German! But I think he goes too far for me." It was a straw in the wind.

By Friday morning the majority of his princely colleagues had slept on their spontaneous emotional response, and simmered down con-siderably.

The seven Electors of the Holy Roman Empire of the German Nation were the real territorial magnates and de facto powers of the lands of Germany, which made up the largest physical unit in Europe but lacked any effective political unity. The Emperor did not possess the realm; it possessed him for a venerated but in practice much restricted figurehead, who had no hereditary claim. The Emperor was *elected,* by the said greater princes of the nation, the hereditary sovereigns of Saxony, Bohemia, Brandenburg, and the Rhenish Palatinate, and the

Archbishops of Mainz, Cologne, and Trier, who thus had the title of
Electors. Their feudal antecedents as immediate subordinates and
frontier guardians to the imperial crown were commemorated by the
titular offices of imperial butler, steward, marshall and so forth; but
they had acquired almost complete independence by means of generic
immunity to the charge of treason. Alone in Germany their territories
were held intact against perpetual fission by the law of primogeniture; and in between elections also it was the Electoral College or
"Union" which maintained the nearest approximate to a central government. More often than not the King of Bohemia was identical with
the Emperor (notably when the Emperor was a Habsburg) so that
his electoral function was invalidated. The Saxon Elector, who in the
person of Frederick III, the Wise, had been in office all of thirty-five
years, ranked senior of the remaining six.

But they ranked second of the three Estates. The clergy formed
the first Estate; the higher nobility came next, and below them stood
a conglomerate of Free Towns and Free Knighthood—towns and
knights, that is, who did not owe allegiance to any intermediate lords
between themselves and the imperial crown. Thus at the Imperial Diet
the archbishops and bishops represented the clergy, the princes, dukes,
and landgraves represented themselves, lesser nobility and unattached
towns sent delegations. Above them all, however, rose the symbol of
empire itself, the anointed Emperor, soul of fealty, fountain of honours,
mana of the state and only legitimate warlord, wielding still a numinous
power out of all proportion to his actual dominion. Edicts were promulgated in his name and seldom if ever counter to his influence, though
nevertheless they had first to be ratified by the Estates as a whole, and
the Emperor's will alone did not necessarily carry the decision.

It took experience and a cool head to ride the Diet and keep
steering, watchful against foreign piracy moreover, with a view to
port—any kind of port. For every bracing peak of outright drama there
were vast stretches of tediously rolling swell. And then you might be
stranded anyway, or sunk without trace, to no purpose.

On Friday 19 April Emperor Charles, fifth of that name in succession
to Charlemagne, bade the German princes to a conference first thing
in the morning, asked what they proposed to be done about the heretic,
and when they hedged drew out a little speech he had written all alone,
and which he now read to them, in French. He was twenty-one years

old, very earnest, with a deceptively adenoidal look, besetting problems, and complex sensibilities wherein Luther had got him altogether on the raw.

"I am descended from a long line of Christian emperors of this noble German nation, and of the Most Catholic kings of Spain, the archdukes of Austria, and the dukes of Burgundy. They were all faithful to the death, to the Church of Rome, and defended the Catholic faith and the honour of God. I am resolved to follow in their steps. One single friar who goes counter to all Christianity for a thousand years must be wrong. Therefore I am resolved to stake my lands, my friends, my body, my blood, my life, and my soul. Not only I, but you of this noble German nation, would be forever disgraced if by our negligence not only heresy but the very suspicion of heresy were to endure. After having listened yesterday to the obstinate assertions of Luther, I regret that I have so long delayed in proceeding against him and his false teaching. I will have nothing more to do with him. He may have his safe-conduct for returning home, but without preaching or making any disturbances. I shall now institute proceedings against him as a notorious heretic, and herewith ask you to declare yourselves."

It was a touching document in its own sincere way, and absolutely devastating in its effect upon his audience. The princes trooped off noticeably green about the gills—or "corpse-hued," as the fashionable adjective had it. They had drawn the intended inference—a threat of excommunication by association. Although the ban of Church and state was not what it used to be, having been employed too indiscriminately and too often in the more recent past, the threat retained considerable deterrent force. For a prince with all his dominions to be placed under interdict meant that he was laid wide open to attack, spoliation, and dethronement, even should he in the event manage to counteract the economic sanctions which were implicit in the measure.

In the afternoon of the 19th the Legate Aleandro ascertained that all six Electors had decided to declare against Luther.

In the night of 19–20 April two placards appeared, on the door of the town hall and in other public places, one designed to shake Luther ("You are condemned by the Pope. You are condemned by the Emperor. Frederick also will condemn you and spew you out. O you fool Luther! You have the effrontery to harp on old errors without

finding anything new to say for yourself!"), one designed to shake
Luther's enemies.

"We, four hundred knights, have sworn not to abandon the just
man Luther, and to declare war on the princes and the Romanists,
particularly the Archbishop of Mainz. I may write poorly but intend
great destruction. With eight thousand men we shall fight. *Bundschuh,
Bundschuh, Bundschuh!"*

The *Bundschuh*—tie-shoe, footgear of the common man—was the
emblem of peasant revolt, which more than once in recent decades
had wrought bloody havoc; the footloose petty knighthood was the
endemic plague of the land. A vaunted alliance of the two was well
designed indeed to terrify. There were all those knights encamped outside the ramparts, and the populace within had shown already where
its sympathies lay.

The luckless Archbishop of Mainz whom the placard singled out
(as had fate singled him out to be an unwilling lever in the whole
Luther affair) lost no time in sending his brother, the Elector of Brandenburg, to the Emperor, with a most urgent recommendation that Luther
be granted another hearing, this time before theological experts. The
Emperor refused. This was early in the morning of the 20th. Not many
hours later, the combined Estates submitted a petition to the Emperor,
endorsing that of the Hohenzollern brothers; and in the afternoon the
promised electoral declaration was seen to bear only four signatures
instead of six as confidently expected. The Elector of Saxony and the
Elector Palatine had after all thought better of it.

The Emperor was no fool, his advisers were not fools. "Uncle Fred's"
proved reputation for incorruptibility and unpredictability obviously
did not place him beyond manipulation and calculation. A man's neck,
if he will stick that out, stops at the shoulders.

Elector Frederick might be loth to lose the professor who had made
his university a paying proposition, he might have been allowing his
court fool to caricature "the little red-hats" alias prelates at the Diet
during intermissions—but he hated armed conflict ("You will only lose
six men." "One would be too many."), and for himself remained
devoted to the orthodox faith. He had already put it on record that,
while believing that Luther had been hard done by and that Luther had
every right to a fair trial such as was not denied even to parricides,
he, the Elector, was in no way *bound* to the interests of a subject of
his. Attempted bribery or coercion unfailingly made Frederick dig his

heels in; but if left alone he was quite liable to sit still and do nothing. His abstention from the desired vote was no doubt characteristic: probity would not allow him to declare explicitly against Luther, but it did not compel him to act for Luther.

Had the Emperor known it, Frederick indeed was writing to his brother who had been nagging him to take positive action in Luther's behalf: "Were it in my power, I should be quite willing to help Martinus secure his rights. . . . But I think he will inevitably be laid under the ban, and in future anybody who so much as hints that he sympathizes with him will be classed as a heretic too. Doubtless God will not forsake a just cause." Over to God. Of course Frederick had the power, then as before and afterwards, but he was tired of the whole thing. For him, it had been going on four or five years now, and not for want of other business.

Everybody had other business, galore. Everybody tired of Diets rather easily—that was why Diets so often broke up inconclusively. In this instance, the proper business of the Diet was on the contrary already done. Emperor Charles himself was on the brink of war in Italy and his presence was urgently required in the Netherlands, his family affairs which were ipso facto grave affairs of state cried out for immediate attention, in Hungary and France and Portugal and Sweden and in England; and his heart was in Spain, his financial life pulse in America. More disciplined than many members of the Diet, the Emperor decided on a policy of procrastination.

Emperor Charles kept the Estates waiting two days before answering their petition to the effect that his own opinion was unchanged as was also his intention to have no further dealings with the heretic, but that he would give them three days' grace to persuade Luther to recant, on their own. It was a masterly move. The Emperor thus got the credit of magnanimity, the appearance of impeccable reasonableness and of having infinite time to sit it out against the flagging representatives, and that without any slur on his valour and determination, or ultimate risk, either. For either Luther would finally recant or the imperial edict of condemnation would go through. Either way, that would be that.

"All Germany is in revolt. Nine tenths shout, 'Luther!' as their warcry, the tenth shouts, 'Death to the court of Rome!'" So ran another frantic despatch of Aleandro. It had little basis in fact: Worms was not "all Germany," and the very selective sample of national representation was melting away, quietly going home. For every loud-mouthed ruffian in the street there were a dozen respectable burghers sitting tight, on the fence. There had been no further communications signed *Bundschuh;* an anonymous scrap of paper found in the Emperor's quarters, with the tag, "Vae terrae ubi puer rex est," Woe to the land whose king is a child, was beneath notice. The Legate Aleandro was hysterical, and yet he was right. All along, since 1517, it had been the ungrounded fears of the papacy which had brought to pass just what it feared.

Emperor Charles was anything but hysterical. He appraised the situation sanely and correctly, but he was wrong.

Luther in a manner was granted what he had always asked for: a hearing in committee before experts, under rather more considerate treatment than meted out to him hitherto. He was treated almost as an equal, rather than as a recalcitrant yokel, by the experts— who, however, were all a priori hostile ones—and offered concessions which even a year ago would have satisfied him as perfectly genuine reasons for climbing down. Jokes were bandied, tears were shed—but still his examiners failed to prove their point *from the Bible,* still fell back always on papal infallibility as such, and so did not succeed in persuading him to recant without conviction.

The talks of 23, 24, and 25 April were far more arduous for Luther than his tour de force of the 18th; but they went on behind closed doors and were unlikely to stir imagination outside. From every point of view they were an anticlimax. The Diet continued to diminish.

On the 25th deadlock was conceded, and in the evening Luther received his congé. He was informed that the Emperor now had no choice but to prosecute, though in accordance with the Emperor's initial promise Luther should return to Wittenberg under safe-conduct. Luther knew as well as anybody else that the Council of Constance, which had condemned Hus, had laid it down for the guidance of the then Emperor and others in the future that safe-conduct granted to heretics was not binding.

Though he knew what was coming, Luther again felt the shock of the news when come it did. He asked to be excused for a moment, went out of the room, then returned to acknowledge the imperial order in due, smooth, mannerly form. He topped this by sitting down to sum up the sequence of events for the benefit of his friend the town apothecary of Wittenberg, Lucas Cranach, as follows:

"I was asked, 'Are these books yours?' 'Yes.' 'Do you recant?' 'No.' 'Then get out!'" Well, it was no lie.

He said goodbye to the sick knight to whom he had administered the last rites and who had recovered.

On the morning of 26 April, having made a hearty meal of toast and malmsey, the condemned man left the town of Worms, unnoticed and unsung.

"I don't want to go against God, but I don't want to get into trouble with the Emperor either," were Elector Frederick's last recorded words before his own departure.

Aleandro, in calmer spirits, and the Emperor's ministers were working on the final draft of the imperial ban.

"Luther has slung mud at marriage, disparaged confession, and denied the body and blood of our Lord. He makes the sacraments depend on the faith of the recipient. He is pagan in his denial of free will. This devil in monk's clothing has brought together hoary errors into one stinking puddle laced with inventions of his own. He denies the power of the keys and encourages the laity to wash their hands in the blood of the clergy. His teaching incites to rebellion, schism, war, murder, robbery, arson, and the extermination of Christianity. He lives the life of a beast. He has burnt the canon law. He despises alike the papal ban and the sword. He does more harm to the civil than to the ecclesiastical power [German Estates please note]. We have laboured with him, but he recognizes only the authority of Scripture, which he twists to his own convenience. We have given him twenty-one days, dating from April the twenty-fifth. Thereafter Luther is to be regarded as a convicted heretic. When the time is up, no one is to harbour him. His followers also are to be outlawed. His books are to be expunged from the memory of man."

"Praise God for giving us such a devout emperor," Aleandro effervesced, Charles having approved the wording. "May God preserve him in all his holy ways, who has already earned perpetual glory and eternal reward on high. I was just about to recite a paean from Ovid when it occurred to me that this is a religious occasion. Therefore: blessed be the Holy Trinity."

The Emperor held back his signature until the Diet was quite reduced to a reliable rump of yes-men. Then the edict of outlawry went through. But the publication of it was muted by the repercussions of the news meanwhile received, that on a detour to visit relations in a small mountain village of the Thuringian Forest Friar Martin had been ambushed by persons unknown, and at the point of drawn crossbows hauled brutally from his tumbril, out of sight of his escort. The body was said to have been found down a salt mine not far from the scene of the crime.

The calculated anticlimax had been spoiled. The lingering, unspectacular exit of the "single friar" after his great solo was more than made up for: now the reverberations, and with them the heroic image, swelled to legendary proportions. People that had never seen, heard, or even particularly thought of Martin Luther, now wept for him and loved him who had testified for the indomitable human spirit, against the mightiest powers upon earth, at Worms.

Now his story really spread, well and truly and in every tongue.

✳

3. The Sources of the Image

Inside the public figure, the living model for the icon and the caricature—what was he like?

The outer man at all events should not be difficult to pin down. He was of middle height and, true to a regional type, "black like my parents," who were of Thuringian peasant stock, swarthy, round-skulled, with dark hair and deep-set eyes. So far the description would fit many; yet it is the distinguishing feature of Luther's eyes which immediately worries us that want our information to come with a certificate of objectivity. In the son the family eyes were described as quite extraordinarily alight, demonically so by his enemies and radiant with endearing genius by his friends. But how can we trust descriptions that one and all date only from a time when Luther was already famous? when, in other words, there had to be—and all along to have been—something outwardly remarkable about the man?

Unfortunately there is no such thing as truly objective vision. Even the most honest portrait cannot but partake of the subjective reactions of the portraitist; even the inanimate camera will traduce, flatter, or score an outright miss, more often than not. More than any other feature the "expression" of a person's eye—a mere gelatine ball whose contours cannot themselves move or alter—lies in the eye of the beholder.

And yet—when the eyes are closed or blind, the human face becomes deficient, enigmatic. This is a proof if you like, that there is more to the gelatine ball than can be physically assayed. But what?

Objectivity, our seal of veracity, resides only in the concrete and measurable, it would seem. But everything is not concrete and measurable; far from it. Concrete facts and tangible data are only ingredients of truth, scattered in disorder until the subjective mind is allowed to bring them into cohesion. Truth, it has been demonstrated over and over, is what we make it, and the value of it to ourselves does not rest in a final absoluteness which is in any case impossible of attainment, but in the use we make of it. Like it or not, so long as there is human consciousness, so long are apprehension and evaluation of all things man-centred.

Luther achieved an ingenious synthesis. He contrived to reconcile the objective fact that man is a tiny, transitory, worthless and presumptuous speck in an infinity beyond grasp, with the built-in subjective urge to orient and harness that infinity to that speck. He made it, so to speak, all right both ways; and men were thankful to believe him. With his own particular subjective objectivity, he carefully submitted his every conclusion to every concrete test—as he conceived of the matter. For the very concept of concreteness is as variable as that of beauty.

Most of the information concerning Luther's character and mentality in the last analysis came from himself, directly and indirectly. He was the soul of truthfulness: he was unable to be otherwise, that was his fundamental trouble; he was too literal-minded, to lie. But he himself knew only too well the inexhaustible layers of human self-deception, where to be truthful is not necessarily to be accurate. As for his looks—"like a cow staring at a new gate," he commented, acquiescently, on his later portraits. The earliest likeness, a drawing made in 1520 for reproduction as publicity material, accords with the contemporaneous accounts of a haggard vigour—but here, too, the static eyes give no definite testimony.

Ah: it is in the shape and play of the surrounding skin and muscle that the impassive organ of sight obtains its apparent individual quality, bespeaking tone and temper of the personality in conjunction with physical make-up and habitual employment. So after all it is a safe assumption that Luther's eyes did flash and shine, glinting mobile from the shadows of a protuberant bone structure and brows bunched from concentration, activated in the facial gesticulations of a communicative nature and a lively mind as very amply evidenced.

"The Emperor Charles talks less in a year than I in one day."

Words were Luther's medium and his element. They were live

entities to him, fraught with specific meaning, no mere conventional signals. He wrestled with the word, devoured and digested it, examined the result and strove to render it productive. Intake was to him inseparable from output. An irresistible analogy presents itself, in view of his lifelong minor fascination with the excretory functions. Likewise the major obsession of his youth, that secret, overwhelming sense of guilt which was then equated with the fear of God, would tend to be aligned with toilet training in a later day. But he was not alone in either, and one swallow does not make a summer: one facet, however valid or seductive, can never reflect the whole of any story.

Whatever the psychosomatic assonances, his inner intellectual struggles certainly hung upon words. "One little word shall slay him," he sang with militant confidence, in his celebrated battle hymn of Faith. One little word drove him to distraction, from the dawn of thinking consciousness till well on in manhood; a word, one word, brought him relief at last. On the basis of one word, one missing syllable, he would eventually throw his entire cause—which he believed to be the cau e of God—in jeopardy.

The words in question were: "faith," "love," "justice," and "is."

In the beginning was the word, love. That word first stuck in his throat, he could not swallow it. He could not believe in the love of God and so could not return it. "Love God? I hated him!" He hated God because he was afraid of him. There was a stained-glass window in the church of the small town where he grew up, depicting Christ the stern King with the sword of justice, so like a rod, only the more awful. All he could feel in face of Christ was terror. Justice and punishment were one. If he did not love God as it was an article of faith he should, he would be justly punished; and how could God love him who was so bad that he could not love God? God was omniscient and could not be deceived. One could not get away with lip-service. The young Luther, man and boy, used to shudder before the crucifix; the host, in which the living presence of the Deity was miraculously made flesh again, filled him with nausea. Hating God was the ultimate blasphemy, which united all creation against the reprobate. He was hopelessly damned.

Not that it showed on the surface. On the surface, animation overlaid his chronic suffering with seeming extrovert appeal; also, activity could deaden it nicely. Nobody can be miserable all the time, not even Luther who had not got it in him to do anything by halves. It was particularly in slack periods, when he was not taken up with some compelling task, that the terrible depressions gained the upper hand.

Luther was the man who first coined the phrase, "When I rest I rust." Rust to him was corrosion as well as failure of function. At a time when he knew better than to envisage paradise in concrete terms, and when he was long past those early agonies—even then he once betrayed the same unallayed need to be active, active. "Whatever shall we find to *do* in heaven?" Touché.

To paint heaven as a convincingly desirable place has taxed even the greatest creative talents, whereas hell presents nothing like such difficulties to the imagination. And tortures which present-day imagination may shrink from contemplating were then an accepted part of the actual scene. Executions were public; malefactors were boiled in oil, incinerated, lopped, disembowelled, broken on the wheel—not every day and everywhere at once, but sufficient unto every region and generation; meanwhile every highway had its gibbets, with rotting human remains displaced only by the next delinquent. It was perhaps not pleasant; but such was life; and such was justice, squared with punishment.

Fear ruled the universe, all governance and training were by terror. Men bent more thought on evil than on beatitude and were more concerned about purgatory than heaven. Deterrence overshadowed the reward: the immediate prize for good behaviour was to get off unpunished; beyond that the final goal was ephemerally remote.

The all-embracing religious symbolism of the Middle Ages, which rested in an inversion of the material and spiritual spheres, rendered the concrete world a mere, illusory reflection of the abstract realm of the spirit which alone possessed true reality. Thus the materialization of "purgatory" and "hell" was a by-product of the de-materialization of carnal, mortal existence. But it had worked too well, the wheel had come full circle. The inversionist technique had so affected thought itself that the faculty of apprehension divorced from substance had become lost. Godhead, sanctity, mercy, merit, grace and faith were seen as substances; sin, evil, guilt, damnation were *absence* of the substances that save.

Religious endeavour therefore centred on the provision and perpetual replenishment of those substances. The merits, compounded of the sanctity and works of Christ and the saints (the saints being those already ascended to eternal bliss) had laid up a treasury of grace, on

high, for mankind to draw on and help add to, towards individual
and universal salvation.

To amend any lack in oneself of the saving substances was a
matter of concrete action, wherein intention and effort played equal
parts. Access to the heavenly stockpile was by sacrifice—not of
burnt-offerings as of old but still in kind: by prayer, fasting, and a
variety of other ascetic practices, or in the shape of alms. Sacrifice of
self was best of all. And the surest way to accomplish this, covering
the whole range of pious "works," was by forsaking the world and
entering a religious order. From having been designed originally
as "schools for the service of God," cloisters had become ideally a
species of spiritual sanatoria for the perfection of the individual soul.

It was in line with this that Luther acted, at the age of twenty-one,
when suddenly one day his anxieties were brought to acute eruption—
by a real, concrete thunderbolt. Walking across country in a summer
storm, he was thrown to the ground by a flash of lightning. He was
thrown to the ground and smelled the earth—the earth to which quite
recently a friend no older than himself had been committed: so might
he be lying dead at this moment, struck down in the flower of his
sinfulness, eternally rejected without appeal. He had already had one
warning, when he had accidentally stabbed himself in the thigh and
nearly bled to death. Who would risk a third time? "Holy Anna, I will
be a monk!" the young man cried out, invoking as his witness the
patron saint of miners.

He came from a mining community and had embarked on a promising worldly career by the study of law, when this happened. Within
a fortnight he made good his vow and joined the Order of his choice.
The Augustinian Friars unlike sundry others enjoyed a high reputation
in the district, and they had recently reformed themselves for greater
austerity. Austerity was what he wanted. It was the sacrificial cure,
the purgative of human corruption.

At first all went well. "I can say from personal experience—and
many people I know have told me the same—that never is Satan so
quiet as during one's first year in the monastery." Although his
devotional curriculum was strictly regulated and mortifications in excess
of prescription were forbidden—and although in accordance with
tradition the novice's seniors made his training period a small purgatory
of petty persecution—the zest of a new life and purpose carried him
through on the crest of enthusiasm. Also, he knew that at the end of

the first year on making his final profession the fully-fledged religious acceded to the same state of purity as the newly baptized infant, with the human heritage of original sin all washed away. Moreover he had heard that this blessing could be procured again and again, by simply renewing one's resolution to keep the three vows of obedience, poverty, and chastity well and faithfully.

But with him the benison either did not take or else wore off too quickly. In the second year his old "afflictions" stirred afresh. Though now, too, he might indulge his thirst for self-mortification to his heart's content, his heart refused to be contented.

"If ever monk got to heaven by monkery, I can safely say I would have made it. All who were my fellows in the cloister will vouch for it that had I gone on so I should have killed myself with pious exercises."

What was wrong? What, treading as he was the straightest road to heaven, kept him apparently as far away from it as ever?

The cloister encouraged introspection and helped to exaggerate the tendency where it was already active. Among the innumerable, fixed duties of the monastic rule confession ranked a prime means of spiritual education. Absolution from guilt, divine forgiveness of sin, was automatic upon repentance—but it was also conditional on repentance. If repentance were imperfect, absolution could not come into effect; and unconfessed sins obviously could not be forgiven. Other people might be able to leave it at the good intention and hope for the best, but not he who was ever in the grip of the significance of words. The young Father Martin began to worry more and more about the quality of his repentance and what sins he might not have left out. No sooner had he made confession and received the assurance of God's mercy from the lips of his priest, than the balm evaporated from his heart again as he bethought himself of offences and impurities he had forgotten, and he would run back for another bout. His anguish was nothing if not logical and perceptive. It was his misfortune that his faculties in that respect were keen beyond the ordinary.

Exposed to the two occupational diseases of his calling, accidie—sloth and torpor of the spirit—and scruple, he had a natural immunity to the former but by the same token a high degree of proneness to the latter. The germ caught on and flourished. His superiors were not unduly perturbed: the scarifying zeal of the new broom was no uncommon phenomenon in young brethren. But with Martin it did not get better, it got worse.

"My poor confessors!" They tried everything—sternly bidding him curtail the self-analysis (he sometimes confessed for six hours at a stretch, day after day), kindly reminding him of God's command to hope, helpfully contrasting his condition with really hard cases—but, "They were no good to me."

They did not understand—or did they? "My son, God is not angry with you: it is you who are angry with God." They admitted having had no personal experience of such sufferings, "No, indeed: but to you clearly they are meat and drink." They could not see the point: "Come with a catalogue of real sins, if you want to trouble Christ for help. Commit parricide, sacrilege, adultery—but meantime stop niggling." They resorted to lame comfort such as, "Son, perhaps God is steeling you for greater trials. Perhaps this is his way of teaching you courage." Perhaps. These exhortations soothed him momentarily, just as momentarily he would feel cleansed by the formula of absolution. Then the cycle renewed itself and panic came again.

For the well-meant advice in fact never touched on that fearful logic of his seeming foolishness. If sin be the intrinsic nature of man, how could one ever hope to come to the end of sins? How could one ever hope to be aware of and recognize each one? how reach rock bottom, in a bottomless pit of iniquity? how then repent completely, and be completely forgiven? (Much later only did it come to him that, "to diagnose smallpox you do not have to probe each pustule, nor do you heal each separately.") Yet it was expressly laid down that total repentance and forgiveness were attainable, and others evidently managed to their satisfaction. It must be that he had been singled out for incurable doom.

One ray of hope kept shining. Once he completed the next stage and became ordained to the priesthood—if indeed God would sanction his promotion to a special class of beings uniquely endowed with the power to perform the miracle of transubstantiation which even the angels could not work—surely then he would himself be transformed at last and would cease to tremble?

He all but fainted when he celebrated his first mass, in the consciousness of the dread, divine presence, wishing to run and hide himself. But he got through. The marvel was done.

And then his father did his best to ruin it all.

*

4. Background Material

Hans Luder, or Lüder, or Lytter, or Ludher was born in 1459, six years after the fall of Constantinople to the Turks and the appearance of the first printed Bible: two exceedingly portentous events—so that he was twenty-four years old on the birth of his second son and forty-eight in 1507 when Martin became a priest—at the village of Möhra, by the western foothills of the Thuringian Forest, in the County of Mansfeld which was a part of the electoral principality of Saxony. In his career there was illustrated a compendium of social history—not excluding the unsettled spelling of the family name: orthography was yet anybody's guess, till such time as the dialect-colouring of Hans' son's enunciation would set a pattern of standardization.

The Luders belonged to a class of free, that is land-owning peasants, on a stable level of adequate prosperity which kept descendants of theirs rooted to the spot into the twentieth century. They paid rent, but only on their fiefs, not on their bodies like the serf peasantry, and were taxed on their draught animals but able to sell, exchange, and bequeath property at their own will. They were independent from the intermediate district seigniories and owed fealty only to the provincial sovereign himself, enjoyed a fair degree of self-government and retained certain community rights to woods, meadows, and streams, intermarried in the endeavour to keep the land together, and to the same end passed their farms on undivided, always to the youngest son. Ultimogeniture was the forerunner in Germany of primogeniture, which as yet operated only in some of the greater principalities; entail in any form being an exception to the rule, so that throughout the

Empire holdings and suzerainty were being whittled into splinters by continual partition under the law of equal inheritance by all descendants of one father. But the elder sons of families like the Luder kindred had to subsist either as serving men to the single heir or by hiring themselves out elsewhere—preferably the latter, if they wanted to marry and have progeny of their own, so long as they could find berths to make that possible. The Luders evidently were particularly fortunate, or particularly enterprising and determined: where other families gradually disappeared the Luders not only stuck but spread, all along the border.

Time was, and that in the none too distant past, when it was next to impossible to change from one social and occupational category to another. Feudalism had its points of similarity to oriental caste systems. But towards the end of the Middle Ages the old rigid bounds first stretched and then broke down, and a novel mobility began to mix up the populations. Hans Luder availed himself of this. He was the eldest of four brothers—Big Hans, Little Hans, Veit, and Heinz—who until the retirement of their father, Heine, lived together on the family farm. Although Heine Luder did not die till 1510, he abdicated in favour of Heinz in the early 1480s; Veit married into another farm, Little Hans stayed on (and became the family black sheep: with no fewer than eleven convictions to his name between 1499 and 1513), and Big Hans emigrated with his pregnant young wife Margarete née Ziegler and their first baby.

They went to Eisleben, hub of the country's burgeoning copper industry, where Hans got employment as an unskilled labourer in the mines. Only about a month after the move, his second son was born shortly before midnight on 10 November 1483, according to the register—neither parents nor son were ever quite sure of the year, later on, though being firm on hour and day.

The day was the Eve of St. Martin, patron saint of feasting and so, by inverted extension of the idea, also of reformed drunkards. St. Martin's Day marked the peak of the autumn slaughtering. Every household that possessed any—and all save the poorest had at least a pig—killed such livestock as it would not be possible to keep alive through the winter, since fodder was very scarce, to preserve as much as could be processed for food to last over the long, lean season till next harvest. What would not keep had to be eaten right away: so this was one time in the year when everybody got enough and more, before Nature closed down for the duration.

Martin's astrological horoscope would not be cast until decades after the event, but the homelier, terrestrial constellations surrounding his birth stared his coevals in the face, then and there. He drew his first breath in an atmosphere redolent of blood and fire, appetizing kitchen fumes and alcoholic cheer, amid bleak boding overlaid with boisterousness, and under the auspices of the sainted Bishop of Tours who had spread the gospel among the wild tribes of Gaul—in whose name the infant was duly christened the first thing in the morning.

Hans Luder did not do well enough in Eisleben to settle, and moved on to the town of Mansfeld some seven months later. Here at last he prospered, although in the shortest feasible time his children increased to the number of nine not counting those that died in early infancy and blurred in memory. In the space of six years he worked his way up through shaft and foundry to buy shares in two modest smelting works, and eventually ended up part-owner of six mines and two furnaces, as well as representative to the town council.

Not so very long before, a working man was wedded to his manual trade and lucky to keep body and soul together on his wage. But meanwhile increasing supplies of gold and silver to the Western world had fostered an increasing use of money in place of former goods-exchange, and had given rise to the practice of accumulating and investing capital—for all that in theory this was still frowned on by the Church under the head of usury as defined in the Bible. It had become possible for a worker paid in coin instead of consumer goods to save and put his savings into enterprises paying other workers to produce something more than the equivalent of their wages. The phenomenon of surplus value had appeared, money had come alive and like every living thing could breed, modern capitalism was engendered. Hans again exemplified a trend of the times.

This took much toil and scraping—while all round there was constant example of others who had likewise gone ahead but slipped back, brought down lower than they had started out by one of any number of chancy circumstances. There was no social security except what a man might build up for himself, by his own efforts or also by the issue of his body. Hans Luder, quite clear as to what he was about, invested in the future of his second son, whose mental abilities soon appeared manifest. Martin was put to school at age four—so small that an older boy sometimes carried him, in kindness—and was kept at school even after he had reached the properly bread-winning age of twelve (admittedly he had on the side tried his hand down the mine, but without marked aptitude).

In the heyday of mediaeval feudalism there had been almost as many sets of common-law as there were domains, each claiming suzerainty and the right of private coinage and private war. Most countries which had come to evolve into unified commonwealths where war, mint, and justice were the monopolies of one paramount ruler, had adopted a ready-made overall law code, the Corpus Iuris Civilis of the bygone Roman Empire; and with that there had come into being a new professional class of as it were disinterested administrators, belonging neither to the landed aristocracy nor to the clergy with its extra-territorial loyalties, yet capable of attaining to high position and contracting profitable marriages. The obvious long-term goal for a bright boy like Martin was the legal profession.

By degrees Hans found it less hard financially to prolong Martin's education, even to the extent of making him a small allowance after he had become a university student—but that was not to say he found it easy. The most stringent economy and unremitting domestic industry continued to prevail in the parental home. But when Martin graduated master of arts, the father let himself go in pride and joy: not only did he insist on addressing so learned a personage formally as a superior, making the rest of the family do the same, but he went to the reckless expense of presenting him with a copy of the Codex Corpus Iuris—since now Martin's ultimate training for the law was to begin. And then in the first semester of his legal studies the son from one day to the next announced that he was going to throw up everything and become a friar.

Hans Luder was not an even-tempered man—or rather, his temper was more evenly irascible than otherwise. Not but that he could be merry and expansive in his cups: however, most of the time he was screwed up to teeth-gritting tension. Martin always professed great love and reverence for his father who he said "meant well," and was prostrated when the old man died, though having often suffered by his father's harshness. Even to those who were accustomed to his outbursts, Hans' furious anger now was unprecedented. Pointedly dropping the formal address he let Martin know that all was at an end between them and that his mother, brothers, sisters, uncles, aunts, and grandparents also would have nothing more to do with him— unless he instantly revoked his wayward purpose, to go on with his studies and fall in with the arrangements for an excellent marriage which the father was in the middle of negotiating for him. A celibate begging-friar would be no son of his.

The Luder family were perfectly good Christians, in the sense that they believed everything they should, said their prayers, paid their tithes, and were regular in all other obligatory religious observances; without being like Martin preoccupied with the problem of salvation or doubts of their righteousness. Certainly they feared God and had their tussles with the Devil (having several times sustained injuries by witchcraft at the hands of a wicked neighbour), but they knew what one had to do about that, did it, and were at peace. They gave alms when they had to, like everybody else, since charity was a religious duty; but they did not particularly relish beggars and mendicant friars anymore than did most people. Anti-clericalism was rife, albeit mostly in ribald form. People might sneer and snigger, mutter and talk big behind the priest's back; but while doing so they made the sign of the cross as a precaution, and to his face meekly ceded due respects. Hans, it is true, during an illness once, when the priest enjoined him to make an extra offering to the Church in order to get well, replied that he had better things to do with his hard-earned money and would prefer to die and leave it intact to his heirs for whom he had been working all his life as a good father should. But he had nothing against the Church, heaven forbid. He merely did not want to lose to it his hopes of a snug old age, prestige, and grandchildren. A philoprogenitive strain ran strong in the family.

Martin if the truth were known would not have minded going back on his rash vow; he had not experienced the serenity he had looked for upon his decision and felt rather uneasy about it now. But while he hated the thought of breaking with his family, his father's rage naturally stiffened his intention.

A second message from home put him out of his quandary. Two younger brothers of his had died suddenly of plague, and all Mansfeld had advised Hans to "offer something holy to God" and let Martin go lest the sickness get him too. "With reluctance and sadness" Hans intimated his consent and Martin started his novitiate in restored harmony with his relations.

It was a great day when a young priest celebrated mass for the first time. All his family and friends were invited to attend and join in a banquet afterwards; of course they would also bring presents to the church where the event took place. By the kind co-operation of Martin's prior his first mass was postponed for a month to a date more convenient for his father, who arrived in fine fettle with a company twenty horses strong. Hans donated twenty gulden to the priory kitchen —a handsome sum by any standards. At table Martin, happy and talkative with the blessed relief of having performed the complicated ritual without hitch, started telling his father about the thunderstorm. They had been drinking; sleeping dogs had better been left to lie. His wound re-opened, Hans flared up, "Well, let's just hope the whole thing wasn't a trick of the Devil!"

Like son, like father: it only needed Martin's shocked contradiction to rouse Hans' pugnacity to the full. Yes, here he sat, the son, all holy and complacent—had he never heard the commandment, then, about honouring one's father and mother? well, and what was he doing about that? leaving his father and mother to fend for themselves in their old age, to starve for all he cared, that's what. He went on in this vein, right there in the refectory in front of the prior and assembled brethren: excruciatingly.

But there was more to the painful scene than embarrassment.

Martin's father had raised a valid doubt. There was no telling where a vision or a prompting inner voice came from—one would never know, until the day that one appeared before the judgment seat of God. In the perpetual contest of Good and Evil the rules of the game gave every licence to the Adversary. In the Garden of Eden Satan might have appeared in serpent form, but to Adam and Eve's more sophisticated posterity he more often assumed the guise of saints and angels. Then why not the guise of lightning, why not by the illusion of a heart responding to divine inspiration? It would make sense, from that angle—Martin's persistent sensation of God's enmity.

He must brace himself and carry on. But the gnawing worm was fastened in his heart.

At all events he was lucky in his superiors, whose constructive sympathy was nourished by the promise which they saw in him. "A new St. Paul!" one of his preceptors enthused to the nuns of the nearby foundation of Mühlhausen. With an insight born of age-old collective experience, they now systematically deprived him of opportunities to brood. Immediately after his ordination the brand-new priest was made to go back to school.

✳

5. Syllabus of Learning

The field of education was one of several in which the Church and the more articulate sections of the laity were just then heading for outright clash. Throughout the Christian era the field had been entirely in the hands of religious authority, which indeed could claim to have pioneered it. The most articulate section of the laity were the humanists, waxing ever louder in condemning the ideological stranglehold.

Ecclesiastical authority was at a loss to understand what they were talking about. Education was Christian education. Anything else was misinformed, pernicious. How could anybody call the Church the foe of popular instruction? Who but the Church had provided the facilities for it? Where but in the monastic communities that survived the prolonged chaos after the Barbarian invasions and the disintegration of Imperial Rome, had the art of letters and the books of olden days, had the very languages of learning been preserved? For what other purpose had the rather shoddy invention of printing been encouraged, not to mention village schools at which the children of the people might be taught to read and write without prejudice to their future occupations—why but in order to disseminate the desirable modicum of religious knowledge with a desirable degree of uniformity: since Christendom was one single spiritual country where men of all nations were compatriots? Would humanism itself have come to flower, without the vital support of a succession of Roman pontiffs? The trouble with the humanists was—as the name implied, under which they had chosen to bracket their diversity—their trouble was that they regarded every-

thing in the light of human interest, instead of leaving all things geared
to divinity which was the proper study of mankind.

The acknowledged king and high priest of humanism in transalpine
Europe, Erasmus of Rotterdam, talked as if the millennium would be
here as soon as "every ploughboy could whistle the Psalms at his
work." What on earth and in the name of heaven would be the point
of that, when as everybody knew very well the Psalms were only
ritual incantations? what would the ploughboy do with Psalms outside
church? Let the ploughboy get his catechism well into his skull, that
took drumming enough. Let him be instructed in his basic creed and
duties and drilled in the correct responses at divine service and in the
confessional: that would be the day, when he could do all that! and
when, indeed, all parish priests not only got the liturgy right themselves
but knew what they were chanting.

Did the humanists then think they were educating the people, with
crude diatribes in verse and prose, in the base vernacular jargons
which had no relation to grammar, and defied spelling? By all means let
the people have that entertainment, of puzzling out such stuff sound by
sound according to the idiosyncrasies of local pronunciations: but do
not talk of literature. For that matter, in the short period that printed
books had been going, there had been repeated attempts at producing
vernacular editions of parts of the Bible: and where had these caught
on? Not anywhere. Not in England, not in France, not in Germany
where these attempts had been most numerous, nor yet in Spain where
scholars were now working on a polyglot version comprising as many
as four languages (Latin, Greek, Hebrew, Aramaic) but wisely omit-
ting the demotic, seeing that all these translations had been proved of
interest only to intellectuals. The humanists, with their critical passion
for Greek and Hebrew, were inconsistent.

With their passion for Greek culture in particular, the humanists
ought to give credit where it was due: did not the pagan Greek
philosopher Aristotle rule the academic roost of Christendom? And who
were the ones to attack Aristotle's three-hundred-year-old enthronement? The humanists, forsooth.

· To be sure, the Northern humanists were different from those of
the romance-cultivated South (to take only a major distinction and
leaving further sub-divisions aside). In the South the artistic, technical, and cognitive achievements of classical thought dominated humanist research; in the North its spiritual application seemed to be

coming uppermost. So who was altogether confusing the whole issue, the very meaning, of education? The humanists, particularly of the Germanic North. Luckily they were at loggerheads among themselves. Let them fight it out, while the stable orthodox majority got on with it in practice—with popular education which no one could deny was on the upgrade anyhow.

Even a glorified mining village like Mansfeld had a municipal school, where anyone might enter and—in the words of its old boy Martin Luther—"study for twenty years, nay forty, and come out knowing neither Latin nor German." Pupils ranging from infants to adolescents were taught all together in one room, by rote and by rod. ("We learned precisely nothing for misery and woe. . . . Whoever loved a schoolmaster? . . . Talk of the hangman!")

How should they have come out knowing German? That was what they spoke already; that was not a language, it was not a subject of knowledge, and not what was taught. Education and latinity were one. And like so much else, education was tacitly treated as a kind of magical substance: you uttered certain formulae and went through certain motions, and if it was done properly you acquired it.

Thus the illiterate tyro was started off from scratch on primers in a foreign language and also was set to copying Latin texts to learn to write. He was given mnemonic tags to recite, in Latin words but without meaning, and taught to sing portions of the Latin liturgy, of which a general précis was however supplied. All this was done by constant repetition aloud and in chorus, with constant thrashings to speed memory and comprehension, not simply to maintain discipline. The pupils were used to punishment; everyone believed in beating exactly as we do in vitamins, and no decent, responsible parent or guardian would have dispensed with a device so essential to successful child-rearing. But in the schoolroom the child was more than sated with it. Luther remembered that when still quite a young child he was flogged fifteen times in one day—in mistake as it happened, because a new dominie confused the lessons proper to each grade.

There were three grades: primarians, Donatists, and Alexandrians —the latter two named after their respective textbooks. In the second grade one took up conjugation and declension, and in the third went on to syntax—if one ever got so far: Luther did not pass beyond the second grade in eight years. One would imagine that these lower schools were effective, selective grids: the wonder being that anybody ever learned anything there, at all. Yet an astonishing number of children did learn enough to fill the higher schools. In the space of little over a hundred years no fewer than a dozen universities had sprung up in Germany.

At thirteen Martin was sent away from home to another school, in Magdeburg. One cannot tell whether in spite of his slow progress at Mansfeld he nevertheless appeared to warrant continued schooling, or whether Hans' obstinacy alone was behind this.

An important function of the lower schools was to furnish local churches with choir boys; hence the emphasis on singing. Martin was very fond of and susceptible to music; this was the one part of the curriculum which he enjoyed. Boys attending school away from home were expected to earn their board—all but the most well-to-do—by singing for alms from door to door. In this they had numerous competitors: mendicant friars, pilgrims, cripples, and the very poor in general, apart from the organized guilds of those who made begging their entire profession. Beggars were as much part of the landscape as trees and as unavoidable an expenditure as tithe and toll—save in that there were no fixed rates for charity and it was mostly broken meats that went into the collecting sacks, not money. "Crumb-seekers" was the name given to the troops of schoolboys singing for their keep.

Axiomatically, no disgrace attached to begging. Axiomatically, poverty was a condition of holiness, and giving others the opportunity for charitable "works" was to confer a benefit on them. However—holy persons embraced poverty as a sacrifice and beggary as a penance; the pious givers often got a little tired of the ceaseless petitioners for their bounty; horror and pity and ridicule attached to the cripples, an aura of delinquency to the professionals; the begging friars were become a byword for rapacity, nosiness, and underhand lechery. Begging in practice was not quite the honoured occupation it was cracked up to be. Humility for the sake of heavenly treasure remained all too closely akin to humiliation, on earth. Anyhow "crumb-seeking" was the custom, and no doubt had some educational value: by way of preparation for an adult climate wherein sensitivity and hanging-back were folly rather than refinement, and bringing boys in touch with people of every class.

Mansfeld was not much of a place. Magdeburg was a cathedral town and also a busy river port. After a year spent there Martin was shifted again, to Eisenach, a town again different in character, on the edge of rugged mountain lands and studded, surrounded, commanded by the palaces and fortresses of a warlike feudal past. In Eisenach at last he began to go ahead. The quality of the teaching at the school attached to the parish church of St. George was out of the common, under an uncommon sort of principal who unfailingly removed his cap in class and demanded the same of his staff: formally to salute the great men of the future who were budding on the benches.

Martin always made friends easily, but in Eisenach for the first time this redounded to his material benefit. His singing attracted the notice of a woman belonging to one of the most respected families in the town. At her suggestion he was offered free board at the family table, in return for taking a young son of the household to school and watching over him in school hours.

This household was not only by far the most cultivated of any Martin had yet encountered, it was also much the most devout. Religion, to the family-complex of Kotta and Schalbe, was not simply a matter of canny, primitive observance. Among these prosperous, gentler folk ideas and feeling had scope as well as leisure of expression. They not only prayed and gave, they conversed. Their lives were ruled by the thought of eternity, not harassed by everlasting thoughts of the morrow: because today was already secure, on a solid foundation of comfortable yesterdays.

They were of the merchant class, at once creatures and carriers of the expanding resources of an expanding world, so that even their mundane concerns touched on farther spheres than the narrow daily round. People of their kind were, if not the initial builders, the liberators and developers of the great towns, many of whose houses were now rising higher than any other secular structures and putting in the shade the dwellings of princes. They possessed movable furniture, not merely some fixed planks of bed and board; their windows were of glass, not simply holes that either let the weather in along with the light of day or must be shuttered. Their domestic chattels were not confined to articles of utility but included ornaments and reading matter, sometimes even a bound book. These were the people who read, not because they had to on pain of whipping. They were the ones that the current spate of moralists, satirists, pamphleteers, and retailers of anecdote and legend catered for. They were the salt of the cities and the backbone of the advancing bourgeoisie.

Martin was happy in Eisenach, where he stayed for three years and unnoticingly, smoothly went through the process of juvenile reaction against the primary environment—in his case towards a subtler religiosity and a now growing appetite for intellectual pursuits. He got to the top of the school and left, certified an expert latinist who was thoroughly familiar with the fables of Aesop, the comedies of Terence, and a collection of moral maxims by one Pseudo-Cato. These qualifications gave him the right of entry to a university.

In May 1501, seventeen years old, "Martinus Ludher ex Mansfeldt" was inscribed on the rolls of the arts faculty of Erfurt University, one of the oldest German centres of learning and at that time the highest in repute. Set, in the spring, within brilliantly flowering hills, adorned with greater and finer buildings than he had ever seen, and pervaded with immense civic pride in the focal academic institution, Erfurt appeared to him "a new Bethlehem."

Life at college was a great deal more strict than at the lower schools, and the syllabus abruptly went a very great deal farther. Students were attached to hospices run much like monasteries (though the one he joined was nicknamed "the Beer-bag"). Their day was minutely ordered and supervised, and the obligatory lectures, dictations, recitations, and disputations were on grammar, syntax, dialectics, logic, for the bachelor's degree; to which became added natural philosophy, metaphysics, moral philosophy, geometry and arithmetic, music, planetary astronomy, and perspective, for the master's examination. Geography and history were yet amateur provinces, except insofar as scraps of such information came automatically with the accredited subjects. Apart from the disputations, and the lapsed presidency of the rod, the methods of instruction were not radically different from what obtained in the lower schools: but instruction was intensified and the matter to be absorbed was more divers and more demanding.

There were "free" lectures—for which, that is to say, special permission had to be obtained—on classical literature and "languages," i.e. Greek and Hebrew: the humanists had made sufficient strides to win so much concession. Technical activities, involving experiment and practical research, remained relegated to the sphere of the artisan; there was no place for anything like that in the halls of higher learning. Art and science were yet synonymous. What today is classed as fine art came in the category of craft which covered all manual skills. The "Queen of Arts" was mathematics, the "Queen of Sciences" was theology, in the definitions drawn up by St. Augustine eleven centuries before.

The universities were secular institutions, but with a strongly ecclesiastical flavour. *Universitates magistorum et scholarium*—that is, corporate communities of teachers and scholars forming *studia generales* or centres of instruction for all—were a mediaeval compound of the Graeco-Roman academies and the early monastic training schools exclusively for clerics. Their comprehensive title notwithstanding, the universities had been designed for adult education from the start—indeed, to start with had served only adults of mature age. Although in some instances medical or legal studies might have furnished the germ of such centres, they were licensed by ecclesiastical decree.

Four principal faculties were recognized: theology, canon law and civil law, medicine, and philosophy or "the arts" of the *trivium* (grammar, logic, rhetoric) and *quadrivium* (arithmetic, geometry, music, astronomy)—called the Seven Liberal Arts in distinction from the Practical Arts of the three superior faculties. Only graduates from the standard arts course were admitted to these. Again, since they were Latin-Christian theology, law, medicine, and Christian-slanted arts, the first and foremost not only dominated over the rest but entered into them.

The University of Paris was mother and model of nearly all those of central and northern Europe, whose statutes as a rule opened with a formal eulogy of the venerable parent. Under the parent scheme the arts faculty had been sub-divided into four "nations" of both professors and students: the "French" nation, lumping Spanish, Italian and also Greek members with the indigenous; the "Picard" nation of north-eastern France and Flanders; the "Norman," sturdily unadulterated; and the "English" which included anyone from Ireland, Scotland, and Germany. The rector was elected by the four nations of the faculty of arts, each headed by a proctor, not by the deans actually heading the faculties; and the chancellor, representing the patron-church, in his official capacity was reduced more or less to the function of a figurehead though being individually a member of the theological faculty. Only "regents," masters engaged in teaching, had the vote. The chancellor however conferred the licence to teach on candidates successfully passing their examinations: the examination system and the academic degree, then, both hailed from Paris too, as did the collegiate organization and quasi-monastic regimen of the student bodies. The Paris fashion owed its liberties largely to the favour of popes wishing to ensure the loyalty of the first transalpine bastion of orthodox ideological leadership.

Subsequent offspring of Paris in the home countries of the various "nations" inherited a measure of democratic constitution, together with subject matter, teaching methods, and a certain independence from the townships that housed them. But the latter aspect cut two ways, in that the universities' privileges gave rise to the traditional hostility of town and gown whilst simultaneously causing the universities to be vigilant of their independence also vis-à-vis the Church which had sponsored that independence. Still at many universities the rector had to be a man in holy orders, and owing to the widespread usage of converting ecclesiastical benefices to the financial support of universities, dignitaries of the ecclesiastical hierarchy frequently doubled the higher university posts.

In the course of the preceding twenty or thirty years the humanistic studies—studies revolving round the condition, quests, past, and achievements of man, rather than round matters metaphysical—which had been initiated by the influx of Greek scholars into southern and western Europe after the fall of Constantinople, had gained some ground at Erfurt as they had done elsewhere. But humanism was a voluntary affiliation, without a decided academic pigeonhole. Luther during his student days made sorties into the humanistic circles among his fellows but was not impelled to join. He liked authority and distrusted independence; he preferred getting his teeth into the tough food of abstraction, to what he deemed the facile diet of actuality.

This did not stop him taking part in the regular meetings between the inmates of different colleges and subscribers to different points of view; his argumentative zest and his singing and playing the lute rather caused him to be looked upon as an asset to the student fellowships.

Sometime in his second year at Erfurt he came across a complete Bible in the university library, tethered by a chain like all the books: even printed books were too precious to take any risks with. Until then Luther had known only the Sunday Gospels. He was amazed at the wealth of other material and captivated by the Old Testament story of Hannah the mother of Samuel—which was all he had time to glance at, as the bell went and he had to hurry off to a lecture. "How fortunate I would be if I could own such a volume!" He bought the nearest procurable thing he could afford, a book of sermons, just for the luxury of possession.

He took both his bachelor's and master's degrees in the minimum time, and graduated second out of seventeen on 7 January 1505, aged twenty-one.

"Oh, what a majestic and glorious thing it was when the master's degrees were conferred on them and torches were carried before them and they were honoured!"—for the whole town participated in the celebrations. "I hold there is no temporal, worldly joy equal to it!" Luther still thrilled to the memory long after, when he had tasted many more of the joys of the world.

At the time, of course, he turned his back on the world soon afterwards.

Academic studies were at an end; however, now he could peruse the Bible from cover to cover. Hand in hand with the cathartic of confession, imbibing the salutary influences of the Scriptures was incumbent on the neophyte, and the professed religious kept it up. Then, after his ordination, he was directed to resume academic work where he had left off at his graduation to *magister artium,* but now to read theology in place of law. Like many monasteries, the Augustinian priory of Erfurt had its own high school, and on days when they had lectures students were excused divine service which took place seven times in every twenty-four hours.

The importance attached to study was matched by the teeming abstruseness of the training material, which required undivided attention. The chief textbooks in standard use were the celebrated *Sentences* of Peter Lombard, a vast twelfth-century compilation of doctrine as defined by the Fathers of the Church from earliest times, and the subsequent tomes of commentary on that work, notably by Gabriel Biel, Peter d'Ailly, William of Occam, and Duns Scotus. Also available were the works of the Order's patron, St. Augustine, and those of St. Thomas Aquinas, which latter however were not prescribed reading at Erfurt. There was enough to go on with for anyone desiring strenuous intellectual application. This was just what Luther wanted; he was delighted with the difficult stuff and apparently forged through it with an ease which at once astounded his superiors and vindicated their perspicacity.

After less than eighteen months of this he was sent out on his first teaching job: seconded to lecture on logic and ethics at the University of Wittenberg, which had been founded six years earlier and advertised its merits with a glowing prospectus: "The air is excellent, the plague is entirely absent, and the cost of living low. . . . Here one may acquire not only learning but also the best manners. . . . Not even Padua and Bologna possess a finer galaxy of savants. . . ."

At Erfurt, however, they did not think much of this, and Father Martin received small credit for his one semester's sojourn, when he was recalled to Erfurt to assist at the Augustinian school. In Wittenberg he had scarcely had the time to write so much as a letter, yet back in Erfurt he found himself working harder still, as he had now to give his first lectures in theology. Again that was just as he wanted it: theology was his new passion, and preferably he would have nothing further to do with the lesser subjects, ever.

He was not to press on in peace. 1510 turned out to be Erfurt's "mad year." Right at the start, in January, the town he had lauded as a new Bethlehem was disgraced by civic disorders, with a rebellion of the labouring population against the municipal government. There were bloody riots and lynch-justice; the chief building of the university with its splendid library was destroyed by the people who had formerly displayed such gratifying reverence of learning. Luther would never forget the outrages he had witnessed.

Before that year was out, his occupation was changed once more. In November he was sent on a mission to Rome. While this was only in the capacity of associate to an older friar, it was nonetheless an honour as well as an exalted relaxation. Visiting Holy Rome, the capital of Christendom, was an experience from which the traveller brought back assured spiritual benefits, the proverbially broadened mind, and extra status.

What the two emissaries failed to bring back, after an absence of five months, was a conclusion of the business in hand.

The whole institution of Christian monasticism having been conceived as a vehicle of spiritual reform, in a sense its whole history was one of recurrent reformations.

Hermits seeking union with the Deity by solitary withdrawal from the sensual world had existed in the Middle East long before Christ, as had colonies of such ascetics. But in the third and fourth centuries A.D. corporate hermitages under Christian auspices had proliferated (till Satan complained to St. Anthony of monastic overcrowding in the desert places which for ages past had been the undisputed stamping ground of devils), and had gradually outgrown their first purpose. Not least by way of missionary activities, these enclaves once devoted to sheer contemplation had come to extend spiritual and social services to the laity; and intercourse with the outside world had inevitably eroded the simplicity of the initial scheme.

So from time to time through the ensuing centuries new Orders had been founded, with fresh rules calculated to refresh basic principles: St. Benedict, St. Bernard of Clairvaux, St. Dominic, St. Francis of Assisi were among the creators of such Orders, which in turn came to require periodical spring cleaning.

The Order of Augustinian Hermits furnished a current instance. Five years before Martin Luther was moved to enter, the Saxon Congregation of the Augustinians had carried out a programme of purification, mainly to restore austerities that had lapsed. Now in 1510 it was proposed to amalgamate the seven priories which had reformed themselves, with some twenty unreformed in the province. The proposal emanated from the Vicar-general of the Order, Dr. Johann von Staupitz, who was also Superior of the Saxon Congregation and professor of Biblical lectures and dean of the theological faculty at Wittenberg. Dr. Staupitz had the Bishop's authority for in this manner diffusing the spirit of Augustinian regeneration; but the reformed priories were loth to give up their distinction, and resisted. An appeal to the Curia was their only hope; and this was the errand of Fathers Johann Lang and Martin Luther.

But the Curia temporized, on the chance that the dispute would right itself (as in fact it eventually did), and the two emissaries returned home to irate conferences and recriminations. Their official rôle of spokesmen for the rebel faction being at an end, they cast their vote—a minority vote of two—in support of Dr. Staupitz, and were "transferred" from Erfurt with a black mark against their names. In Dr. Staupitz's books, however, naturally that mark was of another colour. He made arrangements for the admission of the two white sheep to a new Augustinian priory then in process of building at Wittenberg.

They had shown courage under pressure of unpopularity combined with pressure from within themselves of all those ineluctable community values which seep into the fabric of the soul. They had done this on the side of vested authority, against the stream of strong contemporary anti-authoritarian trends. Dr. Staupitz was a shrewd man, as well as a loyal; he was a competent assessor of character and talent. He began to take a particular interest in Luther, who soon learned to cling to him in father's stead.

The upshot of the Augustinian controversy was that on the eve of his coming up for re-election Dr. Staupitz cut his losses and withdrew the project of amalgamation. He was returned to his old office of Vicar-general and gracefully accepted an invitation to shift his see to Nuremberg (the priories of Nuremberg and Erfurt had been co-leaders of the opposition to him) in token that bygones should be bygones. He had occupied the Wittenberg chair of Biblical lectures since the foundation of that university, but had not very consistently discharged its active duties. Now he really was stationed too far away, and admitted being too busy to do justice to it. He designated Father Martinus as his successor—that is, he went through the motions of recommending him as per protocol, with the invincible determination to get his way.

He had hard work of it, not least with the professor elect himself.

"I submitted fifteen arguments to Dr. Staupitz, to let me off, but they did no good. Finally when I said, 'You will kill me. I shall not live three months,' he answered, 'Fine. The Lord above has large affairs on hand: he can use clever men up there with him.'"

Staupitz won. On 19 October 1512, in a three-hour ceremony at the castle church of Wittenberg which served for all important university occasions, Martin Luther took the doctor's oath and accepted, first a closed and then an opened Bible, together with the doctor's cap and doctor's ring: "I swear obedience and due reverence to the dean and the masters of the theological faculty, and promise to do all I can to promote the welfare of the university and particularly of the theological faculty; not to take the degree elsewhere—" he ought by rights to have taken it at Erfurt, it being considered an affront for a graduate of one university to pledge ultimate allegiance to another—"not to teach vain and foreign doctrines which are condemned by the Church and hurtful to pious ears, but to inform the dean within eight days if I hear of their being taught by anyone; to maintain the customs, liberties, and privileges of the theological faculty to the best of my ability, God helping me, and the holy evangelists." He was then formally licensed "to defend the evangelical truth with all my strength."

He had had some experience of teaching, but not with the core of the evangelical truth, and not in the posture of supreme academic elevation—he who knew himself at heart blind and floundering as ever.

"Oh, how frightened I was!" for he had to study intensively to keep ahead of his students: even more so than is normally the case, since the subject was entirely new to him. The science of theology in which he held the top degree was not taught from the Bible but from the exegetical writings of the Church Fathers and their commentarists. Although he now knew the Scriptures well enough as an oracular text for hieratic recitation or elaborate allegorical paraphrase, as regards didactic interpretation it was "a book with seven seals." As regards preaching, which also was a part of his new duties, he considered himself totally unfitted both in temperament and inclination, and sweated blood when first compelled to practise on his brethren.

＊

6. The Terrain

High thinking grew on a compost of urban squalor.

The respected doctors of the *Leucorea*—the University of "White-hill," Witten-Berg, fashionably hellenized—these virtuosos disporting themselves with élan about what Erasmus called the intellectual mazes of contemporary divinity: these dignified figures, gowned and capped in the uniforms of their lofty calling, which they wore day in, day out unto disintegration, who washed their hands but little else though certainly shaving every Saturday without fail, who ate with their fingers unless the fare were soup—like everybody else they trod unpaved, rutted streets littered with slop and refuse. A modern picnic site has nothing on the average mediaeval town. True, there were then no tins to rust and moulder in the open, bottles and paper were too precious to be thrown away, and pigs and dogs ate up any food waste that might be lying about. But meanwhile anything from the casual ex-crement of man and beast to the residues of brewing, fulling, dyeing, tanning—all highly odoriferous industries—was to be found around those neatly gabled houses which would become the shrines of future nostalgia for a happier past: just as the catacombs represented a bygone golden age to the mediaeval Christian.

Sanitation, water supply, and lighting are the elements of civiliza-tion, *pace* our shamefaced quips about the importance which our own culture accords to plumbing. In all climes, it was always with the formation of larger communities—towns—that the necessity of solving those three problems (which are not so acute in compact isolation) begot advances in social consciousness as well as social organization, insensibly leading to development of thought in general as well as of technological progress.

As regards sanitation, to be sure there were privies inside those snug little houses, or at least manure heaps and sludge ponds within their precincts, and there was the dump outside the town between the wall and the river Elbe, for carcases unfit for consumption and the bodies of criminals who had forfeited burial—where also farm produce was brought to market thrice a week, fairs were held twice a year, and the guilds put on their mystery plays on the days of their patron saints. There was a public bath house with a common pool, where people sluiced each other's backs with dishpans and gambolled with the municipal prostitutes.

As regards water—you could dig a well, if you owned the space and hit the right spot; mostly domestic supplies had to be fetched and carried from the river or the public well. In Wittenberg they had an additional amenity, in the shape of two springs which were piped in through the town wall, to fill a ditch apiece all along the two main streets (which as a matter of fact were paved with cobbles and periodically swept). You could draw water from these as well as drown your surplus cats and dogs—after all, it was *running* water. Those were the days, indeed! when folk were hardy: for anyone who survived infancy at all had by then accumulated a rich treasury of antibodies. Even so the plague, despite the boast of the university prospectus, made regular visitations and regularly took its toll.

People were intimately acquainted with the facts of life and death, including slaughter for food: if you wanted bacon, you had yourself to slit the throat of your own pig, not squeamishly pretend that the dish that comes to table has no connection with a living creature. People were accustomed to blood-curdling noises and inured to evil smells, referring to themselves with matter-of-fact candour as stinking carcases and recognizing in the odours of organic decay the welcome proximity of human habitation. The atmosphere might not be sweet, but it was home. Professors lecturing to crowded classes were equipped with posies of scented flowers to sniff. Not so preachers; but then the air inside the churches was ameliorated by incense and the perfume of melting beeswax. (Luther in conversation a few years hence: "Was the church full?" "It stank." Answer enough.)

As regards artificial illumination, there were tallow candles and rushlights—everything home-made—for domestic use, to augment the sheen from the hearth fire in households where close work like reading or writing might be carried on after dark, or when there was a party. Oil, derived in northern countries from linseed, poppyseed, and nuts, was hardly worth the effort of extraction save on a very minor scale for medicaments and painter's colours: hence painters belonged to the apothecaries' guild, and Wittenberg's town pharmacist Lucas Cranach was also the town artist. Olive oil was a costly import, reserved for sacramental function. Street lighting there was none. The night-watchman carried a lanthorn—a flame enclosed in panes of trans-lucent *horn*. Otherwise, for those able to command attendants, there were torches, clubs of resinous or pitch-coated wood which stayed alight in almost all weathers, though the flying sparks endangered the houses which were for the most part thatched and built of clay in timber frames. But nobody without very pressing need—or without nefarious intent, thus taking his life and salvation in his hands anyway —had much desire to go out at night, the time of demons, wolves, and footpads. Curfew was no hardship, it was a safety device.

A fine town was a town of respectable size and variety of trades; excellence was reckoned by the number of churches and public build-ings. Erfurt, with some nineteen thousand inhabitants, extensively en-gaged in manufacturing leather, cloth, beer, and musical instruments, possessed two collegiate churches besides the cathedral and the great church of St. Severus, half a dozen parish churches, eight monasteries, two nunneries, two citadels, and several tall and handsome municipal and university buildings. Wittenberg on the hill of white sand whence it had got its name had a parish church, a castle church, some chapels, a chapter house, two monastic foundations (the Grey Cloister of the grey-clad Franciscans and the Black Cloister of the black-habited Augustinians), each also with a church, a castle, a town hall, and a nucleus of university premises. Out of under three thousand inhabitants, rate-paying burghers numbered nearly four hundred. The chief in-dustry was brewing, the guilds of bakers, shoemakers, tailors, cloth-makers, wagoners were represented albeit not in great strength; sub-sistence agriculture was equal to requirement, and the town derived a steady income from a monopoly in salt.

It could have been worse. Yet Wittenberg was not accounted a fine town. There were larger, admittedly, but there were also smaller and less enterprising. To be held up as "poor, wretched, filthy," a "stinking sand-dune," "dunghill," "carrion pit" (notwithstanding the gallant phrases of the university prospectus concerning this "Gem of Thuringia")—the state of salubrity of what was after all the capital of Electoral Saxony must have been low indeed. Even Luther, whose personal standards of elegance and comfort were not high, never ceased to wonder what might have possessed the sovereign to select Wittenberg as a suitable site for a university. And Luther had been to Rome.

Rome absolutely stank to high heaven. If Wittenberg was called filthy, what would you say about Rome, where one walked ankle-deep in mud and ordure, knee-deep in ubiquitous debris, inhaling the miasmata of stagnant waters and once-proud ruins polluted for centuries past as mass latrines? A ruin was not then an object of romantic regard.

Rome was a marvellous place for sacred monuments and associations, special altars and meritorious opportunities; the graves were there of the Apostles Peter and Paul and thousands of martyrs, and the Holy See, with the Holy Father when in residence and not away on military campaign: but in every plain, mundane respect Rome was terrible. As a town pure and simple it did not compare with Nuremberg and Ulm, where Luther had stayed in transit, and which were yet looked down upon in Italy for upstart centres of industrial commerce: it had made his blood boil.

But there it was. There were, under such general and particular conditions, men creating noble works of art, men devoting their whole dirt-beset lives to the most disciplined of mental precision work, men investigating the secrets of Nature, men bent with all their powers on charting the realms of the spirit. There were none so few of them, either; and their kind was multiplying fast even in Germany, reputed the back of beyond.

Germany now had thirteen universities, half of them sprung up within the last fifty years and the latest only four years after Wittenberg, which itself had barely entered on its second decade of life. Until 1379 there had been none. Italy, immediate heiress of classical civilization and recognized queen of Western culture, whose earliest Christian universities moreover dated back to the ninth century, had only two more than thirteen. France, ranking a close rival to Italy and leading in the northern field with the Sorbonne of Paris, had fourteen. Spain, though enriched by transfusions of Moorish learning and the new wealth of the Indies, had an effective five out of a nominal eight. England had two; Scotland had three; there were two in

Scandinavia and two in Hungary, one in Bohemia, one in Austria, one in Portugal, one in Switzerland.

The major territorial units outside Italy, of which Germany was the largest, with the exception of Germany had all long since achieved centralization under one single royal crown. The German Empire was not a state nor in any true sense a union of states, merely an assemblage. It was a political anachronism, an administrative free-for-all, an economic mess, a theatre of conflicting interests. Yet now the very cause of this had begun to lend impetus to a spurt of cultural advancement: the many sovereign states of the Empire were competing for prestige as well as for power. As well as a palace, a mint, and an army, it was good to have a university.

The Holy Roman Empire of the German Nation was an invention of the tenth century, planned to figure at once as the inheritor of Imperial Rome and the secular mainstay of the Holy Roman Catholic Church. On both counts it remained a beautiful thought. Geographically its frontiers—from the Alps to the North and Baltic Seas, from the Rhine to the eastern Danube basin—were distinct, linguistically its main dialects belonged to one Teutonic family, in point of religion it subscribed to one faith, in point of fealty it had one symbolic head. But that was as far as integrity went. No emperor had ever yet been strong enough to convert his title into an enduring fact and actually rule the countries that paid him homage—and as for acting as the arm of the papacy, rare were the periods when Emperor and Pope had not been mutually antagonistic. Yet the Emperor was, if not appointed, crowned and consecrated by the Pope who had custody of the imperial regalia, in Rome; and the Pope treated Germany—or so the German Estates avowed—as his "private milch-cow."

The Church, a supra-national body, yet had its autonomous territorial enclaves everywhere in Christendom. In countries under an effective central monarchy ecclesiastical encroachments had gradually become restricted, compared with Germany where the unamended dissipation of secular power sapped the necessary force to exact concessions. In Germany the Church owned no less than a third of the land, besides levying a high tax in kind on the whole country: the tithe, a tenth of everything, which the ecclesiastical authorities interpreted very generously in their favour. In addition to the fees charged by the officials and ministers of the Church for every service to the laity, there was further skimming of the national income by systematic collections of all manner of "voluntary" contributions. On top of that all Church property, produce, and persons were exempt from all and any secular taxation, including toll and customs duties, as well as from secular jurisdiction. There was nothing they gave gratis in return. The hostile estimate of 1,400,000 monks and nuns in Germany at that time may have been exaggerated, but then it did not count other clergy, nor a host of demi-clergy and hangers-on that shared in the clerical benefits. The attested number of clerics in Worms, out of a total population of 7000, was 1500; and the minister at Strassburg (among whose prebendaries, as Erasmus put it, Jesus Christ would never have got in, lacking the required number of quarterings to his escutcheon) alone maintained 137 ecclesiastics. Most of these privileged persons did nothing but read private masses (i.e. services without a congregation), or sing and pray in seclusion. Neither magnates nor communes had any say in ecclesiastical appointments which they stood to defray, except by the uncertain backways of pull and bribery; they could not compel absentee incumbents to discharge their duties. Money "grew dearer every day" as the country was bled white of specie, and the Curia to which it all went made no bones about the contempt in which it held "the drunken Germans." Drunk or sober, high and low, the Germans felt they had had about enough of this. In fact, as not infrequently happens, the protracted experience of contempt levelled at them as a race had stimulated the response of increasing self-awareness, which from defensive truckling turned to wishful vain-glory.

Psychological connotations apart, the specific grievances of Germany against Rome were perfectly concrete and reasonable—sufficiently so to be endorsed by many German churchmen and to have won the official promise of the Holy See that the matter should be looked into. It had come up at Diet after Diet for at least a hundred years, finally detailed in a transaction of 1461 under the head of the "Hundred German Gravamina" which, shelved again and again ever since, had become a standing lever in power politics at large.

For a matter of such dimensions could not be settled by the personal diplomacy even of emperors and popes; it required a General Council of the Church, and in spite of world-wide pressure there had not been one since 1442. The advice of the Legate Aleandro to Pope

Leo X expressed what had in fact long been the curial policy: "Never refuse a Council, never grant one. For thus you will be able continually to stave it off." Still wider issues were involved than the German Gravamina. A complete overhauling of the Church which bravely styled itself *ecclesia semper reformanda,* the ever-(self-)reforming, was being mooted on all sides, not least within its own ranks. What was more, one reform proposal which had very large sections of clergy and laity behind it, was a restoration of supreme authority to the General Council which latterly had been declared a merely advisory body whose recommendations the Pope might adopt or veto at will. Between the poles of international opinion there stretched a great gamut of finer shades of difference, nowhere in more seething permutations than within the German Empire.

One of the stoutest spokesmen for the German Gravamina, and certainly the most long-standing, was Elector Frederick of Saxony. He was an institution. For a provincial sovereign, he had travelled exceptionally widely, even having made the grand pilgrimage to the Holy Sepulchre at Jerusalem which took some doing. Tending to be taciturn, his silence received full measure in benefit of the doubt and his word carried the more weight when it was uttered. The aura of experience hung about him, and he was believed to have the ear of Emperor Maximilian.

Luther penned the following picture of Germany's elder statesman at home: "The Elector Frederick was a wise, just, capable, and skilful ruler, who hated all display, hypocrisy, and sham. . . . He was a real father to the fatherland, he ruled well and kept both cellar and garret full. He held his officials and servants to strict account. When visiting any of his castles, he would pay for his food and lodging like any other guest [sic], that the stewards might not afterwards put in exorbitant bills for his entertainment. Thus it came about that he left his country large treasures and supplies. . . . He gathered in with shovels and gave out with spoons. . . . It was his habit to allow his counsellors to express their advice and then going and doing the exact opposite. . . . This he did not learn, nor was he trained to it, but he had the gift naturally . . . for he was born one of God's miracles."

Seen through the rose-tinted spectacles of obituary regard, moreover with didactic purport, the picture contrasts oddly with the graphic portraits of the prince, of which Lucas Cranach painted and engraved innumerable specimens, and which show a doleful, pendulous, worried countenance, bespeaking—one would guess—frustration rather than aplomb. Both impressions are wrong. Frederick had an equable nature and all in all a satisfying life; and Luther's seeming naïveté and awkwardness in expressing himself on his Elector owed not a little to the proper attitude towards a gift horse. In the event, Luther had much to thank Elector Frederick for, but not always thanks to the Elector's intentions; and while the Elector was alive Luther had not always either cause or inclination to be so uncritical.

"He led a pure life and never married," Luther observed further in appreciation of Elector Frederick. Well, he never married, it was true; and true, too, that the University of Wittenberg was his darling child.

The rule against division of electoral territories had been broken in Saxony. Since 1485 there were two Saxonies, then divided between two brothers into an Electorate and a Dukedom. The Elector had the greater dignity, but the Duke held much of the better and more developed land, and the University of Leipzig, established 1427, also had gone with the ducal portion. A sensible gap was left in Electoral Saxony, which Frederick decided to fill—where else (to answer Luther's rhetorical question) but in his capital city, under his own eye? He went about it with wonted circumspection and with his wonted, enviable ability to act on two different levels. He was an exceedingly devout, obedient son of Rome, and he was at the same time a German nationalist. He contrived on the one hand that his foundation was licensed by an imperial charter and not by a papal charter as were all the rest, and on the other to obtain the usual papal permission to appropriate certain neighbouring ecclesiastical benefices towards financing it.

In and around Wittenberg he had no fewer than twenty-three such benefices to draw on (another excellent reason for the choice of site). The learned Vicar-general of the Augustinian Order was a childhood friend of the Elector, and his learned court physician Dr. Pollich was a noted humanist, previously professor at Leipzig. With Dr. von Staupitz as principal consultant, Dr. Pollich for organizing rector, and several other professors of standing lured away from Erfurt and Cologne, the new university was inaugurated in 1502—in the expressed hope that it should be not merely a school but an intellectual tribunal "which shall resolve all queries which we and the peoples of other countries round about may submit, to the relief of every doubt," as the Elector said in his opening address.

Manifestly devoid of the normal ambitions of aggrandisement, he was considered an enigma among the crowned heads of Europe; but all the time he had his quiet delusions of grandeur. He was determined to make Wittenberg a German Paris, by here setting up a formidable rival to the august Sorbonne, and a German Rome, with the aid of a collection of relics which he was steadily building up to be the biggest in the realm.

Relics were more than sacred curios. They were material particles of sanctity, from which emanated spiritual advantages to the beholder and revenue to the repository where they were to be visited and worshipped. What with diligent purchases and complimentary gifts from other monarchs, the Wittenberg collection had recently grown to 17,433 exhibits, among them 9 thorns from the Saviour's crown (1 certified to have drawn blood), 35 splinters of the Cross, straw and hay from the Manger, 1 piece of the Christ Child's swaddling clothes, 1 piece of bread left over from the Last Supper, 1 vial of the Blessed Virgin's milk, 1 twig from the burning bush of Moses, 1 tooth of St. Jerome, 4 pieces of St. Chrysostom, 4 pieces of St. Augustine and 6 of St. Bernard, 204 parts and 1 whole body of the Holy Innocents of Bethlehem, and a piece of the stone from which Jesus had taken off on his Ascent to heaven. (The Elector had an illustrated catalogue made by the indefatigable Lucas Cranach.)

But it was an uphill struggle. A Rome was not built in a day and neither was the status of a Sorbonne. A brand-new university might have much to offer in freshness and drive, but the pioneering spirit was damped by a certain hostility wafting from nearby Leipzig and Erfurt, and also by financial straits. Although matters had been managed so adroitly that only seven out of twenty-two professorial salaries came out of the Elector's purse, still the university failed to pay its way. Enrolments, promising to begin with, did not accelerate and soon began to fall off—particularly after there had come into existence an even newer university, offering an alternative choice to students of sufficient enterprise or indigence. This was the University of Frankfurt-on-Oder, founded in 1506 by the neighbouring Elector of Brandenburg, with whom the Elector of Saxony lived in chronic neighbourly disharmony. By 1510 the influx of students from outside Wittenberg was virtually at a standstill.

The university was dedicated to St. Augustine, the father of Latin theology, and the local Augustinian cloister was to furnish a backbone of teaching staff as well as the lecture theatre for the theological faculty, until further notice. But even the requisite rebuilding and extension of that cloister pined for want of funds. Dr. Staupitz had continually to cajole the Elector for money or at least bricks, without making very appreciable headway.

When Dr. Staupitz proposed to pass on his chair to a young unknown from Erfurt, for all his glowing recommendations the same difficulty obtruded. The promotion fees for the doctor's degree amounted to fifty gulden, a sum far beyond anything Luther or the impecunious priory could raise. Staupitz had no ready money either, and the Elector was slow to spend—even by the spoonful!—until he could make quite sure of the right dividend. Negotiations dragged on for the best part of a year, before it occurred to Staupitz to give an undertaking that "Martinus shall be responsible for the lectureship on the Bible for the rest of his life." The Elector produced the fifty gulden.

Naturally he desired to keep an eye on his investment and hear how the new man was working out. He was too old a hand at academic politics, too, to rely entirely on academic informants. Not only was the competitive spirit of the universities among themselves mirrored within the individual institutions, but there were too many differences of professional outlook even within one faculty—if that faculty were the theological one—to permit of objective judgment. Firm in faith and wise in title, Frederick knew little more of theology than the name —that name being legion.

But he had great confidence in his chaplain-librarian cum secretary, Georgius Spalatinus (né George Burckhardt, from Spalt near Nuremberg)—decidedly not one of the Elector's counsellors whom Luther had in mind when he praised the Elector's fine disregard of counsel. Spalatin and Martinus were of an age and had met in their student days at Erfurt, without any special resulting intimacy, however, as Spalatin was deeply involved in the humanistic circle at the time. Now, in Wittenberg, they made up for it; and Spalatin was able confidently to reassure his master that the new professor was perfectly sound.

Such were the sovereign preoccupations at Wittenberg, "A poor, unsightly place with small, old, ugly, squat houses, more like a dilapidated village . . . not worthy of being called a town [even] in Germany . . . without vineyards or orchards . . . with an atmosphere like that of a beer cellar, most unhealthy and disagreeable, smoky and cold," whose people were "uncouth, besotted, gluttonous barbarians," of "utterly provincial apparel," and dwelling altogether "on the outskirts of civilization," by various reports including the verdict of Luther, who in a moment of leisure addressed to it this doggerel:

"Sändicken, Sändicken, du bist ein Ländicken!
Wenn ick di arbeit, bist du licht,
Wenn ich di meye, so finde ick nicht."

Which may be translated, albeit anaemically, as follows,

What a land! nothing but sand!
You're easy to sow,
But bring nothing to mow.

Like everyone in his time, he automatically appraised Nature in terms of agriculture; though equally taking it for granted that man does not live by the fruits of the earth alone.

7. The Pathway of Religion

The Jews had started it, by identifying godhead with the spirit, aspirations, ethical progress, and ultimate prospects of a nation, in contrast to the deities of paganism whose relationship with humanity was entirely arbitrary and inconsequential. In his mature form the Jewish God was at once mana, hero, leader, and moral instructor of his chosen people to whom all others should be subject in everlasting peace and rectitude, according to his covenant with Abraham, the archetypal exemplar of total faith. By their sins Abraham's descendants had forfeited the millennium, but they were to have another chance. If they became purified by suffering and repentance, labouring afresh for perfect virtue, they should be reinstated agents of the kingdom of God through the offices of an Anointed One mysteriously incorporating the regeneration of his race.

Jesus was a teacher who strove to reform a creed the true spiritual content of which was becoming stifled by formal externalization in a mass of concrete gestures and material tokens. The severance of Christianity from Judaism occurred over the question whether the Anointed One, the Messiah, the Christ had already appeared in the person of Jesus or whether he were yet to come. Among those who believed in the Christ Jesus, the principle of salvation became denationalized. First, the emphasis of regeneration shifted to the individual particles composing the aggregate mass of the people on which it had previously rested, and second, all humanity irrespective of nation became eligible. The kingdom of God became a truly universal and egalitarian scheme. All men were brothers, all souls were equal, and all lived for the one end, of liberation in God. The triad axiom of revolutions had been formulated.

This was chiefly the doing of St. Paul, originally Saul, a hellenized Jew of Tarsus owning Roman citizenship, and contemporary of Jesus though outliving and never having met him in the flesh. Starting out an orthodox Judaic scholar and as such militant in persecuting the heretic messianic sect, he had however encountered Jesus in a vision which converted him to the Christian belief. With typical convert's zeal, henceforward Paul devoted himself utterly to propagating that faith. Paul's interpretation of the teaching of Jesus—conditioned as it was by all his background, circumstances, and make-up—became accepted as the only correct one, as certainly it was the most comprehensive, telling, satisfying, and dynamic.

Jesus by humanizing and at the same time abstracting an eternal ethic which he wished to render completely accessible to ordinary people, had thereby become the founder of a new religion. Paul was its first theologian, as well as its first xenophile missionary and first international organizer. He was quadrilingual, literate in demotic Aramaic and hieratic Hebrew as a Jew, in Greek as a native of Asia Minor, and in Latin as a citizen of Imperial Rome. Jesus having left a number of disciples in Judaea, Paul concentrated on the gentiles of the surrounding civilization. Lacking a Paul, the Jews of Jewish Palestine finally rejected the Christian heresy; having a Paul to power it, the momentum of Christianity abroad finally carried it to ideological victory throughout the Roman Empire.

Yet it was Simon, originally a Hebrew fisherman of Galilee, called Cephas or Petrus, "the rock," who became the first accredited shepherd of the Christian flock. St. Peter after a chequered peripatetic career spent the last twenty-five years of his life as bishop, i.e. spiritual overseer, of the *communio sanctorum,* the fellowship of saints (meaning believers in Christ) of the city of Rome, who met periodically in *ecclesia,* assembly, at a house thereby consecrated to the Lord (*Kyriakon*=kirk, *Kirche,* church, etc.), which Lord's-house eventually gave its name to the general concept of the Church as the government of Christendom; in the same way as the name of Peter descended as a commemorative honorific to his successors in office.

St. Peter had never been an intellectual like Paul nor was he an organizer. He was a preaching evangelist in the footsteps of the Lord whom he had known in person; he had been Jesus' chief lieutenant, had witnessed his arrest and trial, and although too frightened to be present at the crucifixion, had been among the first to see him resurrected. Peter was the human link par excellence, in whom human weakness rose step by struggling step to perfect strength and courage, and so designated deputy leader: "Thou art Peter, and upon this rock I will build my [holy community]," and, "I will give unto thee the keys of the kingdom of heaven,"—the two crucial statements on which the bishopric of Rome based its position. Peter the senior apostle, representing at once the humanity of man and his divine potential, was the primary minister or appointed servant to the Christian community at large. In the name of St. Peter subsequent bishops of Rome acquired lasting pre-eminence over the bishops of other local churches. The city of Rome, after all, was the heart and hub of the Roman Empire, the great commonwealth which eventually adopted Christianity for its official religion.

It was not until A.D 313 that the Roman Emperor Constantine formally discarded the old gods of Greece and Rome in favour of the monotheistic importation. But in the meantime Greek and Roman influences had wrought some characteristic modifications upon Christian thought, not least by bringing to it those classical modes of enquiry into ultimate principles which had been foreign to the Jewish cast of spirituality. By the same token, a variety of subdivisions had evolved within the wide "community of saints," putting forward different interpretations of different aspects of the faith, to which they gave differing importance.

Furthermore, from a fairly numerous selection of written accounts of the life and teaching of the Christ, four—one in Aramaic and three in Greek—had emerged as the most serviceable, mutually complementary, and authoritative. These were now *the* Gospels; the rest either disappeared or lingered relegated to the realm of apocryphal writings. About the same time the books of the Hebrew-Aramaic Old Testament had been brought together in a Greek translation, by a syndicate of seventy scholars according to tradition, and therefore known as the Septuagint. During the last quarter of the fourth century a translation of the whole of Scripture into the common language of the Roman populations was commissioned by the then Bishop of Rome, Damasus I, from a Dalmatian savant and redoubtable linguist named Jerome. The Vulgate, St. Jerome's rendering of the Sacred Books into the vulgar tongue, from the now somewhat specialized language of literary education, which was Greek, became the authorized version.

Jerome incidentally was the first saint canonized for his services to the Church rather than for martyrdom or otherwise outstanding saintliness: the idea of sainthood also had undergone changes; from a categorical label sainthood had become a particular title. Another saint of the same generation was Augustine, Bishop of Hippo, who died during the siege of that city by the Barbarian invaders—on the eve, thus, of the so-called Dark Ages—having first become the founder of Latin-Western theology. St. Augustine's definitions of the Christian dogma and of essential principles of divinity, in a synthesis of Jewish fundamentals and Greek speculative metaphysics, at once digested and superseded the kindred works of preceding "Fathers" of the Christian Church.

The word father in its forms of *pappas, papa, pope* gained currency in the course of the fourth and fifth centuries as an appellation of bishops—bishops now being the administrative heads of territorial churches whose full-time ministers had concurrently taken on the character of a priesthood. The Bishop of Rome, who for some time remained one of a council of all bishops, did not become the one and only Pope and primate till much later still—although once he had attained that position it had retrospective effect upon his predecessors. Thus the first all-out missionary campaign to christianize the large tracts of heathen territory in the central and northern portions of the Empire was initiated by *Pope* Gregory I, the Great, who flourished from around 540 to 604, and introduced yet another element into Christianity.

For Gregory had the eminently practical notion that to burn down pagan sanctuaries and depose pagan deities was not enough: much wiser to convert them, too, to the new faith. He directed the missions wherever possible to erect their places of worship on the sites of the old and to adjust the dates of Christian festivals so that they might coincide with former pagan high feasts. But this had unforeseen implications. Heathen deities and heathen rites and superstitions (superstition being the name of discredited beliefs) went along with the converted altars and holy days, pouring much of their substance into the Christian melting pot there to form an insoluble alloy. Some of the old gods took on the guise of saints; the great feasts of the winter solstice and the spring merged with those of the birth and the death and resurrection of Christ.

Insensibly the prime pagan factors of idolatry, magic, and barter (specifically anathematized in Judaeo-Christian ideology) re-entered by the back door under cover of saint-worship, crypto-talismans, and pious donations. In other words, the saints whose intercession with the Deity was sought, by degrees received divine honours in their own right; relics of their earthly existence—as well as the rites of baptism and chrysm, and the very eucharist which symbolically repeated the redemptive act of Jesus—acquired the repute of bestowing sanctity by touch; and the designedly spiritual exercise of making sacrifices grew to be confused with purchasing divine favour.

By degrees also the idea of orthodoxy partook of material power. Heresy, once merely a difference of opinion, became a delict of much the same order as treason in the temporal sphere. Dissidences with a relatively small following were suppressed; but where such a following was too large to be controlled there ensued guarded co-existence under the name of schism. The great schism as between the churches of the Eastern or Greek half of the now divided Roman Empire and the churches of the Western, Latin half finally took place—after a long period of wrestling and wrangling—in the year 1054. Each corresponding half of the Christian Church valiantly retained for itself the adjectives "orthodox" and "catholic"; the operative distinction lay in the words "Greek" and "Latin."

This marked a decisive turning point for the bishopric of Rome, already re-named papacy. The Greek churches continued to be ruled by a supreme council of all "patriarchs" together, the Latin churches also had their General Council but simultaneously acknowledged the supremacy of one Pope, *the* holy father and vicar of Christ in succession to St. Peter.

As the countries of the politically defunct West-Roman Empire recovered from the Barbarian invasions under which it had disintegrated, and the scheme of restoring that Empire under the central governance of Frankish kings was launched, the papacy recollected a most important document. This was a charter, called the Donation of Constantine, by which the Emperor of that name upon shifting his capital to his new city of Constantinople in the Eastern half of the Empire had made over to the Bishop of Rome absolute, temporal as well as spiritual dominion not only over the city of Rome itself but the entire territories of the Western Empire. The Donation happily confirmed the meanwhile accomplished fact that the Church—the spiritual community—had evolved into a concrete, terrestrial institution with all the trappings, moreover, of a terrestrial state.

Spiritual authority to be implemented on an international scale demanded a commensurate physical apparatus, in turn requiring wealth and landed independence. So, since the central monarchy of the papal state embodied simultaneously the Church's religious jurisdiction everywhere in Western Christendom, its as it were spiritual consulates in other, national states formed physical cysts, foreign bodies of extra-territorial autonomy, in all the countries committed to the Latin or Roman persuasion. But on the basis of the Donation of Constantine the papacy claimed veritable, feudal suzerainty over the whole of the formerly West-Roman territories, with the addition of all island countries of the earth. (Thus Pope Calixtus III could make Henry II of England a present of Ireland, and Pope Alexander VI in like manner halved the Indies between the monarchs of Spain and Portugal.) Many canon lawyers were of opinion that the dream of many a pope, of real world dominion, was fully briefed and justified—an attitude perfectly described by the term of Caesaro-papalism. Part and parcel of the world-wide drive of the later Middle Ages towards central monarchy, Caesaro-papal pretensions of course went counter to those of the secular, national states.

The papacy had experienced a severe set-back between 1309 and 1417, when for the best part of a century the Roman pontiffs had resided not in Rome but, captive to the French monarchy, at Avignon, followed by a period when pontiffs had come in pairs, each one sponsored by a contending secular power, each claiming to be the sole legitimate successor of St. Peter, and each excommunicating the rival-pope complete with everybody who obeyed him. All this had aggravated the prevailing popular disillusionment upon the failure of the Crusades to appropriate the Holy Land to Christendom, and it had also shaken the credit of the papacy in the economic sense. The papacy was as often compromised by dependence on its bankers, and as rarely solvent, as any other monarchy.

The only pope since the reconstitution of the Roman See to have balanced the budget was the execrated Borgia, Alexander VI—in whose person the papacy had indeed attained to a stark and novel glamour, of concentrated wickedness. The flamboyant figure of the Borgia pope had united every conceivable papal shortcoming in one choice bouquet. Contrary to the cliché that Alexander was another nail in the coffin of the papacy he was a godsend to it: a luminous, broad-backed scapegoat, a scale-setter by comparison with whom other sinful popes, past and future, dwindled to petty proportions. Notwithstanding his financial feat, Alexander had however sacrificed the interests of the papal state to those of his abounding family; and his successor Julius II had the heavy but rewarding task of renewing the campaign for real world dominion, from scratch. Julius, it must be said, also was built on a heroic scale, larger than life in point of all those qualities which at that moment were most needed in the supreme leader of such a movement, and restored the prestige of his holy office.

As Alexander had done too, albeit desultorily, Julius ran up the time-honoured flag of Reform, once again, which over the centuries had so often ushered in ecclesiastical improvements, now in the way of moral rearmament, now in technical and administrative directions.

Reformations must needs be preceded by self-criticism; and the trouble with self-criticism is that everybody else will catch the echo and hurl it back with compound interest. The trouble with concessions is that by relieving an immediate strain they will, not appease but envigorate the cry for redress. Revolutions do not break out at the peak of unendurable conditions but directly things become a little better, not when tyranny is at its height but as soon as it begins to relax. The more openly the Church acknowledged that it was in need of reformation, the louder grew the clamour from outside against its acknowledged defects. The clamour had reached a universal high in the course of the fifteenth century and was swelling still, as the promised General Council was continually deferred.

For meanwhile the printing press had appeared on the scene. Where once every line of writing had had to be copied out by hand, for further dissemination—a costly as well as a laborious business—now literature of any shape, form, and length could be transmitted on an enormously larger scale. Literacy increased and so did the pooling of information and cumulative cross-fertilization of ideas. The defects of the Church, from whatever point of view, and whether set out in serious memoranda, tracts, or entertaining satire, circulated ever faster and more furiously, in print.

Critics, including those themselves in holy orders, inveighed freely against malpractices which had become standard usage, such as the buying and selling of benefices, the levying of annates (payment to Rome of the first year's revenues of every bishopric at every investiture, by which a diocese could be quickly ruined if there happened to be a rapid turnover of incumbents), plural office and absenteeism, and the galloping abuses of the licensed commutation of spiritual dues into money payments. On the score of moral turpitude, there was no mincing of words either: the Holy See was a cesspool of graft, prelates were worldly and power-hungry, unchaste and mostly homosexual at that; convents were hives of sloth, ignorance, greed and concupiscence; the bulk of parish priests (a survey made for Julius II put it at 98 per cent) was illiterate, with a deserved reputation for superstition, predatoriness, and whoring. True, there were dedicated prelates, religious Orders stringently guarding their purity, good and pious parish priests; but these stood out as glaring exceptions. And true, the laity was nothing to write home about, deep in depravity of every sort: but if the spiritual leadership were wanting, how could the state of the modern world be other than degenerate?

Few of these indictments were new. But never had they been proclaimed so widely. Of old, there were two leading schools of thought as to the root cause of all ecclesiastical evils. One blamed the Donation of Constantine, which had inveigled the Church—an entity not of this world—into the false position of mundane aggrandisement. The other blamed the Queen of Sciences, theology, for having overlaid the plain gospel truth with a mountain of philosophical accretions which had completely obscured it and smothered the life out of religion.

Both schools of thought had in common the basic idea that current modern decadence was due to the lapse of Christianity from the clear-cut simplicity of its beginnings. Reformers from St. Benedict to St. Francis of Assisi had centred their programmes on a return to the style of life led by the band of Jesus and the early Christians. They and all would-be reformers from St. Augustine to Savonarola had drawn their inspiration straight from the Word of God as revealed to the evangelists and especially St. Paul.

With the arrival of humanism as an all-European intellectual movement, these twin-schools got fresh grist to their mill. But they would not thank you for calling them schools. School, schoolman, and scholasticism had become bad words. What was more, "theology" and "theologian" were becoming blackened with the same ink-clogged brush.

✳

8. The Pathway of Theology

"A scab of a fellow, theology incarnate."

Thus wrote the great Erasmus—not as it happened about Luther of whose obscure existence he was unaware—but he might have meant him, a highly qualified professional theologian steeped in the scholastic tradition.

Erasmus' friend Sir Thomas More had this to say, "A man might as soon obtain bodily nourishment by milking a he-goat into a sieve as spiritual nourishment by reading the schoolmen."

Luther could have borne this out, but yet feared that the fault lay with his spirit and not with the food.

"One might sooner find one's way about a labyrinth than through the intellectual mazes of the Realists, Nominalists, Thomists, Albertists, Occamists, Scotists," gibed Erasmus.

As a matter of fact Erasmus was being unfair. Thomism and Realism were one and the same, and Occamism and Nominalism were one and the same; although the Scotists while differing from the Thomists in an important particular were nevertheless in coalition with them and so answered to the name of Realists also; while the Occamists-Nominalists were known additionally as Modernists. To cite Albertism on top of the rest was the height of disingenuous duplication: as well might Erasmus have brought in Aristotelianism, separately. But that did not occur to him; that really did go without saying.

The pedigree of sixteenth-century orthodox theology was as follows: ALBERTUS Magnus (called *Doctor Universalis*, 1193–1230) established dialectics as the "science of sciences" in the West, by the methods of ARISTOTLE (called *The* Philosopher, 384–22 B.C.), which Albertus' more famous pupil St. THOMAS Aquinas (called *Doctor Angelicus* though inheriting the by-name of *Doctor Universalis* for good measure, 1225–74) wedded so firmly with the "Queen of Sciences," divinity, that even Thomas' detractor John Duns SCOTUS (called *Doctor Subtilis,* c.1270–1308) and their joint opponent William of OCCAM (called *Doctor Invincibilis,* 1299–1349) were yet full-blooded offspring of the marriage. For something like three hundred years theology was scholasticism. Scholasticism was the knowledge of God by rational means through a system of analytical debate.

The Latin universities owed their existence to the rediscovery of dialectic, as the sovereign tool of intelligent apprehension, which co-incided with the growth of a belief that supernatural truth like any other was accessible by human reason. Previous to that the Christian approach to comprehension of the scheme of things had been guided by what one may roughly call the philosophy of resignation, based on myth and mystic acceptance of the occult, of oriental Neoplatonism with christological infusions—St. Augustine (354–430) being the mas-ter-welder of that compound. The excitement which was caused by the new positive approach, the passionate enthusiasm with which it was taken up, have as many parallels in the fields of science and technology as there have been epoch-making recognitions and in-ventions.

Training the mind to understand the ways of God by meticulous enquiry and argumentation demanded a different type of school from the old spiritual gymnasia teaching but the axioms of revelation along with the receptivity to them. So on that highest plane of learning, where the springs of all knowledge were contained, the word school now became synonymous with the new type of schooling which was provided by the special schools or universities. *Scholasticism* was the divinity of reason and logic, the *schoolmen* were those who pursued it—to the farthest ends of syllogism and conceptual anatomy.

This was where Aristotle came in, the pagan Greek, father of formal logic and applied philosophy, disciple of Plato and prize product of that archetypal garden school of Athens, *Akademos,* which stamped its trademark on intellectual endeavour for all time. Having coined the terminology of categories and superadded a comprehensive system of definitions in which physics, metaphysics, ethics, religion, substance and attribute, matter and idea, poetry and politics, species and essences and accidents, all had their fully classified positions, Aristotle was God's gift to rational theology.

Ironically, this was the work of the Crusades, that débâcle of morality and civilization, which however brought a semi-barbaric Latin Christendom in contact with the world of Islam, then flourishing in the cultural inheritance of ancient Greece. Although, thanks to the late-Roman commentarist Boetius, some Latin compends of the Aristotelian formulae had resisted oblivion in the Dark Ages, these rested virtually dormant until the return in strength of Greek philosophy—via Latin translations of Arabic translations. From the sudden embarrassment of riches flooding a parched field with all the mainstreams of classical thought at once, the Aristotelian discipline at length emerged as the most attractive to the cerebrative mind and the most adaptable to Christian uses.

The cerebrative mind, cultured in the turgid reaches of mediaeval symbology, had relatively little difficulty in so naturalizing "The Philosopher" of the fourth century B.C. *Before Christ* was a helpful denomination, to start with: already room had been made in a special zone between heaven and hell for "good" heathen who could not be held responsible for their unbaptized state and had in no other way earned eternal damnation. Up to a point, intimations of Christ could be read into Aristotle's utterances, as easily as into those of the Old Testament chroniclers and prophets. What absolutely would not fit could be left out, dismissed on the score of The Philosopher's unavoidable blindness to a light that had never dawned on classical Attica.

Or so discrepancies were treated by some thinkers. Some remained adamant in denying that dialectic could be applied to supernatural causes at all, and sharply resected the boundaries of reason. Others toiled undeterred to free reason from every last impediment and prove the total utility of logic. Between these extremes there were innumerable gradations as well as points of occasional congruence. Three centuries of Aristotelian ascendancy afforded ample time for growth, grafts, and mutations—all safely rooted still in orthodox dogma, dogma comprising the fundamental articles of the Faith as laid down in the canons of the Church. Within that reserve, a good deal of cold war might be carried on among the factions, but let the citadel be attacked in any particle and they would all fire together.

By the end of the fifteenth century, the big battalions had stabilized behind the leads of Thomas Aquinas and Duns Scotus on the one hand and William of Occam on the other. Aquinas was the genius who had actually encompassed the longed-for total harmony of reason and faith; Scotus had somewhat disrupted this by introducing the will as a third primary; Occam while upholding the technique and the validity of philosophy showed it and religion to be elements apart.

Thomism allied with Scotism had ruled the halls of learning for two hundred years, while Occamism had had to struggle for official recognition until 1481—i.e. very recently: hence the Occamist epithet of Modernism. Thomism-Scotism was further characterized as Realism, and Occamism-Modernism as Nominalism, after two branches of theory supporting divergent answers to Aristotle's original enquiry into the nature of genera and species, to which they respectively subscribed. Realism affirmed the substantial reality of genera or universals, Nominalism denied this and declared universals mere names, conventions like algebraic symbols, for expressing the summary qualities of substantial particulars.

Realism broadly speaking thus upheld the supremacy of abstraction, Nominalism embodied an essential distrust of abstraction. Thomism had unintentionally favoured the hypertrophy of logic for logic's sake, Occamism unintentionally foreshadowed a preference for observation and experiment. Still they employed the same methods; viewed from the outside, there was little to distinguish them in action, so to speak. The opposition, when it came to birth in turn, to scholasticism as a whole, could fairly lump Thomists and Occamists together, with all their sub-groups, as crabbed, absurd, spirit-dousing sophistry-mongers. For such they had become, at all events, in their most massive manifestations.

What then was the significant difference of content for the follower of one or the other official line? In the long run, the Thomist postulate of complete compatibility of reason and faith though so attractive was unsatisfactory, precisely because it must infinitely multiply dialectical contortions which were necessary if all things apprehensible had to be brought into alignment with the fixed, infallible teaching of the Church: resulting in the paradox that the more concrete phenomena were uncovered, whether in the realms of history or the natural sciences, the remoter and more rarefied became the abstract, explanatory apologiae. To keep what could be intelligently apprehended and what could not, in separate compartments, seemed more reasonable and more practical—as indeed it was, so long as all ultimate testing for truth happened exclusively in the mind. However, Thomism based virtue on understanding, since making the will dependent on the intellect; Scotism had the intellect subordinate to the will, placing the onus of understanding on effect; Occamism made the *human* will decisive, with the will of God appearing as a secondary effect in the form of grace. There were also three different interpretations of Predestination—God's eternal foreknowledge of all things, God's unchangeable decision that some men shall be happy and some unhappy, God's eternal and unchangeable election of some men to everlasting life and rejection of others—distinctions which do not seem to affect the net result in any case. Furthermore, the Realists placing reason above revelation believed that the General Council of the Church was the supreme authority in spiritual matters, while the Modernists placing supernatural ethic above everything recognized the Pope as the absolute head of Christendom. The older universities tended to cling to Thomism-Scotism-Realism, the younger to adopt Occamism-Nominalism-Modernism.

But meanwhile the gravediggers of scholasticism had rolled up their sleeves and were tunnelling away, from opposite directions: progressive and reactionist. The one was humanism and mysticism was the other.

Humanism, too, had got its starting impetus by the Eastern route although only with the transplantation of the hellenic heritage to the West did it come into full spate; and mysticism never had gone quite out of fashion, especially in the brooding North where the occidental variant had put forth bright, green shoots.

For the humanists the interest of Aristotle lay in his scientific maxims rather than the technique by which they were arrived at. To speculative enquiry they opposed critical enquiry. With the recovery of ancient languages other than Latin, of ancient learning other than metaphysic, and with that the disclosure of historic vistas other than an amorphous Past where Moses, Alexander, Julius Caesar, Charlemagne—as also Noah, Romulus, King Arthur—rubbed shoulders in a kaleidoscopic throng, opened up an entire virgin territory: textual and historical research.

While the traditionalists still went on refining the interior ramifications of meaning, the new liberals began to explore the actual records. Instead of debating the precise composition of the Trinity (which incidentally was what the Greek and Roman Churches had quarrelled over), the precise mechanism of the virgin birth, the precise provenance of grace and precise spiritual chemistry of the sacraments, the humanist investigation went after facts and circumstantial evidence. Dogma ipso facto was unflawed and endless dissection of the infinite could not add anything to it, whereas man's knowledge of his own world and antecedents, now that it was beginning to expand again, was seen to be clearly capable of improvement.

Mysticism was impartially hostile to scholasticism and humanism, both: seeking experience of the divine instead of understanding, by the pure medium of feeling, beyond the ever-equivocal one of word-bound thought. The mystic road to salvation was by meditation, contemplation, rapture—suspension however temporary of the separateness of man and God. Neither logic nor classical erudition could be of the slightest use here.

Not but that humanism and mysticism had each its own subsections too. Humanism was in fact united only in a common love of classical culture: the house of Man like the house of God had many, many mansions. Mysticism was principally divided on the nature of the soul's eventual union with the Deity: whether this were a meeting of the divine particle with the Whole, or the submersion and dissolution of the particle in the Whole. Scholasticism, when all was said, had benefited them both, by acting as a general whetstone to the human intellect and the means of human expression.

Well and good: but this did not exhaust the relevant divisions and permutations. For instance: Luther had been reared in the Occamist school of Erfurt, but had willy-nilly imbibed humanist ideas at the same place and time. As an Augustinian Friar later on he was expected to be proficient in the teachings of St. Augustine. Occamism-Nominalism-Modernism with certain idiosyncratic local-Augustinian modifications was the prevailing line at the new University of Wittenberg—where the rector was however a pillar of humanism, with a Leipzig-Occamist background, and the dean of the theological faculty was a

Thomist with strong leanings towards German Mysticism, while the most vocal professor on that faculty, Dr. Karlstadt, was a humanistic Thomist.

Erasmus may be forgiven his satirical exuberance. He made his point, and it was taken.

※

9. The Metamorphosis

Luther as can be imagined had much trouble with his Occamism, in the light of which his spirit's stubborn failure to be nourished unto health was a serious default of will: something to feel well and truly guilty about. He had trouble with his Augustinianism too, not because Augustine's doctrine of Predestination might seem to contradict the unlimited potentiality of the human will as postulated by Occam— contradictions, bless you, were child's play to the skilled scholastic— but because it did *not* contradict his instinctive antipathy to God.

"Is it not against all natural reason that God out of his mere whim should desert men, harden them, damn them, as if he delighted in the sins and torments of the wretched for eternity—he who is said to be of such mercy and goodness? Rather, does this not appear wicked, cruel, intolerably unjust?" But God *was* good, merciful, and the essence of justice; not to believe this was blasphemy. The vicious circle spiralled, on and on.

He had some trouble sorting out his reactions to humanism. On the one hand he remained convinced of the frivolity of the humanist preoccupation with transitory things which was matched by the frequent stylistic levity, and underlined by the not infrequently appalling academic manners, of the "new" scholars. On the other hand he had come round to agreeing that it was vitally necessary to apply critical research to the primary sources of the higher science.

Erasmus of Rotterdam had published some new translations of a number of patristic texts showing up beyond any doubt the errors and misconstructions which had slipped into the hitherto accepted

versions, at the hands of successive copyists and less than perfect
linguists. It hardly bore thinking of, how many more of such pregnant
corruptions of important original documents there might not be about.
Or rather, it was almost pointless to think of anything else before the
whole field had been thoroughly cleared up. In Italy, where money
and books abounded, great strides had been made already in this
direction; but the overwhelming majority of those books were in manuscript, scant copies existing, and in any case the German Emperor's
present wars in Italy had closed the frontier of bibliopole traffic. The
frontier was not closed to private travellers, whatever their nationality,
and there was an unceasing stream of book-hungry students to the
Italian libraries: but still they were only a small percentage of those
having the same interest. Not everybody's circumstances permitted
them to wander off into foreign parts at will; as it was many fell by
the wayside and never came back. One had to be thankful for those
that got through and lived to bring back copies they had made themselves, and to put out careful subsequent editions in print.

Erasmus had been to Italy as he had been practically everywhere
else, and whatever one might think of his polemical and satirical
writings, his learning and editorial penetration were justly admired the
world over. For the matter of that, Erasmus' lambent strictures on the
follies of the world, the immoralities of clergy, and the injustices perpetrated by the ecclesiastical bureaucracy, though one might deplore
the gay, popular form in which he couched them, never missed the
mark. Popular, incidentally, was a relative term, as the author wrote
in Latin: but in language at once so terse and elegant that it fairly
put to shame the handling of it in approved, serious-minded quarters—
and to repeat, when he was serious, his work was unimpeachably
authoritative.

Born in Flanders and now well on in his forties, Desiderius Erasmus
was the epitomal citizen of the world and epitome of unfading intellectual youth and vigour. Physically he was small and chronically
wilting, with just the wise, spare, quizzical face one would picture to
fit his literary personality; and both gastrically and emotionally sensitive to a degree. He was one of a tiny handful of writers in the
Western world able to live on their writings, and held a unique position—something between enfant terrible and philosopher king: a
charming nuisance, and a meritocrat. So, too, he liked to think of himself: a stimulating gadfly, yet serene and detached; a catalyst, but

uninvolved. So far he was having it all his own way; his sarcasm and invective were tolerated smilingly as those of a licensed buffoon, while his scholarly productions were received with enlightened acclaim.

Luther could not but be imbued with so general an attitude, and could not but wish there were more men equipped as Erasmus. He had joined in the local agitation to establish a regular faculty of classics at the University of Wittenberg, where Greek and Hebrew should be taught systematically instead of students being left to fend for themselves in these subjects aside from the occasional lectures given by travelling humanist luminaries. Yes, he himself was trying to improve his meagre Greek and learn the rudiments of Hebrew—for he was having trouble with the Bible, as well.

Though he knew the Bible practically by heart, having read in it every day of his life as a friar, from the teaching point of view he was finding it very difficult to break down. His task was to demonstrate the christological unity of the whole Scriptures, their complete, organic coherence from Genesis to the resurrection and the apostolic Epistles.

"I am here," he opened his first professorial lecture, on the Psalms —the Psalms, forming the framework of divine office, were so familiar to everyone as to be made the usual topic for beginners, "I am here because I have been so instructed. I confess plainly that to this day there are some Psalms which I have never managed to understand. I can only hope that the Lord will now enlighten me through you and for you, that I may become capable of interpreting them."

A small note of originality was struck: this was to be a joint expedition of discovery, not a well-worn conducted tour. But it came from an honest sense of deficiency, nothing else.

His preaching, on which he had embarked in such mortal stagefright, left nothing to be desired in conventional competence. The earliest extant sermon in his hand was an irreproachable specimen of the common run. Based on the text, "Moab is the cook-pot of my hope" (Psalm 60:8), it explained that the cook-pot represents the world, the three legs of the pot being the three evil lusts (lust of the flesh, lust of the eyes, and lust of ambition), and Christ the cook. The cook is cooking a savoury dish of martyrs for the angels. He puts a lid on the pot by allowing temptation to hot up, so that the saints may generate a goodly steam of prayer—and so on and so forth, neglecting no possible analogy to kitchen process. A good preacher, for the parish to be proud of, was someone who could run allegorical rings round alike the plainest and the least intelligible Biblical quotation, ad infinitum.

So that was easy for him; too easy, he felt, though hardly knowing why. He put down the ineluctable shadow of uneasiness to his old spiritual malady which Dr. Staupitz was seeking to combat by the exigencies of nursing the spirits of others. Meantime to prepare his lecture courses and extract the hidden Christian meanings from the books of the Old Testament, Luther covered the big Vulgate which was his constant working material, with careful notes. In spite of the value of books, annotating was not frowned upon: perhaps it counted as embellishment and possible assistance to successive readers. A finely produced volume like the one he used had large margins with the lines of text spaced widely apart, and Luther's script was no defacement. He wrote the small, clear hand of methodical thought deriving encouragement from the aesthetic satisfaction of well-formed, as it were self-respecting letters. In the same neat, disciplined writing, however, he set down irritable exclamations like, "Pig-theologer!" and "rancid Aristotle!" in the Augustinian library copies of standard textbooks, against particularly unhelpful scholastic passages. He, too, was falling out of humour more and more with traditional theology.

If nothing else, the occupational therapy devised for his protégé by the Vicar-general was teaching Luther self-assurance. Further jobs were piled on him, so that before long he acted also as director of studies at the cloister and district vicar for eleven Saxon Augustinian priories, in addition to his lectureship, parish duties, and conventual post, which was that of reader in the refectory.

"I could do with two secretaries. I seem to do nothing all day long but write letters: so if I keep repeating myself, you will understand. I am preacher, lecturer, reader; I am every day asked to preach at the town church; I am director of studies; I am area supervisor which as you know means being prior eleven times over: I am inspector of fishponds at Leitzkau and arbitrator at Torgau! I am lecturing on Paul and gathering material for a commentary on the Psalms which the Elector wants me to bring out, and then as I say, letters, letters, letters. I hardly get time for my prayers or to say mass—and of course there are all the usual temptations of the flesh, the world, and the devil, for such an idle man!"

He was able to joke about it; the Devil scarcely had an opportunity for his wonted whispering when Luther knelt at prayer, "Friend, what do you want to do that for? What is the point? Listen. See how quiet it is here; not a sound. Can you really think there is Anyone about, taking the slightest notice of you?" Quiet, what quiet? The most he could do was to let his obligatory daily devotions accumulate to be discharged in one twenty-four-hour marathon at the week-end without pause for sleep and food, let alone satanic back-chat. True, he was building up a habit of insomnia and disrupting his digestion, but he had not the leisure to worry about that either.

There were other things disrupted for him besides. Many small monkish inhibitions, so attentively inculcated from the first day of a man's novitiate, fell away. How was a man with so many extra-mural posts to go on walking everywhere with head bowed, eyes downcast, hands confined in the sleeves of his black cowl, never smiling, much less laughing in public, and except at set times communicate with his brethren only in sign language? The times when he was not talking audibly were the exceptions. Eyes on the ground, decorously prisoned hands, small, stilted steps were impracticable for someone always in a hurry, always behind schedule, yet continually having to accommodate extra responsibilities. A smile, a jest, a guffaw would be invaluable supplements to judicious sternness, in dealing with the misdemeanours and squabbles of a whole monastic district. He was becoming quite well-known about the neighbourhood and well-liked in the town.

The correspondent to whom he wrote that letter about his activities was Father Lang—whom he had had the pleasant power to appoint prior of the Erfurt monastery they had both been thrown out of.

"You write that you began to lecture on the Sentences yesterday," the letter chatted on. "I shall start expounding Galatians tomorrow—"

Running idly off the pen, here was in fact a significant bit of gossip. The *Sentences* of Peter Lombard—a twelfth-century bishop of Paris and pupil of Abelard the foremost outrider of rational theology—was, to coin a phrase, the bible of scholasticism. It was a compendium of patristic doctrine set out in logical sequence. Designed by the compiler to be definitive, the book had in the event spawned that vast progeny of commentaries which the progressives were deriding, and on which Luther was even now turning his back—with a few parting shots in delicate penmanship but no uncertain terms, "Maggots!" "Parasite-philosophers!" "Fetid logicians!"

Luther had begun to cull from the Psalms and Paul's Epistles the soul-elixir of which he had despaired. In his memory, later on, there was nothing gradual about it. Then a process, of which evidence survived in his study notes, had faded out of consciousness and only the dazzling moment of achievement lived on—just as he tended to remember the time before that as one of solid misery, except by default: "I know a man," he would say, in stylistic assonance to Paul, "who suffered such torments of hell as no tongue or pen can describe and no one who has not felt them could imagine. If they had lasted longer than the tenth part of an hour at a time, he would have perished altogether and his bones would have crumbled to ashes." Exactly: *if* they had lasted longer, without respite, he would have perished.

There was a phrase, echoing throughout the Psalms and the Pauline Epistles: *thy righteousness.* Writing on the Psalms at the Elector's behest, his pen stuck at the words, *In thy righteousness deliver me.* In the Vulgate it read, *In iustitia tua libera me.* It turned on the word he feared and hated above all: *iustitia,* justice, which in the German form *Gerechtigkeit* moreover signified both righteousness/virtue and judicial equity: the word by which he was damned.

"The word used to give me such a seasickness—to speak with decorum—that I would hardly have been sorry if somebody had made away with me. . . . ay, even today I am as though transfixed when I hear God called 'the just.' . . ."

This time it did not let him rest, and did not let him escape. Strongly drawn though he had long felt to St. Paul, he had never brought himself to study the Epistle to the Romans, in which *iustitia dei* was so much the theme-song. This time he girt himself to tackle it. He found, *The just shall live by faith,* and halted. It meant nothing, and yet he sensed that the vital clue, somehow, was here.

So he "raged with a wounded and confused spirit and beat importunately at that passage in Paul, thirsting with a most ardent desire to know. . . . And then at last, God being merciful, as I meditated day and night on the words, *For therein is the righteousness of God revealed, as it is written, The just shall live by faith,* there all at once I began to understand the justice of God as that by which the just live by the gift of God, which is faith: that passive justice with which the merciful God endues us in form of faith, thus justifying, rendering us righteous. . . . The Church Fathers always expounded the *iustus deus* as that [aspect of God] in which he avenges and punishes, not as that which maketh man just. . . . Now at this I experienced such relief and easement, as if I were reborn and had

entered through open gates into paradise itself. The whole Bible all
at once looked different. I ran through it in my mind, as much of it as
I could remember, and gathered together a great number of similar
expressions, corroborating what had come to me. As much as I had
hated that word, the *righteousness of God,* before, so much the
more dear and sweet it was to me now, so that this passage in Paul
became for me in very truth the gate of heaven."

For, with justice/righteousness the unconditional gift of God, virtue
would flow from it but never could precede, much less earn, what is
pure grace. If grace was identical with faith, then neither reason nor
will nor deserts could have anything to do with it; merit ceased to have
any meaning on the human level. Merit was with God alone, and
in the gift of God alone. Out of his infinite goodness and mercy,
God bestowed his grace on the infinite, incurable imperfection which
was man. Man was saved; man *is* saved.

"And then, what a game began!" Luther recollected vividly. "The
words came up to me on every side jostling one another and smiling
in agreement—" everywhere he looked, he found: St. Augustine,
even St. Bernard, even the German Mystics to whom Staupitz had
once or twice referred him, fruitlessly (and of course St. Paul, over
and over)—all affirmed his wondrous recognition.

The words jostling one another, smiling, Luther overflowed with
happiness that demanded to be communicated. Every circumstantial
detail surrounding the climactic moment was precious to memory,
and important. *"Dise Kunst,"* wrote Luther without guile, *"hatt mir
d. S.S. auf diss Cl. eingeben,"*—this art was imparted to me by the
S.S. on this cl.—little guessing as he marvelled untiringly at his rebirth
that he was unleashing centuries of controversy.

"S.S." for Sanctus Spiritus, the Holy Ghost, was a familiar enough
abbreviation. Not so "Cl." which did not refer to a religious concept.
Two witnesses who heard him talk about it said he said *cloaca,*
and "Clo" remained a latterday German euphemism for the privy, also
called "Locus"—as in *locus secretus monachorum,* the secret place of
the monks, so quoted by a third witness. But the fourth transcriber
of Luther's relevant table-talk makes it *hypocaustum,* a place heated
from below, such as a Roman bath of antiquity, and such as the
ramshackle Wittenberg priory, which fourteen years after this event
was still incomplete, was unlikely to boast. Might "hypocaustum" have
been another euphemism, for a shaft-disposal of gaseous matter?

Luther also sometimes spoke of the debated place as "the tower room," a frequent location of privies in his day. The hopeful interpretation of "Cl." as *capitulum,* chapter, falls to the ground if the location was a tower or rather turret which was all the priory ran to; also a chapter meeting would scarcely be conducive to undisturbed meditation. As for the suggestion of "Cl."=*cella,* his cell and study, this is rendered dubious by the fact that he had to consult the Bible "in my mind" instead of rushing forthwith to the book which was always on his desk.

The picture of the man of God straining at both ends—an image right after Luther's heart and right out of his favourite colloquial vocabulary—offends the squeamish hero-worshipper as much as it delights the debunker.

To Luther, defecation was not a discreditable secret—more likely, indeed, something to shout about for joy since he suffered a great deal from constipation. ("Dominus percussit me in posteriora gravi dolore; tam dura sunt excrementa ut multa vi usque ad sudorem extrudere cogar: et quo diu tuis differo, magis durescunt," he lamented in his correspondence, with dignity—not for nothing would the medical profession cling to Latin jargon longest of all!) Had Luther experienced such touchingly heartfelt "relief and easement" from, say, earache, his would-be defenders and detractors would think nothing of it.

Does it not seem fitting and even—"to speak with decorum," Luther's favourite phrase when about to be indecorous—even beautiful, that he should have been vouchsafed that tremendous sense of "rebirth" by "opened gates" to paradisiac peace and achievement, through and through? That would make it, to speak with decorum, official.

∗

10. "Our" Practical Theology

Once again a new discovery proved the epidemic exhilaration of pioneering. The "Tower Theology" or "Theology of Justification" or "Anti-Merit Theology," of which Luther's sudden insight was the kernel and the spark, made rapid headway. In its light, just as he described, everything was re-illuminated, falling into a new, gapless pattern; all he had to do now was to map it out in greater detail and pass on the method. For that was it: a question of new methodology, to reveal eternal facts in pristine clarity. Surely simple once you knew how, it was a matter of disinterring the buried treasure of God's Word and restoring it to full employment as a practical guide to salvation. By this the dichotomy of religion and theology was overcome, and pure science became science applied. Students and colleagues waxed keen to try their hands at it.

One day it would be shown that expositions of Romans by sixty doctors of the Western Church from the time of Ambrosiaster (a fourth-century commentary on the Epistles of Paul, which was attributed to St. Ambrose until Erasmus conclusively disproved this) had interpreted *iustitia dei* in exactly the same sense as Luther's, which he claimed to be so novel.

Maybe so, but it was news to Luther and to everyone around him. What were sixty doctors, spread over twelve centuries of torrential exegesis? There were no reference libraries of classified books, and most of the said expositions never found their way into print. Luther who could unashamedly confess, "Before I actually read Augustine, I had very little use for him," who never "actually read" the prince of schoolmen St. Thomas Aquinas (rejected by the Occamists) at all, and who was inevitably ignorant of huge tracts of theological literature such as no single mind could possibly assimilate even in a lifetime of doing nothing else whatever—Luther had not come across those sixty doctors. The person who dug them up and brought them forward against Luther was Heinrich Denifle, a papal archivist of the nineteenth century, no earlier, who—like Luther himself once he had formulated his thesis and began to cast about for authorities to buttress it—knew what he was looking for.

For Luther, it was of great importance that his discovery was not in itself new and that he should have the best of authorities to fall back on, in merely re-stating an absolute, universal truth. He would have been only too pleased to enroll another sixty doctors against the vindictive, mercenary Deity of the great mass of lesser schoolmen. (Had he looked, he could even have drawn support from Aquinas.) He was only too happy to give credit to any help he had received, witting and unwitting—from the teachers of his youth, from the un-flagging resource of Dr. Staupitz, from the very pear tree in the yard of the Wittenberg priory under whose branches he and his mentor were wont to hold their colloquies.

"Our theology and that of Augustine are carrying all before them!" he wrote in breathless jubilation, again to his friend Lang at Erfurt. "And they reign in our university, and it is the Lord's doing, and Aristotle is going down, maybe into permanent discredit! It is wonder-ful"—for whom it might concern!—"how out of favour are the lectures on the Sentences. Lecturers who don't take the line of the Bible and St. Augustine simply speak to empty places!"

For that was the corollary of "our" theology—nay the be-all and end-all of it—to treat the Bible as a working manual of faith rather than a dictionary of incantation and abstruse symbolism. It did indeed transform the Biblical lecture course at Wittenberg. Allegory went by the board; and while it was essential to the theory of non-negotiable spiritual commodities to emphasize the entirely abstract nature of con-cepts like justice, merit, faith, grace, and penitence, abstractionist analysis was at an end.

It was all laid down, St. Paul had stated it once for all, and never more succinctly than in Galatians which was Luther's perpetual main-stay:

"There be some that trouble you, and would pervert the gospel of Christ [i.e. by embroidering on the original message]. But," so Paul had written with patiently controlled exasperation, "though we or an angel from heaven preach any other gospel unto you than that which we have preached unto you, let him be accursed. . . . Christ has redeemed us from the curse of the law [i.e. outward religious acts like circumcision and observance of food taboos: Christianity at the time of Paul's directive being still regarded as a movement of Judaic reformation]. . . . Before faith came, we were kept under the law, shut up unto the faith which should afterwards be revealed. Wherefore the law was our schoolmaster to bring us unto Christ, that we might be justified by faith [the divine gift of grace]. But after that faith is come we are no longer under a schoolmaster. For ye are all children of God by faith in Jesus Christ. For as many of you as have been baptized in Christ, have put on Christ. There is neither Jew nor Greek, there is neither bond nor free, there is neither male nor female: for ye are all one in Christ Jesus. And if ye be Christ's, then are ye Abraham's seed, and heirs according to the promise." What could be clearer? ("See how large a letter I have written unto you in mine own hand!" the harassed Apostle had remarked in passing, to end crustily, "From henceforth let no man trouble me.") In a nutshell, the Epistle contained Luther's entire position, in its entirety yet unknown to himself. St. Paul was very near to him.

They were all becoming most real to him, his distant forerunners on the road to God. There was no more cook-pot of Moab. For a specimen of his revolutionary, realistic exposition of Biblical texts for popular consumption, his narration of the testing of Abraham is unsurpassed:

"Abraham was told by God that he must sacrifice the son of his old age by a miracle, the seed through which he was to become the father of kings and of a great nation. Abraham turned pale. Not only would he lose his son, but God appeared to be a liar. He had said, 'In Isaac shall be thy seed,' but now he said, 'Kill Isaac.' Who would not hate a God so cruel and inconsistent? How Abraham longed to talk it over with someone! But he well knew that if he mentioned it to anyone he would be dissuaded. . . . The spot designated for the sacrifice, Mount Moriah, was some distance away: 'And Abraham rose up early in the morning, and saddled his ass, and took two of his young men with him, and Isaac his son, and clave the wood for the burnt-offering. . . .' He was thinking all the time that these logs would consume his child. With these very sticks he was picking up the boy would be burned. In such a terrible case should he not take time to think it over? Could he not tell Sarah? With what inner tears he suffered! He girt the ass, so preoccupied he hardly knew what he was doing.

"He took two serving men and Isaac his son. In that moment everything else died to him. . . . If he had known that this was only a trial, he would not have been tried. Such is the nature of our trials that while they last we cannot see to the end. 'Then on the third day Abraham lifted up his eyes, and saw the place afar off.' What a battle he had been through in those three days! There Abraham left the servants and the ass, and he laid the wood upon Isaac and himself took the torch and the sacrificial knife. All the time he was thinking: Isaac, if you knew, if your mother knew. . . . Then said Isaac: My father. And he said: yes, my son. And Isaac said: Father, here is the fire and here the wood, but where is the lamb? He called him father and was solicitous lest he had overlooked something! And Abraham said: God will himself provide a lamb, my son.

"When they were come to the mount, Abraham built the altar and laid on the wood, and then he had to tell Isaac. The boy was stupefied. He must have protested. . . . And Abraham must have answered that God would fulfil his promise even out of ashes. Then Abraham bound his son and laid him upon the wood. The father raised his knife. The boy bared his throat. If God had slept one instant, the boy would have been dead. I could not have watched. I cannot bear to follow it through in my imagination. . . . Never in history was there such obedience, save only in Christ. But God was watching, and all the angels too. The father raised his knife. The boy did not flinch. The angel cried: 'Abraham, Abraham!' "—only just in time.

Luther breathed so much life into the age-old suspense story which had long shrivelled into a mere hieratic fable, that he nearly overreached himself, for a listener cried out: "I don't believe it! God would not have had the heart to act like that!" But Luther turned the interruption to account, saying quietly, "But he did," thus rounding off the tale of faith and mystery.

People from outlying districts came to the town church of Wittenberg to hear him. Matriculations began to rise. Some of the older universities began to take notice.

Luther himself was taking notice of all manner of things which in his previous, essentially egocentric struggle for enlightenment he had passed over as extraneous. His doctorate, which once he had deprecated as an external frill, now was become a commission straight from God. "Who compelled the Lord to make me a doctor? Since he did it of his own will, let come what may!" never mind if the Sententiary lectures of the faculty whose customs he had sworn to uphold all his life were unattended by his doing. But the sacred mandate did not end there. His parish work also showed the effect of the new, practical approach. Right and left, he began to censure and exhort, not only in the confessional but from the pulpit.

"Practical analogy to the present makes the Bible easier to understand," he explained, warning unauthorized persons against speaking out as he did. "I, by papal authority, hold a public teaching office. Accordingly it is my official duty to strike out against all wrongs of which I become aware, even if the wrong is done by persons in high places."

Plus ça change: nobody thinks of anything these days but his material profit. Everyone is out to make money and to get as much as he can for nothing. Bricklayers work as though they were asleep, the merchants trick the public, peasants likewise laze and cheat, lawyers care only about forms and fees. Clergymen snore through the liturgy, lords temporal and spiritual vie for worldly power and possessions, Christian nations are forever at each other's throats to the same end, Holy Rome is all unholy dolce vita; and burghers letting their nubile daughters attend the revels of the student population are asking for trouble: plus c'est la même chose. It was all old stuff even then, that too; only to Luther, again, his own awakened interest and sense of responsibility were new. So long as criticism was not accompanied by sedition, as in the unfortunate case of Savonarola, or attack upon dogma, as in that of Hus, it passed under the head of pastoral fair comment.

If anything it increased Dr. Martinus' popularity. It looked as if he were being instrumental in putting Wittenberg on the academic map at last, and here he was catering for the people as well—"in such stout German!", too. He cared, he really cared. For castigation bespeaks paternal regard: the secret of the success of forceful moralists through the ages, whether or no the cathartic of contrition which they offer be accepted. If some of his views were a little eccentric, that was only to be expected.

11. The Gothic Frontier

It was less difficult for Luther to make his audiences, as it were, experience the prehistoric herdsmen who were the Jewish patriarchs than it is for us to get the feel of the people of Luther's Germany a mere four and a half centuries ago. The patriarchal characters personify two fundamental human preoccupations: God and progeny, easily translatable into any time and clime. Luther's mediaeval Germans, so near and yet so far, were more complex, multifarious, and documented, and they almost defy imaginative understanding in an environment which contrary to superficial appearances had almost more alien features than points of similarity to the present.

The patriarchs are legendary. That—had Luther's Germans been able to appreciate the distinction—would have been enough to make a bond. The German climate was all living legends and fabulous simplifications. The Gothic reality was sporting stranger plots and characters than those of fiction—that "romantic" fiction which had already appropriated the elements of the weird and wonderful, the bizarre, heroic, irregular, and picturesque under the etymological label of the Gallic South. Far more than on the culturally superior soil of France, those prime elements of Romance lived a still active life in the old happy hunting grounds of Northern barbarism.

Ah, the snug towns with their industries and universities, fields, vineyards and orchards, were oases in a jungle of pristine rawness. For every garden there were leagues of murky forest, for every sure waterway there were a thousand death traps along what bore the courtesy title of roads, for every outpost of human civilization there were a million strongholds of ghosts and sprites. For every cathedral there were scores of castles, eyries of prey poised in strategic isolation and unsoftened violence; for every law-abiding citizenry there was a band of outlaws, for every priest a witch, a wolf to every sheepfold and a bear to every wooded wilderness.

Germany was the land of fairytales, teeming with magic and anthropomorphic spirits as ever Hellas or Central Africa—but without the soaring serenity of the one or the sun-baked fatalism of the other. Here the mind of man could not rise above the besetting supernatural caprice, but neither was it willing to lie down under that. The luxuries of an alien ethic like the Christian and the alien ideals of hellenic questing, had to be paid for on an endless instalment plan, making ease and relaxation impossible.

Germany was a land of ingrained tribal conflict—ever yearning for elusive peace and order, ever spoiling for a quarrel; with the dream of a single national leadership offset by alert parochial jealousies, and where ideological miscegenation had never yet resulted in a settled synthesis. But with what the biologists call hybrid vigour, it was highly fecund in production of protean variants and oddities.

At the top, Maximilian I, the "Emperor Max" of frenetic German hero-worship, is almost impossible to assess without first splitting him in two and taking each half at a time without reference to the other. That also was more easily accomplished in the day of Luther, when the individual man and the position which he occupied were perfectly understood to be things apart. Strangely enough, the same minds which baulked at the insubstantiality of spiritual values had no difficulty at all in mentally separating the abstract concepts of "accident" and "class." In most such cases it was a matter of distinguishing between sacrosanctity of office and shortcomings in the individual occupier; with this idol of the German nation one would say it was the other way round.

Maximilian of Habsburg, sixth elected Roman Emperor of his kindred since 1273, was a most attractive, lovable, and fascinating person in himself. As an emperor—whether one stressed his Roman or his German attribute—as an emperor he was, with due respect, a wash-out. As a Habsburg and Archduke of Austria he did very well for himself and his dynasty; as an athlete and sportsman he excelled; as a patron of art and literature he was almost Italian; as a warrior he combined generalship with spectacular personal bravery; as a man he was unusually civilized, tolerant, affable, humorous; as an author he was versatile, beguilingly fanciful, and (for an emperor) prolific. Even as a politician the only fault that Machiavelli, the expert in this field, found with Maximilian was that his consistent perfidy was insufficiently systematic. For as an emperor, in the end result, it did not get him anywhere.

Perhaps an inability for systematic planning (except in matters of straightforward dynastic import) was the crucial flaw. The glorious Max was full of good ideas and splendid intentions, which wove about him such an aureole of credit that the eye was blinded to the absence of corresponding achievement. He was not ineffectual like his predecessor (who had not been deposed simply because the Electors could not think of anybody to put in his place, at the time), but most of his attempts turned into something else. He was resolved on administrative reformation of the Empire, and in effect he undermined it. He declared for the German Gravamina and ecclesiastical reform—yet that objective got lost in a sort of elaborate shortcut to it: the notion of Caesaro-papalism in reverse, as the Emperor thought of achieving universal monarchy by seating himself in the chair of St. Peter and donning the papal tiara on top of the imperial crown. He really worked quite hard for peace within the Empire—which was to say that he was continually involved in intra-imperial warfare; he worked, too, to restore the power of central law, but to win the indispensable support of the princes for this had to make concessions which in the event defeated the purpose. Having once cleared his property of Styria of Turkish invaders, he proclaimed it the supreme ambition of his life to drive the Infidel right out of Europe; instead of which in the event he embroiled the Empire in wars with France, Flanders, Hungary, Poland, Venice, Switzerland, and very nearly with England as he assisted Perkin Warbeck in his bid for the English throne. He was the emblem and heart, the totem of German nationalism, though in almost continuous conflict with now one, now the other, now all the German Estates, and flagrantly neglecting the German interest altogether, in favour of his personal and Habsburg interests, except when he needed German money.

But he spoke the German language, and he was dubbed "the Last of the Knights." German nationalism, like Christian reformism, was looking back to an illusory past. Chivalry, the ruthless ethic of a feudal régime based upon the needs and uses of the horse, had become transmuted into that pretty, aesthetic concept of pure courage, generosity, and honour with which it is still identified today. Maximilian *was* at heart a relic of feudalism: and that was the ultimate cause of his fantastic popularity and of his actual failures.

Yet the strangest of all these factors was that the proper conditions of nostalgia were still wanting. Chivalry, de mortuis nil nisi bonum, the real old chivalry was still very much alive and packed a nasty kick. To call Emperor Max the last of the knights was wishful thinking, in a manner. The knighthood of Germany, more especially in the Franconian heart of the Empire, were its bane.

Its epitome was not Maximilian but Götz von Berlichingen "of the iron hand"—a real, artificial right hand of iron, jointed and riveted and with fingernails delicately incised—a petty nobleman of Württemberg, whom Goethe immortalized, and who best characterized himself with the shout of, "Go to! good luck to you!" addressed to some wolves closing in on a flock of sheep as he rode by. For he and his merry men rode by on exactly similar business, and the foregone conclusion of the wolves' success was a good omen. Götz spoke for all his kind, who lived by banditry and feuds.

The real emperor of the Germans—as a popular saying had it—was Franz von Sickingen, the undisputed leader of that breed.

The position of the free knighthood of Germany was peculiar and equivocal. They were free in the same sense as certain imperial cities, in that they owed allegiance only to the apex of fealty and symbol of the state, the Emperor, and were thus independent of the territorial princes. But they had lost the genuine independence of material security, together with their ancient feudal function as a kind of special militia to the Emperor, by the growth in civil and territorial power of those princes during the later Middle Ages. They had no organic services to perform and therefore no protection, either. As a caste, they were clamouring for revision of a system wherein, without specific accommodation, they could neither live nor die. Bankrupt, bristling and unstable, they formed a floating stratum of unrest which periodically coalesced in private wars such as had died out in other countries.

."Centaurs," one of their number described them, "utterly lacking in education and human feeling. . . . Let no one envy the life of knights! Even were my fortune ample, still I should be without any hope of security. We live, not in decent houses, but in fields, forests, and fortresses. We exist by the labours of poverty-stricken peasants . . . and the yield is extremely meagre in proportion to the labour. Somebody like me has to attach himself to some prince, otherwise everyone will look upon one as fair game. But even when I do form such an attachment, it is fretted by constant anxiety. The moment I venture from home I am in danger of crossing the path of those who are at feud with my overlord, whoever he may be, and of being set upon and carried off: and almost certainly half of what I do possess will be forfeit as ransom. One cannot go unarmed beyond two yokes of land. So we have to keep up a large establishment of horses, arms, and retainers, at great cost which we cannot afford. We can't go visiting, hunting, or fishing save in full armour. Then also there are constant quarrels between our underlings and those of others, which have to be handled with the utmost discretion, as firmness may lead to war and the slightest sign of softness will be interpreted as weakness and will step up the other side's demands a hundredfold. And among what manner of folk does all this go on? Not among mutual strangers as you might think but among neighbours, relatives, between members of the same household, even between brothers. Such are our romantic delights. One's castle needs to be, not fair, but firm, hemmed in by moat and wall, narrow and dark inside, draughty and cold, crowded with cattle, stores, and armaments, not to mention the dogs and their dung everywhere—sweet aroma I can tell you. Horsemen go in and out, you don't know what thieves and cut-throats. The noise is incessant, what with bleating of sheep and lowing of cattle, dogs barking, men shouting, the squeak and rattle of barrows and wagons, and the howling of the wolves in the woods. Day and night it is the same, there is no peace, no rest, no end of anxiety and vigilance. . . ."

Born 1481 in just such an environment, as the only son among a brood of daughters, small of stature but wiry and fiery, Franz von Sickingen while yet in his teens became known as a redoubtable free lance and before he was much more than twenty had made himself the illegitimate "emperor" of Germany: able any time he liked to lead into the field an army of twenty thousand, which was more than the titular Emperor could usually manage to squeeze out of the Estates in months of bargaining. Franz von Sickingen need but call, and knights and men rushed to his standard, to live off the land of the oppressed for whom they went to war, and then again off the lands of the oppressors. He did not have to wrestle for every German penny by long and complicated negotiations; he grabbed what he needed, then as occasion offered might sell his services to the Emperor or to a confederation of towns, and would come out laden with honours as well as with spoils, even though currently under the imperial ban and uniformly abominated as a scourge of land and people. Blackmail, protection money, bribes (without warranty) came to him as easily as that flair for military organization and tactics to which he owed his ascendancy; and though thinking big he would never disdain the smallest opportunity of highway robbery and ransom. He was a simple man, untroubled by doubt or indecision, and his simplicity was as much of an asset to him as his very evident luck.

His merry band had a habit of cutting off the right hands of the abject civilians whom they robbed, for no better reason than to leave their mark; when people begged them to cut off their left hands instead, it only irritated them. The knighthood considered the free commonalty, and the merchants most of all, as usurpers of a prosperity which the knights in fact had never boasted even in their heyday.

If Sickingen waylaid a caravan and had to leave the booty lying where his victims left it, pending transport to headquarters at his fortress of Ebernburg, there was no need to post guards: nobody, least of all the terrified owners, would touch the prize. If Sickingen announced his temporary alliance with any warring faction in the country, that cause was as good as won. And if Sickingen now took up the cudgels for humanism and education, that just about settled that.

Not that this "centaur" in any way amended his own "utter lack of education and humanity," as his friend Hutten had put it in the eloquent description of the knightly state, quoted above. But he *had* made friends with Hutten, that was the point; and any friend of Hutten's was a friend of his.

Ulrich von Hutten also was of knightly estate, and he was a poet. "What do you mean, men like us?" he briskly took up an acquaintance, once, in conversation. "Do you mean us knights, or us intellectuals?" The day of wonders was not past, not by any means, in Germany.

Once upon a time there was a duke—another Ulrich—who came into his heritage at eleven years old and won the Emperor's niece in marriage. This Duke Ulrich of Württemberg had everything else besides to make a man happy: a rich country, youth, health, strength, good looks, personality, the fond goodwill of his subjects, the earnest care of honest advisers, the friendship of his vassals. The only gifts which the good fairies had withheld from his cradle were sense and sensibility; and so he proceeded to squander the rest. He overspent his revenues; his peasantry rose in revolt from his unjust exactions, his townsfolk were alienated by his touchy tyranny, his advisers by browbeating and disregard; his allies washed their hands of his un-realistic egoism and got along without him. Only his intimate friends still loved him.

One day the Duke fell in love with the wife of a vassal and boon companion. The husband remonstrated, whereupon the Duke went down on his knees and in tears besought the other to condone the relationship, because he (the Duke) could not live without it.

Not long after the Duke noticed what looked very like his own wife's betrothal ring on the finger of his mistress' husband. That was different.

The Duke took his friend out riding, and when they came to a dark wood taxed him with his infidelity, slew him, went home to bran-dish the bloody murder weapon over his own wife as she lay in bed, and repair to the bed of the victim's widow.

He really thought that he would get away with it. He knew his Duchess was the Emperor's niece and sister to the Duke of Bavaria, he knew that she was not of a forbearing disposition, and must have known, as she did, that her illustrious uncle was hunting in the vicinity; he knew perfectly well that the murdered man's kindred were very numerous and very proud. What he did not know—nor would have cared about had he known—was that a younger son of this now envenomed tribe, whose name was Hutten, had turned to writing.

As was to have been expected, the Duchess fled for succour to the Emperor and got her brothers up in arms against her husband, while the proud and numerous Huttens rallied all their friends and liegemen for a punitive expedition. As was not to be expected, the writing runt of the Hutten tribe threw his sharp pen into the fray to such effect that presently Duke Ulrich acquired the singular distinction of facing a united Empire, all out for his blood. He saved his life but nothing else, and disappeared for the time being among the mercenary riff-raff of a foreign country.

The moral of that Gothic true-story—yet to be continued—was that the pen had made its debut as an edged tool, acknowledged worthy partner of the sword by that very section of the German people who were in the best position to know.

Those younger sons of the petty nobility who had nothing but their swords to call their own were the latterday knights errants, the world their tilting ground. But while the concrete pickings of that world diminished for them so that they had to snap and snarl like wolves indeed to get their quotas of the prey, other types of prize came on the market. The Italian Renaissance having freed the intellectual arts from chair-borne bondage to the clergy, the riches of knowledge and the laurels of creative endeavour were coming within reach and—more important—within the admissible ambitions of the noble. The discoveries, or re-discoveries, of classical learning which accelerated day by day in mounting chain reaction, spelt adventure writ large albeit of a new kind. Or perhaps it was not so new as all that: the quest of Parsifal for the holy grail, along with other epic material, had been restored to literary ken and showed that the knightly ideal could be reconciled with arcane spiritual values, without drawing charges of effeminacy. For the new-old learning was daily forging antiquarian tools to apply nearer home and reveal the existence of cultures of the non-classical past, such as had been dismissed hitherto as a contradiction in terms. Everywhere one looked there was treasure to be dug up.

"It is a joy to be alive!" cried Ulrich von Hutten who, God knows, had a pretty comfortless time of it physically. It was like the Gold Rush. Not a few of the ragged wolf cubs joined in, swelling the flood of wandering scholars to Italy. Emperor Max, the soul of virile chivalry, had done his bit to render letters and learning honourable secular occupations, not least by reviving the mediaeval institution of poetic laureateship.

Naturally the Poet's Crown was modernized to meet present trends and was bestowed for more than straightforward technical skill and output as of old—rather like a Nobel Prize—although these of course entered into the award. The first to be invested with it was, appropriately, one who had acted as a leading scout in the pilgrimage of German scholars to Italy, and who had returned with a perfected system of Latin prosody which, voraciously adopted, gave an immense boost to native poetics. He was the son of a vintner—or grape-treader=*Kel-*

terer—hence called Celtes in preference to Konrad Pickel; and he it was who had additionally done the spadework of archaeological and literary excavations in Germany.

Ulrich von Hutten was Celtes' successor to the laurel. Born 1488 in the usual knightly circumstances he so feelingly denounced, but sickly as a child and therefore convent-educated, he broke out of the cloister to escape the compulsion of holy orders and hurled himself into the humanistic pilgrimage. He was made for it. Puny of body, with a cast of features reminiscent of what is often associated with spinal deformity, Hutten possessed invincible stamina, triumphing again and again over an almost monotonous pattern of assault and robbery inflicted on him, and over chronic pennilessness and syphilis. The fallow talents of generations of bucolic knighthood burst forth into sudden, concerted fertility in this scion; what Sickingen was on the gangster front, Hutten was on the siege ladder to Parnassus. His device, *Ich hab's gewagt*, I have dared, stood fitly for his literary epigraph as well.

His writings ranged from lyric verse and humanistic dissertations to patriotic manifestos, satire, and unvarnished political polemics which earned him so fierce a hatred in the quarters under attack that his path came to be beset with secret warrants and assassins—never quite catching up with him. Into a brief, footloose, hunted, unprovided and improvident life Hutten crammed enough excitements for a substantial picaresque romance; he died free, of his own spirochaeta, argumentative to the last breath.

Characteristically he had himself portrayed in knight's armour but with the Poet's Crown upon his head; he was as proud of the one calling as of the other, though no less conscious—perhaps no less proud?—of the creature discomforts of both. His humanist apprenticeship was served in the "Poets' Circle," also known as the Mutianic Club, a brilliant constellation round the leading light of Konrad Mutianus (Muth) Rufus, a red-haired canon of Gotha near Erfurt, who there kept open house for wandering students and settled graduates alike.

Mutianus was probably the most original and potent single force in German humanism. Teaching was his inborn métier, the young were his passionate concern, and ethic was his sovereign theme. He wrote and preached untiringly against religious formalism, himself seldom celebrated mass, derided aural confession and fasting, and on the debated subject of relic-worship issued the following audacious statement:

"I will not adore the coat or beard or foreskin of Christ, but only the living God himself who has left us neither coat nor beard nor foreskin on this earth. The true body of Christ resides in peace and goodwill, not in some wafer: your eucharist is only mutual love in the hearts of men."

His influence spawned learned societies throughout Germany; and from the Poets' Circle in particular there sprang the literate vanguard of the national reform movement in all its diversity. Canon Mutianus himself it is true advocated only internal reformation of the Church, but among his disciples there were those who nimbly linked this with external reformation vis-à-vis secular society, and others going farther still, by attacking the Church as such.

"Three things are sold in Rome," Hutten summed up the radical position, "namely Christ, ecclesiastical preferment, and women. Three things are hateful to Rome: a General Council, the reformation of the Church, and the opening of German eyes. Three ills I pray the Lord for Rome: pestilence, famine, and war."

Three things Hutten had brought back from Rome: patriotism irritated to a high degree of inflammation, artistic maturity, and a paper by Lorenzo Valla, a distinguished clerical professor of Pavia and Naples in the preceding century, who among other irrefutable critiques had exposed the Donation of Constantine as a forgery inserted into the canonical decretals some five hundred years after the alleged donor's demise.

Erasmus was to make good use of that document—but in the meantime it did not cause such a stir as, accustomed to modern mass-communications, one would imagine today. The works of Valla had not caused sufficient stir in Italy, where they had been available since 1440, to have become so much as known abroad, till Hutten republished a part of them. Publication and publicity had as yet little correlation. Printing had enormously improved the chances of reception, but distribution remained erratic and to some extent fortuitous, especially so when it was a matter of small editions aimed at a narrow but scattered field of specialists.

There was many a slip and many a gap, too, between authority and enforcement. Authority was absolute and the Law was totalitarian, but for want of speedy intelligence and co-ordination the transgressor had a to us surprising latitude: first catch your hare, and before that, run him to earth. It was different with crimes like murder, theft, or failure to pay one's taxes, which were noted on the spot; but the humanists of whatever cloth and colour were preaching, writing, publishing away against a tyranny which was a fact and which yet left them largely unmolested. Every now and then somebody was made an example of—as one might, or might not, catch a disease that is in the air. But the Establishment was on the warpath, to remedy this lax state of affairs.

The ecclesiastical Establishment was largely run by the Dominican Friars, whom nobody loved except their fellow-Dominicans, and certainly not their rival mendicants of St. Augustine.

✳

12. The Reuchlin Affair

The Augustinian Friar Martin Luther, like most thinking churchmen, agreed with much of the humanist-inspired criticism concerning ecclesiastical wrongs—especially with regard to rancid Aristotelian pig-theology, hagiolatry and relic-worship, and the other excrescences of outward ritual; and he agreed that the Dominicans, who controlled most of the older universities, stood by these wrongs from sheer, benighted, egotistical conservatism. Proved to the hilt times out of number, this vicious defensiveness was demonstrated as never before in a matter on which he received express enquiries. For although, in 1515, the name of Martin Luther was not included by the visiting compiler of a Dictionary of Authors which was meant to cover also minor and potential celebrities, his local and district reputation was sufficiently established for his expert judgment to be sought.

The Reuchlin scandal, which had its muted beginning and end respectively in 1510 and 1520 but rose to a furor of public participation midway, set several unexpected precedents.

Johannes Reuchlin, born 1455, just under thirty years before Luther, was the effective founder of Greek and Hebrew studies in Germany. The son of a poor message-bearer of Pforzheim, his outstanding intelligence had early attracted patrons and teachers who sped his higher education in France and Italy. In Paris he had sat at the feet of the noted emigré Greek Hermonymus of Sparta, together with Lefèvre of Étaples (the man who was to do for France what Reuchlin did for Germany); Reuchlin and Lefèvre drank, too, from the same fountain at the Medicean Academy of Florence, where they were privileged to fill up with classical learning under the then greatest living hellenist of all, Argyropulous. (Argyropulous extravagantly complimented the young Reuchlin with the words, "Alas! Hellas, driven from her home, has fled across the Alps!") However, while Lefèvre was first and last a theologian and besides producing new critical editions of the non-metaphysical works of Aristotle devoted himself to direct Biblical studies along humanist lines, Reuchlin steered clear of clerical affiliations and was first and last a philologist. Unlike Lefèvre, Reuchlin had no private means and had to make a living variously as interpreter to travelling noblemen, as a calligrapher and copyist of Greek, and writer of elementary schoolbooks, the while he pursued his major studies. Through his acquaintance with the Habsburg Emperor Frederick's Jewish physician, he became interested in the cabalistic line of Jewish theosophy, and took to Hebrew like a duck to water.

Before long Reuchlin was the foremost Christian authority on that language. In 1506 he produced *De Rudimentis Hebraicis,* the first-ever Latin grammar and dictionary of the Hebrew language, at great expense as much of the type had to be specially cast, and with scant returns as there was great shortage of Hebrew books in Germany owing to Emperor Maximilian's Italian wars, so that few German savants had any immediate practical use for Reuchlin's high-priced lexicon. Like Erasmus Reuchlin believed that education was the whole secret of wisdom and virtue; and Erasmus added to Argyropulous' compliment, praising Reuchlin as a modern St. Jerome (Jerome having been fluent in six languages). Reuchlin capped this by uncovering a number of dubious passages in St. Jerome's Latin Vulgate.

Beginning at Basel, he held a succession of university lectureships, and proceeded to combine his grammarian teaching with a suggested mystic synthesis of Cabbalism and Neoplatonism—in the old hope of reconciling knowledge and faith—and published works affirming the utility to Christian learning of the Jewish Talmudic writings.

Not that it must be imagined for one moment that Reuchlin's academic philo-semitism embraced the living adherents to the Jewish faith. In the mediaeval Christian outlook the Jews were more reprobate than the heathen, having rejected Jesus with their eyes open and stubbornly refusing to see that the Old Testament was a Christian book. It was not because distant ancestors of theirs had consigned Jesus to crucifixion that coeval Jewry was condemned, but because coeval

Jewry still endorsed the crucifixion in refusing to accept Jesus as the Messiah, for whom they continued to wait.

Admittedly a certain confusion on this score reigned in untutored minds, Jewish as well as Christian.

The ancient Jewish colony in the city of Worms, which dated back to the time of Julius Caesar, promulgated the story that *their* forefathers here had voted against the crucifixion, although on account of the great distance the messenger from Worms had arrived at Jerusalem too late; and the common populace, for whom it had all happened in one foggy yesterday, found it simplest to hold present Jews responsible for the past, especially in view of their unpopular functions in present society. As the Jews were by law debarred from owning or even working on the land, as well as from almost every manual trade, while Christians were forbidden to lend money at interest yet with the importunate growth of capitalist enterprise needed to borrow, Jews could only trade in second-hand goods and money, glad to get employment from suzerains even in the detested capacity of tax-gatherers and financial agents. It never struck Reuchlin, either, as it would shortly strike the livelier mind of Luther, that the mainly parasitical subsistence of the Jews in the Christian communities where they were suffered was not of choice but by default.

With their extraordinary combination of self-consciousness, God-consciousness, and perseverance, the Jews maintained their identity through thick and thin, fire and sword, national extinction and dispersal. Come persecutions, come missionary attempts, Jewish converts to the Christian faith remained few and far between. In Cologne there was one, baptized Johannes Pfefferkorn, who conceived yet another scheme to persuade the Jews in Germany of their error. Being so essentially the People of the Book—that minutely codified religious lore, the stringent study and observance of which kept them Jewish—the Jews should first of all be deprived of their literature: everything else would follow.

Formerly not merely a Jew but a rabbi, Pfefferkorn at over fifty had gone all the way and taken holy orders, under Dominican auspices. Cologne was the particular German stronghold of the Dominican Order, which since its foundation in 1215 had served all over Europe as the mainstay of orthodoxy and vigilant academic supervisor. From the ranks of the Dominicans had come Albertus Magnus and St. Thomas Aquinas as well as latterly the first missionaries to the Far East and the New World; they it was who kept Thomism inflexibly alive, and they who staffed the sanitary brigade for the extermination of heresy, the Holy Inquisition. They manned the bastion of papal supremacy against conciliar reform—to the extent of declaring that the Church was "born slave to the pope," as wrote the Dominican theologian Giacomo de Vio of Gaeta, styled Gaetanus: so that even under a bad pope there was nothing the whole sacred institution could do but pray. In Germany, however, the Dominican grip had been slipping for some time past, and the Pfefferkorn scheme appeared to offer a sound vehicle for a rousing come-back. He had their full support.

Whether in the hope of forging a cast-iron case or because he was deranged, Pfefferkorn went to the length of accusing his erstwhile co-religionists of worshipping the sun and the moon and practising methodical ritual blasphemies against Christianity. He adduced his proofs from the Talmud. Reuchlin was approached to support Pfefferkorn with the Emperor, that an imperial decree might be obtained to confiscate and burn all Jewish books except the Bible.

Reuchlin was horrified and rose to the defence of the Talmud, his fount of "Hebraic verity," which as such had hitherto been fully licensed under both papal and imperial law. He sent in a memorandum showing that the few Jewish writings which were openly directed against Christianity were outside the authorized Jewish canon and discounted by most Jews themselves, and emphasizing once again that the Talmud was an indispensable reference work for Christian studies. He proposed an ingenious if naïve compromise. Let the Emperor create two Hebrew chairs at every German university and let the Jews of Germany give up their books to equip these, thus repairing the Italian blockade without prejudice to Pfefferkorn's scheme.

But by speaking out in this way Reuchlin had insulted Pfefferkorn's expertise and injured the Dominicans of Cologne in the nervous centre of their status. Pfefferkorn struck back with a pamphlet, *Hand-mirror against the Jews,* in which he added to his reiterated libels the charge that Reuchlin had accepted Jewish bribes. Reuchlin retorted with a pamphlet entitled *Eye-mirror,* in which he for his part repeated that the Talmud contained no such matter as Pfefferkorn claimed; and the Cologne Inquisition launched against him the pride of its arsenal, the charge of heresy. A formal enquiry, of the sort which predictably had but one outcome as a rule, was instituted against Reuchlin on the basis of the *Eye-mirror* and duly condemned the little book.

Reuchlin like Erasmus was a man of peace, though not of gracious living as he was too poor; but at least, "A poor man can lose nothing," he decided—again somewhat optimistically: but he knew so absolutely that what he had written in the *Eye-mirror* had no conceivable theological implications, that he absolutely could not see his life to be in danger. He appealed for a transfer of the case to Rome.

It must be clear to every scholar worthy of the name that the *Eye-mirror* was concerned simply and solely with what was or was not in the Talmud: Reuchlin was not the author of that, nor could he be asked to retract what he had quite correctly said there was in it and acknowledge himself an advocate of "dangerous doctrine." He was entirely a believer in orthodox Christian doctrine, and published solemn protestations to that effect, whilst patiently reiterating the purely technical import of his pamphlet.

To every scholar worthy of the name it was clear. Individual professors at the Dominican-dominated universities from the Sorbonne downwards saw it so; individual prelates and doctors at the Roman Curia saw it, as did the rank and file of European letters. But collectively the higher authorities had to think of their solidarity with the Dominican Inquisition. It was neither the first time nor the last, that an instrument of power was seen to have taken on a power of its own and become capable of backfiring. The ideological police force had grown too strong for easy manipulation by its employers. The Inquisitors in Germany had indicted Reuchlin for heresy, so one had better back them up. Metaphorically sighing, the Sorbonne and its satellites and also the Vatican administration endorsed the verdict, and, after renewed admonitions to withdraw while the going was good, Reuchlin came up for trial in Rome, though not as yet in person. His presence in Rome might never become necessary; he could recant or be excommunicated where he was, in Stuttgart.

Indeed Reuchlin could hardly get away. He was poorer than ever, already up to his ears in debt with the litigation to date, and shaking in his shoes. His situation was hopeless. He could never admit what was not true; it was as cut-and-dried for him as that.

By this time, however, the whole European intelligentsia had begun to stir in the old man's behalf. He was not personally very endearing, and many disagreed with his views—but his private quirks and philological opinions were not the question. Luther, too, deemed Reuchlin's assessment of the value of the Talmud highly exaggerated; but in answer to the Elector's request for an opinion he wrote to Spalatin:

"My opinion concerning the innocent [sic] and most learned Johann Reuchlin and his Cologne enemies, and whether he is guilty of heresy, is as follows. As you know, I have a great esteem for the man, so cannot be called unbiased. Nevertheless, since I am asked I will say what I think, which is that there is nothing dangerous in his writings. I marvel greatly at his opponents, because they make out of something so plain a tangle worse than the Gordian knot; regardless of his constant protestations that he is not setting up articles of faith but simply expressing a technical judgment. This in my view absolves him so completely from suspicion that if he had made a collection of every heresy in the world, in such a purely technical report, I should still hold him sound and pure in the faith which he explicitly professes. If technical judgments are no longer to be free from danger, these inquisitors will be able to pronounce a heretic anyone they like, however orthodox he may be. . . . There are a hundred real evils all around us, wherever one looks idolatry is rampant. These are the things we need to fight with all our strength. But no, we leave them be and worry about alien irrelevancies like the errors of the Jews. Could there be anything more stupid?"

He did not hesitate to proclaim the same opinion in the lecture hall. Others who were not so busy as he proclaimed it in print. It was above all that stupidity of Reuchlin's antagonists which more and more impressed itself on the educated public. As broadside followed broadside in what was becoming known as "the War of Books," the clumsy obtuseness of the anti-Reuchlinist polemics strained credulity: yet seeing was believing.

Reuchlin tried another angle. He published an anthology of testimonials as to his good character and good faith, by all the best people in the academic world—and all exquisitely styled in the choicest Latin, Greek, and Hebrew—under the title *Epistolae illustriorum virorum,* Letters of Famous Men. Very soon there came the expected counter-thrust, albeit with the oddly modest echo of *Epistolae obscurorum virorum,* Letters of Obscure Men. This collection breathed such stupidity and abysmal ineptitude that at first scarcely anybody doubted it was genuine.

Purporting to be the correspondence of a group of anti-Reuchlinist clergy in various provincial backwaters, addressed to Ortwin Gratius, the publicist-in-chief of reactionary Cologne, these letters discussed the topics of the day, naturally from the diehard point of view, and convicted the "authors" of the most obsolescent forms of scholastic logic-chopping, affectation, ignorance, hypocrisy, and corruption to boot. Though they signed themselves by ridiculous names like Tanz-schneiderius (say, Caper-cutterus), Hasenmutius (Rabbit-hearted-nessius), Eitelnarrabianus (Raving-lunaticus), and similar derogatory concoctions, the public was so used to the vaguely comical-sounding professional pseudonyms of learned gentry that the absurdity of this lot did not at once sink in. (Reuchlin answered to the unenchanting aliases of Capnion and Phorcensis; Luther for a short time fancied Eleutherius, "the Free," for himself.)*

The whole language of the Letters was like that: a sort of bastard monstrosity bristling with Latin transliterations of German idioms and syntax. Yet it took people of Erasmus' calibre to penetrate the hoax immediately; the great man fell into such a fit of laughing that he burst an abscess which was to have been lanced that day, so that the physician coming to the door was sent away with thanks. Sir Thomas More flattered the diehards, saying that if the book had had a different title "those dolts" never would have "perceived the nose turned up at them—though longer than the snout of a rhinoceros!" With the title as it was, the dolts did not all tumble to it right away.

When the joke was out, the impact of it was not weakened but redoubled. A translation into appropriately pompous and mangled German did the rest. The nation rocked with mirth—all except Luther and some like-minded purists, who were moved to deprecate the "impudent buffoonery" of the satire as strongly as the bigotry of those against whom it was aimed. As far as Luther was concerned, he enjoyed a good laugh as much as the next man, he welcomed the showing-up of clerical iniquities, and was not above hyperbole and gross invective, himself—but everything in its place. To Luther it was as if, today, a campaign for cancer research or famine relief were to be conducted as a roaring farce.

The anonymous satirists' aim was nonetheless accurate and devastating. A better cause would have wilted under the exuberant scorn now poured out in cataracts on the "Obscurantists" of Cologne the length and breadth of Germany—and the international vocabulary was enriched by a new word. Continued solidarity with Cologne was out

* Whether or not Luther was aware of this, there was a second-century pope of that name.

of the question, and Rome quashed the process against Reuchlin. For the first time a book already stamped heretical was saved from the brand, and the author, if not reimbursed, was reinstated.

The pen, assisted by the printing press, had done it: with some slight assistance, maybe, by the sword of feudal anarchy rattling sympathetically in its rusty scabbard. The protean cause of liberty makes strange bedfellows. Wonders would never cease: Franz von Sickingen let it be known that he was now a champion of unrestricted Hebrew scholarship.

As Erasmus had been the first to deduce from internal evidence in certain portions of the *Letters of Obscure Men,* Ulrich von Hutten was one of the authors.

※

13. "Indulgences, so rightly named!"

Luther as a matter of fact had been acquainted in his youth with the principal author of the *Letters*, Johann Jäger of Dornheim alias Crotus Rubeanus, whom like Spalatin he had known at Erfurt when they were students, and lost sight of since. He knew of him, of course, as a member of the Mutianic Poets' Circle, that most strident, colourful, and popular section of German humanism, for which he had no time whatever.

The general guessing game about the authorship of the satire subsided in the excitement caused by a truly epoch-making literary event. This was the publication in 1516 of the first complete, printed edition of the New Testament in Greek, interleaved with a revised Latin version, by Erasmus of Rotterdam. The international reception accorded to it was comparable to the effect of the news of the splitting of the atom. Among specialists, to be sure: but as with the splitting of the atom, immense practical consequences were foreshadowed. Erasmus himself trusted that his work would start off fresh and accurate vernacular translations everywhere, to enlighten the peoples of the world and so usher in the millennium of universal virtue; and theologians and ministering clergy the world over drew new understanding and inspiration from it.

Luther hailed it like the rest, and found at least one nugget right away. The Greek word *metanoia,* rendered in the Latin of St. Jerome as *poenitentia,* signified change of heart, so that the daunting penal associations of *penitence* could definitely be dismissed. He knew it already, he had already had it all worked out; but it could not be confirmed too often nor too widely clarified. The encouragement it brought him could not have been more opportune.

The eccentricity which some of his parishioners and students deplored in him—though willing to overlook it since eccentricity in some shape if not another was so much the norm: and there were worse— the thing they now did not quite like about him was that bee he had in his bonnet, about what he was pleased to call idolatry. They were not idolaters, they were Christians; idolaters were heathen. It was not a nice thing to say to people, that they were committing idolatry; and if there were other bonnets in other places abuzz with the same species, that made it no better and besides did not concern themselves. It was themselves they were concerned with. But perhaps he would get over it. Or the Elector, being an interested party, would stop him.

Worshipping saints that had lived and died in Christ was not the same as worshipping heathen idols, even if they were both represented in graven images: yet he said it was in no way different. The one were real, the other were false, that was the difference. He himself admitted that the saints were real and holy and entitled to reverence, and that their merits swelled the treasury of heaven. Then how could it be irreverent to pray to the holy saints and ask for a pittance from the treasury in return? What was wrong with availing oneself of special periods when the treasury was open to the mortal public, and of special tokens and coupons by which one could draw on it? Everybody did it, they would have been fools not to, seeing that the bargain sales were decreed in the Holy City and the vouchers bore the Holy Father's seal. Dr. Martin kept on about true contrition being a state of mind, a change of heart: but if the saints could not give it to one, if the Pope could not sell it to one, who could?

It was all very well for him to talk: he had been to Rome, where the dividends flowed all the year round, and doubtless had laid up enough spiritual benefits to last him. People knew people whom he had told about it, saying he would not have missed the experience.

Yes. And the memory was getting sharper all the time. The pious tourist's regulation guide-book (*Mirabilia urbis Romae*) clutched to him, he had "run like a madman" from one sacred monument to the other, industriously scooping up everlasting souvenirs. He had laid up merit for himself on high by praying at as many shrines as time and spending-money allowed him to visit, had bespoken the advocacy of innumerable saints in his behalf, by the simple expedients of touching and venerating relics of them, and had purchased remission of sins in bulk by dint of saying mass, against a fee, at several particularly hallowed altars. Rome held the greatest concentration of holy places outside the Holy Land, including the graves of St. Peter and St. Paul, and the catacombs with the remains of eighty thousand martyrs and forty-six popes, not to mention the Sacred Stair of twenty-eight steps transported hither from the palace of Pilate in Jerusalem, where Jesus had trodden them.

By going up this Stairway on one's knees, kissing each step and saying a Pater noster on each, one could free a soul from purgatory. He had done that, too. Having released his paternal grandfather, he recalled, he had soon run out of souls to whom he had a personal obligation, "downright sorry" that his parents were still among the living and so could not be rescued from the flames while he was at it.

Had he been any better than the Italian priests of whom he said that they celebrated mass with the virtuoso negligence of jugglers: seven masses at one altar within one hour—? It was only a matter of degree. He had taken his time over it ("Before I had got as far as the Gospel, the celebrant beside me had already finished and was calling to me, *Passa, passa!* get a move on, there are others waiting!"); but the mercenary purpose was the same.

"I still believed—dear God, what did I not believe!" He had not doubted, then, that sinful men could wrest decision out of the hands of God, bypass the condition of true repentance which alone could win forgiveness and which none but God could possibly assess, and say who was to come out of purgatory and when: just by going through certain routine motions.

He was dwelling on his memories, agonizing over his parishioners as once upon a time he had about himself—how to wean them away from a course which it had taken himself long enough to see led steeply in the opposite direction from salvation? Every time one of them left after confession, clearly unimpressed by the injunction to sin no more, he could tell what the poor soul was thinking of: next All Saints' Day, when everyone could buy 1443 years' remission of purgatory plus total absolution from both guilt and punishment for all "repented" sins, just round the corner. For Elector Frederick operated a papal concession of plenary indulgence, obtainable annually on that day from an exhibition of the Wittenberg relics in the galleries of the Castle Church, against a moderate entrance fee. How to ram it

home, that it all hinged on a terrible misunderstanding—which alas
was being fostered by ignorant and culpable priests—as to the workings
of Holy Commerce?

Holy Trade, *sacrum negotium*, in the Holy Commodity, *merx sacra*,
of grace—this was official terminology, coined long ago and in no
pejorative sense at the Holy See.

There was nothing wrong with trade, fair exchange as a natural
concomitant of social inter-relations, which was indeed the mediaeval
way of life. The opprobrium at first attaching to the trader who began
to make a whole-time profession and a profit out of an essentially
unproductive, integral side-line—that had disappeared with the growth
of a merchant class which had enriched not merely itself but the nations
and on which the fortunes of the rulers were coming to depend. God,
who was incomparably richer and creator of all things, who never
could make a profit since always willy-nilly giving more than he got—
God was beyond slur. Luther did not think for a moment that the idea
of Holy Trade was an insult to God, any more than he doubted for a
moment that a concept officially classified by such a name existed. What
he thought was that by placing the initiative of Holy Trade with man,
and placing man's part in the bargain on a completely materialistic
basis, men had fatally got hold of the wrong end of the stick.

What exactly was an indulgence? Exactly; that was what Luther
wanted to know, too. That he had certain notions on the subject was
not evidence. The principle seemed plain enough, but what about the
practice, which seemed so confused and contradictory? How was one
to get to the bottom of it, without access to the full corpus of decretals
in the archives of the Vatican? Local copies of the published canon
law were not always unabridged or up to date.

He was right to wonder.

There were aspects of the matter that Luther never knew.

In principle—a principle which Luther necessarily assumed to be as
old as Christianity itself—in principle, an indulgence or lenity was a
remission of temporal punishment as imposed in the name of the
Church by the priest to whom one made confession of one's trespasses.
Guilt was automatically cancelled by divine mercy, which coincided
with repentance, and in token of which the priest pronounced the
formula of absolution. But though forgiven, sin like civil crime must

still be paid for. The Church fixed the price of sin, and what remained unpaid on earth had to be discharged in purgatory, the place where the soul was finally purified of mortal dross before the forgiven sinner could enter upon his assured heritage of eternal bliss.

For this reason the fear of purgatory was far more acute than fear of hell. Only the absolutely unrepentant went to hell, but everybody except saints had to go through purgatory (some theologians held that even saints did not go straight to heaven). Human nature being sinful, men sinned constantly, wittingly and unwittingly, and could not expect to render payment in full during one lifetime.

Moreover, the earthly penances contingent to absolution could be prohibitively severe: years of fasting on bread and water, years of pilgrimage in exile, years of suspension from all social function. In some cases it became so obviously infeasible to exact payment "to the last farthing" (as the revealing analogy ran), that a system had evolved enabling penitents to delegate their punishment and undergo it by proxy (which entailed making it worth the proxy's while), or to commute it into money payments.

At first arrangements of this sort were made available only in special cases; but gradually they became extended to anybody who could pay. At first the payment rescinded only the penances to be performed on earth, but gradually it extended to the undischarged residue payable in pain, Beyond. From this to offering remission of penance as a *reward*, an incentive to pious sacrifices, it was but a step.

Plenary indulgences, total remission of ecclesiastical penalties here and hereafter, became a useful recruiting device for the Crusades against Islam, first employed by Pope Leo IV in 853, and formally approved in comprehensive form by Pope Urban II about 1095, that is at the start of the first all-out Crusade. Again, while at first it was necessary to take the cross and render military service against the Moslem, soon a money contribution to the war was allowed to be sufficient exchange. From a means of raising troops indulgences became a means of raising funds, and insensibly developed into a form of taxation which presently the papacy could no longer do without.

So when the Crusades came to an end Pope Boniface VIII created the jubilee indulgence of 1300, by which total remission was guaranteed to all who would come to visit the graves of the Apostles in Rome daily for a fortnight during a *iubilaeum* year once in every century. Popes Clement VI (1343), Urban VI (1389), and Paul II

(1470) between them finally increased the number of jubilees to one every twenty-five years. Next, of course, the jubilee indulgence was extended to persons who were unable to make the pilgrimage, if they sent money instead.

Public demand met papal need. The laity pressed for more and more ways of evading punishment and of helping one's tormented dead, and the papacy acquired more and more channels of supplementing a perpetual deficit. Eventually there were to be had "confessional letters," a species of spiritual travellers' cheques procuring full absolution anywhere the owner might apply for it, and/or full absolution anytime he was in danger of death, also full absolution four times a year whatever his state of health and moral fibre; and furthermore full absolution under the same conditions for parcelling out among other people whom the purchaser wished so to favour. Such confessional letters were a great boon, as normally the sinner was tied to his parish priest who knew all about him, while sins too grave for the parish priest to deal with would have to be referred to the bishop or higher still, which was a costly, lengthy, and uncertain business. There was an appropriate scale of rates, and also something of a black market, under the misconception that a receipted indulgence could provide an *intending* sinner with absolution for a crime he thereupon went out to commit with an easy heart.

The Curia also doled out the right to issue indulgences to particular sanctuaries in need of repair, or in aid of a new church or a road or a bridge or any other sufficiently important edifice; or to help an insolvent prelate to pay his debts to the Curia; or as a gesture of goodwill to distinguished temporal lords (like the Elector of Saxony). In such cases there was an initial fee payable to the Apostolic Chancery, and either a lump sum by way of inauguration fee or a promise to share the proceeds with the Holy See. Offsetting this, to soothe the grumbling of secular potentates at papal indulgence campaigns which competed with their own, such potentates were sometimes granted a percentage of the collection in their lands.

While the Holy Trade might thus be plied in cynical fashion at times, at the bottom of it was a genuine belief, on both sides, in the spiritual purchasing power of sacrifice. The whole idea of sacrifice, after all, originated in a seeming mercantile transaction between man and the unseen powers he desired to propitiate. And the sacrificial death of Jesus was to *redeem* the world from perdition, the Saviour had *bought* eternal life for mankind with his blood: so, in those commercial words, men had been taught.

Now, in the light of the Theology of Justification this interpretation was all wrong. Grace being a miraculous gift, there was no purchasing it. Not any amount of goodness and "works" would get you into heaven: though by rendering yourself receptive to the heavenly righteousness you might be given grace to be good. But sacrifice turned into sacrilege if it had an eye to reward; and the notion that any human agency could interfere in the administration of purgatory was patently absurd. So, Luther deemed, the Holy Father could not be aware of the pernicious nonsense which was being put about in his name. Nowhere in the canon law did it say that the Pope had any jurisdiction outside mortal bounds; and if this seemed to be suggested in some given indulgence-proclamation, any competent ecclesiastical jurist was always able to prove that the wording did not really say what the ignorant laity fondly thought was meant. In the meantime, however, the indulgence-sellers did their level best to keep the ignorant laity in the fond belief that for a consideration the Pope got people out of purgatory. Somebody should bring these "stinking lies" to the Pope's attention.

There was a lot that neither Luther nor even some very competent ecclesiastical jurists knew. Not only did they lack historical information and perspectives which it would take several more centuries fully to disclose, but there were one or two dogmatic declarations on the subject of indulgence which had never been incorporated in the standard books of canon law, remaining in the nature of reserved appendices. In one of these, dated 1477, it was explicitly stated that the Pope had the power to deliver the dead from purgatory (which until 1450 had been as explicitly denied); another, dated 1343, affirmed that the Treasury of Merit was a capital foundation with disbursable dividends. However, in no shape or form had there ever been an official definition of the effect in purgatory of indulgences.

Meanwhile it appeared self-evident to Luther and a great many like-minded priests and theologians that the popular attitude to indulgences was wrong and extremely dangerous to the health of the soul.

One could not stand by forever and look on without lifting a finger to stop people from destroying themselves. Luther was in a difficult position with his sovereign and employer and loving owner of the Wittenberg relics. He had made several attempts to persuade the Elector privately that it was a sin to sell indulgences. The Elector had exercised his celebrated capacity of keeping his own counsel; he had not even replied. Another All Saints' Day was coming round.

Preaching at the town church on the previous day, 31 October 1516, Dr. Martin uttered some general remarks on the nature of indulgences and their relation to penitence. He made the point that only the canonical penalties imposed by the priest at confession were remissible, and emphasized once again that true repentance was a matter of the heart: remorse and payment might go hand in hand, but were disparate and impossible to substitute for one another. He castigated nobody and nothing but the state of mind which seeks evasion of punishment instead of longing for the cathartic action and emulation of Christ inherent in submission to punishment.

The sermon was not well received, either by the congregation or by the Elector. Now he was really going too far. He was cold-shouldered in the town and the Elector withheld a new gown that had been promised him. If anything had been needed to stiffen Luther's resolve, these reactions would have done it. He continued inserting allusions to the topic in successive sermons, and delivered another blast—appropriate to the Lenten season of penitence—on 24 February 1517.

On this occasion he went farther. He dilated on particular aberrations of the indulgence trade which encouraged men to take their sins lightly. ("Ay, when it is evening the pilgrims return home with full indulgence: full of indulgence in beer and wine, full of unchaste thoughts and other moral horrors. . . .") No man could vouch for God, who alone was able to judge of the sinner's degree of contrition on which remission was dependent. If the Pope had power to go over God's head in the matter of purgatory, it followed that the Pope could do more for the dead than for the living, and that he was cruel not to release all dead souls, at once and gratis. Therefore it was wicked to impute such powers to the Pope.

"Indulgences promote an abject servility, for they do nothing but teach the people to flee, to shudder at the punishment of sin instead of at the sin itself. . . . Would that I lied when I say indulgences are rightly named, because to indulge is to permit, and indulgence is now taken as impunity and permission to sin."

Spalatin's efforts at mediation, Dr. Staupitz's moral support, and the material success of "Our Theology" notwithstanding—"your Herr Doctor," in the Elector's weary phrase, looked like becoming very unpopular indeed in Wittenberg.

14. The Great Amateurs

If the Renaissance ideal of the universal man—the man whose mind and sinew could encompass all the human arts—was ever embodied in a living person, that paragon was not Martin Luther. He had no eye for the visual arts. While he would have disputed this as indignantly as do all those who "know what they like," while he was exquisitely sensitive to word and melody and deeply moved by all divine Creation, he had not the first glimmering of appreciation as to what fine art is really about. And so he was not interested in it— although, again, he would have considered himself wickedly slandered had one told him so: for did he not admire sacred statuary especially when it was big and lifelike, pictures when they were of edifying subjects or alternatively portraits one could recognize when one had had time to get used to them, and spacious, well-wrought buildings? When, later on, he cast about for some manual trade which he might learn to keep himself and his family, did he not consider the craft of painting before finally deciding on carpentry? only because he did not think there was adequate art teaching to be had in Wittenberg (what was wrong with Lucas Cranach, Luther's great friend, we may well ask?).

All the same, from that point of view, he did not notice a thing, the time he was in Rome. It was a time when the tourist of our day would give his ears to have been on the spot. True, the hellenic antiquities then being recovered thick and fast from chance excavations and sea-fishing hauls went mostly into private collections—but many were displayed in gardens and not at all inaccessible, particularly when they were yet being cleaned in situ or in the appropriate workshops.

crop of people, then, who trusted themselves to understand anything except the word impossible.

Even the humanist scholars continued to be guided by traditions. Though having learned to despise mediaeval superstitions, together with the knowledge they were wholeheartedly adopting the superstitions of antiquity, instead. To go against any maxims set up by the recognized ancient authorities was in their eyes as unthinkable, as heretical, as was denying any Christian articles of faith in the eyes of religious authority. Only the artists were not satisfied with the crack in the barrier and kept at it to demolish it from end to end, with every conceivable implement at their disposal. For they would not stick to their last. Of necessity they were simultaneously draughtsmen, mathematicians, chemists, metallurgists, geologists, anatomists, historians, engineers—some of them more so than others, that was all. The more proficient they were in these ancillary arts, the better they would be at their main calling: and in general it worked out so. It was unfortunate that in the pursuit of technical perfection they must infringe against all manner of taboos and prohibitions. Dissection of dead bodies (other than dismembering the corpses of saints for distribution as relics) was forbidden; the dividing lines between mathematics and cabalistics, chemistry and witchcraft, exploration of natural phenomena and satanic disruption of sacred mysteries, were indistinct; and going actually beyond the aesthetic of classical realism might well be asking for trouble too. There were moves afoot, notably on the part of the reactionary clergy, to dam the artistic overflow into the out-of-bounds—which included such defections from orthodox formalism as the development of polyphony in music. So long, however, as there were popes in office who applauded these lawless departures of the arts, so long would the repressive moves be blocked. And the popes, almost without exception since the Holy See had shifted back to Rome from Avignon, had magnificently sponsored the new art as well as the new learning.

Julius II, who was pontiff at the time of Luther's Roman visit, stood out head and shoulders in his sponsorship of art just as he did in his other worldly pursuits for the greater glory of the Church; and he was himself no respecter of diplomas. Bramante, whom Pope Julius appointed chief architect of the new St. Peter's, had started his career as a painter. Michelangelo, whom Pope Paul III entrusted with the revision and completion of the stupendous project, was and never wished to be anything but a sculptor.

More than a quarter of a century lay between those two appointments. St. Peter's which had got off to such a flying start proved to be a long time abuilding. There were times when the work flagged and times when it was altogether at a standstill. Why? Why else but for lack of funds.

An enterprise of such dimensions swallowed up commensurate amounts of money. Also, the bigger the enterprise, the bigger the leakages, the peculations, pilfering, overcharges, particularly in view of the permanently disorganized state of the curial economy. Fiscal reforms were among the proposals for an ecclesiastical overhaul; and although few people knew it at the time, the apostolic exchequer and the apostolic privy purse were not always kept strictly apart. Even with moneys collected for a specific cause there was a lot of decrement. Thus the jubilee indulgence of 1500, designated for the war against the Turks, had for the most part gone to Alexander VI's natural son Cesare Borgia; the wars of Julius II had made inroads into the St. Peter's building fund; and now the Medici Pope Leo X had a needy sister and a passion for cards at which he sustained royal losses, apart from a fresh rise in military expenditure. Then, too, a sizable amount of the collections was filtered off before ever the money reached the Holy See, what with the usual cuts incurred by converting foreign currencies and the deductions for the services of the Holy See's conveyancers and commission agents. Finally, the overheads of the very collection-campaigns were fairly high. A crack campaigner like the Dominican Friar Johann Tetzel, for example, commanded a fee of eighty gulden a month plus free maintenance and transport for himself and his party plus ten gulden a month extra for his personal servant. By way of comparison, a councillor of the wealthy town of Leipzig, where Tetzel came from, received a salary of one hundred gulden per annum, or a little over eight gulden a month, the same as the chair of Biblical studies in Wittenberg, without any extras.

But Tetzel, in the St. Peter's indulgence campaign of 1517, eleven years after the foundation stone had been laid, was not paid by the Holy See, was he? That's right, he wasn't. He was paid by the primate and titular chancellor of Germany, the Archbishop of Mainz. For we have barely touched on the financial complications in this context.

Finance, too, was the province of amateurs—though some of its empirical practitioners were making strides in placing it on a professional footing: notably so the banking dynasty of Fugger, who were the principal indulgence agents to the Curia and also the principal creditors of the Archbishop of Mainz.

Pope Leo X, who had succeeded Julius II in 1513 at the age of thirty-seven, was destined for the Church at birth, ordained to the priesthood at age seven, and made a cardinal at thirteen years and three months. Nevertheless he also was an amateur as regards his holy office. His father was Lorenzo the Magnificent, and therefore his chief vocation was that of a statesman, not to call it politician. Not to be too frivolous, one hesitates to say that the papacy was his hobby—nor would that be quite true, since of course the papacy carried incalculable political power. Besides, he was less than enthralled with the working details of the pontificate. His education at his father's brilliant court had been humanistic, theologians and consistories bored him to distraction, and he was fond of outdoor sports. Luther was right in his professed belief that there was a great deal going on behind the Holy Father's back that the Holy Father did not know about. The Holy Father's back was firmly turned on executive matters that did not interest him. From the point of view of papal monarchy, Leo was a good pope, nevertheless.

Nobody would expect a great ruler to waste his time on administrative minutiae. Simony had long been established practice at the Curia; it was one of those things, forbidden in canon law, which yet had come to be taken for granted and indeed would now be very difficult to get rid of. Auctioning bishop's mitres and cardinal's hats was a not unimportant source of revenue, which could not be abandoned from one day to the next without creating further chaos if not ruin within the household of the Church. But the standard buying and selling of benefices to the highest bidder added to the financial tangle. The purchase price often reached such figures that the lucky winner could not possibly put his hands on the necessary cash and would have to raise it by mortgaging the future income from the benefice in question for an immediate loan.

The Archbishop-Elector Albrecht of Mainz was a case in point—a glaring example only because the eventual consequences of his speculation put a deathless spotlight on him, and not otherwise in any way unique. He was a personable and prepossessing young man, wealthy, with some of the best connections in the Empire, a connoisseur of gems, paintings, and fine books, strongly humanist in inclination, and he was being cast for the rôle of German ecclesiastical leadership against Rome by the partisans of Reformation.

Albrecht von Hohenzollern was a scion of the electoral house of Brandenburg—contentious neighbour of the electoral house of Saxony—and in the twenty-fourth year of his age had carried off no fewer than three ecclesiastical prizes. He was Bishop of Halberstadt and Archbishop of Magdeburg as well as Archbishop of Mainz— despite the fact that plural office was canonically illegal and the legal minimum age for episcopal rank was thirty. The German bishoprics were generally filled by members of the leading families of the Empire, and the competition was fierce. In the person of Albrecht, Brandenburg had scored a triple triumph over the rest, and especially over the Saxon candidates for these posts—more especially as the sees of Magdeburg, Halberstadt, and Mainz encircled and partially cut across the Saxonies. But the cost to the victor was steep.

Wealthy he was, but over and above the purchase price of office he had had to pay heavily for dispensation by the Curia from the canonical regulations respecting age and pluralism, to say nothing of the annates immediately falling due to Rome. The annates of Mainz had been levied seven times in recent years; the see was cleaned out for the nonce. He would not have been wealthy anymore had he discharged all the financial obligations for which he had contracted. His debts to the Curia and to the Fugger who had advanced part of the dispensation fees amounted to thirty thousand gulden.

In order to help Albrecht to pay off his debts to the Curia and to the Fugger, the Curia arranged that half the takings in his dioceses from the new St. Peter's Indulgence should go to the Archbishop, and the Fugger saw to it that the indulgence-sellers were accompanied by Fugger accountants. Although of course none of this was mentioned in the archepiscopal bull by which the campaign had to be licensed, there was no outright secrecy about it. The quality of the merchandise was entirely unaffected by the final destination of the money, after all. It was, then, in the interests of everyone including the laity that the best possible salesmen's services be procured. And Tetzel was so good that he was able to charge a separate commission to the Fugger and nobody said a word if he helped himself to the till a little here and there.

Nobody except himself would ever write a kind word about Tetzel —nobody except of all men Luther would write a kind word *to* him when, cynically abandoned by his employers and former comrades, Tetzel lay dying of a broken heart, in black disgrace. No doubt the familiar excuse that Tetzel was only doing his job as ordered, to the best of his ability, must be ruled irrelevant to judgment; the hired assassin is not less a murderer because someone else employs him; and to Luther and all who thought as he did Tetzel was a mass-murderer of souls. From every viewpoint, past and present, Tetzel was immoral (for in point of chastity, too, the less said about him the better). But one must put in a word to defend him against the charge that he worked purely for gain. Tetzel, too, was in his way an enthusiast, an amateur prodigy of the nascent profession of advertising. He loved his work, and he believed in it.

Else he could not have done it so superbly well, holding huge crowds wherever he set up his ambulant trading post with waving banners, fife and drum, the cross of Jesus carried on before, augmented by the arms of the Pope. The wares that he peddled were outstandingly attractive even beyond the run of indulgences, consisting in a new type of certificate which combined plenary indulgence with a confessional letter. Each certificate came with a blank space for filling in with the name of the person to whom it was to be made out, whether dead or living. If dead, the beneficiary was hereby certified in heaven. If living, he was henceforth entitled to instant absolution from all his sins and all punishments before or after death upon producing the document anytime, anywhere, before anybody who could call himself a priest—even if such a priest were illiterate or did not know the bearer's language.

The charges were fixed at twenty-five gulden for monarchs and high prelates, twenty gulden for the next rung of nobles, abbots and the like, six gulden for lesser nobility and clergy, three gulden for merchants and master artisans, one gulden for peasants and workmen. The very poor might contribute by prayers and fastings—always bearing in mind that omniscient God is not deceived as to a person's pecuniary capacity.

All the world agreed that Tetzel was as good as a play; better. He spoke in many voices: on behalf of God, on behalf of St. Peter, and, heartrendingly, for the departed roasting in the flames of purgatory: "Pity us! pity us! Can't you hear our screams and groans—your

fathers and mothers? We bore you, fed and clothed you, brought you up
and left you all our worldly goods: can you then be so callous and
cruel that you won't release us, for the merest pittance?" He would
then step over to the money chest (where stood on guard the recording
clerk of the firm of Fugger) and himself open the sale by purchasing
one of the title deeds to salvation, to exclaim as soon as the money
tinkled in the coffer: "Ah, he is saved, my poor, dear father is
saved at last! Now at last I can be sure he is in heaven, and I need
no longer pray for him." Tetzel's father, if he had been anything like
the son, must have been doing a thriving trade, Beyond, in surplus
bliss.

It must be clear to the meanest intelligence that in possession of
one of the new "papal tickets" one had no further need of any other
afterlife-insurance policies, such as for instance the Wittenberg Indulgence. Elector Frederick forbade Tetzel access to Electoral-Saxon
territory. Tetzel took up a position just the other side of the frontier,
and the Elector's subjects, and the parishioners and even the students
of Dr. Martin, ran across the border with whatever spare cash they
could rake up. They came back blithe and brazen, reporting Tetzel
said a papal ticket would absolve a man even had he violated the
Blessed Virgin; that the pardoner's red cross was equal in holiness to
the cross which had borne Jesus' body; that money contributions were
most assuredly in lieu of spiritual acts. Attempting hecklers were
usually silenced with prophecies of supernatural retribution or Dominican revenge. Who could blame the people for believing what they
were told on such authority? To this day most of us take on trust the
bulk of our information on matters unseen.

The worst of it was that for the duration there was little one could
do about it. Wherever an indulgence preacher was in action, all
gospel preaching was supposed to be suspended; and although there
was not the slightest doubt that Tetzel's reported statements were
arrant and blasphemous falsehoods, the Archbishop's bull which he
displayed on a gold-tasselled velvet cushion made it an offence to
obstruct him.

All this happened within a month or two of Luther's unwelcome
February sermon. The coolness between Elector Frederick and his
Herr Doctor became tempered by their unanimous annoyance. There
was a rapprochement; Luther got his gown. Reports came in from many
quarters, to the effect that Holy Trade, Holy Church, and Holy Father

were becoming objects of ribald mockery among the very public which made a run on the St. Peter's Indulgence. Luther wrote round to a number of the German bishops, begging them to restrain Tetzel in some fashion, but got no satisfaction from any. He discussed the matter with his colleagues of the faculty of canon law. Every one advised him to drop it. The reports about Tetzel were probably exaggerated. In any event, as Luther might see for himself, it was futile to try and stop the fellow.

The summer went by and Tetzel moved on.

Luther started on the new term's lectures, still deeply troubled. He had been made to feel a meddlesome fool; yet it could not be right to do nothing. There was however something he could get on with meanwhile. Scholasticism was now definitely finished at Wittenberg and the Bible was established as the basis of theological instruction. The time was ripe for taking the issue beyond Wittenberg. At the beginning of September Luther published a programme of ninety-seven theses challenging the academic world to a debate on the devaluation of scholastic methods, which he sent round the universities. He waited, and he waited, in extreme suspense. Nothing happened, absolutely nothing. The academic world took no notice whatsoever.

Before he had quite given up hope of some response, he chanced one day upon a little book of specimen sermons for indulgence preachers issued in the name and with the imprint of the arms of the Archbishop of Mainz. It confirmed what one had heard about Tetzel's oratory, in black and white. Impossible to hang back any longer.

With touching trust, considering Luther's so recent fiasco in that line, he decided that the way to give the subject of indulgence a thorough yet entirely decorous airing was by a public disputation, as customary. (Or was it not a case of trustfulness, at all? Might Luther have been hoping subconsciously that this disputation also would come to nothing—so that he would have made a show of doing his duty and thereafter be able to leave ill alone?) Another All Saints' Day was approaching and suggested the date.

So he wrote out another debating programme, this time of ninety-five theses, and took it across the street to the printer Johann Grünenberg who was to run off a few copies as a placard. Nobody else besides Grünenberg and Luther's famulus Agricola né Johann Schneider knew anything about it. Luther "took counsel only with

God"—whether this be suggestive of fear of humiliation or fear of being dissuaded. Shortly before noon on the Eve of All Saints Luther and Agricola took a short walk from the Augustinian cloister to the Castle Church and to the north door there which served as a university notice board nailed his placard of *Ninety-five Theses Concerning the Power and Efficacy of Indulgences.* The text was of course in Latin, with the following preface:

"In the desire and with the purpose of elucidating the truth, a disputation will be held on the subjoined propositions at Wittenberg, under the presidency of the Reverend Father Martinus Luther, Augustinian Friar, master of arts and doctor of sacred theology, and ordinary lecturer upon the same in that place. He asks those who cannot be present and discuss the subject orally to do so by letter."

One copy went off the same day to the Archbishop of Mainz, with a covering letter:

"Father in Christ and Most Illustrious Prince, forgive me that I, the scum of the earth, should dare to approach Your Sublimity. I make so bold because of the fidelity which I owe to Your Paternity. May Your Highness look upon this speck of dust and hear my plea. . . ." After summarizing the reprehensible little book of pardoners' instructions, the writer went on in a rather different tone: "God in heaven, is this the way the souls entrusted to your care are prepared for death? It is high time that you looked into this matter. . . . Indulgences can offer no security but only the remission of external canonical penalties. . . . Christ did not command the preaching of indulgences but of the gospel, and what a horror it is, *what a peril to a bishop,** if he never gives the gospel to his people but only the swindle of indulgences. In these instructions of Your Paternity to the indulgence sellers, issued I am sure *without your knowledge and consent,** indulgences are called the inestimable gift of God for the reconciliation of man to God and the emptying of purgatory. Repentance is declared unnecessary. What can I do, Illustrious Prince, but beseech Your Paternity in the name of Jesus Christ our Lord to suppress utterly these instructions lest someone arise to confute them and *to bring Your Illustrious Sublimity into contempt, which I am afraid is what will happen** if they are not speedily withdrawn. May Your Paternity accept my loyal admonition. I too am one of your sheep. May the Lord Jesus guard you forever. Amen.

* My italics. E.S.

"Wittenberg, 1517, on the Eve of All Saints.

"If you will have a look at my enclosed theses, you will see on what shaky ground the indulgence proclamations rest. Martin Luther, Augustinian Doctor of Theology." That should make the gilded young triple-prelate sit up.

Another copy of the theses with a suitable letter went to Luther's diocesan Bishop Scultetus (Schulze) of Brandenburg, but Luther carefully refrained from sending any to Elector Frederick or even Spalatin—because, as tantalizingly he told the latter, he wished to guard both the Elector and himself against any breath of suspicion of political skulduggery and collusion against the house of Brandenburg.

Alas, he flattered himself, it seemed. Nobody appeared to think anything at all about this second disputation programme either. Nobody came to the debate. Nobody wrote in. Archbishop Albrecht and Bishop Scultetus might never have received their packets. All was silence.

So much for branching out from one's prescribed and settled professional track.

※

15. The Ninety-five Theses

We have to go by what people tell us, and be grateful if they give us so much as Luther left on record. But an abundance of personal testimony narrows the margin of permissible deduction and places one under the obligation to either accept or impugn it wholesale. This becomes a tricky undertaking when the subject's plainly intended, honest statements contradict each other, and that—as plainly—without his realizing it. With a subject like Luther, whose recapitulations frequently touched on the same events at intervals over a period of many years, there are of course the factors of changing outlook and memories reconditioned by distance or nostalgia or the intervening consequences, to be taken into account. Too readily do a subject's friends or enemies select from his utterances what they need to prove either his complete consistency or his muddleheadedness, or hypocrisy, or total disregard for truth. Yet it is a truism that a man is many things, even well below the threshold of schizophrenia, and that his own profound sense of his single, continuous identity is a delusion. As Luther himself emphasized over and over, the human heart is fathomless and man, his inveterate reasoning and rationalizing notwithstanding, is not a rational being.

One tends, as Luther did too, to hurry past the publication of his ninety-seven theses on scholasticism in order to get on to the Ninety-five as soon as possible. That is because of what came out of them; naturally. Nothing very much came out of the former paper, except in that its substance was embedded in the foundations of his entire position. But at the time when he published it, that paper represented to him the fruit of all his being and striving to date, from which should grow a sturdy landmark of a tree of knowledge. The Ninety-five Theses on Indulgences were nothing to do with his professional career; they dealt with an occasional albeit important side-issue, comparable to—let us say—a medical scientist's calling attention to some endemic hygienic ill: it may be his duty but is not his actual job, to do so. For an exciting scientific paper, which he has taken the trouble to produce properly in book form, to sink without trace, will be a most depressing disappointment—though if immediately afterwards an informed humanitarian appeal of his also falls flat, this will additionally ram home his impotence, obscurity, and isolation: the more if his apparent influence in his own little manor had previously lulled him into a sense of carrying due weight. This, to be sure, apart from the fact that both publications have a vital bearing on universal health.

But Luther's Ninety-five were not a publication like the ninety-seven. Although couched in much the same form, the ninety-seven constituted a positive challenge, the Ninety-five a probing invitation; the first were issued in an official, marketable edition, the second were a placard with only a few extra copies for private distribution. He had used only three—one for the Castle Church, one for the Archbishop of Mainz, and one for his own bishop—and had some over. He felt convinced it was good stuff, worth publishing. You never knew.

It ought to be published.

If the Archbishop of Mainz was determined to ignore the communication, publicity would flush him.

Publicity was to be strenuously avoided until one might have ascertained that it was the right thing to publish.

Luther wrapped up the remaining copies and sent them, each with a note asking for the recipients' confidential advice as to publication, to colleagues of his acquaintance at other universities.

He did this on his name-day, 11 November (by accident? hopeful design?), having "waited patiently" since despatching the copies for his spiritual superiors on 31 October. Messengers went on foot and road conditions were at their autumnal worst. As it happened, the missive to the Archbishop of Mainz, who was in residence at Aschaffenburg on Main, did not reach even his court councillors of Magdeburg, who sat at Kalbe on the Saale, until 17 November. So even if the Archbishop's councillors forwarded the packet from Wittenberg right away, Luther would be anticipating its arrival in the hands of the addressee by something like ten days—when he decided to write him off already.

Again he armed himself with patience, waiting for readers' opinions. Again the days went by and he heard nothing.

Then he heard, and with a vengeance. The letters of approbation from the colleagues to whom he had sent his placard, were the least of it. Expressions of enthusiasm came in from people he did not even know, people he had never heard of, people in towns where he had no correspondents. His correspondents before ever writing in reply had taken it upon themselves to publish the placard out of hand. It had been copied out by colleagues of his colleagues and their students till enterprising printers came forward to help them out, with increasingly numerous editions as the sheets sold like the proverbial hot cakes everywhere they appeared on offer. Nobody asked the author— not even for permission to translate the Theses into German, which was promptly done. In Ducal Saxony the Bishop of Merseburg caused the Theses to be posted up on public sites—including churches, and monasteries of varied denominations—to make sure that they were read as widely as possible. Luther's fan-mail from all walks of life included a parcel from Albrecht Dürer of Nuremberg, containing several portfolios of the painter's woodcuts and etchings—a very valuable present as Dürer was acclaimed the king of Northern art—in gratitude, the artist wrote, for the much-needed illumination the to him unknown author of the Theses had provided.

It was too much, too soon. He was getting far more than he had asked for, but had not got what he wanted. It was not at all correct professional procedure. It was awful. He was supposed to be launching an enquiry, not to provide illumination. It was not in him to whine and repine; but he took fright. What ought he to do?

"Within a fortnight," he would relate with unfading astonishment, "the Ninety-five Theses ran throughout all Germany—" and more than that: for Albrecht Dürer was then staying in the Netherlands, and Thomas More in England saw the Theses before November was out, and Erasmus as far away as Basel had got hold of them in book form by early December. How was this to be explained?

"The whole world was complaining about indulgences," Luther essayed, "especially with reference to Tetzel. And since all the bishops and doctors kept silent, and nobody was willing to bell the cat—

for the Inquisitors of the Dominican Order had frightened the whole world with the terror of the stake, and Tetzel himself had menaced several priests who objected to his preaching—and so this Luther was praised because at last somebody had come forward and dared to take a stand in the matter."

Well, it happened, we know that; but even as generalizations go Luther's explanation is hardly good enough. All the world was not complaining about indulgences, on the contrary; only a small portion of the world knew Tetzel. But there it was.

"I myself did not know what the indulgences were," Luther shuddered in retrospect, "and the song threatened to become too high for my voice."

The song was a hit, for reasons which in their entirety never can be fully gauged with such phenomena, and "the whole world" ran away with it right out of the composer's range. Unexpectedly, mysteriously, somehow, it had struck a universal chord which set the whole keyboard of Christian society humming.

And it was some placard, that placard. It had not been drawn up for lay consumption.

Theses 1–4 were concerned with defining the precise meanings of penance and penitence. Theses 5–7 marshalled the general principles by which the respective power or impotence of papal indulgences were to be assayed. Theses 8–29 were concerned with indulgences for the dead and the assumption of papal power over purgatory, Theses 30–40 with indulgences for the living. Theses 41–52 posed a comparison of contributions to the St. Peter's building fund, with other good works (by means of propositions such as, "He who refuses to help a poor man in order to buy a letter of pardon for himself does not gain God's favour but God's wrath"). Theses 53–80 were calculated to assess the relative value of preaching indulgences and preaching the gospel, and also of the Treasury of Merit and the treasure of God's Word. Theses 81–89 cited current arguments put forward by some laity, as Luther had previously given them in his All Saints and Lenten sermons: Why did not the Pope empty purgatory at one sweep, out of Christian love and charity, instead of piecemeal and for money? Why, if it was ruled to be wrong to go on praying for souls released from purgatory, were not the countless benefices suppressed which had been endowed for the purpose of mortuary and anniversary masses in perpetuity? Why did not the Pope, being "rich as Croesus," build St.

Peter's out of his own pocket: why would he wring those of poor believers? What might the Pope be able to bestow on people who in perfect contrition had already won full remission for themselves?— Theses 90 and 91 proposed that to muzzle such objections without answering them was a grave mistake and also would not work. Theses 92–95, however, were only a summing-up of the foregoing, albeit sonorous and solemn.

One cannot tell, centuries after, whether those artless queries of the laity had really been uttered or whether their provenance was so to speak rhetorical. Certainly there were many lay folk like Dürer who had been worrying about the rights and wrongs of indulgences and now considered their doubts at rest. It is equally certain that most people took the ninety-five debating-propositions not merely as a critique but simultaneously as laying down the law. What can never be certain is how, in the secret reaches of his heart, Luther had initially meant them to be read. Then and always he protested that he only wanted to find out what the law was and to that end had set up a series of disputable points. But his similar ninety-seven debating-propositions against scholastic theology had not been offered in any such tentative spirit. But then again, they would never have been taken up by people outside the specialist circle.

Sober reflection damped the elation of Luther's friends, who began to share his misgivings. With encouragement from Staupitz, he sat down between academic chores at the beginning of the new year to write an explanatory elaboration of the Theses which, under the title of *Resolutiones disputationum de indulgentiarum virtute* and with a request for unsparing criticism, he sent to Bishop Scultetus. After about a month the Bishop acknowledged receipt and wrote to say he would examine the *Resolutions* as soon as he had time.

Meanwhile the opposition mustered. The Archbishop of Mainz, when his slow-travelling copy of the Theses was at last to hand, passed it on to the University of Mainz, which passed it back to him, whereupon he passed it higher up, to Rome. As for placing an injunction on the author until further notice, the Archbishop hinted to his council that he had no desire to stir up the Augustinian Order, which was very strong in the neighbourhood. Indulgences were Tetzel's department, the whole fracas was Tetzel's business really: let Tetzel see about stopping Luther's mouth. What was Tetzel a Dominican for? Tetzel jumped to it with alacrity and announced, "Within three weeks I shall have the heretic in the fire, so he can go to heaven in a bath cap," meaning the ashes would as usual be gathered in a bag and thrown into the river.

The heretic. The horrid word, avoided like the name of plague, was out. The mere suspicion of heresy was legally enough to start off a formal process against the person to whom it attached and smirch his associates. Unaware of Archbishop Albrecht's gratifying estimate of Augustinian power, Luther's prior begged him to withdraw, so as not to bring their Order into disgrace: "Already other Orders, especially the Dominicans, are dancing for joy that now the Augustinians too will burn!" the prior urged, remembering four Dominicans of Bern who had been burnt for blasphemy a few years ago—to the dancing self-complacence of other Orders as one cannot but infer. From the University of Erfurt came loud repudiation of its "presumptuous and conceited," absconding graduate. "Everything you say is true, dear Brother," a fellow-Augustinian from Hamburg said to Luther, "but you will accomplish nothing. Go back to your cell and say, 'God have mercy on me.'", and a close friend on the Wittenberg faculty of canon law clinched it with, "If you will write against the Pope, do you really expect they'll stand for it?"

He had not written one word against the Pope; in Thesis 91 it was posited that pardoners like Tetzel maligned the Pope. He was no more a heretic than Reuchlin—less, for he had made no sort of statement; what reason had he to hide and pray for mercy? The Wittenberg faculty of theology pronounced his *Resolutions* blameless, and word came from Bishop Scultetus too that he could find nothing wrong or un-Catholic in Luther's paper (though would he please hold back publication for the time being?). And there was Tetzel, pouring out abuse unadulterated by scholarly refutation even though he wrote in collaboration with two professors having equal rank with Luther. This was because Tetzel did not himself own a doctor's degree—not for want of pressing offers, Tetzel averred in his foreword, he just had never had time or inclination to accept, that was all. The lack was hastily remedied, that he might henceforth be free to combat Luther without the delays occasioned by learned collaborators living as far away as Frankfurt and Ingolstadt.

Bishop Scultetus' unexpectedly amiable message constrained Luther to silence—which scrupulous obedience in turn impressed his diocesan so favourably that almost at once he revoked the embargo. Luther had already prepared a German version of the *Resolutions:* a twenty-point abstract for the people, entitled *Sermon on Indulgences and Grace;* and directly Bishop Scultetus' permission came through he published both it and the Latin *Resolutions.*

Perhaps Bishop Scultetus had not in fact read them—unless he simply failed to understand the implications. Both "explanations" of the Theses went slightly farther than the original. Luther had not stood still. He was incapable of confining himself to a stationary paraphrase of something he had already said. While as before stressing his willing subjection to papal authority, he now made several additional statements—yes, statements. One was that the Church of Rome had not always been supreme over all other territorial churches, another was that burning heretics at the stake "though no doubt convenient" was against the will of God as expressed in Scripture, also that Christ did not wish "that the salvation of mankind should rest in the power of one man," and finally there was the conclusion, "The Church needs reformation," which however, "God will bring about in his own good time."

Resolutions and *Sermon* both went into several editions and supplanted the *Theses* as desired. Tetzel by return replied with another violent attack in which not only Luther but also Elector Frederick was threatened with the stake. Luther hit back in kind.

"Pestilent heretic," "stinking brand," "infamous, blaspheming scoundrel," was he? "Thousands of scholastic teachers" were against him, were they? And it was definitely better, was it, to buy an indulgence than to give alms to a poor man in extreme need?

"If it were only me that he insulted, I would gladly bear it. But it is not to be borne that he treats the Scriptures as a sow does a sack of oat straw. . . . When he cites such thousands of scholastic teachers—if he had troubled to look them up, he would have found three or four, the rest being only their parrots. . . . If a Christian man is not to help another before he helps himself, then Christian love is worth less than the comradeship that exists among brute beasts. . . . When such people, who do not know the Bible and who understand neither Latin nor German, insult me with such extreme slander, it is no more to me than as if an ass were braying at me. . . . When he offers to prove his teaching by bludgeon, fire, and water, I, poor

and with Spalatin in constant attendance on him he too held fast to it that all Luther wanted was an enquiry.

The people who were getting worried and did not mind showing it were the Dominicans. The closest friend of the Pope's chief minister and kinsman, Cardinal Giulio de Medici, was a Saxon Dominican; and the leading theologian at the Curia, Cardinal Gaetanus, was General of the Dominican Order. Having lodged their formal denunciation of Luther for heresy, with the Holy See, the German Dominicans pressed for action. Cardinal Giulio to get a little peace dropped a hint to the Vice-magistrate in Rome of the Augustinian Order to tell the Vicar-general of the Saxon Congregation of Augustinians to order Friar Martin to be quiet. Such a hint, such a message, such an order, relayed from the summit, should suffice. It was being suggested in various other quarters of the Church that the best way of silencing the obstreperous friar was to give him what he was asking for: a definitive official statement as to the power and efficacy of indulgence. But that was really too much. Rome really could not be expected to produce the equivalent of a white paper to answer some remarks made by the equivalent of a half-educated native schoolmaster in some colonial village. Such was the view, natural in the circumstances, on the summit of Rome.

*

16. Trial Heat

The Vicar-general of the Saxon Augustinians was still Dr. Staupitz. He had an excellent opportunity to discharge his commission from the Vice-magistrate, at the triennial chapter meeting of his Congregation, April–May 1518. The meeting was held at Heidelberg, the chief city of the Palatinate and seat of the university of that province.

Luther being due to report on his term as district vicar, which ended herewith, had first to obtain leave of absence from his university, as usual through Spalatin—it was well for both the Elector and his professor, now, that they could honestly say they had never had so much as five minutes' conversation. Spalatin made up for that. The Theology of Justification had won him heart and soul, and he had come to regard Martin as a veritable apostle, long before anybody else arrived at the comparison. Nothing would please him better, Spalatin avowed, than to devote his life to serving Luther's interests; and although he and Luther did not always see eye to eye as to what was in Luther's best interests, Spalatin was as good as his word.

The Elector demurred, "We do not like to have him long away from his lectures," but could hardly refuse; the Dominicans were helping Luther with him too. Tetzel and company lately had begun to cast aspersions at Elector Frederick's darling university itself, together with renewed threats and attempts to harass the princely patron. If they wanted him to disown or coerce Luther into unconditional surrender, they were going the wrong way about it. Laughable as were their unilateral attacks on the leading magnate of the Empire, who was on excellent terms with the Holy See, their rumoured boasts that

Luther if he ventured outside his own country would soon find out his mistake, could not be simply laughed off. But neither could they be allowed to intimidate anyone in Wittenberg. So Luther went with the Elector's blessing, instructions to take every precaution for his safety on the road, and a bundle of high-powered letters of introduction to serve him en route.

As Spalatin had impressed upon him the wisdom of travelling incognito, Luther made no use of these credentials till he got to Würzburg. He was in fact very nervous. This was the first time in years of travelling outside his own Saxon district, and would be the first time that he faced, in person, the theological representatives of the outside world, since the indulgence row. If the attitude of his prior and brethren in Wittenberg was anything to go by, the chances were that he was going to be disciplined: he was a monk and under vow of absolute obedience to his Order. The favourable attitude of his academic colleagues at home was nothing to go by; as witness *Our Theology*," they had already made it their own. "Our Theology," which would have another and a priori better chance at the Augustinian congress of being propagated outside Wittenberg, was in jeopardy. Its being propagated by a friar in disgrace would scarcely recommend it. The material damage no less than the insult to Tetzel at the hands of the student hooligans, also still preyed on Luther's frugal and respectability-loving mind (for eight hundred pamphlets however scurrilous represented no cheap merchandise); where previously his cause had been morally foolproof, his supporters at all events had put themselves in the wrong.

To their mutual surprise, Luther and the reigning prince of Würzburg, Bishop Lorenz, got on famously. So taken was the Bishop with "that devout and most worthy man, Dr. Martinus," that he wished him to go the rest of the way under armed escort at the Bishop's expense—but this Dr. Martinus would not have. He was determined to show his trust in God, and not to involve in his uncertain affairs one who might afterwards have cause to regret it.

A greater surprise awaited him in Heidelberg. Staupitz had had the gratuitous courtesy of having him made president of the public gala disputations held in honour of the occasion at the great chapter hall. Honour—he found himself treated as a guest of honour, altogether. Even Staupitz's friendship could not account for the fact, much less arrange it, that he who stood denounced by the Dominicans as a heretic scored a quite astonishing personal triumph at the disputations *with his theology*. The Dominican allegation, and for that matter the indulgence-controversy, never so much as came up in public. Naturally Luther and Staupitz had some private talks about the business; but that was as far as it went. The congress which he had dreaded was the most agreeable thing that had ever happened to him; it was like a dream.

Writing as promised to allay Spalatin's anxieties, Luther detailed joyfully, "The Count Palatine, too, has been treating me extraordinarily well. He entertained me with Father Staupitz and our Lang (who is the new district vicar!). We had a wonderful time together, conversing happily, eating and drinking, and viewing all the treasures of the chapel and the armoury, and being shown over this whole, truly royal and remarkable castle. Nothing was omitted that kindness could prompt. The doctors also heard my disputation with evident pleasure and debated with me so modestly [sic] that they made themselves very dear to me. For although the theology seemed strange to them at first, they discussed it perceptively and skilfully—with the exception of one very young one, who raised a great laugh when he blurted out, 'If the common people were here to hear you, they would surely stone you to death!' "

There were other young men in the thronged auditorium who responded otherwise—namely with instantaneous hero-worship. One of them, Martin Bucer from Alsace, who was himself a Dominican Friar, reported hot from the conference, with all the fervour of the convert:

"Though our [Dominican] chief men assailed him with all their might, their wiles were not able to make him yield one inch. . . . His charm in answering is amazing, his patience in listening is inexhaustible. His acuteness reminds one strongly of St. Paul. With answers that are as succinct as they are to the point, drawn entirely from the Holy Scriptures, he dazzles everyone with admiration. . . . The next day I had a confidential chat with him alone and afterwards shared his meal with him, which was moderate though seasoned with delicious conversation. Whatever I asked him, he explained to me most lucidly. He is quite in agreement with Erasmus. [A good thing Luther was not looking over Bucer's shoulder as he wrote this! Like everybody else he admired Erasmus' scholarship and literary finesse, but his opinions about humanism as such were unchanged.] But he surpasses him in that what Erasmus only insinuates, he teaches freely and directly. I wish I had time now to write more—you know he is the one who put an end to the rule of scholasticism in Wittenberg and who has brought it to pass that the Greek language, Jerome, Augustine, and Paul are taught there as a regular thing!"

At Heidelberg, it was Luther's theology which decided people overwhelmingly in his favour also as regards his stand against the Dominicans of the Cologne party. On all intelligent persons, other Dominicans not excluded, the enlightening impression it produced reflected on his general probity and reasoning; and here as in Wittenberg the young in particular drew the immediate practical conclusion and went over to his teaching without reservations. So far from being ostracized Luther had at one stroke won enough outside adherents to be able to write home:

"As Christ, when the Jews rejected him, went over to the gentiles, so I now confidently hope that the true theology of Christ, which those who have grown old in Occamism reject, will pass to the younger generation."

So far from being finished, he had gone up in the world. Staupitz insisted that on the return journey Luther travel by wagon, paid for by his Augustinian fellow-passengers; it would not do for the star of the congress to tramp back as he had come.

Answering the usual excited bombardment of questions with which the returning traveller is met at home, Luther summed up his experience thus: "I went on foot. I came back in a wagon." That told them everything.

*

17. Controversial Leapfrog

People in Wittenberg remarked on it, how much healthier Luther looked after he had been to Heidelberg: fairly blooming.

He got back on 15 May and next morning, Sunday, preached in the Castle Church, on the subject of excommunication. However pertinent and timely, and never mind if the text was that of the appointed lesson ("They shall put you out of the synagogues," John 16:2), the sermon was a clear act of defiance.

The papal ban was the essential instrument of ecclesiastical power. It was the sovereign mechanism of the rule of fear. Being debarred from holy communion was to be consigned to eternal damnation—to hell, real, literal hell. It also entailed ejection from the temporal community; it was social death as well as the death of the soul. And it had become a lever of despotism and extortion.

Anyone who failed to pay tithe or any other Church tax on the dot was excommunicated: which meant excommunication for anybody associating with him thereafter; and if he did not pay up on the second reminder, his whole family—even if they had ceased to associate with him—were excommunicated as well. No allowances were made, no account was taken of excuses, no matter how demonstrable. At harvest time, when the large tithe fell due, "bans fly about by the hundred like bats," as Luther put it, and the German countryside swarmed with troops of vagrants who were dispossessed and excommunicated peasantry. If on the other hand a town council declined to excuse an ecclesiastical foundation within its domain from paying import duty or brew-tax like everybody else, or a suzerain arrested a subject even remotely connected with the clergy, even for a capital crime—out flew the bats, and town or castle was laid under interdict. Almost the entire business correspondence between secular and clerical local authorities had to do with bans, which could of course be lifted if and when the excommunicate came to heel. When it was a case of excommunication for non-payment and the defaulter could not pay—well, that was too bad; in a case like that of Luther, all he had to do was to apologize for his writings against indulgences and indulgence-sellers, withdraw them, and atone, to escape excommunication.

Not that there was as yet any word of this from Rome, but Tetzel and his partisans were staunchly bruiting about the imminent destruction of their presumptuous critic. If it had needed this, the Dominican lobby were underlining what they had made plain enough in the Reuchlin affair: that criticism levelled at themselves was a matter for punishment not argument. Yet their refusal to answer Luther save by vituperation was strengthening the impression that his criticism was unanswerable. Indulgence sales in Germany were declining. So long as it was only Tetzel against Luther, so long as there was no decisive statement from the Holy See, so long must the position be regarded as uncertain. So long as it was not certain that money put into the box bought what it was meant for, and that the intended purchase was not in fact a sin, it would be an unnecessary risk to carry on with the practice. Such contributions being voluntary, one could not be excommunicated for withholding them.

Luther had not had it all his own way on the return journey from Heidelberg; he had encountered the expected opposition of Occamites and Thomists, notably in Erfurt, and received further instalments of Dominican-inspired abuse. This in a way was exactly what he needed to turn the satisfactions of Heidelberg into a stimulating rather than a merely soothing experience.

When it was done, people might wonder that he had not touched on this, a far more urgent and radical issue than the question of indulgence, earlier. Up to now, however, he had concerned himself with reform only in the context of education, his professional brief: academic education and moral education. Actual doctrine and institutions he too accepted as unassailable: hence the absurdity of calling him a heretic. He had not attacked the principle of indulgence, only its practical misapplication. Now the acute threat to himself, of ex-communication, had brought the principle of that into closer, sharper, more imaginative focus. He knew, and also had it on the authority of his bishop and colleagues, that his views were irreproachably orthodox; therefore, should he be excommunicated for his views, excommunica-tion could have no validity. If the Church could say a man was damned when he was not, then the Church had no right to say so; if it had not the right it had not the power. Even yet he was not concerned with the material injustices perpetrated by means of the ban, but rather, with the mental confusion and spiritual despair which the arbitrary handling of it must occasion to souls innocent as his own of any religious defection.

He therefore could not wait to stand up in the pulpit and tell the world that excommunication could only exclude a person from the out-ward fellowship of the Church, never from the inner fellowship of Faith which was beyond the control of any outside agency whatsoever. There was nothing for the soul to be afraid of, in the ban. Hence, "If you are unjustly banned for the sake of truth and right, you may by no means stop doing what has drawn this upon you. If in consequence you die without the sacrament, if your corpse is thrown into uncon-secrated ground . . . happy are you! Blessed is he who dies under such an unjust ban! For inasmuch as he has remained faithful, he shall gain the crown of life."

What he was saying was, not merely as heretofore that the Pope's powers of intercession with the Deity were limited, but that the Pope had no power to damn. What did that mean, but that the Pope had no power, period? Indeed this was precisely the conclusion Luther had now come to. *Power* was with God alone. Power was nothing to do with the Church. The Pope was but its chief ministering servant, like St. Peter the fisherman whose shoes he wore. Look it up in the Bible, look it up in the Fathers: there it was, right there.

Imaginably, the sermon caused a stir not only among the laity but also on the academic side; so much so that the university forth-with arranged to hold a disputation on the subject. But then the dis-putation was postponed; the subject was too important not to allow people ample time to marshall their ideas and their sources.

In the event, the time allowance benefitted the opposition. One might have thought that Luther's sermon as it stood would be quite enough to get things moving against him at last in Rome; but the

German Dominicans wanted to make sure. Some "dreadful spies" of theirs had been lurking among the congregation on that Sunday, and hastened to elaborate their notes into a pamphlet of spurious theses, which were forwarded to Rome as Luther's work, well ahead of his own published version of the real sermon. Whether or no the real sermon would have gone down any better in Rome, the clumsy extravagancies and offensive garnish of the false theses came up high on the agenda of the general chapter of the Dominican Order then meeting at Rome; and papal authority was now obtained to start regular proceedings against Luther for heresy. The Curia's chief consultant on matters of faith was called upon to give an opinion of the Ninety-five Theses which had started all the trouble, for the purpose of framing the formal indictment. This was in mid-June.

About the same time as the Dominican congress opened in Rome, Luther on Staupitz's advice had written to the Pope. The purpose was to depose at headquarters an authorized copy of the *Resolutions* on the Ninety-five Theses, as a proof of Luther's orthodoxy and loyalty in the teeth of the Tetzelites' wild accusations. With it went a letter which neither Staupitz nor Luther were so naïve as to trust the Pope would actually see, but which nevertheless the Pope was more likely to see than one addressed to somebody else.

In the first draft of this letter Luther dealt at length with the claims and threats of the German Dominicans, adding that the writer would not have presumed to trouble the Holy Father were it not necessary to show these people that they could not frighten him. "I lay my work at your feet, Holy Father, with the utmost confidence. Whatever your decision may be, it will have its origin in Jesus, without whom you cannot propose or state anything. . . . May he, the Lord, preserve and guide you, not according to your pleasure or that of any man, but according to *his* will, which alone is good and to be praised eternally."

The draft was shown to Spalatin and as a result substantially altered. The counter-accusations against the Tetzelites were deleted, as was also a passage declaring that Luther did not care what happened to his books. Instead, some defensive compliments to Luther's temporal sovereign were inserted: ". . . If I were as they describe me, the illustrious Elector of Saxony certainly would not suffer such a pestiferous boil in his university, for he is probably the greatest living champion of Catholic truth in the world. . . ." and the appeal for paternal judgment became less assertive: "For my own protection, let my book go out under the safeguard of your name, Holy Father, so that everyone may realize with what pure intentions I have sought to fathom the nature of ecclesiastical power and in what reverence I hold it. . . . Most Holy Father, I cast myself at your feet. . . . Raise me or slay me, summon me hither or thither, approve or reprove me as you please. I will listen to your voice as to the voice of Christ." However, two emendations of a different nature also slipped in. First, Luther drew the attention of the head of the Church to the discrepancy between *metanoia* and *poenitentia* which had so gladdened his spirit on reading Erasmus' Greek Gospels; and at the tail end of all his pliant phrases came the sting, "I cannot recant," which made nonsense of them.

"The Pope," Luther wrote in after years, "never gave me a really bad moment except at the start when sylvan Sylvester wrote against me and it said on the title page 'by the Master of the Sacred Palace.' Then thought I, Horrors! has the business come before the Pope?" Well, was not that what he had wanted? Yes; but the difference between wanting a thing and getting it can be as poignant as any, between expectation and impact.

Although—if only with deference to the endless layers of the psyche—one has to take with a grain of salt Luther's reiterated belief that the Pope knew not what his underlings were doing in his name, it was nevertheless true that he distinguished between the human person and the office-bearer, with reference to the Pope no less than to the Archbishop of Mainz (or for that matter to Elector Frederick who went on clinging to his relics in the most unenlightened way). He revered and stood in awe of the head of the Church even when he could not respect its policy in certain particulars. Apart from his keen appreciation of the sacrosanctity of office, per se, Luther's in-grained love for authority continued undiminished: it hurt him more than anybody, to go against authority. That was why, having stren-uously to nerve himself to do so, he could then display an almost excessive degree of nerve in the act.

The person whom he ridiculed as "sylvan Sylvester" was the curial expert who had been entrusted with framing the indictment of Luther for his trial in Rome, named Sylvester Mazzolini da Prierio —Prierias for short, with the title of Master of the Sacred Palace.

Prierias was a Dominican, a strict Thomist of the old school, sixty-two years old, with a long and vicariously distinguished record of service at the Vatican. Incidentally, his voice had been the only dissenting one on the committee of cardinals which had quashed the process against Reuchlin; but that small defeat had shaken neither his position nor his aplomb.

Prierias became the first in a relay of curial delegates girding themselves, with a negligence born of super-confidence, to show whom it might concern how one dealt with a bucolic nonentity like the "mini-friar" (*fraterculus*) of Wittenberg. Instead of producing the required deposition, he elected to take a short-cut, and published—unprecedentedly—a printed polemic under his weighty name and title: "O horrors!" was precisely the effect he anticipated. So beyond a few quotations from Thomas Aquinas, Prierias, too, did not trouble himself with arguments, relying mainly on invective ("son of a bitch," "libeller and calumniator," "leper with a brain of brass and nose of iron") and untenable hyperbole ("the Church's authority is greater than the authority of Scripture," "the Pope's word is the oracle of God"). He himself was so pleased with his brainchild as to advertise in the introduction that it was the fruit of a mere three days' work.

The Pope's private comment was he wished to God Prierias had taken three months over it. Luther, having read beyond the alarming title page, heaved a sigh of relief: "But our Lord God was merciful, for that bacchant wrote such rubbish one could only laugh." The Master of the Sacred Palace fell even below the standard of Tetzel; and Luther caused no little embarrassment by re-publishing the papal expert's pamphlet verbatim conjointly with his own reply. For his part, Luther apologized, he had taken only two days for it as against Prierias' three: but if his opponent would deign to write something less flippant next time, he too would give a more polished retort. Meanwhile he contented himself with quoting the canon law that there was no infallibility on earth save only in Scripture, and pointing out once again, "Even now I am only taking part in a disputation."

A disputation takes two. Even now the Holy See was not having any. Prierias might have made a sorry hash of his expertise, but he was the Curia's own, and one would hardly jettison him for asserting that the Pope *was* infallible. His charge, of dangerous doctrine and revolt against papal authority, was upheld, and the canonical trial went forward. Irrespective of the theological niceties, the theses based on his sermon about excommunication conclusively showed Luther to be propounding dangerous and rebellious opinions indeed. A citation went out commanding Luther to appear in Rome within sixty days, there to answer the charges before a papal tribunal.

"I thought," said Luther, sadly, "the Pope would *protect* me." Did he? Did he, truly so? He thought that was what he thought, perhaps. But he evidently did not even trust the Pope to ensure due process of justice. Nor did anybody else. Anybody in receipt of a citation to Rome for trial would move heaven and earth not to go. Through Spalatin, Luther immediately lodged a petition with Elector Frederick, to obtain from the Pope a transfer of the trial to German territory. Prospects were not good, but better than they would have been before the Reuchlin case.

It was now August. There was no immediate reply from the Elector. The Elector was away in Augsburg, where the Imperial Diet of that year 1518 was assembled, in the presence of Emperor Maximilian and a special papal delegation, to deal with large, world affairs.

The weeks went by, still no word came.

Luther did not appear to be repining; one might have thought he was not worrying, at all. With his wonted capacity for enthusiasm—which at this juncture one might almost mistake for volatility—he was giving vent to great excitement about the latest addition to the University of Wittenberg. The newly established chair of Greek had been filled and its first incumbent arrived on 25 August: Master Philippus Melanchthon, "a shrimp with a twitch in one shoulder," also afflicted by a stammer, and only in his twenty-second year, but a great-nephew of Reuchlin who had recommended him. Reuchlin had not promised too much: as soon as the shy, awkward young man opened his mouth for more than smalltalk, he was—so Luther diligently broadcast—"like the boy Jesus in the temple! There is no one else living so gifted!" He was diligent, too, in befriending the newcomer and extolling the pleasure and benefit to himself of "our Grecian's" companionship. Perhaps it helped to take his mind off waiting.

In any case, Luther was not idle. With his reply to Prierias—reprinting the attack as a part of the defence—he had stumbled on a mode of combat which made his writings in this matter tantamount to ringside reports: so much so that the general public was now constantly on tenterhooks as though for the next instalment of a gripping serial.

18. Blind Men's Buff

No use being impatient; bootless to tie oneself in knots of speculation about temporal happenings which no one could hope to gauge
till they were all finished and done with, if then. All quarters operated
very largely in the dark and very much in insulated compartments.

News travelled slowly; general intelligence was hard to come by.
Sometimes it is true the mysterious grapevine of technologically primitive societies proved astonishingly effective; sometimes to be sure some
particular, printed communication got around with unaccountable
speed. But such was not the rule.

The mails went on foot and there was no regular postal service.
Special messengers might go on horseback, but there was not any
permanent system of fixed remount stations. Apart from beacons held
in readiness for specific events like invasion by sea or the death or
accession of a sovereign, the channels of transmission were entirely
occasional. Highways were meagre and nobody shouldered the responsibility for them; the peasants sometimes quarried or improvised
marlpits in the road; repairs were likewise improvised at need. Knights,
peasants on the run, or unemployed mercenaries favoured the main
routes for ambush. There were few public inns and none too many
convents where the passing stranger might find overnight accommodation; his own cloak draped over a bush often was the only roof he
could rely on. Hardihood was as necessary for travelling equipment
as the money to buy food—when there was food to spare for him
where he called in.

The messengers of popes, princes, and bankers, though well provisioned, were not less subject to accidents and not less at the mercy of guides in foreign parts. There were no handy maps and no phrase-books in foreign dialects. Spies had no wings and no electrical appliances; their orbit of reconnaissance was narrow, and the inevitable time lag cooled the hottest tips.

From day to day, nay from week to week the Holy See did not know what was going on at the German Diet, and the papal legate to the German Diet did not know what was going on in Rome. From month to month the Emperor had only the sketchiest knowledge how his wars were going when he was not himself at the front. By the time he learned of some lawless outbreak inside the Empire, the incident might be over or it might have spread. As for the progress of the Turks to east and west, and the internal balance of Infidel power which had a great deal of bearing on that situation—reports might get through, now tolerably prompt, now tardy, or they might not.

The German representatives might be in closer touch with home but were dependent on the wit and vision of what deputies they had there left in charge. For the representatives of towns and knighthood this was no problem; but the prelates and great nobles tended to bring virtually their whole political households with them to the Diet. The Elector of Saxony had his quota of jurists and councillors at Augsburg as well as his secretary Spalatin: but Spalatin had nothing to tell his friend in Wittenberg till there was something to tell. It was not that the Elector had forgotten Luther's petition. Extremely busy though he was, he discussed it daily with his entourage, from every angle: only that the angles seemed inexhaustible.

While the Diet acted as a sounding board and news exchange for the legislators of the Empire, the principal business of 1518 concerned the project of a new Crusade against Islam—a grand "General Passage" as of old—which had been mooted perennially since the fall of Outremer in 1291, and all genuine attempts at which had ceased since the 1450s. Now in the last six years the situation, from the Western point of view, had rather seriously deteriorated. Under Sultan Selim the Turks had almost doubled their dominions, with the acquisition of Egypt, Syria, the Hejaz, and Kurdistan, in Africa and Asia, and the borderlands of Carinthia, Croatia, Hungary, Poland in Europe, not to mention their hold on the Dalmatian seaboard. Thus the Turks' strategic position was at once too good and too precarious for Western comfort: having penetrated so far afield, the Turks by the same token must push on to ensure against being pushed back. The West had better get in first, for a change—now or never.

Pope Leo X proposed to realize the project, for which so many of his predecessors had laboured in vain. His proposals were: 1. a general truce between all the powers of Christendom, himself to be acting arbitrator; 2. leadership of Holy War to be shared by the Emperor and the King of France, who should also furnish the necessary armies; 3. England, Spain, and Portugal to furnish the necessary navies; 4. a universal tax to finance the enterprise. Needless to say it was 4. which particularly put everybody off (yet without which the whole scheme must once more collapse). France, England, Spain, Portugal jibbed. Only the Emperor showed any inclination to accede to the papal plan: to the stark amazement of the German princes.

Emperor Maximilian had his reasons, two of them eminently practical, one romantic. To take the latter first, "the last of the knights" had, he confessed, known no dearer wish from earliest youth than to do battle against the Infidel. But also he had been trying for some time to levy an overall imperial tax which had fallen into practical though not statutory desuetude: the crusading tax would restore the appropriate machinery to easy running order. Furthermore, he had never had the time to have himself crowned. The last of the knights retained enough of the mediaeval mentality to feel uneasy for the lack. In mediaeval theory, the Emperor elect was merely *King* of Rome until the Pope in person had set the Holy Roman crown upon his head; and although Maximilian was not the first to have managed without that and found it infeasible now as ever to go to Rome for it, he had in his old age thought of a way round the difficulty. He was negotiating with the Holy See to have the sacred regalia sent out to him on loan across the Alps, for the German primate (Albrecht of Mainz) to invest him with them, as the Pope's proxy. Regarding the matter dispassionately, it was not very likely that the Holy See would consent to this in the end; but there was no harm in letting him try, with an eye to some quid pro quo.

Maximilian was the more interested in his belated coronation at this point because he was also deep in negotiations with the German princes, to obtain a guarantee for the succession of his grandson Charles to the imperial throne. As a preliminary he wished to have Charles elected King of Rome before he, Maximilian, died: and there could not well be a new King of Rome so long as the Emperor himself still bore the lesser title, technically.

These dynastic considerations, which followed in the well-worn groove of Habsburg endeavours to secure the imperial dignity as a true family adjunct, prejudiced the Emperor's position both with the papacy and the German Estates. In a somewhat suppliant posture, his hands were somewhat tied in relation to either. And as Maximilian's reign had seen an immense spurt of increase in the Habsburg possessions, the rest of Europe was commensurately alert against any further Habsburg aggrandisement and intent on blocking the future election of yet another Habsburg. The papacy entirely shared that prejudice, and the German Estates were not untouched with it.

The papal legate to the Diet of Augsburg, whose mission was to push through a definitive imperial proclamation of Holy War plus the requisite universal levy, was Cardinal "Cajetan"—in the whittled Northern adaptation of his by-name Gaetanus. Cardinal Cajetan was a dyed-in-the-wool Thomist Dominican like Prierias, only much the latter's intellectual superior. (And so he ought to be: his mother when pregnant of him had been vouchsafed a prophetic dream in which the portly saint Aquinas came down from heaven to act as personal tutor to the coming child.) He had proved his worth as a scholar, teacher, author, debater, and parliamentarian—more especially in inflicting a crushing defeat on the conciliar party within the Church—before Leo X in an unprecedented mass elevation of thirty-one new cardinals had raised Cajetan among them to this dignity. Albrecht of Mainz also was one of this batch, which was not unconnected with a conspiracy of cardinals to assassinate the Pope, discovered in the nick of time the previous year. So the dignity was still shining new, and Cajetan loved and much insisted on it: but that did not detract from his capabilities and earnest dedication. He worked as hard as any man could to succeed in his task.

That the mission did not prosper was no fault of Cajetan's. Like the governments of France, England, Portugal and Spain, the German Estates would not hear of a universal levy. They went so far as to submit the unheard-of argument that "the people" would never stand for it: what good would it do, to decree such a war tax and then be unable to collect it?, so the delegates countered the Emperor's baffled, feudal thunder and the Cardinal Legate's politer suasion. The very fact

"The world hates the truth. By such hate was Christ crucified, and as far as I can see to be crucified is all you can now expect. Therefore flee while there is still time. Come to me that we may live and die together: the Archbishop of Salzburg is willing."

Staupitz's letter left Salzburg on 14 September. Eighteen days before that and four days after the orders for Luther's arrest had left Rome, it was learned in Augsburg that the Emperor's talks with the Electors in behalf of his grandson had come to a halt. The electoral vote had to be unanimous. Five of the Electoral College had been more or less brought round to the Emperor's wishes for his grandson; one, however, had categorically refused to subscribe. That one was the Elector Frederick of Saxony. His importance to the Holy See instantly shot up. To keep the Habsburgs out next time, everything should be done to keep the Senior Elector to his refusal. But the Holy See away in Rome did not know that yet; only Cardinal Cajetan in Augsburg knew.

He knew more before that same day, 27 August, was out. On that day, too, the Estates of the German nation gave their final answer concerning the proposed crusade. The answer was no. The No was barbed and loaded as never before in a transaction of the kind. The Estates explained at length that the nation had no money left to give, being constantly sucked dry by Church impositions: *let the German Gravamina be redressed,* then perhaps another time the Pope's proposals might get a more favourable hearing. Meanwhile, should the Germans feel like fighting the Turks, it would be under secular steam. ("The Turks we need to fight are in Italy!" Hutten had written in a pamphlet which enjoyed a big circulation at the Diet.) Nor was the Emperor spared, in this belligerent declaration. A long list of complaints and demands was included, with regard to the present state of the imperial administration, which had sunk into a slough of impotence, so that there was neither justice nor security to be had inside the realm except what every man might try to get for himself.

No Emperor had ever participated in a less satisfactory session of the German Diet, than Emperor Max, the idol of the Germans.

Cajetan conveyed the news to Rome post haste, so that as early as 3 September it was decided at the Curia to bestow on the Elector of Saxony the Golden Rose, the highest distinction in the Pope's gift, which Frederick the Wise had hankered after and made play for, for years. That should keep him happy, amenable, and anti-Charles of Habsburg.

But meanwhile on 29 August Cajetan had had occasion to write again. On that day Frederick the Wise had finally made up his mind to intercede for Luther: the old man's wisdom was not such an empty honorific.

Frederick sent his compliments to the Cardinal at the Fugger house where Cajetan was staying and asked him to meet Luther here. Seeing that he, such an erudite and eminent representative of the Curia, happened to be on the spot in Germany, was this not a heaven-sent opportunity to examine Martinus "in a fatherly and not in a judicial way"—so that the matter might be cleared up swiftly and quietly, as the Elector was sure it would be under such conditions—seeing that the finest of universities, namely that of Wittenberg, had expressed complete confidence in the orthodoxy of the profes-sor—? Should the examination nevertheless go against him, he, the Elector, "would be the first to punish Martinus"; though to be sure the order of extradition would have to be suspended for the nonce.

The order was suspended. Cajetan's recommendation to that effect was received and confirmed in Rome on 10 September. He was able to show his revised instructions to the Elector on 20 September. On 21 September Spalatin acquainted Luther with the concession that had thus been gained for him, the Diet dispersed, and Elector Frederick left Augsburg on 22 September. Staupitz's impassioned warning reached Luther on 23 September; the official order to present himself at Augsburg for examination by the Cardinal Legate reached him on the 25th, when as ordered he at once departed from Wittenberg. It took him till 7 October to get to Augsburg.

It would seem to be introducing an entirely superfluous flourish of complication (which moreover was entirely inconsequential), that before they parted Emperor Max dropped a cryptic hint to Elector Frederick, "to look well to that monk of his" who might come in useful one of these days, presumably against the papacy. But it helps to give additional atmosphere, does it not?

Another footnote, seemingly unconnected with the immediate events at Augsburg, is however very much in place. Some time before, Luther had lighted on a manuscript of sermons by an anonymous disciple of the German Mystic Johann Tauler (d.1361). In the bad old days of Luther's "afflictions," his mentor Staupitz had referred him to Tauler, without benefit; but now in this little book Luther found to his delight much that was to the point of his own theology, and had it printed with a glowing introduction. In spring 1518 a complete copy of the original work came into his hands and impelled him to publish an accordingly amplified edition, to which he gave the title of *A German Theology*. This appeared in June, with a foreword pointing the crass contrast of such genuine, god-loving piety with the rantings of Luther's opponents. The contrast was what the foreword made it (two years later Luther changed his views about German Mysticism); the foreword was what people mostly read, and in some cases it was the title which attracted readers to the foreword. Among the latter was Ulrich von Hutten, whose nationalism derived a new orientation from the perusal.

19. Confrontation

For the second time Luther rode in a cart, though not for any gratifying reason. He was so ill with violent bowel trouble that he had to hire transport for the last three miles to Augsburg and entered the great city in a state of complete physical prostration.

"All the way I saw the stake before my eyes. 'I go to my death,' I told myself, 'What a disgrace to my dear parents!'"

The orders for his arrest and hauling to Rome in chains had not been rescinded; in Augsburg he would be very nearly as friendless and unprotected as in Rome, against the Cardinal Legate with a great train befitting his rank and the powerful papalist sympathies of the House of Fugger. All Luther's fine equanimity, upon Prierias' having put the enemy so gloriously in the wrong, had evaporated. Cardinal Cajetan as a former general of the Dominican Order and renownedly serious theologian was the real thing, and would in all probability make short work of him. The legal adviser whom Elector Frederick had detailed to Luther's assistance during the forthcoming interview had not turned up. The only bright spot was that he had been able to borrow a cowl, a brand-new one, precious rarity—so that at least he would not look too much the part of the "mangy friar" in the current parlance of his foes.

Once he had arrived things began to look a little better. His host, the prior of the Carmelite monastery of St. Anna, had him put straight to bed, and the two Saxon councillors who he had been told would remain in Augsburg for him proved to be there. They insisted that he must not move until letters of safe-conduct from the city council and the imperial chancery were procured for him, and sent appropriate word to the Fugger residence. The Cardinal professed himself deeply offended that anyone should so distrust him, the representative of the Holy Father; and meantime put the interval to good advantage, completing his two weeks' careful study of Luther's publications with a detailed, written refutation of them. The patient also rallied. It seemed he was not so friendless even in this, the proudest city of the Empire. Numbers of Augsburg notables came in to introduce themselves and converse with him most amiably, among them the celebrated humanist and antiquarian Konrad Peutinger, intimate friend of Albrecht Dürer and Emperor Max, and a visitor from Ingolstadt University, its vice-chancellor Professor Johann Maier (of Eck) Eckius—whose call gave Luther particular pleasure.

Professor Eckius had been one of the few scholars outside Wittenberg who eventually took some notice of the ninety-seven theses, with a resulting friendly correspondence; but then, to Luther's most painful surprise, he had come forward as one of Tetzel's earlier collaborators, and they had been engaged in intermittent skirmish ever since. To have the man now paying him a social call and civilly discussing arrangements for an orderly disputation sometime soon, was cheering. Within a day or two Luther was on his feet again, not to say on his toes.

So also was the Cardinal. The Emperor was gone, the unprofitable Diet was as if it had never been, and here was his chance to vindicate his ingenuity in a subsidiary matter which yet offered no unworthy challenge. For his orders were, either to procure the friar's recantation or else deliver him to Rome regardless of the promise made to Elector Frederick that any necessary punishment of Luther should be left to Luther's sovereign; and at the same time to keep Elector Frederick in good humour. The Cardinal rose to the contradictory assignment with corresponding zest. Unlike Prierias, he felt—just like Prierias—that he would give a thumping demonstration how to handle an affair of this sort.

There was in Cardinal Cajetan's retinue another armchair strategist spoiling to try his hand at it. His name was Urban de Serralonga, and he made an independent sortie to the Carmelite cloister, only a stone's throw from the Fugger house. Kindness, he thought, would do the trick. Having come, as he told Luther, to coach him in correct deportment towards a cardinal, he talked as one should to a simple soul: come, now, all that Luther was asked to do was to pronounce six letters, r-e-v-o-c-o, I recant: well? was that so difficult? was it worth so much fuss and bother, baulking at one little word? What, Luther said he had come all this way for the purpose of defending his opinions? "Dear, dear! You're set on a tournament, are you? Honestly, dear fellow, you are taking the whole question of indulgences much too seriously. Why not teach something, even if it is not strictly true, that brings in money? For that matter, the Pope's power is so great that he can put articles of faith in and out of force by a mere wink. What does the Pope care about Germany anyhow?"

"So this go-between," Luther exulted fuming, in a transcript of the interlude for Spalatin, "has put new heart into me. Give my regards to my friends in Wittenberg and tell them to be of good courage." Nevertheless he wrote some provisional farewell letters as well, under the same date (including one to his young friend "the new Grecian" Melanchthon in which he said his chief regret, if he were now to be slaughtered as a sacrifice, would be not seeing him again). For that day the letters of safe-conduct had arrived, and next morning, 12 October, Luther with five other friars went to wait upon Cardinal Cajetan at the house of the Fugger.

The Fugger house was reckoned one of the wonders of the world, surpassing any princely palace of the North, with cellars full of gold, apartments full of works of art and comfortable seats, and a turret roofed half-way down in solid silver coins. It was one of the sights of Augsburg, which no traveller of distinction would willingly miss; Master Jakob Fugger—surnamed, one feels unnecessarily, "the Rich"—did not disdain showing such visitors round. ("My lord fully expected a goodly parting present," an attendant to one noble tourist wrote after their exhaustive circuit of the Fugger domain, "But all we came away with was a goodly hangover.") Very important persons with large entourages always lodged with the Fugger when in Augsburg; not even the great Dominican cloister nearby could compete in point of space and entertainment.

Not but that Cardinal Cajetan had brought along extra furnishings—his demands in this respect, for his sojourn in Germany, had made the curial Master of the Wardrobe smile, according to a talkative official. Decked in satin, brocade, velvet, and gold gallooning, and surrounded by a throng of courtiers similarly apparelled, he received Luther against a background of portable wall-hangings in crimson damask encircling the whole audience chamber. The mangy friar in his borrowed black gown had never seen the like. He remembered to go through the prescribed motions.

"First I prostrated myself full length. When he commanded me to arise, I got up only to my knees. Only when he beckoned again did I stand up. First of all I humbly asked his pardon for having delayed till I had the safe-conduct and then assured him all I wanted was to hear the truth from his lips."

The Cardinal replied so graciously that for a moment all Luther's affectionate nature welled to meet the magnificent father-figure. But then the Cardinal opened up with a comprehensive restatement of his commission: this was to be an examination, not a debate; with the sole object of obtaining from the examinee a recantation of his errors and the promise to be good in future. With that Cajetan had stepped on to Luther's ground and on his combined professional and emotional reflexes. Crimson damask and filial yearnings notwithstanding, Luther snapped back just as if he were at home, that he had not made the arduous journey to Augsburg to do what he could have done perfectly well at Wittenberg; so would the Cardinal kindly get on with telling him what his alleged errors were.

The Cardinal smiled. The dazzling spectators tittered ("in true Italian style," Luther remarked in his account of the proceedings, which apparently were punctuated throughout by gusts of Italian merriment). Very well, said the Cardinal; that should not take long. There was no need to go through Luther's Theses one by one; two crucial points would suffice: one, Luther's denial that the treasure of the Church was identical with the merits of Christ and the saints; two, his assertion that Justification was by faith and not by sacrament. Regarding the first, Pope Clement VI's Bull *Unigenitus* of 1343, which the Cardinal would quote as the friar was perhaps unacquainted with the text, categorically affirmed that identity for all time; and regarding the second—well really, that *was* out and out heresy: "This you have to recant whether you want to or not. For on the basis of this one passage everything else you have said or may say is to be condemned."

Of course, since it was the basis of everything he had to say, Justification by Faith was to Luther not an opinion but a fact of facts, given by St. Paul. It was the absolute kernel of Christianity, utterly indisputable; nothing anyone might quote against it had the slightest cogency. If anybody was a heretic, it was he who attempted to assail that immutable truth, whether he be a cardinal or the meanest village priest. If the Bull *Unigenitus* contradicted Scripture— then assuredly it was not Scripture that was wrong.

Well might the Roman courtiers laugh—now to applaud their master, now in derision of the friar. The encounter had its comic side. The contestants spoke each to deaf ears. In effect, neither cared what the other said—except in that Luther kept on demanding scriptural chapter and verse for the Cardinal's assertions, while the Cardinal kept on asserting that papal authority was above Scripture, Church Fathers, General Councils, and all things else. "Show me that it says so in the Bible!" "Recant, because it is the will of the Pope!" So they went on throughout the interview, with Luther quoting Scripture and Cajetan quoting *Unigenitus,* immovably at cross purposes. The Cardinal kept his temper, poise, and manners longer than the friar, who truth to tell behaved rather badly, blustering and quibbling like any pig-theologer, forsooth; but in the end he too was lured into a very tantrum, shouting incautiously, to hell with the Council of Basel and to the devil with the whole Sorbonne (Luther having cited these in proof that popes could err). With the Cardinal's end of the seesaw thus plunging to the bottom, Luther's end swung up to the heights of seemly dignity; so that it was the examinee who suggested quietly that they adjourn, reflect, and resume tomorrow; and withdrew in tolerably good order. At all events he had achieved that the examination had turned into precisely what Cajetan had declared at the outset it was not going to be: a wrangle.

Next day the Italian sense of humour was tickled afresh, as Luther came to the second interview armed with a written statement and a whole procession of supporters, swelled by the Saxon councillors, Dr. Staupitz (just arrived), and the great Peutinger whose standing in Augsburg outranked even that of the Fugger brothers. Cajetan smiled to see the array, and smiled again to hear Luther read his statement, while the courtiers laughed. The gist of the statement was that, not being conscious of having taught anything contrary to the Word of God, patristic doctrine, or reason, Luther was nevertheless aware that he like all men could err, and would be glad to submit either to a public disputation or to the considered judgment of the Universities of Basel, Freiburg, Louvain, and Paris. After a renewed access of quotations from the Bible on the one hand and *Unigenitus* on the other, Luther said he would answer only in writing henceforth: "We are not getting anywhere like this, I've argued quite enough with you," and the Cardinal exploded, "I am not arguing with you, little brother!"

Although by Staupitz's bland, diplomatic intervention the Cardinal was prevailed on to give Luther a third chance, the impression among Luther's friends was that his case was lost. Only the two Saxon councillors, one of whom was his brother-in-law, reappeared with Luther on the following day—bravely, to prevent his being arrested and abducted then and there. The rest of yesterday's procession now judged the Fugger house too unhealthy territory.

That third interview was the most heated though not essentially very different from the previous ones: Cardinal and friar tried to shout each other down with quotations from Bull and Bible, and parted each in the belief that he had had the best of it.

Admittedly the Cardinal had the last word. "Recant!" he cried in dismissal. "I am authorized by the Pope to place you and all your patrons under the ban and all places which receive you under interdict. Get out and don't let me see you again unless you will recant!"

"That's shaken his confidence," the Cardinal said afterwards, at the same time as Luther was writing to Spalatin: "So his confidence was shattered, and while he still went on shouting, 'Recant! Recant!' I turned and went."

But this was where the element of comedy ended. Staupitz and another Augustinian, whom Cajetan sent for after dinner, could see nothing funny in the situation—not even in a remark the Cardinal let slip: "Whatever happens, I'm not going to have him here again. I don't like the look in his eyes." The Cardinal's intention was to strike the iron while as he thought it was hot and induce the shaken friar's conclusive capitulation through his friends. Certainly the pair came away convinced of the Cardinal's determination to destroy him.

Luther was, comparatively speaking, undaunted. "I shall not retract one syllable. Instead, I am going to have my defence printed, that he may be refuted before all the Christian world. I am also preparing an appeal to the Pope and the next General Council."

Staupitz was beside himself with worry. He was scouring the town to raise money for Luther to escape—out of the country, out of the Empire, to France or Switzerland where the judiciary power of the papacy had no such grip as here: but not a soul in the whole of wealthy Augsburg, it seemed, had any ready cash, though all agreed with fervour that instant flight was Luther's only hope. Staupitz gave up; he no longer felt safe in Augsburg, himself. He formally released Luther from his vow of obedience to the Augustinian Order—ostensibly to free his hands but, as Luther felt with sorrow, disowning him too ("I was excommunicated thrice over: the first time by Staupitz. . . ."), and left.

The two Saxon councillors stuck it out with Luther one more day. Witnessed by them and in the presence of a notary, he registered his appeal to "the Pope ill-informed who shall become the Pope better-informed," for a hearing before a fully qualified commission *not* in Rome where the Pope himself had barely escaped assassination only last year.

The councillors took their leave, but Luther wanted to hang on and wait a little longer for a possible message from the Cardinal, whom he had sent notice of his own departure. There was no reply. The Fugger house, hub of news and rumour, was suddenly enshrouded in complete silence, most ominous and unnerving. To stay any longer would be madness—or, worse, vainglory, *courting* martyrdom.

Luther still had friends in Augsburg who wished him well even if they could find no hard cash to show their feelings. At dead of night, a canon of the cathedral smuggled him out by a postern in the town wall; a mounted city messenger was waiting with a second horse. Just as he was, without breeches or boots, the monk got into the saddle; the messenger, who never said a word, spurred his horse, and the horse with Luther on it gamely followed, away, away.

The ride remained a vivid nightmare in Luther's memory for years. He had never sat a horse before, and this one they have given him was a stiff trotter. The marvel was that he stayed on at all, what with the darkness and the hilly country; yet he got as far as Monheim, some fifty kilometres. There, however, he sank straight from the saddle into a dead sleep, in the straw of the stable.

He rested one day, rode on the next, found that it had been just as well, since at Nuremberg he saw a copy of the papal order for his immediate arrest, continued north, lost his way, found it again, and finally arrived in Wittenberg on the first anniversary of the posting of the Ninety-five Theses. It being Sunday, his first act was to celebrate mass ("So holy was I still at that time!"), his second to start writing a full account of the Augsburg interviews for publication as soon as might be, his third to consider plans for going into exile. That he would be excommunicated was now certain, which made him an embarrassment to his sovereign and a menace to all his associates.

His prospects were to say the least unsettled, his proper work which he loved and considered of the first importance was indefinitely disrupted. He had conceived a searing, ghastly doubt at Augsburg—in face of the blasphemous Italian laughter every time he quoted Holy Writ and the monstrous claims for the papacy, of Cajetan: "I whisper it in your ear," he confided to Melanchthon. "The Pope may be Antichrist." Short of actually burning at the stake, matters could not have been worse, for Luther, than they were at this dark and foggy moment.

Yet at this moment he experienced a tranquillity he had not known before. "I feel so contented and so peaceful," he wrote, wonderingly.

How could that be?

Cardinal Cajetan was chafing under a sense of dissatisfaction, perplexity, indecision. That was the reason for his silence.

How could that be so?

The strange, unrealized thing was that Luther had won this, his first round face to face with the adversary, at Augsburg. They only sensed this, Cardinal and friar; though Cajetan was unpleasantly aware that he had allowed himself to be goaded, not only to debate, but into going too far, with regard to those claims of his, for papal supremacy. At the same time the nub of the whole wretched business, the question of indulgence, had been scarcely touched on, much less resolved (an omission which indeed formed Luther's strongest argument in the defence which he was even now composing).

Until he heard from Rome again, particularly in connection with the Elector of Saxony, the Cardinal was at a loss whether to implement the order for Luther's arrest before forwarding his appeal. Whilst awaiting instructions, he drafted a suggested papal statement concerning the concept and scope of indulgences, and sent it in. The draft was adopted almost as it stood, and was published on 8 November in Bull-form under the title *Cum postquam*.

In the Bull *Cum postquam* the principle of Indulgence was defined as affecting only canonical penalties, being entirely discrete from penalties imposed by God, and the Pope's relevant powers were narrowed down to petitioning God for remissions through and by the Treasury of Merit—that is, without the capacity of dispensing the treasure on his own authority. This was exactly what Luther had posited originally, just over a year ago; it was this which had brought down upon him the wrath of Tetzel and the Dominicans, for whom at that juncture the idea of Justification by Faith was an incidental irritation. The Bull *Cum postquam* put pardon-preachers like Tetzel straightway out of business; it caused Tetzel himself to be cast off incontinently by the forces he had called to war and which now continued the war without him. Otherwise—apart from giving a certain mental relief to orthodox persons who had been loyally swallowing their doubts about abuses that were herewith terminated—the Bull, coming when it did, did no particular good.

Had it come out twelve months, eight months, even five months earlier—yes: had such a draft been to hand when Luther was at Augsburg—it is very possible that Martin Luther would be giving straightforward lecture courses and straightforward spiritual advice, as it were, to this day.

But he conceded that *Cum postquam* was an intelligent, methodical, scholarly piece of work—so far as it went.

The story of Luther's ride, breechless, unspurred, bounced black and blue, caused much amusement in a good many circles. It brought an engaging, rueful tinge to the growing image of an incorruptible.

*

20. The Third Contender

All this time, the prospective bearer of the Golden Rose to Elector Frederick of Saxony had been waiting, booted and spurred, ready to set out from Rome. The rose itself, wrought in gold and precious stones, together with an ornate papal testimonial extolling the virtues of the recipient, lay wrapped and sealed while various extras to go with it accumulated between September and mid-November. The extras were: a charter increasing the annual indulgence of Wittenberg by a hundred years for every separate bone in Frederick's collection of relics; blank patents of appointment for five papal notaries and house prelates, five counts of the Lateran, ten official poets, ten doctors of theology; and ditto dispensation from the ecclesiastical disabilities of illegitimate birth, for any two persons of the Elector's choice—*pace* Luther's ingenuous "He led a pure life and never married," Elector Frederick had two natural sons whose welfare and advancement he was known to have very much at heart.

The person who had secured the rôle of courier was a Vatican chamberlain named Karl von Miltitz. By birth a Saxon nobleman distantly related to Elector Frederick, Miltitz was also a cousin of the Saxon Dominican Nikoläus von Schönberg, who was chief confidant to the Pope's chief confidant Cardinal Medici; and under Schönberg's wing he had ensconced himself in Rome. His niche was cosy but not lucrative: titular Gentleman of the Papal Chamber, Miltitz made a desultory living as a notary, occasional commission agent in the relic trade, and hanger-on of the younger set of socialite prelates. His personal qualities seemed calculated to cancel each other out: ambition and quick-wittedness were offset by a sanguine and indolent temper, as were his dreams of grandeur by an innate penchant for the line of least resistance. But he was always short of money, and this saved him from stagnating.

Like everybody else in curial circles, Miltitz had his ideas about the Luther affair, which ideas he was able to present persuasively to his protector. Schönberg like Miltitz was all too conversant with the Roman tendency to underestimate the Germans, and appreciated the force of Miltitz's argument that it was time somebody who knew the language, the people, and the national climate took a hand. So Schönberg saw to it that the coveted commission to convey the Golden Rose to its destination went to Miltitz rather than as usual to an Italian cleric. The job was an easy, pleasant, and normally rewarding one, since nuncios on such errands would be fêted and cosseted all along their way, their luggage commonly containing an assortment of minor charters, patents, and dispensations for distribution where they were liable to do most good. One could hardly avoid perquisites and windfalls such as accrued from ascertaining whether the papal honours thus in one's bestowal were indeed deserved. The Curia, after all, set the tone: as regards the Golden Rose for Frederick, Miltitz was instructed to delay handing it over until, in close consultation with Cajetan, it was ascertained that Frederick would do the right thing in respect of his Wittenberg monk.

For Cajetan had now come to life again, and by the middle of November Frederick had a letter from the Cardinal, to say that the process against Luther for heresy was going ahead, that a Bull of Excommunication was in preparation, and that unless he wished to abandon honour, conscience, and immunity the Elector should make haste to hand over "the son of perdition" or at least expel him from his dominions.

It was the Elector's turn again, to shroud himself in silence. He was now on circuit through his realm, moving from castle to castle. His correspondents never knew if and when he received their communications—not till he was good and ready at the end of interminable deliberation with his advisers.

Elector Frederick was as averse from putting pen to paper (even by the vicarious hand of secretaries) as not only Luther but also most of those who had any part in these events were addicted to committing themselves in writing. Frederick's official correspondence was confined to the minimum, his thought processes went largely unrecorded, and seldom was there any word about the course of the discussions in his cabinet save in the upshot—if upshot there were. For many problems will settle themselves, with procrastination. At all events he evidently commanded exceptional loyalty in his counsellors: there were few if any leakages without his consent. As a result the springs of many of his actions remained forever obscure and subject to unending guesswork. Luther's pious summing-up of him as "one of God's wonders" sensibly left it at that.

Miltitz however was an amateur psychologist as well as—now that he was getting the opportunity—an amateur diplomat, and confidently pursued his private analysis of the whole situation. He planned to solve it all on the human level, never mind about theology, power politics, and that Dominican preoccupation with status which would brook no other terms of reference than either victory or defeat. Rather, a reconciliation was what Miltitz had in mind; and one cannot say that on the face of it his notion was unapt.

He left for Augsburg at last about the same time as the Elector of Saxony received Cajetan's letter directing him to get rid of Luther (which, without comment but requesting Luther's comment, he had passed on to Luther in Wittenberg, on 19 November). Miltitz was no less adept than the Elector in making haste slowly, so that when he reached Augsburg the Cardinal Legate, having had to follow Emperor Maximilian to Innsbruck for an important Austrian Diet meeting, was gone. Theoretically Miltitz should have followed his Roman superior, but he had the best of excuses, in that he had already spent all his travelling allowance. He knew from experience that nothing elicits tardier response than a demand for additional funds, and that therefore there was no hurry to notify the Cardinal Legate in Austria of his arrival in Germany. He deposited Elector Frederick's precious Golden Rose and the entire, weighty diplomatic bag in the fabulous strong-room of the Fugger house, and settled down to look around and listen while he waited. He also talked. He talked, as he had done previously in Nuremberg and elsewhere on his route, inside information about the papal court—which, lending him the cachet of a bosom friend of the Holy Father's, he had found a highly remunerative way of singing for one's supper.

In self-sufficient Nuremberg especially he had noted enough of Lutheran sympathies to enable him to send statistics to Rome: not more than one German out of every four was on the Pope's side; an army twenty-five thousand strong would not suffice to bring Luther to Rome. With equal assurance he now related Pope Leo's reaction to Tetzel's sales slogan ("As soon as coin in coffer rings/The soul from purgatory springs"): trembling with rage all over, the Holy Father had cried out, *"O porcaccio!* the swine!" As for Prierias, His Holiness only spoke of the fellow as "that utter clod." Who knows, it may have been true at that. In any event, Miltitz was having the time of his life. He had never enjoyed so much consideration on either side of the Alps.

Whether by good luck or calculation, he fell in with the Saxon Elector's councillor Degenhard Pfeffinger, an old acquaintance who happened to have business in Augsburg, and got himself invited to stay with the latter on his country estate till Rome replenished his purse. This was at the end of November. He stayed a month, and did not waste his time.

Just when Miltitz and Pfeffinger were getting together, Luther prepared in earnest to leave Wittenberg. He had replied to the Elector's last missive with a lengthy, acute, and impressive set of "comments" on Cajetan's letter. But the Elector had not replied to his concluding statement that, although to command the Elector to surrender Luther was to command him to do murder, he, Luther, would willingly remove himself and "go wherever the God of mercy would have me—that no evil may befall Your Excellency on my account." Silence. Luther preached a farewell sermon in the town church, to a lamenting congregation, on 25 November. On 28 November he said goodbye to the university in Corpus Christi Chapel, the customary venue for this ceremony. That afternoon he got his answer. The Elector approved his decision and accepted his offer.

Luther took it well. "Let father and mother forsake me: the Lord will care for me." There was still a lot to do and tidy up; he set the date of his departure for 1 December and invited his friends to a last supper by way of send-off on that evening.

They were at table when a note was brought in, from Spalatin who was still away from Wittenberg with the Elector, conveying his master's surprise to hear that Luther had not yet left, and asking him to hurry up about it.

Luther insisted that he was not shocked: merely a little taken aback, he said—the message was so sudden. He was going anyway; he might, him at Altenburg, Miltitz slaughtered the fatted calf, in the form of Tetzel, whom he caused to be arraigned for immorality and embezzlement (with the connivance of the Fugger agency and the Dominican Inquisition looking the other way); he was convinced that Tetzel was the only stumbling block, and sacrificing Tetzel the only prerequisite, to an agreement with Luther. And he convinced practically everyone else concerned. Even Luther was now feeling tired and jaded; reaction after the last twelve months had caught up with him, and he welcomed the hope that he might be able to get on with his work in peace again quite soon.

He arrived at Altenburg on 4 January—the Elector having whisked himself off to the next castle on his itinerary directly the arrangement had been made—and with Councillor von Feilitzsch and some others of the electoral court for witnesses held speech with the papal nuncio for two days.

Luther found it in him to write kindly to Tetzel as the once imposing pardon-preacher cum inquisitor lay pining away from his shattering downfall: "Do not take it too much to heart. Your fault is not the origin of all this: the child has another father altogether." Luther's sense of justice in this instance was undimmed by any lurking consciousness of less than faultless conduct on his side. In the instance of Miltitz it was to be otherwise; there he fell in with the subsequent chorus of sneers, devoid of charity. There the fault, which he could not forgive, lay in himself.

With suggestive venom Luther would relate in after days how "Herr Carolus" had tried to bamboozle him with flattery—with a rhapsody of back-handed admiration: Luther's case had made more trouble for the Curia than anything in a hundred years, the Curia would rather lose ten thousand ducats than have the case continue, at every inn where Miltitz had stopped on his travels Luther's name was praised—and so on and so forth; how Miltitz had wept ("Crocodile tears!") and, believe it or not, kissed him ("Ay: the Judas kiss!").

"I pretended that I did not see through all these Italian shams."

He pretended most successfully.

At the end of the first day of the talks Luther agreed to the following: to let the controversy die, provided the other side held its peace too; to write a letter of apology to the Pope, for having ex-

pressed himself so drastically here and there; to publish an announcement to the same effect for general distribution, in which he would
also exhort everyone to show continued obedience to the Roman
Church; to commit his case for judgment by a German archbishop.

It was not a bad day's work for such a transparent nincompoop as
Miltitz subsequently was made out to be—was it? Luther set the tone,
he gave out the cue. He surely was ashamed. It was not so vile, that
Miltitz had gone all out to flatter him, as it was that Luther had allowed
himself to be flattered; or so one cannot but suspect. Of course he was
also very tired. He would be just as glad as the Curia to have the
whole thing end.

He drafted the desired letter to the Pope overnight; but the one thing
that was missing from it was a certain little six-letter word, r-e-v-o-c-o,
without which Miltitz knew in his heart Luther's apology would appear
valueless in Rome. So on the second day the agreement was whittled
down to the two main points: the cease-fire, and submission to an
archepiscopal judgment. Miltitz let the other two points drop, for the
moment. They could be raised again afterwards, or might then be unnecessary. The truce alone would be a bright feather in his cap; he
was the first who had got some results, and quick results, no need
to spoil them now. He was so pleased with Luther that he accompanied
him part of the way back, a craftsman who could hardly bear to
let go of his handiwork to the customer.

The customers however had to be advised with all speed of the
completion of the order in its first phase. Considering that Cajetan
had reported Luther to be obdurately intransigent, and that Luther
had begun seriously to think Holy Rome had been captured by
the Antichrist—and considering that Rome had been pushed to the
point of compulsion, to excommunicate Luther, when Rome wanted
to do nothing that could possibly upset the Elector of Saxony—considering all this, that first phase was quite an achievement.

And so it was regarded, not in the least by Miltitz himself only.
The achievement was the more striking for a development of world-
shaking nature, initiated on 12 January, by the sudden death of
Emperor Max: meaning that now there was an imperial election
to think about. Miltitz had made it possible for the Holy See to forget
about Luther's case until the election should be safely over; particularly
as the Saxon Elector—vice-emperor for the duration of the interim!—
was thus to be kept happy and unruffled too.

Nobody was more pleased than Luther, to think that he could now relax for a spell, without having had to violate his conscience in any way; unless it were Miltitz.

Miltitz was on top of the world. Money was no object, for the time being. He was wined and dined and listened to respectfully, travelling hither and thither with a free hand to negotiate phase the second, which was to find the right archbishop, one who would be acceptable to all concerned, for the job of arbiter. Herein too he encountered no great difficulty; the first choice of both Luther and Elector Frederick, when Miltitz had asked them to make some suggestions, was Archbishop Richard von Grciffenklau, Elector of Trier. Greiffenklau (whose name might be translated as either griffin's-claw or grasping-claw according to taste) was an old friend of Elector Frederick, a fine, upstanding, massive, hard-drinking, hard-riding, very lordly lord and prelate, having little use for the Archbishop-Elector of Mainz, and not much either for Emperor Max's grandson Charles as a candidate for the imperial crown—so that the Holy See, too, ought to like the look of him for the part of (provisional) judge. Even Cajetan thought so, with whom Miltitz made contact at last after more than six months. Greiffenklau intimated that in principle he might be willing but would prefer to have a definite request from Rome before carving the necessary time and attention out of the ticklish pre-election period, which needed all he could give it of concentration.

Miltitz tried variously to speed matters up on his own, but the election fever was against him, especially as the truce was on; for himself meantime he really had nothing to complain of, and he was not really any such obsessional type as some people.

Some people, like Luther for instance, tired early of the truce. "When I rest I rust." He had had a breather, and that was all he wanted; this looked like turning into a right long rest. His mind would not rest; ideas were churning inside him, and he was debarred from letting them out. He could not even write anything in support of the popular German candidate to the Holy Roman monarchy, "our Charles" since Our Max's grandson: for the reasons informing Luther's recommendation would inevitably have borne on the controversial views which he was not to air.

Some people remained unexcited over the election. They having nothing to do with it were ill-conditioned to work up a very heated academic interest in it. Their obsessions were academic in the proper sense: to do with academies, academic status and preoccupations, academic contests and trophies.

Such a man was Professor Eckius of Ingolstadt, who last August had made arrangements with Luther in Augsburg for a contest he had every expectation of winning, and who had good Dominican connections.

✳

21. The Fourth Round: The Champions

In February 1519 Professor Eckius of Ingolstadt challenged Professor Karlstadt of Wittenberg to a disputation to be held on neutral territory, or at all events on territory to which neither of them was attached by professional ties, at Leipzig.

Andreas Rudolf Bodenstein, better known by the name of his native town of Karlstadt in Bohemia, was Luther's immediate senior in age and years of service at Wittenberg University. He had arrived there from Cologne seven years before Luther, had presided over Luther's promotion to the doctorate and personally placed the doctor's cap on Luther's head. At that time, 1512, Karlstadt held also the posts of archdeacon, canon of the collegiate church of All Saints, and expected to become provost of the same; his academic reputation, too, was well-established. Although exposed in his earliest environment to the dangerous influences of the Hussite heresy, which had both its birthplace and last redoubt in Bohemia, he had been brought up a good Catholic and educated a good Thomist, touched with humanism.

In his second seven years at Wittenberg Karlstadt's nose was twice put out of joint, first by Luther and then by the boy-wonder Melanchthon. With Luther this happened gradually; at first blush there was nothing to distinguish him so particularly; he was neither so disappointing outwardly nor so startlingly brilliant as Melanchthon. Luther was well enough, for an Occamist and protégé of nice, old, smooth, easy-going Dr. Staupitz, into whose well-worn shoes he stepped without ado; whereas Master Philippus Melanchthon né Schwarzerd came in amid fanfare, sponsored by his kinsman "the phoenix of German learning"

(Reuchlin wrote: "I know among Germans no one who excels him in Greek except Erasmus of Rotterdam who is in any case a Dutchman. In Latin Melanchthon excels everybody.") and installed to build up a newly created chair. Anyhow, both had the benefit of personal pull.

When Luther first came out with his Theology of Justification by Faith, Karlstadt very naturally opposed it. But after a visit to Rome— whether or no that had anything to do with the change—he was converted and displayed to the full what one may call the Saulus-Paulus syndrome. When Luther stepped into the limelight of the indulgence controversy, Karlstadt leapt to the defence of his colleague, with a vehement attack on Dr. Eckius who had just then joined forces with the yet degree-less Tetzel. But Luther had to put his oar in, and at Augsburg, without Karlstadt, Eckius and Luther had fixed up for Karlstadt and Eckius to debate the question of gospel-teaching versus Scholasticism, at some date yet to be settled.

Meanwhile Master Philip had made his appearance and was gathering effusive acclaim. People could not say enough about his intellect, erudition, and didactic endowments; Luther's voice was piercing in his praise, and he as good as made it obligatory for his own students to attend Melanchthon's early morning lectures to start their day. In no time Melanchthon had a permanent class of four hundred, with visiting audiences of "sometimes nearly two thousand, sometimes with many persons of rank among them. He lectures on a wide range of subjects, including Hebrew, Latin, Greek, rhetoric, physics, and philosophy . . . and by the quality of his teaching accomplishes as much in each of all these subjects as other professors do in just one," it was reported.

The scrawny prodigy was not yet twenty-two, and looked much less. He had attained the baccalaureate at fourteen and passed the master of arts degree with distinction at fifteen, but had then been denied the actual title "on account of his youth and boyish appearance." Even so they had had to let him have it at seventeen—but Melanchthon ever afterwards stood out against all importuning to let himself be made a doctor, although between eighteen and twenty-one he had published more work than many produced in a lifetime, including an extremely valuable new Greek lexicon. Erasmus generously prophesied that this young man would eclipse all the humanists of the world, the prophet himself not excluded. The young man could have taken his pick of the universities, which vied to offer him employment, offers which in consultation with his great-uncle he sifted from the point of view of maximum liberty and scope. From his short list of Ingolstadt, Leipzig, and Wittenberg, Philip finally opted for the last, at exactly half the salary of the former—even though they raised their bids at the eleventh hour, when he passed through on his way to Wittenberg. Young and poor as he was, he already owned an impressive library, too. ("For without books," great-uncle Reuchlin explained to Elector Frederick, because the new professor was delayed waiting transport for his books, "one can neither rightly teach nor read, especially in a university.") Poor he was, and poor he stayed; Luther continually tried to use his influence on the Elector to increase Melanchthon's minute stipend and allow him some assistants as he was excessively burdened with teaching so many. Melanchthon having come to Wittenberg of his own free will in preference to Ingolstadt and Leipzig, and showing every sign of liking his work, the Elector saw no reason to coddle him.

But as the year 1519 opened, the Elector did see himself forced to delve into his coffers, to build a large new lecture hall especially for the use of the theological faculty. In the course of the last few months the student enrolment had taken such an upward bound that newcomers could not find anything like enough accommodation in the town, which was crowded beyond the existing capacity of bursaries and private lodgings. Foreigners were coming in—Tyrolese, Alsatians, Walloons, Bohemians, Scots, and growing numbers of German graduates long since past their student days, teachers and preachers who resigned their respectable positions elsewhere on purpose to take a course of studies in Wittenberg. All at once Wittenberg had expanded to parity with the formerly largest German universities, Cologne and Leipzig, and—so Leipzig was heard to be complaining—was now drawing ahead of them. As for Ingolstadt, there they had trouble enough to keep up.

Wittenberg had become peculiarly associated with evangelical science, and it was the crying need of the theological faculty to which Elector Frederick had at length to open his tight fist. Nevertheless—and despite thankfully boasting about such effective divine action on behalf of Our Theology—the leading light of this insisted on attributing the steep rise of Wittenberg to Master Philippus as much as anyone. Luther, who possessed among his undeniable faults the undeniable and exceptional virtue of total freedom from academic jealousy—Luther loved talent when he saw it. Luther the anti-humanist and anti-rationalist really believed in the power of a beautiful mind. He believed there was nothing like it, that everybody else was as susceptible to it as he, and he really thought that learning coupled with insight (the right kind of insight) must move mountains.

It was a little hard on Karlstadt, who was a declared and designated "champion of Luther," and as such shared most of the theological teaching with him, the others on the faculty coming a long way behind in the esteem of the students—when Melanchthon was not even a theologian, the merest spectator albeit a sympathetic one, from his chair in the arts department. Karlstadt was nearly twice Melanchthon's age and had been a doctor since before the little chap was well out of his nonage.

The Elector might be treating Melanchthon with complacent negligence, but there was no question whom he regarded as the most important person at the university—and, again, that was not Karlstadt. It seemed there was nothing Luther could not get away with. He had never stopped denouncing the Wittenberg Indulgence and charging the sovereign with foolish and self-seeking ambition apropos his relics; he even trespassed on ground outside his province, politely asking his "most gracious and dear Prince" to reconsider a new tax which would do the prince's popularity no good either on earth or in heaven. The Elector had strictly forbidden Luther to publish his *Acta Augusta,* the blow-by-blow account of the transactions at Augsburg between Luther and Cajetan; Luther—with the excuse that he had thought he was going into exile anyway—had published. The Elector was most annoyed, yet the very next thing was that he went against his favourite policy of enigmatic silence and discharged a letter at the Curia—the first and only one he ever wrote on Luther's behalf—with an outright refusal to deliver him to Rome or banish him for alleged and yet unproven heresy.

One would allow that it behoved Luther to show some gratitude ("I have seen the admirable words of our Most Illustrious Prince. Dear God, with what joy I read and re-read them!"); but was it necessary to go to the lengths of, "I have never thought of deserting the Pope. I am quite satisfied that he is called the lord of the world, and that he is that,"?—even if the passage continued, "One has to honour and endure the Sultan, too, on account of the power with which he is invested. As long as the Pope does not confuse his decrees with the gospel, I will not stir as much as a hair, even if he strips me of everything. Accordingly I will adhere rigidly to the pact—" the Altenburg pact, that he would publish nothing further in the controversy.

"These two months I have done nothing new and just stood still," Luther grieved, in proof of his rigid adherence. He complied with the Elector's request to publish after all the general advertisement which Miltitz had waived, telling the laity to do nothing drastic in connection with Luther's past strictures on the Church: *Doctor Martinus Luther's Instruction on Several Articles Ascribed and Assigned to him by his Detractors.* While only laymen would take what he said therein about saint worship, indulgences, good works, and all the rest, as unexceptionably Catholic, there was no getting around the conclusion:

". . . The Roman Church is undoubtedly esteemed by God more than any other church, for in Rome Peter and Paul, forty-six popes, and many hundred thousands of martyrs spilled their blood. If present conditions in Rome are unfortunately such that they might be better, neither this nor any reason whatsoever can be or become sufficient to tear loose from Rome. On the contrary, the worse conditions become there, the more one should help and cling to the Church. . . . We should be intent only upon unity, and should take good care not to resist papal commandments."

In other words, forget it, do nothing. Karlstadt, nurtured in Bohemia, would have shown himself of sterner stuff.

Not that Karlstadt was a Bohemian in the ideological sense of the word. Heaven forbid. The very name of Bohemia was, in all Roman Catholic circles, what the name of any communist country would become in the twentieth century on the opposite side of the fence. It raised the hackles, forced up adrenalin production, and made the flesh crawl. To be called a Hussite, when one was not, was a deadly insult; to be seriously accused of it was a death warrant. Johann Hus of Prague, the founder of the Bohemian heresy, had been burnt; but his doctrine had never died in the country of origin. On the contrary, the followers of Hus had declared open war on the Roman Church and in the none too distant past created frightful havoc in the German lands which they invaded, especially Saxony. In spite of severe setbacks since, they retained considerable influence in Bohemia, and their secret agents or crypto-missionaries were hunted in every corner of the Empire, with reason. The final solution to the Bohemian heresy was part of the programme for "reform in head and members" of the Church which the elusive, next General Council was supposed to deal with; and it had likewise figured in Leo X's design of 1518 for a new crusade, together with a scheme to heal the Great Schism which divided the Eastern or Greek Church from the Church of Rome.

Schism was a great evil, but heresy, which was schism in small, was worse.

While no one in his senses would even dream of linking Professor Karlstadt with the heresy which stained his native country, the moral fervour and pugnacity with which it impregnated the Bohemian atmosphere were, as the saying goes, in his blood.

When the challenge finally came through, from Professor Eckius of Ingolstadt to Professor Karlstadt of Wittenberg for a debate under the somewhat unwilling aegis of the authorities of Leipzig—Professor Luther stepped in, and Professor Melanchthon was not far behind. It was true that as the circumstances had developed this was not to be avoided—not without dishonour; but again, it was a little hard on Luther's champion, that now Luther had to come and champion him.

The pact of Altenburg, Miltitz's chef d'oeuvre, miscarried in the third month, and Eckius was the abortifacient.

*

22. The Fourth Round: Whose Victory?

Eckius' challenge in the approved manner consisted of twelve propositions—which, however, were seen to have very little to do with the
points on which he and Karlstadt had been clashing. The very opening one constituted a direct attack on Luther's Ninety-five Theses, and
the other eleven also were entirely concerned with utterances of
Luther's; with Luther's proposition in his *Resolutions* that, "The Roman Church at the time of Gregory did not as yet possess sovereignty
over the Greek Church," for pièce de résistance.

This it was impossible for Luther to ignore. In an open letter to
Karlstadt he announced that Eckius had placed him under the necessity
of joining Karlstadt in the forthcoming debate at Leipzig. Eckius
thereupon wrote to him to say that Luther had indeed understood
his, Eckius', theses quite correctly, and that he was counting on
Luther's presence as the real author of all the false teaching which
was rife at Wittenberg. With this letter in hand, Luther overbore the
remonstrances of Elector Frederick, Bishop Scultetus, and his friends
in Wittenberg.

"Let my friends think me mad. If I go down to destruction, no
one will be harmed by it. The Wittenbergers do not need me any
longer—" for Bible Theology was in swing, and he had begun to
think that God might have sent him as a mere outrider to the coming
man, Master Philippus. "Do you hold me unworthy of martyrdom?
I have to die sometime."

He announced that he was definitely going to Leipzig with Karlstadt.
The only trouble about that was a grave failure in courtesy and proto-

col: it behoved Luther first of all to ask permission of the sovereign of Ducal Saxony, to which Leipzig belonged. Duke George of Saxony, Elector Frederick's cousin, was much incensed and announced that he for his part would not have Luther in Leipzig without a formal petition to this end by Eckius. Eckius, republishing his debating programme under the frankly provocative title of *Theses against Luther to be disputed at Leipzig,* deliberately played on Luther's nerves by holding back the required petition and not answering Luther's repeated letters urging him to get the matter settled. As little as three weeks before the disputation, fixed for 27 June, there was still no word, so that Luther could not apply for the necessary safe-conducts.

But at least Eckius had herewith released him from the unbearable constraint of "doing nothing new," in Luther's heartfelt complaint. His preparations for meeting Eckius' challenge produced six-fold fruit, ready for the printer—too much at one time for Master Grünenberg's press to cope with: two Leipzig printers jumped into the breach. There were four treatises and two commentaries: *On the Double Righteousness, On the Marriage Estate, On the Contemplation of the Blessed Passion of Christ;* and the *German Exposition of the Lord's Prayer for Simple Laymen,* with the first part of an old project, *Studies in the Psalms,* which a week or so later were followed by *Commentary on the Epistle to the Galatians* and *Treatise on Prayer in Rogation Week.* Luther, who hardly felt alive when he had not some piece of writing on the stocks, and whose thinking progressed best under the stimulus of publication, immediately sang a different tune: "Now I am constantly growing and advancing!"

The cardinal points of advance in the foregoing spate were 1. that the command, "Resist not evil" does not apply to the government in the fight against crime (*Double Righteousness*), 2. that bringing up children is better than leaving them in order to go on pilgrimage (*Marriage Estate*), 3. that thinking one's self into the position of Christ during his life and suffering (as advocated by the mystics) was a selfish-sensuous form of appreciating the divine (*Contemplation of the Blessed Passion*); the remaining four papers were devoted to further elaborations of practical, pastoral theology, with apposite references to the nature and locus standi of the papacy—such as, "A command of the Pope is binding only when it is in accord with the glory of God," and, "The papacy is only a human, earthly arrangement, not a divine institution."

Just in case he did not get a hearing at Leipzig—determined to go, with or without permission, he did not know what might happen—Luther composed for good measure a defence of his proposition concerning the origin of papal primacy, for publication in case of accidents. In this he pointed out that the New Testament makes no distinction between presbyters and bishops, that until the time of Emperor Constantine IV (669–83) the Roman primacy had had no legal existence, and that "the Church" is not a visible institution identical with the kingdom of God, but the spiritual community of all believers, to which the whole of the priesthood stands in the relationship of servitors. "But people like Eckius make of the kingdom of faith a realm of visible things in that they give it a visible head." Nevertheless—and in spite of the warning that Antichrist appeared to be reigning at the Curia, Luther was yet far from abrogating the papacy; and he went to some pains to show that *honouring* the Pope was perfectly all right.

However, the last thing Eckius wished was to be done out of asserting the superiority of Ingolstadt over upstart Wittenberg. He had good hopes of success, as he had made something of a corner in disputations, and saw to it that Duke George's permission came through in time, with attendant safe-conducts.

Without that, Leipzig would surely have refused admittance to the Wittenberg contingent. As it was, the reception was as ungracious as possible. Eckius, though also representing a rival university, was ostentatiously honoured (apart from the particular hostility of the Leipzig authorities to Luther, Eckius bore letters of high recommendation from the Fugger, whom he had done great service in proving that their canonically anathematized financial operations were—if one looked hard enough—canonically licit). The Wittenberg contingent of two open carts—the leading vehicle occupied by Karlstadt and a towering quantity of huge books, the second by the honorary rector of Wittenberg with Luther and Melanchthon—accompanied by nearly two hundred students armed with spears and halberds, was jeered as it entered the town. Great was the joy of the townsfolk and Leipzig's own students, when a wheel came off Karlstadt's cart and the poor man fell out and badly sprained both thumbs.

Everything that could be done, with the aid of red tape, official slights, and chicanery, to contribute to the discomfort of the Wittenbergers, was lavished on them. Yet nothing was spared to render the contest, which was to go on for seventeen days, a gala occasion.

First there was the ceremonial of welcoming the disputants in the great lecture hall of the university, then came a festival mass with twelve-part singing in St. Thomas' Church, followed by a reception in the tapestried court room of the ducal residence, Castle Pleissenburg, with a two-hour address on "The Art and Method of Disputation, especially on Matters Theological" by the Leipzig professor of poetry who had a bad cold. The opening culminated in a performance of the hymn *Veni Sancte Spiritus,* given by the St. Thomas' Church choir and the massed pipers of the town. The court fool of Duke George was in evidence, as yet reserved, for light entertainment as needful.

It was very needful. The disputants were enjoined to speak slowly so that the recording secretaries could keep up with them; and once everybody had got used to the large and distinguished audience (including Duke George, with one of the best beards in Germany) and the decorations (including a banner depicting St. George the dragon-slayer for Eckius' lecturing desk and a banner depicting St. Martin for the desk of the Wittenberg disputant), the opposing factions in the auditorium accused one another of sleeping through most of the proceedings. Again, the present-day mind finds it difficult to see how anybody could ever keep awake during disputations of this sort, where every thought was framed in dialectical safeguards against traps so that transcripts read not unlike exhaustively conscientious legal contracts of today, and where moreover all rhetorical moves were as carefully formalized as those of classical ballet; but the art had many passionate aficionados.

The cough-racked professor of poetry, Mosellanus, described the principals: "Martinus is of middle height, emaciated from care and study so that you can almost count all his bones through his skin. But he is in the vigour of manhood, his voice rings clear and distinct. He has the Scriptures by heart and commands sufficient Greek and Hebrew. A perfect forest of ideas and words is at his command. He is affable and friendly, not a bit austere or arrogant. In company he is vivacious, jocose, always cheerful and gay. Everyone chides him for being a little too insolent in his strictures and more caustic than is prudent or becoming. This can be said of Karlstadt too, though in a lesser degree. He is smaller than Luther, with the complexion of a smoked herring. His accent is thick and unpleasing. His memory is not so quick, but he is quicker to anger. Eck is a great, tall, thick-set fellow. The truly German voice that resounds from his powerful chest would do credit to a town crier or tragedian: but it is more noisy than distinct. His physiognomy puts one in mind of a butcher or a mercenary soldier rather than a theologian. As far as intellect is concerned, he has a phenomenal memory. If he had an equally acute understanding, he would be perfect. But he lacks quickness of comprehension and clarity of judgment, qualities without which all the other talents go for nothing. . . ."

There is no doubt in which direction Mosellanus' sympathies were inclining—nor that in extemporaneous argument neither of his Wittenberg opponents was a match for Eckius. Mosellanus omitted to mention Eckius' gift of fluent repartee, which coupled with that phenomenal memory gave him an immense advantage. Karlstadt's memory dried up completely—he said pathetically that it must have trickled away with the blood-letting which the local surgeon had prescribed to make him better after his fall; and after a week's tussle on the subject of human depravity, he had to give up. It cannot have helped him, to know that everybody was waiting tensely for the main event —which was not *his* bout with the Ingolstadt professor.

Luther mounted the rostrum with a posy of pinks in one hand (which gossip swiftly enlarged into a wreath and garlands) and his silver ring on the other (which rumour embellished with a capsule containing his helpmeet, the Devil). The story was quite true, that when during the preceding week he had gone to mass at the university church the officiating Dominicans on recognizing him had rushed away the monstrance with the sacrament to a place of safety from contamination, and he knew that "fiend" and "rascally viper" were among the kinder epithets applied to him here in the ducal palace. Together with that contrary optimism which drew strength from the despondency of others on his behalf as well as from the animosity of others, Luther possessed a curious fatalism in face of hatred and contempt. It saddened and infuriated yet never seemed to hurt him when former friends turned into malevolent detractors. So long as he could feel confidently at one with God, no other relationships really mattered. Therefore his righteous indignation at the wrong-headedness of Eckius was unsapped by emotional pangs at the duplicity of one with whom only a few months ago he had conversed in the friendliest fashion.

Ah, but it was all up with his good opinion of the other. Where he had used to respect Eckius as an able scholar, Luther now saw in him only an unoriginal and superficial thinker, a mediocre Latinist and a poor speaker in the German language withal, whose mnemonic facility and "gift of the gab" could not impress him. Finding that the Ingolstadt professor of theology was amazingly unversed in the Bible, Luther did not recognize Eckius' pouncing verbal triumphs as such. He waited his turn and then scored a victory of his own, to which Eckius was similarly immune. In a way it was Augsburg all over again.

Others noticed what Eckius' opponents had no means of checking till for purposes of rejoinder it was too late: namely, that he frequently misquoted his citations to suit his arguments. Melanchthon, emphatically an "idle spectator," kept both Karlstadt and Luther supplied with ammunition against that phenomenal but unreliable memory, and on several occasions drew Eckius' fire: "You keep out of this, little Philip, you dusty grammarian, you conceited nephew of Reuchlin!"

("Philip's opinion and authority mean more to me than several thousand miserable Ecks," Luther wrote to Spalatin. "I would not hesitate to yield if he should disagree with me, even though I am a master of arts, philosophy and theology, and adorned with nearly all the rest of Eck's titles." And next term a number of students transferred from Leipzig to Wittenberg, to study under Melanchthon.)

Eckius made another enemy, by his treatment of Duke George's one-eyed court fool. He insulted and mimicked the fool's disability, and the fool thereafter burlesqued him at every turn—welcome comic relief for the spectators, which however did not damage Eckius so much as it benefitted both contestants with the weary audience. In the words of one faithful spectator, "This debate might have gone on forever, had not Duke George called a halt," for the Duke now needed his palace to entertain the Elector of Brandenburg who was coming on a state visit.

The debate was thus wound up on 14 July—yet the high-spot had occurred on 5 July, only the second day of the Eckius v. Luther event, on the subject of the nature of the papacy. ("What difference does it make," Duke George asked pertinently, "whether the Pope is pope by divine right or human right? He is pope just the same, isn't he?")

repaired to the university library to look up the acts of the Council
of Constance, which had tried and condemned Hus. Eckius' memory
had practised no deceit this time: it was as he had said. But there
was more to it than that. Among the relevant articles of Hus which
the Council had ruled heretical there was one which was a direct
paraphrase of St. Augustine.

At two o'clock when the session was resumed Luther stood up
and said, "Among the articles of Johann Hus I find many which are
plainly Christian and evangelical, and which therefore the Universal
Church cannot condemn."

Sensation. Duke George uttered an oath. Luther's friends reeled
with the shock which for himself he had neutralized by embracing
it at once. For himself, he might be ignorant of vanity—to name no
other deterrent emotion: but one must remember that the wounds of
the Hussite invasions of Saxony were yet scarcely healed, and that the
word Hus was the worst term of opprobrium in the vocabulary. Eckius
pressed his advantage, and Luther helped him staunchly by getting
himself into ever deeper water—or so it appeared to his opponents.
In Luther's own eyes he was getting on to ever firmer ground. Soon
he would say, "We are all Hussites. Augustine and Paul were Hussites."
Even without that, Eckius was so well satisfied that he lowered his
stentorian voice to a note of suavity: "Reverend Father, if indeed you
believe that a lawfully instituted Council can err, then I am afraid I
must regard you as a heathen and a publican."

That finished Luther with Duke George of Saxony, and, despite
Mosellanus' valiant statement to the contrary, with the majority of the
audience. But the debate was not finished, for nearly ten days more.
And then Karlstadt had another innings, for another two days, on
the question whether the human will, without divine grace, be able
to work anything but sin. Then Duke George had his court room
cleared in earnest, for the imminent state visit. He sent Eckius a fine
stag and to Karlstadt, magnanimously, a hind—but to Luther not so
much as a bowl of gruel. Eckius was invited to stay on and meet
the noble visitors, who were coming fresh from the imperial election
at Frankfurt.

Leipzig was quiet again. The Wittenberg students with their daggers
and their halberds and frequent noisy demonstrations had long since
run out of money and gone home; the Leipzig students, who had given

as good as they got, were under control; the thirty-four armed guards stationed round Eckius' quarters were withdrawn. At Ingolstadt there was rejoicing. At Wittenberg there were congratulations all round too.

Luther had been driven into a corner so that he had had to acknowledge himself a heretic. Only, to Luther at this stage it had become luminously clear that the heresy was on the other foot. Eckius knew that he had won. Luther knew he had not been defeated: more, that he could not be defeated. He was certain of that now as he had not been before.

He was burning, surging with writing to be done.

Wittenberg and Ingolstadt and Leipzig were full of it all—perhaps hardly to the exclusion of other news, but still almost to the extent of forgetting events on a less lofty plane.

23. The Election

Planes of importance are like all things relative, and outside the universities which were particularly involved with the fresh twist in the religious controversy, the election issue dwarfed all others—up to precisely this moment of late summer 1519. The election was now over; Germany had a new emperor. One could take up the threads again, with a view to weaving them into the next piece set up on the loom of time.

Duke George jumped to it. Not being a member of the Electoral College and so statutorily barred from intercourse with those that were, during the most crucial period, he had passed the time with other things; but as soon as the result was out he cleared his palace for political conferences to get his future orientation straight. The Elector of Brandenburg as an immediate participant in this, the event of the century, would be able to fill in Duke George's sketchier information, as to how the business had gone and what guiding inferences were thus to be drawn regarding the international outlook.

Why, what had the rest of the world to do with an internal transaction which was moreover confined to seven specific German princes? Everything.

The Holy See, for one, exercised an influence on the event which was none the weaker for being indirect. Its influence was exercised in two conflicting ways. On the one hand, the three spiritual Electors, the Archbishops of Mainz, Cologne, and Trier, were princes of the Church before they were secular rulers. On the other hand, the four temporal Electors (of Saxony, Bohemia, Brandenburg, and the Palatinate) were liable to pull in the opposite direction to the wishes of the Holy See if the Holy See allowed those wishes to become too obvious. Less precipitately than on a previous occasion, but hardly more distinguished for his timing than for his literary judgment in the past, the Master of the Sacred Palace was hatching a new declaration of papal omnipotence, which in Prierias' exposition covered the making and unmaking of emperors, not to mention electors and secular legislation in general. Tact was definitely not his forte. But then, nobody at the Curia thought to stay his pen.

German nationalism ran high, not to say rampant; the German Gravamina blazed, writ large, another Mene, tekel, upharsin. Germany for the Germans, German Charles for Emperor, was the for once concerted cry of humanists, knighthood, and people. Without any vote whether by representation or as individuals, the humanists could write, the radical knights could fight, and the people could palpably manifest a mood—as testified by the Estates at Augsburg, where the reference to public opinion had so annoyed our beloved and never-to-be-forgotten Emperor Max.

Never-to-be-forgotten Emperor Max had not always nominated German Charles of Spain. Sometimes, especially when he had been considering making himself King of Sweden and/or Pope, he had suggested now the King of Hungary, now the King of Bohemia, now the King of England. But blood proving thicker than water, in the last year of his life he had done everything he could for Charles, down to writing him reams of practical advice. Nothing if not consistent, Maximilian adjured his grandson to discount the popular factor and concentrate entirely on essentials. Money, *"much* money," wrote Maximilian, was the only reliable vote catcher. Charles, at nineteen already heaped with crowns and diadems of every secular description, wished above all things to add to them the thankless but also peerless one which so many of his ancestors had worn; and money was not wanting among his resources.

What with the mineral wealth of Austria and Spanish America, he had more than any other Western monarch. What with the scattered nature of the Habsburg possessions, however, his expenditure also was even greater than that of the others, so that he like lesser men had to fall back on the House of Fugger for such vast immediate outlay as his candidature involved. The House of Fugger, which was beginning to feel the pinch of the waning indulgence trade in Germany, and which already managed the young King of Spain's Austrian mines for him, was not averse from investing in his imperial speculation, and obliged handsomely. Nevertheless, and while money never comes amiss to propaganda, the popular factor—namely the belief of the Germans in Charles' German-ness—weighed most heavily in his favour. One quarter German, one quarter Burgundian, half-Spanish; brought up in Flanders and now bent on rooting himself thoroughly in Spain, *Charles was Maximilian's grandson,* it always came back to that; and as far as his imperial prospects went Maximilian dead was worth more than Maximilian living. For only Maximilian's most admired qualities were now remembered, his shortcomings and outright conflicts with his German subjects were forgotten. In the long run the Electors, who alone had the vote, and who were being offered the strongest inducements to vote against Charles simultaneously with the inducements to vote for him, could not but be affected by the popular factor which Maximilian had despised.

After some bewildering fluctuations of support within and without the Empire for a motley array of possible entrants, the field in the course of spring narrowed to three: King Charles of Spain, King Francis of France, and King Henry VIII of England. The pragmatic Tudor presently dropped out also: the German crown was coming too expensive, he said; the price exceeded both the value and the utility of the merchandise. And then there were two.

It was not just the money, it was not just the brisk peddling in royal brides, to bribe the Electors: candidature was becoming a question also of auxiliary military action. The King of France was well to the fore, with an election budget of three million florins, the bestowal of his sister-in-law Princess Renée, and troops moving into positions of acute discomfort to the Rhenish Electorates of Trier, Cologne, and the Palatinate—in addition to his materially encouraging a whole series of feuds and wars inside Germany. The King of Spain refrained from broadcasting the amount of money he was willing to disburse, but one heard of all manner of indemnities, so-called, which he was paying out to the Electors—and in some cases also to the relatives of Electors. Against the Princess Renée he had his twelve-year-old sister Katherine to offer, and was in receipt of tenders from two separate mercenary armies that had just completed professional engagements in Germany, for the job of "policing" the election zone for him.

No, the King of England had neither money, soldiers and munitions, nor sisters to spare, and his baby daughter Mary, at present betrothed to his French rival's son and heir, was not going to be thrown away on a mere Elector.

The Holy See had favoured England and had to think again. On balance it disliked the solid gains of Habsburg in Naples and Sicily more than the recent and yet minor conquests of Francis I in Italy; and with that trustfulness which never ceases to amaze one in the unscrupulous potentates of the Renaissance, Pope Leo was convinced of Francis' solemn intention to promote the Crusade against the Turks directly he became emperor: three years from now, Francis had sworn, he would be either in Constantinople or dead. Time was running out. To further Francis' suit the Holy See held out a number of wild promises to the Electors, more especially to the Archbishop of Mainz, to whom it was hinted that if all went well he should be the head of a territorial German Church along Gallican lines, that is, with a large measure of independence from Rome. So much candid pressure on behalf of France was bound to arouse every latent anti-Roman suspicion in Germany, and the German nimbus of Charles of Spain glowed ever brighter.

Albrecht of Mainz had long been built up for the part which Rome now dangled over him, at home. For some time past he had had in his employ the bête noire of the Establishment, Ulrich von Hutten, in his (the Archbishop's) persona of humanist Maecenas, which was the one in which Hutten accordingly saw him. He had been rubbed up the wrong way by his fellow-cardinal, Cajetan, at Augsburg, and without a tremor accepted Hutten's dedication to him of a violent polemic against a Crusade under papal auspices, which contained the most scurrilous pen-portrait of Cajetan. He was not on particularly good terms with his fellow-spiritual Elector Greiffenklau of Trier, and through Hutten was in tune if not positively in touch with Franz von Sickingen, scourge of Trier. Sickingen, who could charm the landsknechts of all Germany into his service, was on the warpath and did not mind who knew of it that he expected to play a leading part in the regeneration of the Empire under Charles who was all for it (or so Sickingen thought or had been led to believe), to the tune of amicable correspondence, a proffered pension, and of course hard cash. As the King of France had also been paying Sickingen, it looked very much as if Sickingen would attain his goal of a principality (which would have to come out of somebody's lands), and then who was going to be the most powerful Elector? Not Frederick of Saxony, who possessed no affinity with landsknechts and would not have known what to do with it if he had. Sickingen's plans included a Gallican-style primacy for Albrecht, though probably with some other, evangelical reforms thrown in. Albrecht did not mind that; he was not plagued with adamant convictions; in religious matters, he was willing to be led. The bird in the hand looked more substantial than its twin in the papal bush.

It only needed a few extra presents and "indemnities" from the Habsburg campaign fund, and an imprudently blunt request by the Holy See that Francis not Charles be elected, to swing all three archbishops into line with the desire of the nation. Only the Elector of Brandenburg still prevaricated. He had his own reasons; but the House of Hohenzollern had to wait till 1871 to get what he was after.

The Holy See essayed a last throw. The nuncio extraordinary, Karl von Miltitz, was still pursuing his negotiations on the election fringe, not unsuccessfully, as the Archbishop of Trier had now agreed to form a committee of examiners to deal with Luther. Although this was not necessarily a proof of Miltitz's skill (but rather of the Archbishop's change of front in favour of the candidate whom the papacy did not want), there was no reason to disbelieve his vaunted rapport with the Elector of Saxony.

Elector Frederick the Wise's reputation stood higher than ever before. His function of Imperial Vicar between emperors was the least of it. It was generally known that he had refused all bribes—including the hands of both the Princesses Renée of France and Katherine of Spain—and had even forbidden his officials to accept gratuities from any quarter whatsoever. One must hope that a sense of virtue compensated Frederick's counsellors for going empty-handed where everybody else in their position was gathering windfalls without contingent exertion. At all events, the entire German higher nobility was lost in admiration. Knowing what they knew about each other with that unique exception, they would never support the last-minute candidature of any other German prince; but it was not such a far-fetched notion to put up the Saxon Elector. Even the Elector of Brandenburg might come to regard this as a Solomonic solution.

Miltitz was sent to Elector Frederick with an offer of energetic papal support if he should agree to stand; there was thrown in with this the guarantee of a cardinalate *for any cleric the Elector might wish to name.* Having previously failed to appreciate that Frederick might have a sense of responsibility towards a miserable mendicant, the Holy See now misapprehended the nature and extent of Frederick's attachment to Luther. Besides, Frederick really was too wise to let himself in for a title which, without the necessary power and resources of his own to enforce his will, would have brought him nothing but chagrin and humiliation had he donned it. He declined.

The Holy See gave up and withdrew its opposition before Charles might be elected in the teeth of that.

Be it never so humble, there was scarcely an abode in Germany that did not have one of the cheap woodcut pictures representing Charles, with an artless, rhymed caption praying God to let "the young noble blood" win, with which the realm was inundated. Even the beggars had them. Those who had nothing to lose, and would not gain; those who had everything to gain, and would not lose—they and everybody in between, were all, all, all for Charles. A hero was needed.

The election finally took place on 28 June 1519 (the day after the Leipzig disputation opened), in Frankfurt on Main, the statutory venue of electoral congress. The town council warned the populace not to take alarm at the tocsin, which would be rung three times when the Electors, robed in scarlet, went into conclave at the dusky chapel tradition set aside for them. "At the sound of the bells, let every man pray God that they may elect an emperor who will be useful to God Almighty, the Holy Empire, and us all."

By unanimous vote the Electors chose Charles, "King of Spain, Sicily, Jerusalem, the Balearic Islands, the Canary Islands, the Indies and the mainland on the far side of the Atlantic, Archduke of Austria, Duke of Burgundy, Brabant, Styria, Carinthia, Carniola, Luxemburg, Limburg, Athens and Patras, Count of Habsburg, Flanders and Tyrol, Count Palatine of Burgundy, Hainault, Pfirt, Roussillon, Landgrave of Alsace, Count of Swabia, Lord of Asia and Africa"—and now also "elected Roman King, future Emperor, semper augustus"; a most puissant monarch, strong enough to enforce the law and keep the peace even in Germany, and to protect the German nation even against the Holy See of Rome.

Charles was in Spain, much occupied. His coronation as Roman King at Aachen, town of Charlemagne, could not take place for another fifteen months. His coronation as Emperor would follow on as soon as ever he presented himself in Rome.

Those that knew no better sighed. It seemed a long time to wait.

*

24. Busy Bodies

Elections in the grand style are like weddings. The excitements of the courtship period shade over into a crescendo of planning for the climax: sufficient unto the day. There can be no serious, preparatory adjustments on any side; apart from certain broad provisions for a presumptive happily-ever-after, all the world has to wait until the thing is done before taking up appropriate positions and attitudes to go on from there. In the case of a major political election, of course, all the world's involvement in the affair is a great deal more acute than that of society at large in any marriage; to strain the analogy just a little, with an empire's espousal of an emperor it was as though all the wedding guests were going to have to live with the young couple.

For all that it was so largely a love match, the broad provisions for the future, from the German point of view, included the precaution of a *Wahlkapitulation,* a set of conditions imposed on the Emperor. There were to be no Diets held anywhere except on German soil, Diets were to be conducted and imperial edicts enacted in the German language, no foreign troops were to be introduced into the Empire under any circumstances, no decisions of policy to be taken without the consent of the Estates, and no German nationals to be tried without a hearing in Germany (Elector Frederick's pertinent insertion); a necessarily somewhat vaguer undertaking to push the German Gravamina went without saying. However, once the Emperor upon accepting these terms had been endowed with the sovereign power, his newly wedded Empire could no longer dictate but would have to resort to other, wilier means of keeping him up to the mark.

The Emperor's former rivals had to show themselves good losers— an enterprise in which Charles adroitly aided them by showing himself a most forbearing winner. He promised to marry the French King's daughter, bore in silence some audible Gallic crowing that his election expenses far surmounted those of France, and—truly a masterstroke— thanked the King of England for his *assistance*. He made a convincing show of forgetting that the Elector of Brandenburg had also tried to run and the Elector of Saxony had been tipped as a better bet on the home stretch; and he reminded the Holy See that his ancestors on both sides had distinguished themselves in pledged championship of the papacy. The honeymoon was on: for everybody desired the good graces of the new Emperor quite as much as he now needed theirs.

The French had more cause for crowing than they knew: the finances of the richest monarch of Europe were in a parlous state. The right hand did not know what the left hand had been spending, and vice versa; the fount of Habsburg wealth, the mines in their hereditary Austrian dominions, was in pawn to the Fugger; the demands of ten distinct and separate territorial parliaments—those of Castile with the recently annexed kingdoms of Navarre and Granada, of Aragon, Valencia, Catalonia, Naples, Sicily and Sardinia, the Netherlands prov- inces and the county of Burgundy, plus the "crown lands" of Austria; not to mention the administrations of the American and North African colonies—were competing in discordant unison for the sovereign's at- tention and subventions. The sooner Charles could get the German Diet to vote him grants of money and military, the better. In the mean- time his ministers were negotiating for the outright purchase of the Duke of Württemberg's sequestered lands, in the heart of the Empire, which would fill a much-felt gap between some of the scattered Habs- burg provinces; for a state visit to England (with a view to a trade pact between England and the Netherlands and a double breach of promise to the French crown, by which it was proposed that Charles not Francis' son should marry Mary Tudor in place of Francis' daughter); and for a possible rapprochement between the papal and Habsburg states in Italy by way of mutual defence against Francis' conquests in the Milanese. Francis, nothing daunted, was wooing Henry VIII as well and putting out feelers towards the Sultan of the Infidels concerning the undesirable increase to the Most Catholic House of Habsburg.

In Leipzig as at all provincial courts, city halls, castles, and chapter houses throughout Germany the local policymakers were confabulating how best to exploit the opportunities of the new reign. Duke George of Saxony and Elector Joachim of Brandenburg would not be averse from scoring over their common neighbour Elector Frederick the Wise—whether by acquisition of territory or of prestige at his expense. Professor Eckius, agog with his victory over the Saxon Elector's pet academics, was yeast to their brew.

In Wittenberg, Elector Frederick lay prostrate from exhaustion after Frankfurt, dangerously ill with fever, gout, stone, and colic, which for nearly eight months kept him hors de combat; while Luther, conversely envigorated after the show-down of Leipzig, resumed his normal work with a will and on top of that produced no fewer than sixteen new publications in six months.

It was not only that he flamed and bubbled with fertile, urgent corollaries of his most recent recognition, not only that he knew he probably had very little time to lose if he wanted to get said what he had to say, and not only that the Elector was too ill to stop him—but that he felt he could now let himself go with a good conscience since without any futher risk to the gospel cause. For Melanchthon had now made that cause his own. Even as Eckius had forced Luther to face at last the only conclusion of his cumulative criticisms and to attack the very institution of the papacy, so had he impelled Melanchthon to forsake his detached, classicist enclosure and jump with both feet into the theological fray. All his scientific curiosity aroused by the contradictory quotations from the Church Fathers and Councils of the past, with which Luther and Eckius had pelted one another, Melanchthon immediately on returning to Wittenberg had immersed himself in intensive study of those sources, parallel with new departures in New Testament research; punctually coming up with incontestable treasure trove. What Luther postulated on a more intuitive basis, Melanchthon proved by meticulous test and watertight argumentation. It was he who formulated the first proper, fundamental axioms of evangelical doctrine, and, in those remaining months of 1519, began to lay out the groundwork of a Lutheran system.

Luther, to be sure, would not allow such an adjective ("What is

Luther? 'My' teaching is not mine."), and rather exulted, "See how this little Grecian now outdoes me even in theology! Now all and sundry know him for the miracle he is, worth many Martins! He is the mightiest foe that Satan and scholasticism ever had: he has the power and by it will conquer. Amen."

But while the marvellous little Grecian applied himself to the methodical task of building up a perfect theory for the teachings of Luther—which he thereby extended, with inexorable logic, beyond Luther's boldest dreams till then—it was Luther's spontaneous outpourings that got through to every section of society and gripped the imagination. Whether the response be affirmative or hostile, response was forthcoming at every hand, and seldom in moderation. Luther and specialist intelligentsia after him might place Melanchthon above him in intellect and erudition, and allot altogether greater importance, in any lasting sense, to Melanchthon's consolidatory work: but it was Luther who had the instinctive, resistless, human approach, who had the passion and trenchancy, the gift of words and an equally individual command of two languages totally different in character and so demanding totally different modes of expression—who had the unfailing knack of topicality and compulsive beguilement—in short everything the writer wishing to be read can possibly desire.

He wrote, in those months, on baptism, on the Lord's Supper, on the ban, on repentance, family life, the ten commandments, preparation for death, consolation in times of illness, the sacrament, the Lord's Prayer, as well as starting on a large project, a book of sermons for all the Sundays and Holy Days of the Church Year, producing a continuation of his *Studies in the Psalms,* three polemics against Eckius, two treatises on economic problems, and putting the finishing touches to the commentary on *Galatians.* "It just flows out; I do not have to press and squeeze."

Nor did it need to be puffed and pushed on the market: the booksellers complained that everything of Luther's was snatched damp off the presses; really, his output and the public demand between them were working the poor printer-publishers to death. What masochists they were, to be sure: recruits to the trade kept coming. As much as "God's latest and best gift to us" benefitted Luther, the trade benefitted by him. There was so much money to be made out of going in for Lutheran production that innumerable artisans changed over to typography and set up presses. For the author took nothing.

"Please get me some copies of my works. This is the only claim I make on my publishers, to let me have some copies now and then; I don't think that is too much for my labours. . . ."

"Work as I may, I can't supply all the presses that demand their food at my hands. As it is I am feeding something like six hundred printers now."

One publisher had offered him a flat payment of four hundred gulden annually, but Luther did not feel morally justified in doing such a thing. On purely moral grounds, he bemoaned the rapacity of another: "There he is, making monstrous profits out of the books I give him to print—I put it at 100 per cent. How different from honest Grünenberg! He said to me the other day, 'Herr Doctor, I am making too much. I shall have to print larger editions and sell them for less.' A God-fearing man; the Lord will bless all his undertakings."

For there was also working for Luther a factor quite outside himself: that long-mounting wave of spiritual emptiness and lassitude among men, from which humanist enthusiasm had already derived much of its dynamic. This gladly flowed towards the reservoir of potential vivifaction which Luther was instrumental in opening up: where the dammed currents would generate power not only for the evangelical movement but also for a Catholic revival. The subject, the meaning, the very stuff of religion had become of surpassing interest once again, among both parties to the religious controversy; giving people's lives a fresh content, with the exhilaration of either joy or anger for a bonus.

The interesting thing is that Luther instigated this by writing. Although by all accounts effective as a preacher, it was not by spoken oratory that he stirred the multitudes: his sermons only gained their greatest impact when they had been printed.

The present-day investigator of any religious phenomenon ignores at his peril the current enquiries into brain-washing, thought-control, and the physiological machinery of charismatic experience. Luther's much-publicized states of anguish, followed by wondrous relief, followed by irresistible access of missionary zeal, can be and have been fitted to the typical picture of mechanistic indoctrination, and also to certain patterns of mental disease. It is not difficult to make out a case for either of these—or any number of others—so long as the alternatives are ruthlessly excluded. But where there are so many imponderables involved as obviously played a major part in the career of Luther,

the facile case history is more hindrance than help in the endeavour
to explain what happened.

With Luther, it is necessary to remember that the initial "brain-
washing" conversion was spontaneous and not induced—indeed every
effort was made from outside to arrest it; and as regards the hysterical
manifestations associated with pathological mental states, there is no
authentic record of trances, pentecostal outbursts, or thaumaturgy in
any shape or form. Luther never even claimed *direct* divine inspiration.
As he put it, he was merely given grace to understand the Word of
God as it had been laid down already for all time; and when at
moments of crisis he "took counsel" with God, God in the same
way merely gave him the grace to see what he should do. God did
not *tell* him. Luther never witnessed a miracle, and he performed
none. He never so much as saw, nor heard, an angel. And he at
no time countenanced the slightest attempt at foisting a personal cult on
him: "Christ has no need of me," he emphasized over and over. "The
people have no need of me, for Christ will do what he wants done,
anyhow. It is just that so long as I am here I have to do his will."

Neither did he employ the notorious demagogic techniques of emotional titillation and hypnotic repetition. His rhetoric being argumentative appealed always to the rational faculties which he denigrated only
as a means of apprehending the divine but considered indispensable
to human relations: therefore was it at its most effectual when the word
was not fugitive but could be mulled over at leisure. Luther was the
first religious leader to avail himself of a mass medium and perhaps
the only one ever to disseminate his message by that medium alone:
unaided by personal canvassing outside his immediate orbit, and without benefit of electronic projection of his personality. Forceful and
magnetic that personality undoubtedly was, but it came to leadership
by accident not calculation, and heedless grit not calculation kept it
there.

Obsessive, we call such disregard of comfort and safety in the
service of a cause beyond self, just as we call unreasonable such
strength of conviction, and glibly minimize martyrdom by linking it
with a perverted craving for pain. As Luther well knew, in this life
and left to its own devices, the poor naked human psyche cannot do
right.

Whatever the contestants and their partisans might think as to who
had carried off the palm of victory in the Leipzig disputation, there

was no official decision till the appointed umpires pronounced their verdict. The Universities of Paris and Erfurt had been chosen but declined to act in that capacity: Erfurt had the grace to say so, Paris simply did not answer. Valuable time having been lost—or gained, depending which side one was on—the Universities of Cologne and Louvain came unbidden to the rescue and condemned the bulk of Luther's views as recorded in the transcripts of his debate with Eckius. Armed with these judgments, and sped with warm recommendations by the Fugger, Duke George of Saxony, and Elector Joachim of Brandenburg, Eckius set out for Rome to help to get the matter moving again at the Curia, towards the end of the year.

Shortly before, Cajetan had arrived back in Rome and put a different complexion on the diplomatic successes of Miltitz as hitherto described by Miltitz. Shortly before that, the Inquisitor Hochstraaten of Cologne had arrived, in the guise of a semi-refugee. His brethren had deemed it politic to dispense with his presence until further notice, as an act of appeasement towards Franz von Sickingen. For shortly after the imperial election Sickingen had formally declared a feud against the Cologne Dominicans, "on behalf and in the interests of the most highly learned and far-famed Doctor Johann Reuchlin," demanding cessation of the Dominicans' continued attacks on that worthy man, an abject apology for the same, and immediate payment of one hundred eleven gulden by way of compensation; or else. As Sickingen showed that he meant it, appearing with an army when there was not instant compliance, Reuchlin at last got some peace and some refundment; and Sickingen in his turn got a tribute from an unlooked-for quarter.

"The world of learning shall never permit the name of Franz von Sickingen to perish, without incurring the smirch of ingratitude." Thus wrote Erasmus of Rotterdam, though not meaning to be quoted. He had not meant to be quoted either when privately registering qualified approval of Luther in a letter to Ulrich von Hutten, which Hutten had incontinently printed.

In the new year the news seeped through the Alpine barrier that Hochstraaten had employed his exile urging the Curia to re-open Reuchlin's case as "but for Reuchlin there would have been no Luther," thus discharging his part of a pincers movement in which Cajetan furnished the other shank.

As soon as this was learned at Sickingen's headquarters of Ebernburg, where Hutten was whiling away the military off season in reading to his unlettered friend from the works of Luther, the author was

True, the most monumental workshop of the moment, the Sistine Chapel where Michelangelo was then immolated painting the ceiling, was kept closed: but it was not impossible to procure an introduction for a peep. Altogether there was so much going on in the whole realm of formative art, in Rome, you could not miss it. Luther did. Among all his impressions of the Eternal City which he listed, besides the religious *mirabilia* there were only the numerous ruins and the heads of Peter and Paul—encased in busts of gold which Luther described as made of wood: so he either had not seen them at all or had not bothered to look when paying his respects to these outstanding relics.

He went through Florence, and noticed nothing. Very well, his mind was all on Rome. But in Rome, even if he was not struck by the general, teeming evidence of artistic activity, how could he have over-looked one of the boldest building projects of all time, which was then sufficiently advanced to fill other visitors with amazement at its grandeur? Luther never said a word about the rebuilding of St. Peter's basilica in Rome—not even at a time when all his utterances turned on this very thing—although he could hardly have helped at least passing by the four great piers of Bramante, already rising up when he was there. A blind man, one would think, could not have over-looked (unless he were also deaf) the traffic of building materials for St. Peter's, passing him, for the work was being pushed ahead so rapidly on such a scale that this traffic must have been virtually constant. Luther, who was so observant in respect of matters which had his interest—him all this passed by indeed.

Those who came nearest to the ideal of all-round genius were the artists of the Italian Renaissance. They broke through the degree-ridden professionalism of the so-called sciences and made themselves elbow-room for limitless amateur productivity. In the Middle Ages it had been forgotten, even as it is forgotten today, that the founders of professional disciplines of every kind are by definition always mu-tinous sports refusing to be tied down in compartments, and refusing to believe what they are told to believe because they are told so. What they did, the reckless talents of that period, probably has never been surpassed. It was not only what they *made,* themselves—which would be miraculous enough: but everything we count on the credit side of human progress—whether in art or in science, outlook and insights and environmental improvements—all this was seeded by a serried brother, can't stop him. I can only offer him my advice that he had better stick to his wine cup and the fire that smokes from a roasting goose, which are more in his line. . . . Since they are so bitten with the desire to burn heretics even for such piffling, un-heretical causes (seeing that the subject of indulgences has nothing whatever to do with faith, salvation, need, or law)—forgive me, dear Heavenly Father, if I cry defiance to my Baalites, just this once! . . ."

It was handed in to Master Grünenberg at white heat, and Luther's second thoughts about his mode of expression came too late. The press "across the street" was working overtime to meet popular demand as well as keep up with the author's concurrent academic and pastoral publications (two bulky and three or four shorter ones).

In Rome, Pope Leo was quoted as saying, on the one hand, "Never mind, it's only a drunken German, who will feel differently when he sobers up," and on the other, "Friar Martin has talent: that is why they're jealous of him. All this fuss is nothing more than the usual monkish rivalry." (Hutten had the same thought. "The monks have gone among the writers now!" he wrote to a friend. "The booksellers are having a field day. I devoutly hope they will cock-fight to the last feather and end up by devouring one another." Erasmus, however, was said to have signified his approval of the Theses.)

Elector Frederick issued an invitation to Tetzel—"safe-conduct, open doors, and all found"—for a public debate with Luther; but Tetzel instead sent eight hundred copies of his rebuttal for distribution in Wittenberg. The students seized the lot and made a bonfire of them. Luther was very much upset.

"The grave injury done to the man by our supporters will surely be laid at my door," he wrote to Lang; and, to his revered old teacher Professor Trutvetter of Erfurt: "Surely you cannot believe I had anything to do with the burning of Tetzel's theses? Do you really think that I, a monk and theologian, have so lost all sense of propriety?" The answer was yes; Trutvetter severed relations.

The Elector was not pleased, either; but he did not hold Luther responsible. The Elector was at pains to show that he was not worried by the talk, emanating from Brandenburg as Luther had feared might happen, that Luther was his instrument of petty spite against the house of Hohenzollern. Nobody who knew the Elector's personal interest in indulgences could seriously entertain such a suggestion, he deemed, that Emperor and Legate pulled shoulder to shoulder hampered their purpose. The Estates had too many unappeased grievances in relation to both, not to misdoubt such a partnership. The moieties of resistance came together and strengthened in unity. It was an object lesson in the positive potential of unity, had anyone then cared to heed and act upon it. As usual, those against whom the negative unity of resistance was manifested saw the threat of an aggressive unity long before their antagonists awakened to its promise. The suzerains of the Empire had come to a point where they could agree on what they did not want; but in what they wanted they yet remained individualistic and divided.

The Emperor was accustomed to his refractory Germans but found it hard to stomach the form which their refractoriness took this time: that they should even mention popular opinion, let alone attribute power to it and cheerfully declare themselves at its mercy! To the last of the knights it seemed a ridiculous excuse; and the Cardinal Legate saw his moment to improve the occasion. He laid before the Emperor the pseudo-Lutheran theses on excommunication which, he showed, were nothing less than an incitement to total anarchy, already bearing fruit, Q.E.D. The Emperor took the point at once and gave Cajetan a personal letter for the Holy See, calling for speediest action against the monk of Wittenberg whose heretical influence was beginning to corrupt "not only the people but the very princes of the Empire."

The Dominican Cardinal's move in passing to make good the set-back to his Order's cause at the hands of Prierias proved shrewdly judged. The imperial letter duly electrified the Holy See. Evidently the affair, which the Holy Father Leo would like to dismiss as a "monkish squabble" even yet, had assumed far graver proportions than one had thought in Rome—seeing that not only had the Emperor heard of it but that he considered it necessary to ask for papal intervention!

Cajetan despatched the imperial letter on 5 August. On 23 August the Curia despatched a triple warrant for Luther's arrest and delivery, in bonds, to Rome: one went to Cajetan, the second to Elector Frederick of Saxony, the third to the provincial of the Saxon Augustinian Congregation. Now, certainly, Spalatin had something to tell him—enjoining him, however, not to give up hope just yet. But then Staupitz, now in Austria, wrote to Martin from Salzburg:

he supposed, finish his meal. He was still eating when a second note arrived, telling him to hold everything until he had seen the Elector who had "some necessary things to discuss" with him. The Elector would let him know when and where. Both notes had been despatched from the same place, Castle Altenburg, at the time interval of their reception.

It certainly was very strange. Luther's friends were thrown into a turmoil of speculation and conflicting advice; but he was growing accustomed now to living in constant suspense and did not mind weathering an anticlimax.

Luther never knew what exactly had happened. Nobody knows anything more than that Miltitz and Pfeffinger had gone into conference and that the loyal councillor informed his Elector as to whom he was entertaining. Nobody knows whether it was at this point or another that Pfeffinger relayed Miltitz's interesting disclosure that Luther might have had an archbishopric and a cardinal's hat, had he named these as his price for recanting, and that the Golden Rose was intended to remain in the Fugger vault so long as it might be deemed advisable to reserve it for dangling over the Elector. Both these intimations, of bluff on the one hand and blackmail on the other, were bound to affect the Elector strongly, on the one hand calming him down and on the other putting his back up; and undoubtedly they were in his possession before very much later in December, although he did not receive Miltitz in audience at Altenburg until the twenty-eighth of that month. Pfeffinger was present at this decisive meeting, to which no future secrecy attached, as the Elector when once he had come to a definite decision was wont to hold to it with adamant fidelity.

Though he wished that the professor—whom not long before he had been unwilling to spare for even a few weeks—might have gone straight to France from Augsburg, and though he did not think he would be able to protect Luther from the consequences of the ban, he had decided to stand by him and also make one more attempt to obviate the ban. After some preliminary fencing, Miltitz formally acquainted the Elector with his plan to reconcile Luther and the Pope, and the Elector formally gave it his blessing. Miltitz wrote to Rome that he had the Wittenberg monk as good as in his pocket, in spite of Cajetan's mismanagement; he got his money and permission to exercise his discretion. Luther having been summoned to talk with

Eckius asserted that the Roman primacy had been instituted by Christ himself; Luther over-reached himself by saying it went back no farther than three hundred years, when Pope Gregory IX, the first systematic organizer of the Dominican Inquisition, had set in motion the necessary legislation. This Luther could not maintain against the evidence of earlier decretals, and he had to extricate himself with some fast sophistry. But—quite apart from the fact that in Jesus' day there had not as yet been any Christian Church at Rome—he absolutely drew the limit at the seventh century, and stuck to his guns there. When Eckius adduced the text of a letter by a first-century bishop of Rome, which stood incorporated in the canon law, Luther by means of reasoned historical criticism impugned its authenticity; and nothing could move him.

(The amateur was right; although the professional research scholars did not prove it till a few decades hence, the text in question belonged to a corpus of spurious insertions, known ever since as the False Decretals. Yet he had not so far even heard about the work of Valla on the false Donation of Constantine.)

Luther's most powerful argumentation rested on the Greek Church, which did not recognize the Bishop of Rome as its head and never had: would Eckius, then, condemn the entire Eastern half of Christendom for heresy? Over-rash in his turn, Eckius said yes; and on this basis Luther had a fine time with him. What? damn the whole Greek Church with all its adherents over fifteen centuries, the Church which had produced the best of the Fathers and many thousands of great saints, none of whom had had so much as a suspicion of the Roman primacy? "Do you and the Pope and his sycophants mean to throw them out of heaven?" It was for Eckius to display some fast footwork and retreat into the circumscribed sphere of the Latin Church, where he did know his way about. And now it was his turn, to have a fine time with Luther.

He fired his bombshell. "I see that you are following the pestiferous errors of John Wyclif, who said, 'It is not necessary for salvation to believe that the Roman Church is above all other Churches,' and likewise the damned and pestilent errors of Johann Hus, who said that Peter neither was nor is the head of the Holy Catholic Church."

You could call Luther a boil, a bastard, a monster, a drunken, mangy, lice-ridden mendicant; but you must not call him Hussite. He roared in furious protest—but in the lunchtime intermission, he surprised to receive a cordial invitation to come and dwell under their protection—an offer which not long after was improved on by one hundred knights willing, not to say spoiling, to muster for his defence.

About the same time as Sickingen had his eyes opened wide to the relevance of the gospel to the political programme of the German radical knighthood, Luther became acquainted with Hutten's edition of Lorenzo Valla's exposure of the forged Donation of Constantine. His suspicions regarding the appropriation of Rome by the powers of evil were confirmed.

At first he was more appalled than triumphant, but then saw that the widest possible publicity must be given to this state of affairs: "To think that the truth has been available for a hundred years!" But yet he did not like to commit himself to Hutten's and Sickingen's invitation —"Christ *may* have inspired them," he wrote to Spalatin; but he was not certain, and preferred not to answer till he was. He could always say afterwards that there had not been any messenger to send, at the time. In Germany it was still winter.

The spring came with earlier vigour in Italy. Pope Leo X welcomed it by taking a vacation, before the end of April, at his hunting lodge in the hills of Magliana, where there was good sport, with an abundance of wild boar.

25. Exsurge, Domine

Suddenly it had come. It had happened after all. Three years after he had first been threatened with the papal ban, two years after the apparent imminence of excommunication had caused him to challenge the whole principle—on 15 June 1520 the papal chancery published the pontifical anathema on Martin Luther, and he heard about it by the end of the month. During the remainder of the summer the rumour was verified, and substantiated by some printed copies clandestinely reaching Germany from Rome. Though formal publication in the Empire was yet to come, there was no doubt. It was true. His Church was casting him out.

"Exsurge, Domine," ran the Bull of condemnation, "Arise, O Lord, and judge thy cause. A wild boar seeks to destroy thy vineyard. Arise, O Peter, and consider the case of the Holy Roman Church, the mother of all churches, consecrated by thy blood. Arise, O Paul, who by thy teaching and death hast and dost illumine the Church. Arise, all ye saints, and the whole universal Church, whose interpretation of Scripture has been assailed. We can scarcely find words to express our grief over the superannuated heresies which have thus been revived in Germany—Germany on whom the popes of old bestowed the Roman imperium, by reason of their very special affection for her: Germany, who was always in the forefront of the war on heresy! Our pastoral duty can no longer neglect the pestiferous infection in our midst. We can no longer tolerate the serpent to crawl through the field of the Lord. The books of Martin Luther which contain his errors are to be examined and burned.

"As for Martin himself, good God, what have we omitted, what have we not done, what have we neglected of paternal charity, that we might recall him from his errors? After we had summoned him, desiring to deal more mildly with him, through our legate and by letter, to renounce his errors, or to come without any hesitation or fear—for perfect love should cast out fear—and after the example of our Saviour and the blessed Apostle Paul, talk not secretly but openly and face to face. We even offered him safe-conduct and money for the journey. If he had come he would certainly, we believe, have seen his errors and repented. Nor would he have found so many evils in the Roman Curia which, relying on the empty rumours of its enemies, he vituperates in unseemly fashion. We should also have taught him more lucidly than light that the Holy Roman pontiffs, though he abuses them beyond all decency, have never erred in their canons or constitutions.

"Yet he has had the temerity to appeal to a future Council although our predecessors Pius II and Julius II placed such appeals under the penalties of heresy. Now therefore we give Martin sixty days in which to submit, dating from the time of the publication of this Bull in his district. Anyone who presumes to infringe our excommunication and anathema will stand under the wrath of Almighty God and of the Apostles Peter and Paul."

Appended were forty-one articles, for the most part copied from the judgments of Cologne and Louvain, on which the charge of heresy was made to rest. They centred on Luther's denial that baptism per se can save, that the Pope can open and shut purgatory, that either Pope or Council has power to supersede the Word of God, that the Pope is the absolute ruler of the Church and the Roman Church absolute mistress over all other churches; on the subject of penance and indulgence, the three commissions which had worked for three months on the final wording had forgotten all about the Bull *Cum postquam* and indicted Luther for statements (made in 1517) which agreed completely with Pope Leo's definitions in that Bull (of 1518). To give it body, the list included such remarks as, "To burn heretics is contrary to the will of the Holy Spirit," "Princes would do well to end mendicancy," and "War against the Turks is resistance to God's visitation." The first of these had the authority of the Apostle Paul ("There must be sects"), the second and third only echoed what Erasmus had been saying with perfect impunity—rightly so, since by no stretch of the imagination could such opinions be said to touch on central dogma: in fact they had no connection at all with tenets of faith and so no possible connection with heresy either. For heresy consisted in deviation from fundamental religious doctrine.

It was, as Luther had found once he had "actually read" Hus, stretching the concept of heresy not a little, to apply it to the Bohemian postulates that all dominion stems alike from God so that secular and spiritual power are alike sacred; that all baptized Christians have alike direct access to God without the intermediary services of a special, professional class of priests; that therefore all should alike partake of the sacred elements during holy communion; and that otherwise all practices seeking to establish the Deity in material manifestations are sinful. "I said," Luther had written recently, "that some of Hus' beliefs were evidently Christian, which I have been asked to retract. I retract. I now say all Hus' beliefs are Christian." The trouble was that as soon as a man was condemned for heresy and his works were burned, these were discredited, prohibited, unread. One shunned one knew not what: there was too much to be read that one should read, and that one never had time to read, to go out of one's way to study the condemned heretics.

Something of the sort had now happened with Luther's writings, at the Curia—though there was an unexpected twist to it. Aesthetically speaking, it was a shame: they could have really got him, they could have made a charge of heresy stick on good, technical grounds— grounds which Luther had plentifully provided in the "new things" written after Leipzig; there had been no need to pad out the instrument of excommunication with feeble, far-fetched quibbles. But these new things, which from the Establishment point of view truly deserved the name of "dangerous doctrine" and which were resounding through Germany to the tune of a truly national concert even now, just had not been read in Rome. The pained surprise the Holy See had lately had occasion to convey to the Archbishop of Mainz, that he, the German primate and in a manner accoucheur to the Luthern controversy, had to this day avoided "actually reading" Luther, was a plain case of the pot calling the kettle black.

There were other curious features about the Bull, not the least of them the plaintive, occasionally almost apologetic note sounding through the thunder. An offer of safe-conduct and journey money had not been received in Wittenberg. If Leo X's predecessors Pius II (1458–64) and Julius II (1503–13) had ruled appeals to future Councils out of order, others, one must assume not less infallible, had allowed them: there were ample precedents. Furthermore, since Luther's heresy was held to be proved, why instead of outright excommunication was he being given one more chance to recant? The Bull itself ran a rider attributing this to "an outburst of Christian compassion from the pious soul of the Holy Father": being nonetheless unusual, on all counts.

In a letter dated 8 July the Holy Father similarly announced to Elector Frederick the Wise what he had done: "Beloved son, we re-joice that you have never shown any favour to the son of iniquity, Martin Luther. We hardly know whether to credit this the more to your sagacity or to your piety. This Luther favours the Bohemians and the Turks, deplores the punishing of heretics, spurns the writings of the holy doctors, the decrees of the oecumenical councils, and the ordinances of the Roman pontiffs, and accepts the opinions of none save himself alone, which no heretic before ever presumed to do. We cannot suffer the scabby sheep longer to infect the flock. Wherefore we have summoned a conclave of venerable brethren. The Holy Spirit also was present, for in such cases he is never absent from our Holy See. We have drawn up a bull, sealed with lead, in which out of the innumerable errors of this man we have selected those in which he perverts the faith, seduces the simple, and relaxes the bonds of obedience, continence, and humility. The abuse he has heaped upon our Holy See we leave to God. We exhort you to induce him to return to sanity and receive our clemency. If however he persists in his madness, put him in prison." It gave the same impression, of unwarranted lenity coupled with insufficient home-work.

Pope Leo never had been greatly interested in the affair, and he was assuredly surrounded with a bevy of incompetents. But the original draft of the Bull, presented to the Pope on his hunting holiday as early as 2 May, had been the work of Eckius, who had shown himself competent enough at Leipzig: competent enough, too, to have wrested the management of this stage in the proceedings from Cardinal Cajetan.

To meet, for these two antagonists of Luther, was to be antagonistic. ("Who let in that animal?" the Cardinal enquired, smelling the air, on the stout professor's first appearance at the conclave.) Cajetan, wishing to build up an inescapable case against Luther once for all, was acting far too circumspectly for Eckius' taste; and Eckius was not backward in reminding everyone that he unlike the Cardinal had worsted Luther in *their* personal encounter.

The chemistry of personal antipathies and competition was certainly at work throughout the deliberations, which had started in December and went on into the middle of June, and the outcome of which was never in doubt save as regards the technical details of presentation. But vanity and back-biting alone were not responsible for the delay. There were shades of difference in the professional opinions of theologians versus canonists versus diplomats, and shades again within the shades. Also, the motivations never came quite clear: for faith, cynicism, and sincere rationalization cut across each other not only in the different groups but also in their individual components. There were those who believed Luther to be a danger to Christian salvation, those who believed him a danger to the Roman Catholic Church, to the papal institution, to Dominican authority, to economic stability, to world peace, to the standing of Ingolstadt University—which accordingly coloured their views concerning his usefulness to Rome's relations with the new Emperor. The one thing which obtained from every point of view was that, as an ostensibly purely religious matter affecting the Empire, the case of Luther was an immediate opening for Church and Emperor to get together. The question remained, how and to what purport.

Small wonder that the Bull *Exsurge, Domine* was a confused document.

This could not comfort or mollify the man against whom it was directed. He might fume and rage and despise its libels and ineptitudes; but it would have been no different had the Bull been well-informed and well-constructed. He might have been desiring a head-on collision, a war to end war; he might now be entirely ready to defy the papal curse, which in any case he abrogated—but yet he was wounded by the non-existent weapon and outraged by the empty insult: that Antichrist should dare do this to God and verity, in him!

Neither did it make the smallest factual difference to the effect of the Bull, that it was a poor piece of work. Literary merit, sound reasoning were not in question; the papal seal was the operative point, excommunication was excommunication, a bull was a bull. It would not be rescinded because it was botched—any more than Luther would have bowed to it had it been a model of the genre.

✳

26. The "Reformation Treatises"

Luther was depressed.

He bethought himself of a most excellent letter of consolation which he had written for the spiritual uplift of Elector Frederick on his sickbed, and asked the Elector for the loan of it, to cheer up the author now. The Elector had recovered and no longer needed it so much, while the author was in the throes of soreness and indecision. He knew he wrote good medicine, and waste not, want not.

Significantly, the muddled Bull heralded on its way to him was meanwhile supplemented by perfectly unequivocal pressures: there had been renewed attempts at stampeding his sovereign and getting the Augustinian Order to take repressive action against Luther. Staupitz, under fire by the Order's General, resigned the vicarship he had held for so many years. The Elector, at last in possession of his Golden Rose —now somewhat devalued—asked Dr. Martin's advice, just as he had done after the Augsburg interview, but with the difference that this time the request was not a means of oblique prompting. Nowadays the Elector meant it. Luther, however, wanted advice himself, in receipt of another tempting offer of demonstrative protection on the part of the radical knighthood, which he still did not know how to answer. God was not noticeably helping. Luther might be destitute of angelic voices (he humbly said that if, as was possible, angels still occasionally conversed with human beings, he alas was not among the ones they honoured), but the voice of the Devil, of human weakness warring against itself, that he heard.

"I am so little able to resist the smallest wave of inner trepidation

that it makes me proof against any amount of onslaughts from outside."
Thus at length he was able to make up his mind: "I am not willing
to fight with bloodshed even for the gospel. The world is conquered
by the Word; by the Word will the Church be served and rebuilt. As
Antichrist arose without the hand of man, so without the hand of
man will he fall."

True up to a point: by the Word, yes; quite without the hand of
man, no.

Elector Frederick took the advice which Luther gave him, to mention
in his answering despatches to the papal agency that Luther was being
besieged with offers of warlike support: he, the Elector, would not care
to create a quasi-Hussite situation, in Saxony.

The relationship between the sovereign and his contentious subject
had subtly changed. Outwardly the same forms were observed between
them; but it looked as if the Elector had resigned himself—or even
as if he gave a secret welcome—to the recognition of a stronger will
than his own. His long illness had taken a great deal out of him.
He still endeavoured to keep Luther out of trouble with, as he thought,
uncontroversial literary commissions, he still did all he could to restrain
and reprove Luther's more reprehensible polemical outbursts; but he
showed no very marked anger or surprise when that did not work.
There was nothing Luther touched, now, that did not turn out to bear
on controversial questions; and when taken to task for importunity and
coarse language he answered back. If every sharp or hasty word
uttered against manifestly dishonourable opponents were a slander
—said Luther—then Jesus Christ and Paul the Apostle would certainly have to be called slanderers.

Luther's busy pastoral and devotional writings between summer of
1519 and spring of 1520, which, had Rome bothered with them, could
have bolstered up the condemnatory Bull with real unorthodox assertions
galore, in a manner helped him to marshall his ideas and see just
what they were. Having been given grace to sketch out a considerable
array of crucial points, he would use all further respite to elaborate
them into a constructive plan to lend virtue to the work of demolition
which he was obliged to prosecute with everything he had.

His notion of the Antichrist differed from the primal Jewish concept
of a personalized antithesis to the christ or messiah, and equally from

that of successive mediaeval Christian thinkers which had identified this or that individual pope with the anti-messiah of Biblical prediction. His view was that "Antichrist," a convenient name for the Force of Evil, had permeated the papacy, analogously to a parasitic disease taking over the whole body without apparent blemish to the shell. The terrible danger of it did not lie in the practical corruptions of the Church but in the claim of papal infallibility by means of which the Bible was to be overset, the Word of God replaced by the decrees of Satan, and all mankind lured to irremediable perdition.

While Antichrist would scarcely be dislodged without a titanic struggle, meanwhile the people must be told the position, armed against the enemy propaganda, and shown how at once to carry on and help in the war effort.

To write out the necessary prescription was lesser, menial work compared with what Philip Melanchthon was doing, but indispensable for all that. In fact, this fell in with one of the important points Luther wished to put across—that there is not any kind of work more holy or more valuable than any other.

"I can just imagine," he wrote in the first of his greater tracts designed for the instruction of the people, the *Sermon on Good Works,* "the people of Nazareth on judgment day. As they come up before Jesus they will ask, 'But wasn't it you that did the carpentry for my house? How do you come to be in this seat of honour?'—"

Ay, that would be their mistake, would it not? It was a mistake to think that prayers, fasting, alms and indulgences purchased entry into paradise; nothing could do that, of course, but performing one's ordinary duties well and faithfully led at least in the right direction. Whatever earthly labour God had called a man to—or a woman for that matter—was a divine vocation by which they served Him who had neither hands nor feet of his own, in this world. Yes: women were just as good as men. In fact, "If you were not a woman, you should wish to be one," in contradiction of the accepted patristic dictum, "Every woman should blush that she is a woman." It was the Luther family passion for progeny at work, fastening on the birth-giving rôle of woman. Hence, too, virginity was by no means superior to motherhood as frequently alleged. "A mother's love mirrors the love of God, which overcomes the filth of sin just as mother-love overcomes a lapful of muck. . . . The milkmaid and the carter of manure serve God better than do idle monks chanting psalms at him."

For God himself does not laze about in unproductive contemplation; he works. He works as a tailor and shoemaker, gardener and cook to all creation, butler even to the myriad sparrows. "The Virgin Mary, after she had heard the amazing news that she was to be the mother of the Saviour, instead of sitting back to preen herself went on with the housework. How strange. The shepherds, too, having seen and adored the Babe, went back to their flocks. Surely that is wrong. Surely the passage would read, 'They went and shaved their heads, fasted, told their rosary beads, and put on monks' hoods.' Instead the Bible tells us, 'They returned.' Where to? To their sheep. The sheep would have been in sorry plight if they hadn't." Vows and exercises for selfish grooming of the soul defeat the purpose. It is what a man or woman has done for others that will count on judgment day. Neither brawn nor brain has any right to despise one the other. "The soldier boasts that it is hard work to ride in armour and endure heat, frost, dust, and thirst. But I'd like to see the horseman who could sit the whole day and look into a book. It is no great trick to hang two legs over a horse"—Luther should know!—"They say writing is just pushing a feather quill, but I notice that they hang their swords low down and put feather quills high in a place of honour on their hats. Writing occupies not just the fist or the foot while the rest of the man may be otherwise engaged, but the whole of him. As for school-teaching, that is such hard work no one ought to be bound to it longer than ten years." The priest's job is to instruct and minister to the people, but there is no call for him to hug a monopoly expertise in this or for the Pope to disdain good advice: Peter, the first pontiff, had not dismissed Jesus' amateur suggestion to cast on the other side. "Had it been me, I might have said, 'Now look here, Master. You are a preacher, and I don't tell you how to preach. Well, I am a fisherman, so kindly do not tell me how to fish.' But Peter was humble, and therefore the Lord made him the fisher of men."

To his coevals it was all new, charmingly and searingly new, both in matter and in manner. The mediaeval, symbolic reverence of the poor and lowly, conforming with the Sermon on the Mount, had long lost any social connotation; praise of poverty and poor-relief were simply part and parcel of the good works by which one acquired merit. There was no doubt who was the greater, the glittering pope or the ragged peasant. If Jesus had worked with his hands, well, that was of a piece with the rest of his carnal impersonation. In practice, manual work was by definition at once the curse and the brand of under-privilege; and the strictly graded structure of society was congruent with a fixed pyramid of worth. True, the German peasant had his transliteration of the English Lollard rhyme, "When Adam delved and Eve span Who was then the gentleman?"—Hus himself, after all, had only followed in the footsteps of Wyclif. But "Who was then the gentle-man?" was a rhetorical question, harking back to Eden without any really forward-looking suggestions for improvement—levelling-down in-stead of levelling-up, a plea rather than a working proposition.

Luther was only interested in working propositions, all his pleading was practical and positive, never passively wishful. Despite his in-termittent groans of overwork, overwork was what he thrived on, and he had no sympathy whatever with contrary tendencies in anybody else whoever they might be. This undoubtedly influenced his attitude to the problem of mendicancy, over and above the fact that mendicancy played so prominent a part under the doctrine of good works. Without troubling to pause for an enquiry into which was the chicken here and which the egg, he saw quite clearly that there was an intimate connection between the alleged meritoriousness of begging-and-almsgiving and a human preference for idleness. Statistics in the sixteenth century were a somewhat hit-or-miss affair, but even if a contemporary estimate, that only one person out of fifteen worked, in Germany, should be unreliable—it still suggests a large enough number of persons who did no work. The consequences to the national morale were easy to discern; and to Luther, the remedy seemed obvious. To see an ill and to see a remedy was one, with Luther, always. If it did not work out, that was another matter—but anyhow that remained to be seen till such remedy had been tried.

So, now it was a pleasant revelation for the milkmaid and the dung-carter to hear that God was a fellow-toiler of theirs; simul-taneously furnishing their masters with a likely lever against that work-shyness which Luther as well as the Italianate disparagers called the endemic plague of Germany.

Though in its impact on the orthodox hierarchy the *Sermon on Good Works* might be likened to, say, the advocacy of birth control in the Catholic Church of today and a manifesto for racial integration in parts of the world today, rolled into one—all in all it helped to endear Luther to increasing sections of the public.

But he was not out to endear himself; his unaltered, chiefest purpose was to endear the evangelical outlook to all men, which could not be done so long as the religious dictatorship of Rome prevailed. So long as man-made decretals ("Say rather: Excretals!") were supposedly capable of over-ruling the decrees of God, so long as any occupier of Peter's chair by virtue of that piece of furniture assumed the powers of a god on earth, so long was a reformation of the Church in any true sense a chimaera. Not only were men prone to error and self-seeking, to which no sort of throne provided any antidote, but as had been seen they did not scruple to commit forgery to perpetuate errors for their own advantage. What was there so magical about an object of utility made of wood and other fibres? why, "an ass or a dog could sit in Peter's chair"; would that render ass or dog infallible and sacrosanct? Well, they had enthroned worse than beast: they had got Antichrist in possession.

Since Antichrist would prevent the Church from reforming itself, there was no remedy but for secular power to step in. Conceived once again as a placard which in the writing turned into a book, an *Open Letter to the Christian Nobility of the German Nation concerning the Reform of Christianity* was Luther's first positive response to the news of the Bull.

He reiterated that Christendom was no outwardly visible kingdom but the spiritual community of souls united in faith. Nowhere in the Bible was it stated to be otherwise; nowhere was it written that the spiritual estate was as a class independent from let alone above temporal governments. "We are all Christians and have baptism, faith, the Spirit, alike in common. If a priest is killed, a land is laid under interdict. Why not if a peasant is killed? Wherein lies this great distinction between two human beings who are both called Christians?" Church and state are one another's keepers; if the Church needs help, the state must render it. If the Church refuses to convoke a Council to reform itself, then the secular authorities must do so and if necessary themselves compose such a council.

Having previously addressed himself to the people at large on a simple, moral level, Luther now called upon the governors of the state to regenerate the Church by relieving it of the administrative functions and paraphernalia through which its corruption had been brought about.

Let the kings, the princes, and the magistrates, then, put an end to pardons, dispensations, annates, jubilees, indulgences and other special levies by which the "fuddled Germans" were systematically despoiled; let them reduce the numbers of holy days, votive masses for the dead, mendicants, cardinals, idle officials, monastic Orders, excommunications, pilgrimages, and canonizations; let clergy answer to civil justice and pay the civil taxes, and let ecclesiastical litigation involving German nationals be conducted in Germany under a national primate.

The ·Pope should be made to give up all worldly pomp, pretensions, and concerns, to divest himself of tiara and kindred flummery; he should have his toe kissed no more, no more receive the sacrament seated, at the length of a golden reed held out by a kneeling cardinal, but stand up for it like any other "stinking sinner." Clerical celibacy must be abolished, education improved and extended; congregations must be given the right to appoint their own pastors. The mass should be purged of idolatrous concomitants, the canon law should be scrapped, the care of the poor should be overhauled and regularized; and while one was about it some sumptuary legislation should be passed. Add an embargo on traffic in money, close down the municipal brothels (run with town funds), tighten up on one or two things more, and the distance to universal salvation would be considerably diminished.

Luther seldom stopped short at the exact purport of his message, he was usually carried away into related though not always at first glance germane detail. Succinctness and tight tabulation were not among the shibboleths of letters in his day: the richer the pudding, the better it would go down; a book of any kind was a lasting possession which should repay endless dipping. Although Luther often took great pains in revising manuscript and reprints, cutting and rearranging hardly entered into this—the main objective being to ensure that no possible angle of illumination was omitted. Exhaustiveness, not compression, was the hallmark of literary clarity; and Luther was acknowledged a past-master at ringing the changes on his motifs.

By no means everything in his *Letter to the Nobility* was wholly new; but the sum added up to a revolutionary conclusion. The mediaeval axiom of the dual nature of society was denied, and the mediaeval unity of culture wherein all human pursuits were under the dictate of the Church was broken up. The implicit proposal for a wholesale social reorganization was of enormous interest to all classes besides the upper crust to whom it was inscribed, and whose thoughts turned at once to a thus justified secularization of the one third of all German territory which was still held absolutely in the hands of the Church. Luther was able to show Spalatin a collection of over thirty letters of appreciation from lords and magistrates all over the country. And he did not know, as we do, that Duke George of Saxony who went all out to get the book suppressed confided privately to a Roman correspondent, "What Luther writes is neither altogether untrue nor uncalled-for. In fact these matters need speaking out about and holding up to the light. If no one mentioned the evils in the Church, the very stones would cry out in the end."

Duke George was a staunch adherent to orthodox Catholicism and staunch hater of Luther; but he was a reigning German sovereign as well.

"God knows Christ commanded all the erudition in the world, but he concentrated above all on expressing himself with childlike simplicity to make sure that even the meanest intelligence could comprehend him. That's what I am after too. If anybody wants proof that I *can* do the other thing—let him come to me in class."

The people and the rulers having received their briefing, it was the turn of the theologians. In Latin now and with the requisite abstruseness, Luther proceeded to expound the basic theory of his case, for the experts.

He called this exposition *A Prelude on the Babylonian Captivity of the Church*—"prelude" because this was only a preliminary essay on the big trumpet that was to bring down the walls of Jericho, and "Babylonian captivity" because under the present circumstances all true Christians were in exile as the Jews at Babylon.

The authority of the Roman Catholic Church, he said, was built on the sacraments as the exclusive channel of grace and on the exclusive control of these by the clergy. The Church had become synonymous with the clergy; the congregation was not considered an integral part of it, merely an outside beneficiary and subject to it.

Cut down on the sacraments, and sacerdotalist dictatorship would be automatically eliminated. The only sacraments—that is visible, outward, ceremonial acts signifying spiritual grace—mentioned in the Bible were baptism and the Lord's Supper. The five which had been added since Biblical times—confirmation, marriage, ordination, penance, and extreme unction—were one and all purely social transactions, embellished with a pseudo-spiritual frill.

Take ordination. This was nothing more than enrolment of a person to the office of ministering priest—an office for which every baptized Christian was eligible and which did not change him in any way, but which had been given the spurious appearance of magically and indelibly transforming him into a special being, member of a caste apart which alone had access to the Deity.

"This is the source of that detestable tyranny over the laity by the clergy who, relying on the external anointing of their hands, the tonsure and the vestments, not only exalt themselves above lay Christians, but even regard them as so many dogs, unworthy to be included with them in the Church. . . . Here Christian brotherhood has expired and shepherds have become wolves. All of us who have been baptized are priests without exception, but those whom we call priests are ministers, chosen from among us that they should act in our name and behalf."

Baptism was the initiation of a person into the spiritual community, but confirmation and extreme unction were only assertions of spiritual control over him on the part of the clergy. Marriage was an affair of the flesh, which was the better for God's blessing, but could not be made in itself a means of grace. Penance, if it had to be said again, depended on inner contrition and could not be encompassed by external formula.

As for the Lord's Supper, this was not a magic but a mystic rite. Holy communion was not an act conferring grace, the mass was not a re-enactment of the crucifixion in which the priest made the Christ anew and then sacrificed him over again—for God is eternally omnipresent and Christ made his sacrifice once for all time. The rite constituted a symbolic manifestation, a repeatable revelation of that omnipresence and sacrifice, through the elements of food and drink; and to have any spiritual effect it required the active factor of faith in the recipient. It did not "take," like medicine or poison or a spell, regardless, as the Antichristian witch-doctors claimed, but necessitated the *experience* of participation.

The test of a sacrament was whether it had been instituted by Christ —who indeed had undergone baptism and had set the example of the Supper, sharing out the bread, "This is my body," and the wine, "This is my blood. Drink ye all of this." "All," in the orthodox interpretation, referred solely to the apostles who were priests of Christ; wherefore only the priesthood was permitted to drink the wine at the mass. Luther, like Hus before him, averred that all believers being priests they should all partake of the blood as they did of the body. The differentiation was entirely arbitrary and not of Christ.

The "erudite" treatise made a very different impact from its "simple" predecessors. Everyone who read it was thunderstruck. But to the Romanists it merely proved beyond the last lingering shadow of a doubt what they had instinctively suspected right from the beginning, long before ever this had dawned on Luther himself: that he was threatening to overthrow the whole Catholic system. To Luther's friends, sympathizers, and benevolent neutrals, however, this was news, and deeply shocking news to many of them. It alienated a great number of those who still looked for a peaceful regeneration within the existing, venerable framework.

The first impression almost everywhere was one of horror and revulsion. Johann Bugenhagen, then a young convert to Luther in Pomerania, was to remember throwing the book from him like a live coal; the Emperor's liberal-minded father confessor, who had as he said enjoyed Luther's work in the past, could not believe the same hand was responsible for *The Babylonian Captivity,* which made him feel as if he had been lashed from head to foot. Erasmus before he had finished reading exclaimed, "A split is now inevitable." Henry VIII in England was so upset that he immediately got some learned friends together with whose help he composed that fierce repudiation of Luther which earned for the King and all his successors to date the title of Defender of the Faith, bestowed in papal recognition of his championship.

The thing that so appalled the orthodox was not the proposed reduction of the sacraments, so much as Luther's denying that a sacrament had intrinsic virtue. According to Luther, no sacrament could save you unless you had faith, yet having faith you would be saved without any sacrament; to treat any act or substance whatsoever as autonomously carrying a spiritual effect was sheer paganism. For contrary believers this was insult to blasphemy.

The thing which so appalled the liberals was that this categorical statement of Luther's position placed it utterly beyond mediation. From merely resisting papal pretensions he had suddenly passed to setting up against Catholicism itself an entire, different, antagonistic concept of religion and religiosity.

However, there were some who changed their minds on second or third reading of the book. Young Bugenhagen (future city pastor of Wittenberg) for one suddenly felt "that the whole world has been blind till now," and others wrote to Luther in the same vein. Many saw in *The Babylonian Captivity* a salutary, clean break, a wholesome burning of boats. Others again succumbed to incurable human optimism: the very force of the blast might well frighten both Luther and the orthodox hierarchy into an eleventh-hour compromise. Among these optimists were an experienced psychologist: the Emperor's confessor, Father Glapion; a professional sceptic: Erasmus of Rotterdam; and that guileless Machiavellian, Karl von Miltitz.

＊

27. Joyeuse Entrée

As long as life goes on, the pendulum of bias will remain in motion; and the bias of conventional outlook swings rhythmically between the extremes of optimism and pessimism. It happens that our present age is favouring the latter, discounting the former with a pitying smile. But in truth neither viewpoint is any more unrealistic than the other. While there is life, anything is possible, with two particular exceptions: the golden mean and the normal person, ever-elusive ideal figments, both.

Anything could happen.

The Joyeuse Entrée of the Emperor elect into his Empire took place on 22 October 1520, a fine and sunny day. Charles was of an age with the century, being less than two months younger than it. He had suffered from ill-health through infancy and adolescence, and had developed commensurate nervous strength. His very notable horsemanship and almost excessive outward self-control were twin-indices of this. Apart from the material affluence in which he had been cradled, the formative influences of his young life were among the worst that modern pediatrics recognizes.

His mother was mad, showing progressively violent signs of insanity before ever he was weaned and sinking into hopeless alienation from the world before he was seven years old. His father died at the same time, having scarcely been acquainted with their six children (five of them born within six years of each other) as he was compelled to restless travels and campaigns ranging between Flanders, Spain, and Austria; while, their fruitful cohabitation notwithstanding, the parents' marital relations were bad—clamantly so. Charles was the second-born and first son; there was little normal sibling interchange in the family, as each child had its own small court and nurses. These baby-courts were not so much composed in the interests of the baby as in due consideration of the Habsburg international vassalage, and were accordingly alive with intrigue; nor were such noble infants expected to make do with anything so niggardly as one single mother substitute even during the suckling stage. The youngest was not born until after the father's death and the mother's complete mental collapse; and this child together with Charles' younger brother was brought up in Spain. The other four when they were to all intents and purposes orphaned in 1506 did then at last receive a stable foster-parent, in the shape of their paternal aunt the Archduchess Margaret of Austria, Emperor Maximilian's daughter whom he appointed regent for the Netherlands at the same time as he committed these grandchildren to her care.

Childless and twice-widowed by the age of twenty-four, Margaret was by the standards of any era a remarkable woman; equally charged with sensuous appeal (her first husband's death after six months of marriage was ascribed to over-indulgence in his connubial rights) and an intrepid temper and intelligence believed to be peculiarly associated with the masculine sex. She gave the children love and educative care as far as time and strenuous political duties permitted: even so she did not live with them in one and the same household, but had her own, modern palace built opposite the ancient ducal residence at Malines which had been allocated to Charles and his three sisters.

The dominant mentors of Charles' later boyhood were Adrian of Utrecht, rector of the University of Louvain, a theologian of great piety, and Guillaume de Croy, Lord of Chièvres, appointed governor and grand chamberlain to Charles at age nine, a Burgundian noble of great worldly wisdom, class-consciousness, and both flair and experience in high diplomacy. Charles particularly attached himself to the latter, on whom his adult persona was largely modelled, and who remained his chief minister and companion till Chièvres died of plague at Worms just after the first Diet of the new reign.

Charles was fortunate in that his closest advisers during the difficult period before, during, and after the imperial election were whole-heartedly devoted to his interests: not excluding his newly appointed confessor Glapion, a French Franciscan formerly in the service of the formerly Francophile Bishop of Liège. Otherwise the Emperor elect was surrounded, as was his whole existence surrounded, by rampant and importunate, multi-lateral self-interest whereby all the world was trying to get the better of him or, through him, of one another. The heir to the heterogeneous Habsburg dominions was no stranger to rebellion and chicane on the part of subject countries, or to the antagonism to his dynasty of other heads of state. He took all that for granted; it was all he knew; and he had early made up his mind to be guided by his conscience, his calling, and his religion—just like Luther. Like Luther, regarding earthly day-to-day developments, Charles would be surprised at practically nothing.

On the eve of his coronation at Aachen Charles' principal problems were a) making the right transition from currying favour with the German Electors to asserting his sacrosanct dignity over them, b) paving the way, his way, for a patently unavoidable clash with France in the none too distant future, c) resisting papal sanctions about to be applied against certain aspects of his rule in Spain and yet also paying his pledged devoirs to supreme apostolic authority—no mean assignment. By necessarily slow stages, he had made his way from Spain to Antwerp, where he had been entertained, if that be the word, by a concourse of conflicting embassies, all having to be held in balance.

His reception at the gateway to the Empire left nothing to be desired. The Electors met him outside Charlemagne's town and paid their homage, to which—impassive and attired in splendour as an idol—he replied through the Archbishop-Cardinal of Salzburg who was his vice-regent in Austria. He then entered Aachen in procession. First came the counts and lords of the Empire, preceded by troops of cavalry and followed by three hundred mercenary foot; then the town councillors of Aachen with their staffs of office and the Duke of Jülich as the regional sovereign with his own four hundred horsemen. Next, flanked by halberdiers and with the unmistakable Emperor riding in the middle, there came all the great magnates and dignitaries of the Empire, Austria, Spain, and Naples; courtiers, knights, soldiers, servants and other attendants to them all completed the magnificent train, scattering gold and silver to the cheering crowds that were doing the honours here for the German people.

In the evening Charles took the coronation oath in accordance with the terms of the *Wahlkapitulation* and early the next morning was anointed, robed, crowned and acclaimed Roman King in the cathedral, the Archbishop of Cologne officiating and Archduchess Margaret watching, proud and happy, the enthronement of her fosterling. Banquets and other ensuing festivities matched the occasion so that it should duly take a fabulous place in the folk-memory for generations to come. Then that halcyon, arrested moment of imperial ascent was over, and the whole substantial phantasmagoria removed bodily to the next stop on Charles V's inaugural progress along the Rhine—Cologne—to resume business as usual, in the standard, summit atmosphere of vertiginous insecurity. It was the element to which the pale, taut, over-propertied young Habsburg had been bred, and where he expected to disport himself with congenital resilience.

It would not have surprised the lowly friar Martin Luther of provincial Wittenberg to know how well-primed with information about his case was the greatest temporal sovereign in Christendom—but only because Martin Luther would not put anything past the power of God. It would have surprised him very much indeed to know that his case had become a fulcrum of international leverage, in the three months that it took the Bull *Exsurge, Domine* to come officially into his hands. But this, being quite outside *his* element, he never knew.

Five months before, in May, the Emperor elect had been notified by his ambassador to the Holy See, "Your Majesty must go to Germany and show some favour to a certain Martin Luther who is attached to the court of Saxony and whose preaching is causing concern at the Roman Curia." In September, therefore, when the Vatican librarian and special nuncio Aleander first arrived at the temporary imperial court in Antwerp with the mission of winning Charles' support for the Bull, Chièvres told him bluntly that one good turn deserved another. The point was that Pope Leo had been giving his support to demands in Spain that the Inquisition, which in that country had become a formidable secret weapon of secular despotism, be detached from crown service. Showing "some favour to a certain Martin Luther" was the Spanish crown's first concrete opportunity of counter-thrust.

At that time, too, it had been thought that the Curia by sending out two separate nuncios for the transmontane publication of the Bull was deliberately trying to stir up trouble in the Empire pour encourager l'Empereur. The choice of Eckius for the second of these, and his reception in the central German territory mapped out for him, lent some force to this theory. The three months' delay in lodging the Bull with Luther was the result of systematic obstruction of the German nuncio on the part of the universities and bishops on his list; not a few of them raised the objection that Eckius as an active participant in the dispute was the last person to have been entrusted with the task. Suddenly it looked as if the Ingolstadt professor was as unpopular in Germany as he had made himself with certain sections of the Holy See. The imperial court might be excused for inferring the poor man had been so unpopular all along, not only in the sensitive nostrils of a Cajetan; they held lives cheap, in Italy.

For Eckius' life was seriously threatened in many places where he wended his way. In Leipzig, where only last year he had been fêted almost like a prince, his appearance with the papal placards was greeted by such storm of hatred that he had to go into hiding—was it any wonder that Luther set no store, either way, by mob demonstrations? At Erfurt, too, where Luther had been persona non grata ever since he transferred his allegiance to Wittenberg, students and townsfolk staged a display of throwing copies of the placard into the river, amid shouts of, "It is a bubble (*bulla*): let's see if it will float!" At Torgau, where Eckius succeeded in having the Bull posted, every copy was torn down again and daubed with filth. But it was not only the fickle populace that behaved in this extraordinary manner; the appropriate authorities themselves were hardly any better. Only three bishops out of something like three dozen—those of Brandenburg, Merseburg, and Meissen—endorsed the publication of *Exsurge, Domine* in their respective residential towns; elsewhere procrastination alternated with refusal on a variety of technical pretexts. It was to be expected that the Elector of Saxony would forbid Eckius' entry for fear of civil disorders, but not that the Duke of Saxony and the Duke of Bavaria would—as they did—follow suit. The luckless nuncio, who must have felt the whole world had gone topsy turvy on him, on his eventual return to Ingolstadt erected a votive tablet in gratitude that he got home alive.

Yet surely the Curia would not have reckoned with, much less calculated for similar resistance to its very own Girolamo Aleandro (Hieronymus Aleander in the hellenist style), a former rector of the University of Paris and thus endowed with a double quantity of authoritative impact—? No.

Aleander had been allotted the Low Countries and the Rhineland, respectively outside and on the periphery of the German Empire proper, to address himself especially to the Emperor and the actual rulers of the commonwealth, besides, of course, publishing the Bull. The reason why this was considered necessary was that by this time Luther's *Sermon on Good Works* and *Letter to the German Nobility* (which with *The Babylonian Captivity,* yet in the making, were justly to become known as the Reformation Treatises) had been at last digested at the Curia. The Curia deduced that from appealing for a hearing to the Pope and to a future Council Luther would now press the same appeal, concerning his own case, upon secular authority. Indeed an "Appeal to Caesar," purposely echoing St. Paul, in Luther's hand was on the way—whether the Curia had advance intimations or merely a logical presentiment of this. In view of the German Gravamina, and seeing that whether he knew it or not Luther's most recent publications had furnished the evangelical movement with a doctrine and incipient tradition of its own, a transfer of his case under secular jurisdiction was an acute danger, to be prevented at all cost.

It was not to be supposed that the Emperor and the spiritual and temporal German princes would offer insult or violence to an Aleander as had the lesser strata to his lesser colleague. At Antwerp the Emperor—leaving the task of improving the occasion to Chièvres—met him graciously enough and authorized the burning of Luther's works, for which the Bull provided, in his, the Emperor's, personal dominions. The order was executed at Louvain and Liège before the imperial court crossed into Germany, and incidently just after *The Babylonian Captivity* had appeared there. But directly Aleander made to follow the court, he too encountered resistance and discourtesy to say the least. Suddenly there were no boats available to ferry him across the river Meuse; he nearly did not get to Aachen in time for the coronation. He was warned to guard against suspicious-looking knights: Hutten wished to kill him.

At Cologne worse awaited him. The humanists of that imperial city, a fraternity which had steadily gained in ebullience by the struggle against the Dominican "obscurantists," flooded the thronged venue with broadsheets in which Aleander was called the son of a Jew, an enemy of the arts and friend to sodomy, a toady and lickspittle, and to top all a mere puppet and mouthpiece of Inquisitor Hochstraaten who had surely forged *Exsurge, Domine*—a document so clumsy and brutal as to bear the stamp of darkest Cologne rather than urbane, enlightened

Rome. Then on top of that the Elector of Saxony flatly refused Aleander's request for an interview, and other princes cold-shouldered
him. Aleander sent for more money, which he explained was needed
for bribes, and meanwhile made another attempt upon the Saxon
Elector, whom he waylaid and bearded at mass—the worst approach
he could have chosen to the ear of that pious Catholic. (Aleander
testified to the Elector's firmness in orthodox faith, adding that, however,
the Elector's entourage were one and all more Lutheran than Luther.)

The Emperor himself proved less accessible to Aleander at Cologne.
There were rumours that through his confessor he was parleying with
Sickingen and Hutten. There were rumours, too, that the imperial
court believed the Holy See to be using the issue in an endeavour to
estrange Charles' Italian subjects from the Habsburg rule, that France
was trying to drive a wedge between Charles and Henry VIII whose
beautiful friendship was in full flower at the moment, and also that
the German princes were weighing the chances of a test case regarding
the *Wahlkapitulation* of their untried Emperor, before the latter's
requisitions went to the Estates at the Diet. Throughout, as a matter
of fact not rumour, the Cortes, Spain's equivalent assembly of Estates,
continued the negotiations with the Holy See about curtailing the
anomalous temporal activities of the Spanish Inquisition; the possibility
that the menace of the German heresy might come in useful, one way
or the other, also over there, was not to be ruled out.

The Emperor let the papal nuncio know that for the present he could
not see his way to promulgating the desired mandate of sequestration,
which must precede the burning of Luther's books in Germany, without
consulting the Diet. From the observer's point of view the situation at
Cologne—stuffed to bursting with lords, embassies, and agents of every
description—became daily more turgid and impenetrable, since wherever
one looked private colloquies were evidently carried on in constantly
changing combinations and permutations; so that nobody could rely today on anybody's yesterday's opinions, to say nothing of what might
not be put forward tomorrow. The most Aleander could do meanwhile
was to keep abreast, as far as possible, of what was going on within
and between the various groups, by bribing everyone in reach from
porters, pages, and secretaries upwards; and at the same time try to
convince each prince he could get hold of that all the others had already
pledged him their full co-operation. While they would scarcely take his

word for it, it helped to sow distrust among them: if you can't control confusion, aggravate it.

Elector Frederick the Wise had got the same idea. He played off Aleander against Eckius and Eckius against Aleander: copies of the initial Roman proclamation having circulated about Germany since mid-summer, and differing materially from the commissions of both nuncios, which moreover differed also from each other—who was the right nuncio and whose the valid instructions? Eckius' had nothing about burning Luther's books before the excommunication came into effect; Aleander's had nothing about Hutten, Melanchthon, and a number of south German humanists known to be bêtes noires of Eckius, all of whom were included in Eckius' rubric of prospective excommunication. In order to defend themselves against the charge of fraud, both men were forced to reveal that they had indeed received different, secret instructions, without each other's knowledge. Speculation as to what the Holy See thought it was about ran higher than ever: although most probably a plain failure of co-ordination was the cause of the disparity. Never mind, Elector Frederick had two further aces up his voluminous, slashed, fur-edged sleeve: the Archbishop-Elector of Trier and yet another papal nuncio—who else but Miltitz?

Last year, through the offices and with the papally accredited authority of Miltitz, the Archbishop of Trier had been approached, and had agreed, to act as chairman of a commission of German ecclesiastics which should thoroughly examine Luther in compliance with the latter's unremitting plea. Having agreed, the Archbishop who was not only a fellow-Elector but also a good friend of Frederick the Wise, was still waiting to form his commission: it would be unforgivably rude and likely to have the gravest consequences to go over his head without so much as a pretence of deferring to him. As for Miltitz, he had never been recalled and Elector Frederick had remained in touch with him all these dragging months: nothing Elector Frederick had done or omitted to do with regard to Luther but had been done or omitted on the advice of Miltitz, papal nuncio. Why, even at this moment the good Miltitz was engaged in another passage of mediation between Dr. Luther and Pope Leo—having first sought out Eckius and told him just what he thought of him, for coming along with his bull and without any by your leave to ruin Miltitz's fine-spun scheme on the brink of its completion. . . .

It was all true, every word of it—as far as it went.

The Babylonian Captivity had come out, first of all at Wittenberg, on 6 October. On 10 October Eckius' special courier had got through to Wittenberg with the official copy of the Bull for Luther.

"This bull condemns Christ himself," Luther announced as he sent it on for Spalatin's perusal. "I am going to act on the assumption that it must be spurious, though I think it is genuine all right."

His reply was already drafted.

"I have heard that the bull against me wandered all over the earth before it came to me, because being a daughter of darkness it feared the light of my face. For this reason and also because it condemns manifestly Christian articles I had my doubts all along whether it really came from Rome and was not rather the offspring of that man of lies, hypocrisy, errors, and heresy, that monster Johann Eck. The suspicion was strengthened when it became known that Eck was the apostle of the bull. Indeed the style and the spittle are Eck's to the life. True, it is not unlikely that where Eck is the apostle there one should find the kingdom of Antichrist. Nevertheless until further notice I will act as though I thought Leo was not responsible—not I hasten to say because I honour the name of Rome, but because I do not consider myself worthy to suffer martyrdom for the truth of God. The cause seeks a worthier martyr. But whoever wrote this bull, he is Antichrist. I protest before God, our Lord Jesus, his sacred angels, and the whole world that with all my heart I repudiate the condemnation of this bull, that I curse and execrate it as sacrilege and blasphemy. This be my recantation.

". . . This bull condemns me on its own authority without any proof from Scripture, whereas I draw all my assertions from the Bible. I ask thee, ignorant Antichrist, dost thou think that with thy naked word thou canst prevail against the armour of Scripture? If this were all it takes, just to say, 'You are wrong because I say so,' what idiot, what ass, what mole, what log of wood would not have power to condemn? The Turks say we are wrong. The Jews say we are wrong. The heretics say we are wrong. So be it. I can distinguish between a mindless piece of paper and the omnipotent Word of God.

"They show their ignorance and bad conscience by their use of the word 'respectively.' My articles are called, '*respectively* some heretical, some erroneous, some scandalous,' as much as to say, 'We don't know which are what,' though they are all condemned together. Well, I wish to be instructed, not respectively, but absolutely and definitely. I demand that they show absolutely, not respectively, distinctly and not confusedly, certainly and not probably, clearly and not obscurely, point by point and not in a bunch, just what is heretical. Let them show where I am a heretic, or dry up. . . . Whether this bull is by Eck or by the Pope, it is the sum of impiety, blasphemy, ignorance, impudence, hypocrisy, lying—in a word, it is Satan and Antichrist.

" . . . You then, Leo X, and you, cardinals, and everyone else who amounts to anything at the Curia: I challenge you and say to your faces, if this bull has in truth gone forth in your name and with your knowledge, I warn you, in virtue of the power which I, like all Christians, have received through baptism, to repent and leave off such Satanic blasphemies, and that right quickly. Unless you do this, know that I, with all who worship Christ, shall consider the See of Rome to be occupied by Satan and to be the throne of Antichrist, and that I will no longer obey nor remain united to him, the chief and deadly foe of Christ. If you persist in your fury, I condemn you to Satan, together with this bull and your decretals. . . . But I forget myself. As I said, I am not yet persuaded that the bull is by the Pope.

" . . . As they excommunicate me for the sacrilege of heresy, so do I excommunicate them in the name of the sacred truth of God. Christ will judge whose excommunication will stand. Amen."

It was ready for press, under the title *Against the Execrable Bull of Antichrist;* but his hand was stayed. Elector Frederick, in renewed communication with Miltitz as indicated, on the eve of departing for Aachen to meet the new Emperor had arranged another conference of Luther and "Herr Karl."

So the two men renewed their acquaintance, at a little place called Lichtenberg midway between Wittenberg and Leipzig (where Miltitz had been attending the Michaelmas Fair and incidentally demolished Eckius—so he said—face to face). If Luther would write a little peace offering for the Holy Father, Miltitz suggested, he would himself take it to Rome and arrange that Eckius got the same treatment as Tetzel before him, plus all the blame for the harsh words lately exchanged between Rome and Wittenberg.

One does not know whether to laugh or cry. Traditionally, again, the laughter is all at Miltitz's expense: that he should have been so naïve. But Elector Frederick the Wise also deemed it a good plan, and Luther—Martin Luther obediently wrote within the next thirty-six hours what *he* deemed the desired dulcet serenade, entitled *Canticle on the Freedom of the Christian.*

"Most blessed father," ran the prefatory address, to the putative author of the "Bull of Antichrist,"—"Most blessed father, in all the controversies of the past three years I have ever been mindful of you, and although your adulators have driven me to appeal to a Council in defiance of the futile decrees of your predecessors Pius and Julius, I have never allowed myself because of their dictatorial stupidity to bear resentment to Your Beatitude. To be sure, I have spoken harshly against impious doctrine, but did not Christ call his adversaries a generation of vipers? Who could have been more biting than the Prophets? I contend with no one about his life, but only about the Word of Truth. I look upon you less as Leo the Lion than as Daniel in the lion's den of Babylon. . . . The Roman Curia deserves not you but Satan himself. . . . But do not think, Father Leo, that when I castigate that seat of pestilence I am inveighing against your person. Beware of the sirens who would make you not a man but half a god. You are a servant of servants. Do not listen to those who say that none can be Christians save by your authority, who make you lord of heaven, hell, and purgatory. They err who put you above a Council and above the Universal Church. They err who make you the sole interpreter of Scripture. I am sending you a tract as an earnest of peace, that you may see the sort of thing with which I could and would more fruitfully occupy myself if your adulators would leave me alone."

It was a measure of how far Luther had come up in the world, that Miltitz professed himself delighted with this specimen of conciliatory composition. This and the tract itself, he said, were exactly what was wanted; the only other thing he, Miltitz, needed now was money—"for without money one cannot travel to Rome, and without money presents one cannot accomplish anything in Rome."

The tract was a restatement for the Pope's especial benefit of the Theology of Justification by Faith together with its ethical implications. It had been claimed against Luther that by denying the meritorious effect of goodness he was destroying all incentive to virtue and setting morality at naught. The *Canticle* was designed to disprove the accusation.

While perfect obedience to God's commandments is beyond mere human beings—Luther said—it does not follow that we should not try at all. All men are sinners, but they are not therefore all evil-doers. "Temptation cannot be avoided: but because we cannot prevent the birds from flying over our heads, there is still no reason why we should let them nest in our hair." Yet, in trying to be good and refusing to let temptation come to roost, man willy-nilly sins again, avoiding sin for selfish reasons as he does. There is, then, no end to sinning save in God, and no true goodness save what comes from God. This it is necessary to recognize. But then, is it not, "wonderful news to believe that salvation lies outside ourselves?" For thus salvation at one stroke ceases to be inattainable. "I am justified and acceptable to God —*even though* there are in me sin, unrighteousness, and fear of death. I have to look beyond my self to see no sin," to understand that righteousness does exist, dwelling in the fount of good if not in the muddy trough that receives the outflow. "No good work can be within the soul, unless the Word and faith reign there. . . . Plainly then faith is enough for the Christian. He has no need for works to be made just. But he is not therefore to be lazy or loose. *Good works do not make a man good, but a good man does good works.*"

But directly good works are adduced as grounds for justification, they are no longer good, but foolish, idle, damnable sins. "Understand that we do not reject good works, but praise them highly. The Apostle Paul said, 'Let this mind be in you which was also in Christ Jesus, who being on an equality with God emptied himself, taking the form of a servant, and becoming obedient unto death.' Paul means that when Christ was fully in the form of God, abounding in salvation so that he had no need of any work or any suffering to become saved, he was not puffed up, did not bask in his fullness of virtue and power, but rather in suffering, working, and dying made himself like unto men, just as though he needed salvation and were not in the form of God. All this he did to serve us. . . . Shall I not then freely, joyously, whole-heartedly do everything that I know will please him? I will give myself as a sort of Christ to my neighbour as Christ gave himself for me. . . . I must even take to myself the sins of others as Christ took my sins to himself. . . . By faith the Christian rises above himself to God and from God falls below himself in love, and thus remains always in God and love."

By doing good without taking credit for it and by sharing willingly in the discredit of sins one has not personally committed—thus alone shall we become enveloped in Christ-like, Christian righteousness.

Dashed off to order but yet a labour of love, Luther's *Canticle on the Freedom of the Christian* was perhaps the best thing he ever wrote. It was to the Lutheran ideology what the Sermon on the Mount was to the teaching of Jesus: the kernel of humanitarian religion, reproduced in a contemporary nutshell. It comprised the triumphant reconciliation of goodness and no-goodness, preternatural justice and natural iniquity, action and determinism, homogenizing despair and hope, forging a spiral of achievement out of a vicious circle. It was the crowning answer to the quest of his tormented youth, the rounded burden of his message: if his life had ended next day, it would not have been short of ripeness.

Only, the Pope never saw the pamphlet or the letter. October 10 to 9 December makes sixty days: Luther met Miltitz 11 October and parted from him on the thirteenth, all to give the dove of peace time to make presentation of the olive branch before the period of grace laid down in the Bull should expire. At the end of November Miltitz was still in Germany. He was still there in the new year. We do not know what happened; whether or no Elector Frederick failed to supply him with "enough minted images" of himself "for the young cardinals in Rome" as requested—Miltitz did not say.

But Luther had the whole lot printed in November, anyhow— *Against the Execrable Bull of Antichrist* and *On the Freedom of the Christian,* kindly letter and all, as usual first in Latin, then in German. The Pope could have read the offering after that; it was available. By then *The Babylonian Captivity* had done its worst—and much, much water had gone down the Rhine, at Cologne.

Surely Luther was enjoying himself then—though we none of us like to be told that we enjoy moments of high tension, overwork, and pregnancy. Most certainly Elector Frederick the Wise enjoyed himself at Cologne.

His stonewalling tactics were fortified by three factors: the Emperor's father confessor, Erasmus of Rotterdam, and gout.

Father Glapion, for reasons which appear beyond analysis, was working for the greater glory of the Emperor. Whether he were, as variously he professed to be, a champion of ecclesiastical reformation along Erasmian-humanist lines, of political reformation in Germany along nationalist-radical lines, as well as a rigid opponent of secular jurisdiction in the context of inter-ecclesiastical matters—all his efforts before and during the Diet of Worms permit of no other single explanation than that Glapion meant the decision, the power, and the credit for settling the Luther affair to go to Charles himself. The general impression afterwards was that he told everybody what they would like to hear and also what a wonderful person was the promising young Emperor—in such a way that everyone concluded Glapion spoke directly for the Emperor. Thus, while scarcely arresting the growth of confusion at Cologne, Glapion injected into it a spreading balm of feasible concord. He has been accused of ambition and duplicity—but there are ambitions and ambitions, and duplicity in politics is unavoidable. Perhaps he really liked and believed in Charles. Perhaps he believed, as Charles did himself, from the heart, in the ideal of universal monarchy.

Why?

Why not? The obvious motive is not necessarily a feint. Like Elector Frederick, Glapion wrote letters and reports when needed but nowhere set down his private thought processes. At all events, he was perfectly open about the blow to his hopes, of *The Babylonian Captivity*. When, therefore, he rallied and gave equal publicity to a belief that the horrifying treatise had in fact increased the hope of an agreement—in that now Luther would only need to withdraw this one piece to be welcomed by the Church as its reformer—Glapion appreciably toned down the effect of the piece at Cologne.

The shock of *The Babylonian Captivity* to Erasmus was greater, since in him disapproval was laced with chagrin: already the malicious mot was making the rounds, that "Erasmus laid the egg which Luther hatched."

Not even Luther could be more irritated to have their names coupled in such complicity. At the very best their mutual approbation, latterly, had been guarded—expedient rather than cordial. For Luther, moderation was of its essence equivocal and craven; for Erasmus, the want of it bespoke a crippled intellect. How then could they two love each other? The times had made them comrades-in-arms, perforce, but hardly wedded partners. To be so represented was too much.

But before Erasmus could declare a divorce, the common enemy of himself and Martin Luther made him think better of it. Cock-a-hoop with the success of Aleander in Flanders, the Dominican authorities of Louvain, where Erasmus happened to be living at the time, followed up the burning of Luther's books with a minor campaign to make the place too hot also for Erasmus. Like many a caustic satirist, Erasmus was himself very thin-skinned; also, the celebrated vision which enabled him to see, not merely two sides of a question but all round it, clearly showed that this was not the moment for a breach of front. When he came to Cologne to lend his name and brain to the party of Catholic moderators, he waited on the Elector of Saxony who, against the consultation fee of a damask gown, asked for the great little man's opinion as to Luther's case.

Erasmus (in Spalatin's recounting) hemmed and hawed at first, then smacked his lips, and abruptly intoned, "Luther has committed two great sins." Pause; consternation. "He has hit the Pope in his crown and the monks in their bellies."

"But," Erasmus continued, joking apart, "the basic cause of the persecution of Luther is the diehards' jealous hatred of sound learning. There is not an honest man among the persecutors. The savage language of the bull certainly does not sound like Leo. All decent, thinking men are up in arms against the deplorable screed. Papal bulls are heavy-calibre instruments, but educated persons attach more weight to arguments drawn from the divine Scripture which does not coerce but instructs. One notes that out of all the universities in Christendom only two have condemned Luther—and have only condemned, not refuted him. I applaud Luther's consistent request to be heard by a commission of impartial experts; even in the Pope's own interests this should be granted."

Nobody could say fairer than that. What was more, Erasmus gave it in writing—jotting down the main heads of the judgment on a piece of paper which he handed to Spalatin as a token of esteem, free of charge. The faculty of detachment, of which Luther thought so little, had its uses—enabling Erasmus as it did to give so eminently fair a verdict. Armed with this, Elector Frederick now felt morally secure in his position, and proceeded fully to earn the new by-name coined for him by Aleander, "the Saxon fox."

Erasmus, whose delicate constitution demanded careful treatment (he could not bear the closed stoves common in Germany but had to have an open fire; he could not bear beer but had to have wine, and not Rhenish wine but only Burgundy; he could not bear fish but must have meat—"My heart is Catholic but my stomach is Lutheran," he would say ruefully when later this became apt)—Erasmus had rather better quarters, at the home of a noble patron, than the Saxon

Elector, who was laid up in a small, dark, frugal hotel, with one leg hugely padded in balsam-tinctured wrappings. His gout had come back. But here, now, in hectic Cologne, it was to his advantage to be virtually immobilized. It placed the onus of canvassing upon others, underlined his reserve with a suggestive physical setting. He did not need to speak personally with anyone he did not wish to see. His councillors went hither and thither—among other errands posting up all over the town printed placards of Luther's *Offer and Protest,* his "Appeal to Caesar" for a fair hearing, which Erasmus had approved.

From his dingy sick-room the senior Elector, courtesy-uncle of the Empire and vice-regent, then pressed renewed representations on the Emperor, mentioning by the way as one patrician to another how contumeliously he had himself been threatened and ordered about by such glorified couriers as Cajetan, Eckius, Aleander, not to mention Tetzel in his day; with the final result that in a private audience on 4 November Charles promised verbally "to grant the monk the lawful course to which he has offered himself, and not to condemn him un-tried."

Although written confirmation of this had yet to follow, on 6 November the Elector politely told Aleander through his councillors, as we would say, to go to hell, and the day after had himself borne off to Wittenberg, there to recuperate for January's Diet.

On 28 November the Emperor wrote: "Beloved Uncle Frederick, We are desirous that you should bring Martin Luther to the Diet to be held at Worms, that there he may be thoroughly examined by competent persons, in order that no injustice may be done nor anything contrary to law."

But between 7 and 28 November, on the 12th to be precise, Aleander staged a burning of Lutheran books at Cologne. As he had bragged in one of his earlier despatches from Louvain: "The Emperor and his ministers saw the bonfire go up ere they rightly realized that they had granted me the mandate."

In contrast to such cagey folk as Father Glapion and Elector Frederick, this plenipotentiary of the Holy See expressed himself so frankly, dotting every shifty i and crossing every discreditable t in his bulky correspondence of 1520–21, that one feels almost guilty to read what assuredly was not meant for the eyes of posterity.

✳

28. "My Best Day's Work"

There was a great deal that Frederick the Wise had kept from "his Herr Doctor" in the course of the year 1520—notably the several repeated attempts to bowl him over by freshly angled curial shock-tactics before the Emperor's advent—because he was aware he could no longer control the man. Perhaps the Elector managed to rise to such heights of foxiness because he had been limbering up at home. To him it might be fairly obvious that the Holy See would have preferred to get the whole thing over and done with, settled well and truly out of court, *without* a bull, and that therefore Luther's chances were improved if he refrained from any further provocative acts in the meantime; but he now knew Luther well enough to apprehend that Luther would have thought it utterly wrong to sit on one's indignation, however politic that might be.

So the Elector had kept quiet about sundry démarches of that sort, which in the event had petered out against the old fox's consistent, would-be obtuse stalling; and also about such interesting bits of gossip as that on first receiving Luther's *Offer and Protest* (in which Luther, naturally, addressed the great Emperor personally just as he did the greater Pope), Charles V's consummate composure had broken down, enough to throw the paper on the ground and trample on it. Spalatin was too loyal to betray what should not be passed on; his loyalty to Luther was amply exercised in working for him all he could.

Nobody had told Luther, either, that his books had been burnt already at Louvain and Liège, in the Emperor's dominions albeit outside the Empire; though if he had thought about it at all he must have surmised, correctly, that token specimens of his writings had been burnt in Rome as soon as *Exsurge, Domine* was published there, in June.

But when the Emperor's invitation came in at Wittenberg, it did so at the same time as the news that no sooner had Elector Frederick's back been turned than Aleander had got his bonfire at Cologne and subsequently at Mainz on the very date of the Emperor's letter. The Elector was beside himself with rage. Now it could be told; the news from Louvain and Liège was all over Germany too.

> "O God, Luther's books they burn,
>   Whereby thy godly truth they spurn,"

Ulrich von Hutten added to his recent German tract in verse, entitled *A Remonstrance and a Warning against the Presumptuous, Unchristian Power of the Bishop of Rome and the Unspiritual Spiritual Estate.*

> "He who for the truth will stand
>   With bans is hounded from the land.*
>   This is not godly and not right.
>   He who against it will not fight
>   Will be with God in dire disgrace.
>   I warn him of his evil case."

and,

> "To Martin Luther wrong is done—
>   O God, be thou our champion.
>   My goods for him I will not spare,
>   My life, my blood for him I dare."

This gives some indication of the effect upon Luther himself. The Elector might feel piqued and fooled (the more as the very person he had thought he had outflanked had thus stolen a march on him)—but Luther and his God, they were the victims.

Because of Luther, later generations would become unable to appreciate the enormity of the deed, to him: to us, what are a few books? and at that only token copies, of only some of them. Because of him, such gestures would lose their force, redounding more to the discredit

---

* Translation by Roland H. Bainton.

of the perpetrators than to the hurt of the victim. But when it happened to Luther, the shame and the horror of it were yet as burning as fire itself: quite apart from the fact that if after that one still did not give in, flesh and blood would soon follow the paper. Burnt, disgraced, desecrated, by the public hangman.

The Bull had been bad enough, but this was injustice on another plane, with breach of faith thrown in. Luther had just written another pamphlet, *Ground and Reason for All the Articles Wrongly Condemned by the Roman Bull:* "I was wrong, I admit it, when I said that indulgences were 'the pious defrauding of the faithful.' I recant and I say, 'Indulgences are the most impious frauds and impositions of the most rascally pontiffs, by which they deceive the souls and destroy the welfare of the faithful.' . . . I was wrong to make any reservations about Johann Hus. I say now that he and all his articles were condemned by Antichrist and his apostles in the synagogue of Satan." Spalatin and the Elector had not seen it so far; but now—publish! go on, publish it immediately, said the Elector.

But there must be something more one could do, some stronger form of retaliation; it irked Luther still to be fighting merely with the pen when the enemy was using the torch. The proof of crime, in the popular mind, is in the execution of the criminal; let his pamphlets be never so widely read, for every one who read and understood his arguments there were yet thousands in whose eyes the flaming action of the papal nuncio carried the last word. Luther between the four walls of his cell confided to Spalatin that he had a good mind to give Rome tit for tat. Spalatin reported back to the castle, and again there was instant response: go ahead, go right ahead and burn the papal decretals, the canon law and what you will! said the Elector.

This time it was Luther who held back. The old fox in his layman's innocence did not quite know what he was saying. Though being so remarkably accomplished in maintaining a complete mental separation of Roman perfidy from Roman spiritual supremacy, of politics from religion, personal honour from impersonal disingenuousness, ideal probity from obligatory opportunism, Frederick the Wise evidently did not see the difference between attacking the papacy and abnegating the canon law.

The papacy was the executive of the Universal Church and as such had been attacked often enough throughout the Middle Ages—as had particular decretals. But the canon law *was* the Church as it then

existed; more than that, the whole existing social system was founded
on that ecclesiastical framework. Canon law was not only valid in civil
law but frequently overlapped with it, frequently indeed prescribing
it. To assail the canon law was to assail the accepted order of the
Western world, no less. And then, too, the canon law was by papal
definition sacrosanct—never mind if Luther had already denied this:
who is there that will even walk under a ladder without some little
tensing of mind and muscle, though disclaiming any superstition? Till
Luther did it, the thing was unthinkable. The usually over-prudent
Elector, temporarily doped with wrath, could not have been thinking.

Oh, Luther did it; he had to. He had to counter deed with deed
and put Truth to the public test of trial by ordeal. Till then, inside
him the echo was never stilled, of his enemies' refrain: "Is everybody
wrong except you?" Till then there would always be the possibility
that Antichrist reigned with impunity because he was not Antichrist
after all. In which case Luther was damned and all who had hearkened
to his voice would be damned with him.

He waited until the sixty days' grace was fully up. Then he told
Melanchthon, and Melanchthon was all with him. Only three weeks
married, Melanchthon went out loyally before sunrise on 10 December and put up the following notice on the door of the parish church:
"Whoever cleaves to the truth of the gospel, let him come at nine
o'clock to the chapel of the Holy Cross outside the walls, where
according to ancient and apostolic usage the impious books of papal
law and scholastic theology will be burned inasmuch as the presumption
of the enemies of the gospel has advanced to such a degree that they
have cast the godly, evangelical books of Luther into the fire. Let all
earnest students, therefore, attend the pious spectacle, for it is now
the time when Antichrist must be exposed."

At the last minute they found that they had not got all the
necessary books as advertised: the canon law and decretals were one
thing, but such works as Aquinas' *Summa,* Lombard's *Sentences,* and
Scotus' *Commentary* were valuable encyclopaedias, which the Augustinian cloister library could ill afford to lose. It was past eight o'clock
when Luther sent his famulus Agricola rushing round the town to ask
various likely university colleagues to let him have their copies, but
they would not either. Between them all they raked up what they
could of books by Luther's opponents over the past three years, that
the holocaust should not look too meagre. They had got four folios

and some dozen smaller books; Agricola suggested one might as well add the printed copy of the Bull *Exsurge, Domine* which was to hand and which nobody wanted anyway.

The friends of the gospel assembled at the Augustinian monastery, in gratifying strength: the professors of the university, and most of the friars. They were joined outside by a body of students and people from the town. So, bearing faggots and torches, they marched in procession to the Elster Gate, beyond which, by the river strand, the Holy Cross marked the area of "spectacles" including executions, with the carrion-pit conveniently near.

Here "a not unknown master of arts," as Agricola, who described the scene, modestly designated himself, made up the pyre and set light to it. As soon as the fire was well away, the same not-unknown fed in the books—first the four great, heavy ones and then the smaller. Luther stood alone, praying silently; very pale, the witnesses remarked, and noticeably trembling at the last. When all the other volumes had been piled on and began to burn he stepped forward and himself added one more booklet—mumbling, so that only those standing closest to him could hear and give him Amen: *"Quoniam tu conturbasti veritatem Dei, conturbet te hodie Dominus in ignem istum,* Because thou hast brought down the truth of God, may the Lord today bring thee down unto this fire!"

The fire burnt well, and there was no thunderbolt nor other heavenly sign that the offering was not acceptable.

Luther pulled himself together and went straight home. The professors and friars went with him. The whole business had taken only a few minutes. But the students made a little more of it. First they sang *Te Deum* and *De profundis,* then fife and drum came out of concealment and headed a raucous, prancing parade back to Wittenberg, where the chanting and shouting and triumphal buffoonery went on for some time longer, with such jolly improvisations as an indulgence skewered on a sword and a six-foot representation of *Exsurge, Domine* dragged through the streets at the end of a pole, by dung-cart. As a climax, the derided objects were ceremoniously burnt. Students would be students. It was not yet known that the booklet Luther had cast into the fire was a real copy of the Bull. Not that that mattered; bulls had been burnt before. The Hussites had done it, Savonarola had done it. No one had ever touched the canon law, the "Alcoran of Antichrist," till Luther did it.

Once it was done, the weight was off his chest. What had needed to be done, had been done; God had let him find the right way to do it. No other action of his in the line of battle so completely satisfied him, all his days. It was the only one with which he did not feel sooner or later that it could have been done better—that he ought to have gone farther, or else not so far: his only coup that would survive a lifetime of post mortems without any holes picked in it by the self-dissector— "The best day's work I ever did," to the end.

Of course he realized there would be repercussions, grave ones. His heart was light—but hardly buoyant with euphoria such as the Elector evinced when he wrote asking the Emperor to overlook Luther's little escapade as Dr. Martin had acted under severe provocation.

Dr. Martin's first step the next day was to curb the light-heartedness of the students, four hundred of them packed into the lecture hall to cheer him to the echo. Gravely, prefacing his customary Latin discourse with a speech in German, he bade them not to mistake yesterday's event for an exhibitionist stunt on a par with an indulgence seller's antics. To act as he had done was the only way of showing the world by one simple, comprehensive demonstration that the Antichrist and his servitors were false and impotent. He had had no choice. But they, too, had only one choice—between hell and martyrdom, the only alternatives. They must either harden their hearts in short-term cowardice or summon the courage to be faithful unto death. He personally had no doubt that the papacy would burn them, every one of its opponents, without succour.

Students would be students: their spirits were not greatly dampened by the homily. Curia, kings, and martyrdom were far away.

Students would be students, the world over. Had Luther, had the Elector, had Aleander known it, in Louvain where the first book-burning had been staged the students had contrived to fob off the hangman with a bundle of scholastic textbooks and old sermons in place of the condemned works of Luther. The hangman could not read.

The hangman of Cologne could not read either, but he was well-primed. He refused to act without an imperial order, in writing. He was at the time surrounded by a mob (of mostly students) threatening to stone him if he lit the pyre. The Archbishop-Elector of Cologne asserted his authority and next day the hangman did as he was told—but again a substitution had been effected, and what he actually burnt was a mixture of orthodox and anti-Lutheran literature and waste paper.

The hangman of Mainz was educated. Torch poised, he turned to the assembled onlookers (students?) and asked, "Have these books been legally condemned?"

"No!" roared the crowd.

"In that case," said the good man, "I cannot burn them," doused his torch and stepped down.

Aleander stormed into the presence of Archbishop Albrecht and demanded a seal of authorization. With this, an unlettered and un-coached sexton was procured to do the job, at an hour when the market place was deserted but for a handful of old women bringing geese for sale, and God knows what he burned, except that it was not any book of Luther's.

But this transpired later. Luther, the Elector, Aleander, and the general public had no inkling of it when it happened; so that in practice as well as intention it made little odds. It could never be more than a private, ironic satisfaction, all things considered. And all the world were not wild and merry university students.

29. Perpetuum Mobile

The deed flashed through the Empire, appropriately, like wildfire. Signal by beacon, it seemed, was yet swifter and surer than print. The ten-minute action on the stand outside the Elster Gate spoke louder and carried yet farther than the words of even best-selling treatises and polemics. How right Luther had been. There was not now a single corner of the realm or one single stratum of imagination, where the issue did not suddenly stand forth illuminated.

"Una cosa grande," the haughty Venetian ambassador at the imperial court wrote with respect, "A prodigious event, the importance of which cannot be over-estimated."

"One hears of nothing but what has happened in Wittenberg," the Nuremberg jurist and humanist Christopher Scheurl, formerly rector of the Leucorea, informed his old colleagues. "Now either the Roman or the Saxon front will have to give."

Among his fellow-liberals there was not much doubt which front that would be; several other prominent Nurembergers in particular, who had previously given Eckius pungent cause to have their names included in his version of the Bull, hastened to make peace overtures to the papacy through him. Reuchlin, to the disgust of his recent paladins Sickingen and Hutten, took shelter under Eckius' roof in Ingolstadt. Hutten indeed was about the only outstanding humanist writer who exulted ringingly at what Luther had now done. Erasmus dissociated himself and decamped from the Empire, and all over Europe others followed suit, severing relations with Wittenberg. In Wittenberg itself some of the elder members of the university, especially in the two law faculties, denounced "the arrogance of the mangy monk"—all at once he was that again.

To do them justice, discretion was not all at the expense of valour but was backed in most of them by genuine distaste and disappointment. Luther's crude, uncouth, ugly prank, as they saw it, was a slap in the face of moderation, showing him up a hopeless extremist who must be written off as an assistant to reform. They could no longer go along with him intellectually, so why should they risk reputation and life with him? Besides, not all men are made of martyr's stuff—as Erasmus for one had the courage to say straight out.

At the courts of the landed nobility and in the municipal council chambers, where tastes were less fastidious and both piety and logical prescience were less incisive, there nevertheless was also considerable recoil. The shades of Hus and Hussite war loomed large.

The radical knighthood were sure to see and snatch at the analogy. They did, and lost very little time. It could not long remain a secret that Hutten and Sickingen had got on to Luther again, with a plan to kidnap the papal nuncio on his way to the Diet and win the senior Elector for a coup d'état which with his support must certainly succeed. Luther owned to Spalatin that he was gratified by the proposal: but temptation was all he needed to make him stand firm once more. "By the Word of God, not by the fist," he repeated, "will Antichrist be destroyed. Rebellion is never right, no matter how just the cause. Moreover, the innocent generally suffer by it more than the guilty, and it generally makes worse what it would improve." (But he regretted later on that he had declined, as far as keeping Aleander from the Diet was concerned.)

None would accuse him of cowardice, who had exposed himself to divine vengeance at the Elster Gate and declined all armed protection against the earthly power he had excommunicated for his part.

That God had not struck him down and that the Pope still had not pronounced the final ban, much less burned him, formed a more widely effective argument for his truth than his conscientious explanation, *Why the Books of the Pope and his Disciples Were Burned.* Herein he showed again that the canon law constituted the same, externalized religious legalism which Jesus had fought and that the portion of the codex known as the decretals served no better purpose than consolidating the supreme power of the bishopric of Rome on a pinnacle of feudal totalitarianism. For not only did the "courtesans" (Hutten's catchy name for the officials of the papal court) demand recognition of the Pope as lord of the earth, they had even worked it out that he was no ordinary man but "in some way [sic] like a god on earth." As the representative of Christ, the curialists upheld, the Pope was above the angels and the Mother of God and therefore entitled to religious veneration though not to worship—nice distinction. Luther's researches had turned up a lovely find, in a gloss to the Augustinian library edition of the decretals which granted to the Pope the actual title of *Dominus deus,* lord god.

Luther needed all he could get in the way of tonic. He was suffering from reaction, once again, and thankful for anything to keep him busy. The delusive, post-orgastic tranquillity had evaporated into his more normal moods, fluctuating between aggressive afflatus and apocalyptic premonitions. He had been all screwed up to meet destruction, either by fire from heaven or fire of faggots; and here he was still—back, pretty well, where he had been before. The top-level tussle about how to deal with him had started all over again.

At the top and at the bottom, the horror of his deed did not prove so conducive to flurry and paralysis as among the intermediate sections. Up above, the principalities and powers—the imperial court, the Curia, the Electors—faced the fact that the one-time esoteric monkish squabble had finally attained priority status on the business agenda; down below, to the mass of the commonalty, the monkish author had acquired all the style and radiance of heroic stature. Insofar as he had some inkling of this, he ought to have been pleased.

He was sad. Staupitz had deserted.

Throughout the negotiations, both before and after Luther's bonfire, pressure from Rome remained unflagging to make Luther abjure the pestilent views which had so contaminated the Empire and its environs that before ever the Diet opened Charles V passed an ordinance prohibiting any discussion of ecclesiastical law at the forthcoming sessions; and Staupitz was one of the channels through which it was attempted to exert pressure. Worn out with it, Staupitz retired altogether from the Augustinian Order and sought quiescent anonymity in the ranks of the Dominicans of Salzburg—old and experienced enough though he was, to know better.

"Don't forsake me!" Luther entreated. "I cry for you like a weaned child for its mother. I beseech you praise the Lord even in me a sinner. Last night I dreamed of you. I thought you were leaving me, and as I was weeping and lamenting most bitterly, you waved your hand and told me to be quiet for you would come back."

Staupitz did not find what he sought in the Dominican haven, being, rather, threatened with inclusive excommunication if he did not a) go on trying his influence on his unnatural, spiritual son, and b) issue a public statement of repudiation.

Staupitz did his best. Luther wrote again: "My dear father, this is no time to cringe, but to cry aloud that our Lord Jesus is being damned and rejected. You exhort me to humility: I exhort you to pride. You have too much humility, as I have too much pride. Father, the matter is too serious for good manners. We see Christ suffer, mocked in all the world: I ask you, should we not fight for our most excellent Saviour, who gave himself for us? Shall we not expose our lives? My father, the danger is greater than many think. Now applies the word of the gospel, 'He who confesses me before men, him will I confess in the presence of my Father, and he who denies me before men, him will I deny.' I write so frankly because I see you waver between Christ and the Pope—who are absolute opposites. If you will not follow, at least leave me to go my way. I am deeply saddened by your submissiveness. This is a different Staupitz from the one I used to know. Don't you remember, when we were at Augsburg, you strengthened me, saying, 'Remember, brother, you started this in the name of the Lord Jesus!' I have never forgotten that, and I say it now to you. . . ."

That was shortly before Worms. There was a world of non-stop gyrations and switchback ups and downs at the record-breaking imperial fair, between December 1520 and April 1521.

The simile is fitting. The transitional atmosphere that was generated by the steadily thickening influx of delegates and observers to Worms before the Diet opened, resembled nothing so much as a World's Fair of diplomacy, in the early, festive stages. While in the midst of tournaments, banquets, displays and revels of every sort, private and semi-official sparring and chaffering went on all the time, a sanguine tenor seemed to predominate. It was one of those curious passages in public life, not unknown in any era, of a certain suspension of disbelief: when momentarily everybody has become thoroughly imbued with his own publicity and—incredibly—with confidence in everybody else's friendly declarations.

Charles V, advancing towards his twenty-first birthday in February, one month after the scheduled beginning of the Diet, felt the rising of imperial sap in him from the fecund virtue of the imperial chrysm. He was Emperor, king of kings, everything told him so, and he was getting used to it.

The Electors savoured still the after-taste of the power by which they had made him emperor; replete with flattery, and with congratulations upon having made him swallow the emended coronation oath. As for their doyen, Uncle Fred, arriving aptly on the feast of Epiphany with gifts for the anointed ruler of the Germans, he knew himself a bigger man for the trouble about his Wittenberg professor.

The Estates saw their hour approaching, when their votes would come into play in connection with the new arrangements for the regency and the subventions this like any other emperor would solicit. At the same time the individual representatives had their eyes on what the Emperor, in honeymoon humour, could give them: honours, privileges, exemptions, sinecures, a helping hand in the game of territorial beggar-your-neighbour; and of course, a vigorous push as promised with regard to the German Gravamina.

The foreign ambassadors spiritual and temporal had virtually carte blanche for an occasion so fraught with unpredictable possibilities and kudos.

The lesser fry and entourage had not yet outworn the bracing newness of their liveries—in a day when uniform rather than the stigma of servitude carried the dignity of being well-dressed: when prince and beggar could exchange identities by exchanging clothes, for a joke or a wager, and get away with it. Scribes, cooks, minstrels, artisans, shopkeepers, petty officials—everyone so much as on the fringe of such a congress stood to gain, maybe a fortune, maybe a pension, maybe a patent of nobility, and certainly anecdotes enough to earn them free drinks for the rest of their lives. A breezy air of propitious dawn overhung the preliminary phases of the Diet, so that you can almost smell it now.

The only person with the necessary entrée who had not a hope of making any good thing out of this, now, was Miltitz. So he must have thought: not a sound was heard of him, where he should have been in his element. One would have thought so, yes, after the Lutheran outrage.*

Hasty conclusion!

As we know, Luther was received in Worms, although not until four months later. The seasoned politicians at whom no one would dare laugh as everyone has laughed these four hundred years at Miltitz, quite outdid that butt of superior humour. Until the day Luther left Worms again, indeed for all we know up to his disappearance, a compromise continued to be pursued, by schemes ranging from the over-ingenious to the over-simple. The objective in effect became narrowed down to making Luther withdraw *The Babylonian Captivity,* by which all faces would be saved and the old catchword of reformation would be unloaded of its new explosive charge. For thus he would have been brought to go through the motions of recantation and submission in the eyes of all the unlearned world, yet without asking the impossible as far as he was concerned; and Reform would have returned to the starting point of modal improvements in the Church, leaving doctrine untouched. But that of course did include the impossible as far as Luther was concerned, once his steps had led him to the doctrinal crux. In conscience, these steps were irreversible. In trepidation or in the larger, material commonsense, retreat was possible, and more, advisable. But he was literally too afraid of his conscience, read God, to yield to physical fear, and his inestimable stock-in-trade of commonsense was severely specialized.

Erasmus, though avowedly not of martyr's stuff, realized that; Aleander, though ruled entirely by that other commonsense, felt it by intuition. Hutten knew it. But nobody else.

On high among the seats of power, *la cosa grande* was tackled comparatively unemotionally. When a week after Luther's bonfire the Emperor rescinded his invitation to Worms, it was not on the grounds of what he had done but ostensibly because it had been brought to the Emperor's attention that the period of grace had already expired. The imperial letter more or less crossed in the post with a letter from

* Miltitz disappeared from the higher reaches of diplomacy but did not depart this life till 1529, when, having enjoyed a continued wandering existence "sojourning at places where people were nice to him and entertained him nicely," he fell into the river Maine and drowned, after a convivial evening.

Elector Frederick in which he declined the invitation anyhow because in view of the book-burnings at Cologne and Mainz Luther's case had been prejudiced.

Very nearly concurrently, the bull of final excommunication upon expiry of the period of grace, *Decet Romanum Pontificem,* was launched against Luther at Rome. But when, the Diet having opened on 27 January, this bull reached Aleander at Worms a fortnight later, it was seen to provide also for the excommunication of Ulrich von Hutten. In that form, the bull was unacceptable. An army of radical knighthood was as though carelessly deployed round about Worms, and in any case Father Glapion was bodily engaged in talks with Hutten and Sickingen at their headquarters of Ebernburg. After a reading of the bull at a plenary session, followed by a three-hour speech of Aleander, followed by discussion of corresponding length, the bull was sent back to Rome for revision. As it had taken well over a month to get to Worms in the first place, it would be a long while coming back again—most probably not before the Diet was over.

In this way one thing which the Curia had been cogently anxious to avoid all along was unnoticingly accomplished. The decision of the Diet, what to do about Luther, must now inevitably precede the fiat of the Curia—implementing Elector Frederick's similarly unnoticing inference that an ecclesiastical verdict alone was no longer enough to condemn even an ecclesiastical defector, without ratification by the temporal executive.

"This monk makes much work," sighed the Ambassador of Frankfurt, as the palaver was resumed, whether to let the monk come to Worms or not.

Aleander reminded the Emperor that apart from the safeguards of imperial rights his coronation oath had included the promise to "preserve the ancient faith, protect the Church, and reverence our Holy Father the Pope." Glapion reminded the Emperor of what as his confessor he had told Charles at the outset of Joyeuse Entrée, namely that heaven would not bless his reign if he failed to further the reformation of the Church in line with the German Gravamina. Beloved Uncle Fred reminded him what was due to the Elector of Saxony in equity and honour. The imperial ministers reminded their young master that the papacy was working undeterred, hand in glove with the French King. The Estates reminded him that they were on the brink, but only on the brink, of giving in to his wishes concerning the regency, and that he would be wanting a great deal of money from the Empire.

As time went on and rosy dawn shaded into humdrum day, as general alacrity lapsed into general querulousness, as the tug of war collected more and more hands pulling at the frayed rope from as many different angles, somehow the basic issues seem to have blurred out of focus. On the papalist side the basic issue was not bringing a refractory monk to his knees but to preserve inviolate the absolute autonomy of the Universal Church—in other words, to defeat any attempt to assert secular jurisdiction, even if that looked like bringing the refractory monk to his knees. Procuring Luther's recantation had become more important than the fundamental terms of reference; the immediate prospect of crushing him at last hid the essential principle. On the side of German representation the basic issue remained the unredressed Grievances for which Luther's 1520 Treatises had constructed an unexampled battering ram; the question of divers amour propre was as usual beside the point and as usual began to overshadow it entirely. Who should decide whether Luther were to come to Worms or not became more important than whether he were to be heard or merely seen: the utilitarian political implications of what he had to say got lost.

In the end decision was effected on a plane that could not have been more remote from the ideological one where Luther was riveted. After all the complications of hole-and-corner to and fro and midnight oil, it was really very simple. The Holy See took back the papal breve, which had already been received in Spain, concerning the severance of the Spanish Inquisition from the Spanish crown, and in return the Emperor agreed to suppress Luther in Germany. Thereupon the German Estates took fresh alarm to see their Emperor in such portentous, happy concord with the Roman vampire, and absolutely refused to underwrite any ban arranged over their heads, as it were, by those two foreign powers, the King of Spain and the Pope.

On 6 March 1521 Charles V signed the following citation: "Honourable, dear, and devoted Luther, Ourself and the Estates of the Holy Roman Empire, assembled at Worms, having resolved to demand an explanation from you on the subject of your doctrines and your books, We forward you a safe-conduct, to ensure your personal immunity from danger. We would have you immediately set forth on your journey hither, so that within twenty days of the receipt of Our mandate you may appear before Us and the Estates. You have neither violence nor snares to fear. Relying upon Our Imperial word, we expect your obedience to Our earnest wish."

One can hardly blame Aleander for being somewhat peeved, "That's no way to write to a heretic!" (He had recently amended his earlier descriptions of Elector Frederick, who from an "excellent, Catholic prince" at Cologne had changed into "a fat hog, with the eyes of a dog, which rarely look one straight in the face," or alternately a basilisk, at Worms.)

However, Aleander need not be perturbed: the Emperor joined in the nuncio's efforts to discourage Luther from obeying the summons. If Luther could be frightened off, or even delayed, he was to be proceeded against under statute as a "disobedient absentee."

Luther was "mightily frightened," he admitted it, and little soothed by a breathless communication from Elector Frederick that if Luther chose to come to Worms now he would do so entirely at his own risk and responsibility: the Elector could not undertake to guarantee his subject's safety.

Naturally, Luther went.

On the face of it, Luther's terse, astringent summary of "what happened to me at Worms"—"'Are these books yours?' 'Yes.' 'Do you retract them?' 'No.' 'Then get out!'"—was not so very far out.

He had tried the same tactics as with Cajetan at Augsburg, but they had been circumvented; he had been stopped from making speeches to the Emperor and Estates, forced to answer Yes or No. The subsequent, impromptu conference in camera, doomed to deadlock on the evangelical issue, did not amount to a regular, official hearing either. His condemnation by the Emperor was assured and but slightly deferred. The German Gravamina had slipped back into the twilight sleep from which they had been roused at Emperor Maximilian's last Diet. In spite of its follies and weaknesses, the papacy had won as it had won at Constance over Hus in 1415.

Not at all. At Constance the Emperor Sigismund who had made and broken the promise of safe-conduct to Hus had done so under the direction of a General Council of the Church, where the temporal power was merely a guest, so to speak. At Worms the papal nuncio was the guest, and even if the verdict had gone against Luther, it had been pronounced by the temporal authority, to the grateful applause of the Church. Luther had in fact won an unprecedented victory though he die of it. Besides, the Edict of Worms which placed Luther under the ban of the Empire was rushed through a rudimentary Diet, leaving every legal loophole for any non-signatories who might afterwards wish to set it aside for themselves. But as yet the dust of battle beclouded the vista.

Something else had happened. Luther really was a modest man and an innocent abroad in many ways. He had so schooled himself in discounting popular favours like the hosannas and "cups of honour" and so forth with which he was now received at places like Leipzig and Erfurt where when last seen he had been met with undisguised disfavour, he was so annoyed with himself that he had not expressed himself more strongly at Worms when he had had the chance of blasting Antichrist right to the Emperor's face—it did not occur to him that he had immeasurably consolidated his hold on the imagination of the people. He did not dream that even now blocks were being cut all over the place, depicting him before the Diet, with the already famous phrase, "Here I stand. . . ." for ubiquitous reproduction.

For all that, like any theatre audience, those who had given him such an ovation upon his performance at the Diet had afterwards gone home and left him to it, a lambent impression had stayed with them; and word of his ordeal fell on ready soil throughout the country, wherever his deed of December had spread the necessary fertilizer.

A little monk scribbling away in his cell was all very fine, a monk who went out on a winter morning and burnt the Pope in book form was a marvel, a monk who stood up all alone in a great palace thronged with potentates—he had the ineluctable, familiar, larger-yet truer-than-life reality of folk myth. And it had taken place at Worms—a town fraught with legendary associations of imperial antiquity, Worms of the Nibelungs, shot through with the magic of Siegfried the dragon-slayer. Had he deliberately staged the tableau that was making the rounds, he could not have chosen a better setting. If he had captured the national imagination with his bonfire, now, in the stance of an incredible defiance, it would not let go of him, for many a long day.

It was spring. It was May—the Maytime of the mediaeval poets and miniaturists, the one idyllic season in the strenuous, exacting year, the annual smile vouchsafed by intractable Nature, when all things burgeoned, gay and fresh and green, when faces softened and hearts swelled even without reason. Luther found he had no wish to die. Nor should he: even in the persecutions under Nero the early Christians had been forbidden to invite martyrdom.

Yet he never entirely ceased to feel guilty for it, and so it is one of the few mysteries of his life when, where, and by whom precisely he let himself be persuaded to play his part in a bogus abduction.

II

PARTURITION

＊

1. Accolade

It was not only the heart-easing spring that did it. On the road back
from Worms Luther did begin to realize that something had happened.
The country people flocking, on busy week-days, to kneel by the
wayside and cry for his blessing as he passed—that was nothing.
"Master Omnes" had acted so with Hus and with Savonarola, and
later on watched without lifting a finger as the martyrs were burned;
any excuse was a good one to get off work on a busy week-day.
But that he was met everywhere by deputations entreating him to
stop and preach the gospel—that was entirely different.

He was under an imperial injunction to refrain from propagating
his doctrines and creating any disturbances whatsoever—but "I have
never pledged myself to chain up the Word of God; nor will I."

Yet before letting himself be "absolutely forced to preach" he every
time gave warning what this might cost the congregation in imperial
displeasure. It was the same in hamlets and towns; at the great
Benedictine Abbey of Hersfeld the Abbot paid Luther royal honours;
at Eisenach, of fond memories, the burghers swept him to the parish
church "in the presence of the minister, who was in a great fright
and called in a notary and witnesses" to register his protest. On a
sudden all the people knew how much they needed the gospel and
were demanding to have it told to them.

At Eisenach, "my ever-dear city of Eisenach," he agreed to the
proposed unconventional arrangements for his safety. He did not
know from what quarter the idea originated; he did not know the
agents who approached him with it—yet they must have been able

to show convincing credentials that they were neither minions of
Charles or Aleander nor of Sickingen and Hutten straining at the
leash to fight for him. Luther never said. Sometimes his later accounts
of the kidnapping were disingenuous—making it appear by a little
juggling with words as if the ambush had been a complete surprise
to himself, "Amsdorf no doubt knew." No doubt, Amsdorf knew:
because Luther had quickly told him, when the horsemen were first
sighted "surging out of the forest," and he himself hastily snatched up
his Hebrew Bible and Greek New Testament in Erasmus' edition,
to be kidnapped with him. The rest of the company were genuinely
ignorant—having thought it only too natural that Luther wanted to
make a detour off the main road to see his old grandmother at Möhra
and his other, numerous kin, maybe for the last time in the flesh;
and reacting with proper laments, imprecations, and helter-skelter
flight, once Luther had been taken, "forced to run like a dog beside
the horse of his captor," as they that got away reported. They liked
their fun and took it where they could, the knights of the garrison
of the Wartburg, where nothing ever happened nowadays.

Time was when the Wartburg had been anything but quiet. Time
was when it was a hub of feudal glory and commotion. Those two
revered bards of German vernacular poetry, Walther von der Vogel-
weide (c.1170–1230) and Wolfram von Eschenbach (d.1220), both
inserted warnings into some of their lyric productions, for folk of
tender ears to stay away from the ceaseless crush and clangour at the
Wartburg. It was a little ungrateful of them: Landgrave Hermann of
Thuringia, then the lord of the great fortress, was a lavish patron of
minstrels as well as of adventurers, lovely ladies, and luxury traders:
sponsor of *Sängerkrieg,* minstrels' contests, he would have to wait
for Richard Wagner to do him truly proud.

Landgrave Ludwig "the Springer" had founded the castle, towering
on top of a precipitous mount, late in the eleventh century. His name
came from a characteristic incident of Ludwig's career. Imprisoned
for the wrongs he did to his subjects, he sprang to freedom from the
window of his gaol which stood on a sheer rock above the river Saale,
swam home, and committed fresh atrocities. His lady remonstrated
with him, whereupon he fell into such wrath that she had to flee
and desert her children. As at dead of night she kissed her baby son
goodbye, the pain of parting made her bite his cheek, so that the next
Landgrave bore the byname, "the Scarred." The lady was let down

by rope to the foot of the Wartburg precipice, and escaped to **Frankfurt**. Landgrave Ludwig continued to sin horribly, in the consciousness that he would get away with it since he had made provision to be buried in a monk's cowl—a favourite offshoot of the indulgence system, by which death-bed salvation was supposedly ensured. ("A garment powerless to kill lice," Erasmus quipped, "is believed to drive away the Devil.")

Family life at the Wartburg was seldom serene but briefly took a turn for the better in the early thirteenth century, when the Princess Elizabeth of Hungary married at the age of four the son of Landgrave Hermann, another Ludwig. Though united for reasons of state, the couple grew to have the greatest love for one another. Their happiness was marred only by Elizabeth's excessive charities (the infant bride evidently reacted strongly against the mundane hurly-burly of her father-in-law's domain). As is well known, her husband in the end forbade her to give alms, then one day met her coming down the mountain with a basket full of bread. He asked her what she had got there and she lied, "Roses," and roses had indeed replaced the contraband when Ludwig looked. At this she told him the truth, and he became henceforth as holy as herself. But then he died on Crusade at Otranto. His wife, scarcely out of her teens, ran shrieking through the castle when the news reached the Wartburg. Soon afterwards, ostensibly to save the family fortunes from her pious depredations, her brother-in-law first deprived her of the regency for her eldest son and then turned her out in the middle of winter with a baby at the breast. Though later succoured by her uncle the Bishop of Bamberg and offered reinstatement to the regency by her late husband's principal vassals, Elizabeth renounced the world and under the paranoid directorship of her confessor the Inquisitor Konrad of Marburg devoted herself to a life of penances and caring for the poor and sick until she died, worn out, aged twenty-four. The poor and sick continued to find miraculous help at her tomb, and she was canonized four years after her death.

The castle had since passed into the possession of the Electors of Saxony. Elector Frederick the Wise did not use it, and it was now little more than a *Wartburg* or watch-castle in truth, a monumental shell wherein the warden and his doughty companions had all too much room and far too much peace. How much the abduction of Luther owed to their initiative has never become clear, either. The only utterance of Elector Frederick which it is possible to stretch into a suggestive connection was that sometime during the uproar over Luther's disappearance he let fall that he did not *want* to know what had happened to the man—and the italics are not necessarily merited. Luther himself, who never afterwards allowed a word of anything but praise of the Elector, promoted the inference that the Elector was behind it all. But after over a month at the Wartburg, he was yet able to write worriedly to Spalatin as to who might be paying for his keep.

"I would not stay here another hour if I felt sure it was at the cost of my guardians. Reflection tells me it must be the prince who is the real paymaster. If so, with all my heart; for if one must be a charge to somebody, let it be a charge upon princes. Prince and thief, you know, are pretty well synonymous terms. But I do wish you would find out and tell me for certain." Prince and thief, synonymous? A joke is a joke; but that little pleasantry does not sound as if Luther had been all that satisfied with the Elector's behaviour towards him at Worms. He added, "It is with great difficulty that I have obtained permission to send you this, so fearful are they of its becoming known where I am."

He gave "them" plenty to do. They had allocated a suite of two chambers for his use, at the top of a flight of stairs hidden behind a stout, iron door which was locked and fastened with chains at night or when visitors came. Here he was confined while the hair grew over the tonsure he had had specially enlarged to appear well turned-out for the Diet, and also on his face. Meanwhile he was forced to wear a hat all the time and a false beard, the guardians using the interval for the sober amusement of drilling him in knightly deportment. His robes had been taken away at once, in the woods, and he who had not worn worldly garb at all for nearly sixteen years now learned to swagger in military costume.

"You would not know me. I hardly recognize myself."

For the guardians had to let him write to Melanchthon, or he would have brought the whole cloak and dagger scheme to nothing. Not only did Luther feel it imperative to let the Wittenberg centre know he was still alive before perchance they lost heart—he was so tortured with constipation it was all the guardians could do to stop him breaking out and going all the way to Erfurt for the nearest medical assistance. On the way to Worms when he had been so ill, his enteritis had been stayed with a "precious water" having, it seemed, well-nigh permanent effect; and being locked up without any real exercise did not help. Melanchthon might manage to get hold of a supply of laxatives from Lucas Cranach's shop.

"I see myself, insentient and hardened," Luther wrote revealingly, "a slave to sloth, rarely getting out a prayer, unable to spare a groan for the Church. . . . I have now gone eight days without devotions or study. . . . I had rather burn on live coals than rot here. . . ."

But he must forget that he was Martin Luther. Junker Georg or Jörg in the emollient dialect of the region—Squire George was the name. So he was introduced to the rest of the garrison when he had got head covering and beard that would not fall off and was allowed out in the castle garth. Relieved of the intolerable burden in his bowels, laved by the balms of the young summer, he breathed again and saw the green world all round with new eyes. "The papalists," he improvised, "only look at Nature as a cow does," not like Squire George. He picked strawberries and listened to the trilling of the birds, which like all music he greatly loved.

They took the risk and let him come out hunting with them. "We have been out for two whole days. I'd always wondered what the royal sport was like. I caught two hares and two miserable little partridges. It is a fine occupation if one has nothing else to do. However, I did not entirely waste my time, for I stoutly theologized amid the snares and hounds, and found a mystery of grief and pain in the very heart of this merry pastime. Is not this hunting the very image of the Devil seeking what poor beasts he may devour by the aid of his nets, his traps, and his trained dogs (by which I mean his bishops and his theologians)? There was an incident which crystallized it. I had saved a poor little rabbit which I picked up, all trembling from its pursuers. After keeping it in my sleeve some time I thought it safe to put it down, but the dogs got scent of it and rushed after it, first broke its leg and then pitilessly killed it. The dogs were the Pope and Satan, destroying the souls which I try to save. . . . I have had enough of such hunting as this. The hunting I shall stick to is for the wolves, bears, foxes—the whole iniquitous horde of Roman beasts that prey upon the world. . . ."

Although the experience did not make him a vegetarian, he grew to dislike the taste of game which he had enjoyed so much in his first weeks at the Wartburg.

He relaxed. "It is well with me here. I sit in quiet. I am so happy with the news from Wittenberg. . . ."

In Germany at large the tale of Luther at Worms was being raised to the heights of a passion play, and pious parodies came out, of Luther's "trial" before his Pilate, Emperor Charles, at the instigation of Caiaphas and Annas, guess who?, and the Elector of Saxony not inappropriately in the part of Peter.

". . . They then went away and published horrible mandates in the name of the Roman pontiff and of the Emperor, but to this day they have not been obeyed," one such pamphlet ended.

That was true enough. Published with the most maladroit timing since just three weeks after Luther's disappearance when popular mourning for the second Christ of the Germans was at its peak, the Edict of Worms which outlawed him, his works, and his associates was completely ignored. The Emperor's Spanish guards put up the proclamation at Worms itself, but elsewhere there was hardly a suzerain or magistrate who did not quietly stuff it in the archives.

"As thy son Jesus Christ had to die at the hands of the priests and rise from the dead and ascend to heaven, even so O Lord do by thy disciple Martin Luther," ran a prayer which Albrecht Dürer set down in his diary. (For, "O God, if Luther is dead, who will now instruct us in the gospel?") Casting Luther in the rôle of Christ tacitly implied a resurrection and held off the collapse of militant ardour in despondency.

If the Edict of Worms was disregarded in the Empire, in Wittenberg they did better than that. In Wittenberg, proudly owning itself "Doctor Martin's town" as it might be Nazareth, and where his jurists quickly pointed out to the Elector that an Edict signed only by a rump Diet was of extremely questionable validity—in Wittenberg they forthwith set about proving the Edict null and void. There Luther's reform proposals were now put into practice.

That was why Luther wrote, "I am so happy with the news from Wittenberg, and give thanks to Christ who has raised up others in my place. I rejoice," he added, bravely, "to see it is not you who need me but I who need you."

He rejoiced, and black depression fell upon him.

"Here I sit, doing nothing. . . ." ". . . Like a free man mocking

prisoners. . . ." ". . . In my idle solitude. . . ." "I hate myself."
"O Lord, take away my life!"

His friends in Wittenberg were taking action and risking their lives
in the open, while he who had given himself up for dead, many
times, skulked in safety. But if he were to join them now he would
increase their danger, and would place many others in jeopardy besides, his guardians and his sovereign among them.

He was not solitary, and anything but inactive. By most people's
lights, he had not an idle moment. Almost from the day of his arrival,
Squire George imperilled security by his constant requirements for
writing materials—who would not think it odd for my lords Sternberg,
Berlepsch, Hund von Altenstein et alia to shop openly for stationery?
Luther had plenty to do and plenty of boon companions; but he
had nobody to talk to about his real state of mind.

He was as distraught as he had ever been in his unenlightened
youth. "Are you alone wise, among all men? What if you are in
error, leading others to damnation?" Now that there was no outside
voice to hurl it at him, the horrid echo ricochetted, back and forth,
back and forth, inside his head.

"Ah, I can tell you it is much easier to fight against the incarnate
Devil—that is, against evil men—than against the very spirit of evil
borne upon the air and in one's soul. Then indeed there are a
thousand battles against Satan." Without the compensating brace of
outer pressure, pressure from within can only end in disintegration.
"I greatly fear God will let Satan have his way with me because I
am so sluggish in prayer." No effort of will could restore the capacity
of prayer.

Once again his native, practical ingenuity came to Luther's aid.
He made an outlet for the pressure and projected it into an externalized
force, with a life of its own that thus left his mind inviolate, intact.
The split was the saving of him. Better by far to fight his thousand
battles against Evil personified, than against all the motes of evil
inextricably pervading one's soul. Better to have Evil come at you with
infantile horseplay, than in nameless, formless subtlety.

How Satan harassed him!—especially at night, when the winds
blew round the castle and the owls and the bats were out and about,
when a bagful of nuts on the table began to rattle and crack of
themselves, and a hundred invisible barrels thundered down the stairs
unhindered by the closed iron door, so that sleep became impossible

and mental anguish rose to the most poignant pitch of schizoid duo-
logue. Poisons taken in the correct dosage have healing properties.

He found Satan could not bear contempt.

"Oh, it's you again, is it?" he trained himself to say, turning over
in bed to present his rear. "Don't mind me, will you? I'm going to
sleep." Being nevertheless drawn into an argument more often than
not, he learned to break that off with, "Oh yes, you know it all,
don't you? you are so holy! quite the theologian, eh? Who do you
think you're talking to? Oh, lick my arse and be gone." If that was
no good, there were stronger measures, like breaking wind or having
at Satan with the chamber pot.

Music also was an excellent repellent, also laughter, and congenial
company; except that there was no chance of the latter at night in bed.

Between June and November Squire George, that useless, idle fellow,
besides swotting to improve his Greek and Hebrew wrote refutations
of two recent Catholic treatises, translated a polemic of Melanchthon's,
which he much admired, into German with a foreword of his own
to supplement "Philip's finer bodkin with my bludgeon," also, "a little
volume in German on Confession, a commentary in German on the
67th Psalm; another, also in German, on the Canticle of Mary; a
third on the 37th Psalm, and a *Consolation to the Church of Witten-*
berg; a commentary in German on the Epistles and Gospels for the
year, and a commentary on the Gospel story of the Ten Lepers,"
not to mention "my books on the Mass, on Vows of Celibacy, on the
Tyrant of Mainz," concerning which he irately tackled Spalatin:

"Why have they not been published? Were they intercepted or have
they been lost? If I thought they had reached you and that you
were sitting on them, nothing would anger me more. If you do have
them, will you instantly abandon your untimely caution: I will have
them printed, I tell you, at Wittenberg or somewhere else. Oh, if I
could be sure you were suppressing them I should be perfectly furious.
Don't tell me the Elector will not permit me to attack the Mainz
hell-hound or that the public peace will be disturbed by what I
write. Rather than let myself be stopped in doing what I think fit,
I would annihilate the whole set of you, prince and all."

The hell-hound tyrant of Mainz had plucked up courage and authorized the preaching of a new indulgence at Halle. Luther wrote
to him direct: ". . . Did you think Luther was dead? Well, he is

not dead. . . . You are now warned; I declare to you—" that, in
short, if the Archbishop did not mend his ways within a fortnight
Luther would publish a pamphlet against him. "Given in my desert,
this Sunday after Catherine. Your humble well-wisher, Martin Luther."

Albrecht von Hohenzollern, German primate, cardinal, and Elector,
replied in his own hand:

"Dear Doctor, I have received your letter and have read it in all
goodwill and friendship. . . . I will henceforth conduct myself, with
God's help, as becomes a good prince and a good priest. I acknowledge fully that I have great need of God's assistance, poor, weak
sinner that I am, sinning each day of my life, and wandering aside
from the right path . . . vile dust of the earth that I am. . . . I am
ever ready to submit to a paternal and Christian reprimand." Etc.,
etc. "Albertus, *manu propria.*"

How could the Devil Doubt not be in retreat, from an embattled
monk wielding such manifest authority? Never till he donned the
accoutrements of knighthood, in hiding and under ban, had Luther
threatened anybody with his own wrath, but only with the wrath
of God.

The secret of his whereabouts was surprisingly well kept. No one
betrayed him, and punctiliously he headed his vast output of communications *From the region of air, From the region of birds, From
the mountain,* or even, in the fullness of poetic licence, *From the Isle
of Patmos,* exile of St. John the Divine.

※

2. First Reforms

No man is master of his heart. Luther found there was something to be said for the existence of Squire George, after all. Like that, one could get a lot of work done. He had great plans, which one would execute in a fraction of the time that otherwise had to be snatched from between university and parish duties.

"Though I should be lost," he wrote again to Melanchthon, "the gospel will lose nothing by that. In Scripture too you now excel me: you are Elisha who succeeds Elijah with a double portion of the Spirit, the which may the Lord Jesus bestow upon you in his mercy."

But although in point of evangelical penetration he considered himself "a dishwasher" to Melanchthon, Melanchthon too could not do everything at once, nor be everywhere at once. Now that there was a right, good, universal hunger for the gospel, it was vital to make relief available. Melanchthon's finer work would be fully appreciated only when everybody knew exactly what he was explaining. Everyone should know the text; if Melanchthon were expected to provide that as well, valuable time and energy would be taken from his more important job. Luther was hoping to translate the Bible so that it made universal sense in German, which had never been the case with previous translations.

Had not Luther been away from Wittenberg, it is doubtful whether practical reforms would then have been instituted. With only himself in authority, the smallest residue of doubt would have stalled action. For all his waxing arrogance, at heart he cherished superior authority with an undying, wistful, unrequited love; for all that he liked to flirt with his peasant origin, at heart he distrusted himself as a man of the people.

Karlstadt was his antithesis. Karlstadt at heart acknowledged no authority superior to his own, and did not trust anybody else to know what to do. Where Luther always thought he jumped into the breach as a stop-gap pending the arrival of proper reinforcements, Karlstadt in a manner was always looking for a breach that should be worthy of his quality.

Karlstadt lacked Luther's staying power, but Luther had the narrower field of vision. While jealousy and ambition were abnormally absent from Luther's make-up but much to the fore in that of Karlstadt, it was Karlstadt who found the purer and more consistent solution of the evangelical issue. Luther's was the nobler soul, yet Karlstadt took the nobler course. Luther's record became blotted as soon as the world of worldly affairs claimed him, Karlstadt's record was washed clean and his career was smashed.

While Melanchthon struggled with the heavy folds of the mantle of Elijah which had fallen on him, it was Karlstadt who introduced reformed practices in Wittenberg.

Having had the scene stolen from him once again at Leipzig, and having attended the Elster Gate bonfire as only one of the spectators, he had not even got an excommunication to himself but was lumped in with the rest of Luther's supporters. He had wavered then, but decided against the distinction of solitary withdrawal from "the Wittenberg Sanhedrin"; instead he published a separate appeal to a future General Council, together with a treatise of his own on the corruptions of the papacy, called *On the Holiness of Popes,* which alas merely shared in the furore caused by Luther's kindred and concurrent writings.

In May 1521, however, Luther was "dead" and King Christian II of Denmark invited the surviving Lutheran doctor of Wittenberg to his country. King Christian had perused Luther's manifesto calling on the secular rulers to take the spiritual power in hand, with the utmost interest; and he was very interested indeed in an appropriate reform of the Church in Scandinavia. The crowns of Norway and Sweden were united with the Danish, if somewhat tenuously, and the King, who was related to the House of Saxony, had every incite-

ment for testing out new weapons to subdue the unsympathetic nobles
and ecclesiastics in his dominions.

Karlstadt immediately proved two things: that the Edict of Worms
was just a piece of paper, and that he was a fast worker when
he had the opportunity. He crossed Germany unimpeded and in
Denmark before the month was out promoted a royal law by which
clerical celibacy was abolished.

As the Lord's Supper was the central rite of Christian worship,
so was celibacy the central feature of priestly vows setting the clergy
apart from the rest of humanity. By striking first at the exclusive magic
of the priest which alone could work the miracle of reconstituting
Christ, the Antichristian concept of a magic ceremony would come
down, bereft of underpinnings. This view was well advanced in
Scandinavia; but Karlstadt's allied proposals for radical changes in the
mass came too soon. The concerted outcry of nobles and clergy was
such that King Christian postponed further reform and shipped Karlstadt home. He was back in Wittenberg in June, and at once began
again where he had left off.

Luther had a specific treatise on celibacy on the stocks, but had
several times had to shelve it. So far, in the major Reformation
Treatises he had simply asserted that marriage is a state ordained
by God's commandment, and that a priest had to have a housekeeper:
"And to put a man and a woman to live together is like bringing
fire to straw and expecting nothing to happen," so that there would
be vile unchastity as long as priests were debarred from godly wedlock.

Karlstadt now produced the necessary elaborations and Scriptural
detail, in a quick succession of publications. He came to the conclusion
that marriage should be not only permitted but made obligatory for
men in holy orders, among whom he included monks.

This startled Luther. Monks did not have female housekeepers,
monks had taken voluntary vows which had nothing to do with
ordination, and he himself was a monk. "Good heavens! wives for
monks? No thank you." Still, he thought it over and decided tentatively that it was up to the individual.

At this juncture three Saxon priests took the plunge and testified
to the belief that "no pope or council ever had the right to inflict
upon the Church a statute injurious to body and soul," and honourably
married their concubines. Orders for their arrest went out from the
Archbishops of Mainz and Magdeburg, but only one, Pastor Jakob

Seidler who had the misfortune of living in Duke George's territory, was apprehended and perished in prison as the first blood witness, thus, of the evangelical revolution. The other two belonged to Electoral Saxony, and Frederick the Wise, though not at all edified by their conduct, said he would not be used as a bum-bailiff and declined to extradite them.

Of course it was being said by the orthodox opposition that the abolition of celibacy aimed at nothing but the satisfaction of unholy lust—just as Aleander said the abrogation of the canon law aimed at nothing but the satisfaction of innate German laziness—to cut down on studies. The earnest reformers barely paused to refute the idea that sex was fun, which in the context of Christian marriage was as nearly beneath their notice as Aleander's aspersion on German diligence, insofar as it was aimed at German savants, anyway.

The three pioneers being secular clergy, not monks, had Luther's unqualified approval, and Melanchthon seconded Karlstadt with an apologia entitled *Priests May Take Wives,* the conclusions of which were formally adopted by the Wittenberg law faculty. After this there was no more holding back. All over Electoral Saxony priests went to the altar. In the Augustinian cloister of Wittenberg one Brother Gabriel Zwilling started a heated agitation against monachism as such, declaring the very cowl an obstacle to salvation.

Now, too, Melanchthon acceded to the popular demand—endorsed by the town council and, very much so, from the Wartburg—that he should preach the gospel in place of the absent leader. "The people need the word, and no one is more richly qualified than Master Philip, to dispense it." Honouring the tenet of the priesthood of all believers, on 22 September 1521 Philip Melanchthon, a married layman, preached in the pulpit of the town church, and afterwards for the first time since Hus celebrated an evangelical Lord's Supper with a select congregation of students, who received the chalice, as well as the wafer, from his hands.

The struggle about the mass began in earnest. Rather than have the ritual altered in any way, as growing numbers of the brothers demanded, the prior of the Wittenberg Augustinians had no more masses celebrated in his monastery at all, for the present. On All Saints' Day the incumbent of the Castle Church, Justus Jonas, preached against the Wittenberg Indulgence and declared the Elector's relics so much rubbish, almost in so many words. Masses for the dead ceased in one religious foundation after another, threatening a landslide of administrative disorder as endowments and stipends must collapse along with their conditional object.

Elector Frederick hurriedly appointed a representative committee of Wittenberg lawyers and theologians, whose verdict was that mass had become so commercialized as to be the greatest sin on earth. The committee recommended that he, the Elector, emulate his famous namesake Emperor Frederick Barbarossa and lead a new crusade—the crusade of evangelism, even if he should be called a heretic for it. "It is better to bear reproach from men on account of God's Word than to be condemned by Christ on the day of judgment," he was sagely advised. At the same time there came threatening growls, not unmixed with glee and greed, from Ducal Saxony: Electoral Saxony was seceding from the Edict of Worms and should be disciplined by imperial force of arms if necessary.

Frederick the Wise was saved from an immediate decision, as the various groups represented on the committee were unable to agree precisely how its general directive should be implemented.

In the meantime Karlstadt and Melanchthon continued to go forward—practice and theory hand in hand—with ancillary reforms of public welfare and morals.

On 13 November Zwilling and twelve other friars resigned from the Augustinian Brotherhood and took lodgings in the town, some with the burghers and some in student bursae—with the result that the agitation against celibacy caught on with the laity so that men in cloister garb began to be hissed in the streets and told to get married. The Franciscan monastery of Wittenberg applied for protection by municipal militia.

Luther at the Wartburg put all other work aside to search the Scriptures, and reluctantly found in favour of Karlstadt and Zwilling. His so-called "Ten-Day Book" (written 21 November–1 December), *On Monastic Vows,* had the homely touch of a preface addressed to his father.

"My dearest father, when I became a monk it was not of mature decision but in the terror excited by a sudden threat of death. When I mentioned this to you some time ago, you exclaimed, 'God grant it was not a delusion of the Devil!' Your words struck me deeply, as though they were the word of God sent by your lips, but I shut my heart against them." The writer went on to recapitulate his father's reproach on the occasion of his first mass, which, he said, he had also hardened his heart to, but which deep down he had never got over. However, all was well that ended well: God had manoeuvred Martin into taking the delusive vows *in order* that he might be thus enabled to discount them. Whilst doing so with all his heart, he, Martin, would stay as he was now: "For what difference does it make whether I wear cowl and tonsure or discard them? My conscience has become free, and that is the real freedom. Thus I am a monk, and yet not a monk, a new creature, not of the Pope but of Christ alone."

Having had to catch up with Karlstadt, Luther neatly turned it to unconscious advantage. He had had it on higher authority in the first place; and with luck the sop of having his name extolled to all Germany in his old age would stop his father's mouth. As a dutiful son he could not have left his parents in suspense regarding his fate, and the abolition of celibacy could not but raise Hans Luther's hopes again, for more grandchildren: if Martin was *obstinatissimus,* where had he got it from?

If Karlstadt had outdistanced the leader, suddenly they were all of them going too slow for the townspeople. A crowd of students and younger burghers rushed the town church on the first Sunday in December, with naked knives beneath their cloaks, hacked the mass books in pieces, chased the ministrants from the altar, and stoned some others engaged in prayer before the statue of the Virgin. Directly the malefactors had been rounded up it was seen that they were no mere isolated band of vandals. The whole, respectable community raised a tumult which was sufficient to release them, unpunished.

The very next day Squire George came riding down from his mountain, in broad daylight and straight through Ducal Saxon territory, but perfectly safe in his impenetrable disguise. Till he dismounted at the door of his friend Amsdorf in Wittenberg, asked for lodging, and revealed his identity, no one would have dreamed the burly, bearded horseman was their sainted exile. Lucas Cranach was fetched under seal of secrecy to make some drawings for a record of the transformation while Luther conferred with the inner circle, Melanchthon, Jonas, Amsdorf, Bugenhagen. There was not time to see and talk to everybody; as it was Spalatin could hardly contain his anxiety to have Luther out of Wittenberg again before, in such a small place as this, his presence became known and compromised the Elector.

Luther concurred; he only wanted to stay overnight and to get back to his work as quickly as possible. He was not worried about Karlstadt or the over-zealous Wittenbergers so much as about his tract *On the Abolition of Private Masses* and his *Blast Against the Archbishop of Mainz* (Albrecht's abject letter had had no concrete sequel), which Spalatin even yet had failed to hand over to Master Grünenberg. Very well, said the spurred and sword-begirt, new Luther, if Spalatin would prefer him to bring out a *Blast* against the Elector, exhorting the sovereign to throw away his relics and sell their gold and silver casings for the benefit of the poor. . . . The pamphlets were released for press.

That was all Luther had really come for. Twenty-four hours was enough to provide him with a sample of the turmoil in the city. The fears of the Franciscan Friars were realized and a riot broke out against them on the evening of Luther's visit; but still he was not worried. Perhaps he would have worried more had there been rioting against the Augustinians. However, the demonstrators were dispersed before anybody came to harm; and Luther deemed a mob so enlightened as to shout for a German liturgy and the right of admission to divine service wherever it be held, could surely be controlled by a few well-chosen words of paternal reprimand. He drafted these, to be published in his name, and left. In addition to a Gospel translation he now also planned a reliable commentary of sermon postils to go with it, for the use of preachers and home devotions.

His appeal to the people of Wittenberg explained that violence was contrary to the will of God and therefore calculated to strengthen the forces of hell; preaching and praying were the only correct means of Christian battle. Also, "I beg that my name be passed over in silence and that men will call themselves not Lutheran but Christian. Saint Paul would not allow Christians to bear the name of Paulists or Peterites. How then can it be that I, a poor stinking carcase, have the children of Christ called after my unhallowed name? Not so, dear friends! Let us root out party names and just be Christians."

The Elector took from this what he needed for his cue and on 19 December published his decision that while discussion might continue no further action was to be taken for the time being in the cause of reform. Preach and pray, as Luther said, by all means.

But Luther had said also, for some time, that mass after the orthodox style was of Antichrist. Now that the evil had been proclaimed,
the townsfolk reasoned, God would not forgive them if it was still
perpetuated. In agreement with the magistrate Karlstadt gave notice
that on New Year's Day, when it was his next turn to conduct
the service at the town church, the canon of the mass would be dispensed with and communion in both kinds administered to the entire
congregation. The Elector replied with an injunction. Karlstadt made
private arrangements with the priest who was on the rota for Christmas Day and circulated the verbal announcement among the populace
that he would be officiating then.

On Christmas Eve crowds collected round the town church, where
old-style mass was about to be celebrated, invaded it blaring popular
songs, smashed the lamps, and shouted down the priest with abuse
and slogans. They then tramped through the streets up to the Castle
Church, arriving in time for the benediction, for which in strident
chorus they returned their cordial wishes of pestilence and hell-fire.

On Christmas Day "the whole town"—some two thousand head
were counted, out of roughly a total twenty-five hundred inhabitants—
came to attend Karlstadt's mass.

Karlstadt appeared without vestments, in a plain, black robe. He
preached briefly, saying that no preparation of fasting and confession
was necessary to receive the sacrament, but that on the contrary such
preparation showed lack of faith in the sacrament's efficacy. "Faith
is all; by faith and heart-felt longing and true contrition alone does
Christ make man a sharer in his blessedness. And if, denying his
intention, you partake of the bread alone without the wine, you commit
mortal sin."

Yet, when he proceeded to the mass, it seemed as if he were going
to go through with it as usual. He said it in Latin as usual. But he
came to the climax much sooner, cutting out as he had promised all
references to the sacrificial aspect of the ceremony. Suddenly he spoke
German, words which had never been heard in that language.

"This is the cup of my blood of the new and eternal testament,
spirit and secret of the faith, shed for you to the remission of sins."

The people did not trust their ears. They had not realized the
moment was here—he had omitted, too, the elevation of the host.
There was breathless silence; some broke out in sweat, some swayed,
it was said, near to fainting.

The minister called upon them to come forward and help themselves to the bread with their own hands and to receive the sacred blood into their own mouths. One man trembled so violently that he dropped the bread, God's body, on the ground.

It was to obviate the danger of this frightful sacrilege that the clumsy laity had been barred from touching the bread and receiving the wine lest any drop be spilled. The man was terror-stricken. Karlstadt told him to pick up the piece. The man could not do it. He stood as though paralyzed, then turned and fled from the church.

Otherwise the first German mass, which Karlstadt not Luther had the privilege of celebrating, was finished without accident or disturbance. He was a very brave man too, who did this. This was one act which it was not given to Luther to perform, where he could only follow, later.

*

3. The "Enthusiastes"

The revolutionary, Luther, was a cogenital conservative. Every fibre of his being revolted from innovations. Because he had had the misfortune to discover that the latterday Church was one gigantic medley of innovations against the authority of its founders, he had been compelled to violate his nature ever since.

Pitifully, he clung to little things, as long as he was able: thus, head bushily overgrown and wearing breastplate, hose, and scarlet cloak, he asseverated his loyalty to tonsure and cowl, in his Ten-Day Book. But the mass was no little thing, it was the biggest thing in the Christian cult. He had proved to his entire satisfaction that all ceremonial was irrelevant and immaterial. Like any other castle, the Wartburg had its chapel, where he could have celebrated mass. He knew the orthodox way was wrong, but he could not bring himself to make a start with something quite new, though that would be right. Was that one reason why all at once he had become incapable of devotion altogether?

He had urged that the unordained believer, Melanchthon, assert the equal priesthood of all men baptized in Christ, by standing up in church to preach. But he was not there when it was done. He was not there when the fast days he abrogated were abolished in fact, when aural confession was discontinued as well as all divine service without communicants, when foundation moneys were diverted to the relief of the poor. He could make the large, symbolic gesture—whether that meant to burn or to face the being burned—but he could not himself make the break from minor, concrete traditions which he had given four solid years of his life to show did not signify in the least. It was not the courage that he lacked; the desire to be top and actually govern was wanting.

When it was done, when somebody had taken it out of his hands and done it, he took it in his stride and thought it well done (and still he was not there, and evidently did not want to be). He was very pleased with them at Wittenberg; he told them so over again. He would give them every possible help and encouragement, with the Word. He thoroughly approved, too, of Karlstadt's marriage, which the latter had announced to round off that momentous Christmas Day—with what was to become an almost stereotype disclaimer on occasions of priest-marriages, namely that the bride was "neither pretty nor rich." However, neither was she old; she was a healthy virgin of fifteen. "I know the girl," wrote Luther, "and I am very pleased."

He could hardly be so pleased when the pace quickened more and more. A few days after Karlstadt's first mass Gabriel Zwilling raised a rabble of iconoclasts to cleanse the temple of graven images which the Lord had forbidden and which Karlstadt said he himself found a distraction from truly spiritual worship. Similar outbreaks followed, and multiplied, concentrically spreading outside Wittenberg. There were people who did not like it and began to make themselves heard.

"Give the people time!" Luther, who was not there, admonished. "It took me three years of constant study, reflection, and discussion to arrive at where I now am. Can the common man, unversed in such dealings, be expected to cover the same distance in three months? Abuses are not eliminated by destroying the object which is abused. Men can go wrong with wine and women. Shall we then prohibit wine and abolish women? Sun, moon, and stars are worshipped by the heathen. Shall we then tear them out of the sky? Such haste and violence betray a lack of confidence in God. Had I wished I might have started dire upheaval at Worms. But while I sat still and drank beer with Philip and Amsdorf, God saw to matters and dealt the papacy a mighty blow. The Word did it all."

On New Year's Day Karlstadt celebrated his new mass again, turn or no turn; the demand for it was such that he agreed to repeat it on Fridays as well as Sundays and holy days henceforth.

In the early days of January 1522 the Wittenberg town council made the reformed religion law, and the prior of the Wittenberg Augustinians officially dissolved his congregation although all brothers wishing to do so were at liberty to stay on in the cloister. In February

Justus Jonas, the minister of the Castle Church, took a wife, neither pretty nor rich, age passed over. Desecrations increased, altars and tomb stones were smashed here and there. Hardly a day passed that either Karlstadt or Zwilling or both did not come up with something new, and quoting Scripture for it. *"Drink ye all of it"* and *"Thou shalt not make unto thee any graven image"* were followed by *"God is a spirit,"* to be worshipped only in the spirit; so away with the material trappings of worship now in their entirety: "Organs, trumpets, flutes belong in the theatre, not in church."

The Puritanical element, too, was quite lacking in Luther. He had nothing against theatrical representations, on the contrary he held that they were useful, educative, emotionally salutary. "If we are to keep away from plays because they often turn upon love," he answered one objection, "then we should on the same principle refuse to read the Bible."

Still the messengers came, from Wittenberg to the Wartburg.

"What shall I do?" asked Melanchthon. "You know better than I," Luther answered. "You are much cleverer and you are on the spot. I think you are doing very well." He did suggest it should be pointed out that music, vestments, candles, incense and the rest, since they did not signify, were logically optional even as tonsure and cowl: for his own part, he could not conceive of public worship without that most divine of God-created glory, music, but he would not force it on those whom it disturbed.

"What shall I do?" asked the Elector. In March there was another Diet, convened at Nuremberg; Duke George of Saxony was about to go to the Estates with a formal protest against a neo-Hussite movement erupting in the Empire which it was the duty of the imperial judiciary to suppress before it got out of control. Elector Frederick, whom the best arguments in the world had been unable to induce to use his military on less problematical occasions, could not see his way to risking bloodshed among his own subjects in a cause so doubtful. He "did not want to go against the Emperor but did not want to get into trouble with God either," just as he had said on leaving Worms. It seemed he was not able to countermand the laws incontinently passed by mere, municipal government, without the use of force: but how could he dare use force, when that might verily be against God?

Luther had comforted Frederick the Wise before, in sickness; he now comforted him on the rack of conflict, thus—

"For many years Your Electoral Grace has been collecting sacred relics in every land. Now God has heard your wish and has sent you without cost or labour to yourself a whole cross, complete with nails, spear, and scourges. I congratulate you on your new relics. Do not be afraid. Stretch out your arms trustfully. Let the nails pierce deep, and be thankful and glad."

(A lesser man might have come to curse the day he ever saw his relics, but not the Elector. He held on to them, come what might. Obstinacy ran not only in the Luther family. A day would come when the Elector got something of his own back on Luther: when Luther positively commanded him to get rid of his relics and the sovereign replied he was under the impression that freedom of conscience was the law under the New Religion. He kept his relics.)

Next it was, *"Be not ye called rabbi,":* no one should any longer study or teach school.

"Dr. Karlstadt," Luther was informed, "is going round the houses of the townsmen, asking everybody how they understand this or that passage in this or that prophet. And when these simple townsmen say to him, 'Herr Doctor, how come you learned gentlemen ask us poor, unlettered folk such questions? Rather should you tell us the meaning,' then Karlstadt answers them with Matthew XI: *Thou hast hid these things from the wise and prudent, and hast revealed them unto babes,* and Luke X likewise. . . . Now Karlstadt and Zwilling give out no learned man should be allowed as preacher or priest in the churches, but only laymen and artisans if they can merely read."

Karlstadt was being consistent. Zwilling (now calling himself Didymus in token of emancipation—Didymus/Zwilling=twin) was hyper-consistent. In order to cancel out his former clerical status and professional learning and thus qualify for officiating in church notwithstanding, Zwilling took to celebrating mass dressed not simply in layman's garb but dressed up as a landsknecht—a mercenary foot soldier. He did not simply keep his hat on during service but wore gaudy feathers in it. And, "The blood of our Lord is served not in a chalice but in a beer mug."

"I see no reason to come down," said Luther. "You can surely deal with it." He was very busy. God was making him do his best work yet, and it was going wonderfully well.

In Wittenberg there was never a dull moment. Enthusiasm was fanned by a group of fascinating strangers calling themselves the Zwickau Prophets, who had first appeared in town during the hectic season of Advent and had not let the grass grow underneath their feet. There were four of them, two clerical defectors and two regulation illiterates—Thomas Münzer, priest, Marx or Marcus Stübner, one-time student of Wittenberg, and Klaus Storch and Thomas Drechsel, weavers—from a place on the Saxon-Bohemian border, which was a centre of industry, commerce, and crypto-Hussism, and which supposedly derived its name of Zwickau from *cygnea* or Swan Lake. They were exceedingly eloquent, colourful, and in constant direct communication with God.

God had told them to come here and lend a hand to Martin Luther, the sooner to build the kingdom of righteousness. God told them every word they were to say, together with the necessary Biblical quotations, and God vouched for it that Martin Luther would be overjoyed at their co-operation.

They caused complete bewilderment and demoralization in the Lutheran deputy-leader. Their doctrine squared with the Lutheran as far as Luther's pronouncements had gone to date; and if the Prophets of Swan Lake went farther than that, so might Luther when he got around to it, for all anybody knew. Luther's admonitions to Karlstadt and Zwilling, discountenancing violence and haste, were well enough: but *in principle* Luther did not disagree with Karlstadt and Zwilling; far from it. It was perfectly possible that he might agree with the four from Zwickau, just as the four were so sure he would. Melanchthon no longer felt sure of anything.

The principal departures in which the Zwickau Prophets went beyond Luther were for the abolition of the Bible itself and of infant baptism.

The Bible, too, was a man-made and material thing, the Prophets argued: else it would have fallen straight from heaven untouched by human hand; and it was manifestly redundant, seeing that the Spirit all the time supplied themselves with accurate reference from it. As for the sacrament of baptism—if a sacrament had no intrinsic power but became efficacious only through the faith of the recipient: what then happened when it was conferred on a recipient yet incapable of conscious faith? Nothing, was the answer. Infant baptism was meaningless and therefore evil.

Now, this was a very delicate point. There had never been any wholly satisfactory ruling on it. St. Augustine and other Fathers of the Church had variously got around it by slightly altering the connotations of baptism, in relation to infants. In infants it might possibly act as a kind of cauterization of original sin, such as was performable without the recipient's consenting awareness. It was difficult not to agree with the Zwickauers that this smacked too much of scholastic quibbling, which Luther would never uphold.

Melanchthon did not know what to think and Luther when first appealed to was not sure either. He recommended circumspection: give him time to examine the problem at leisure, and till then walk warily, "lest their counsel be of God."

It was not so easy to follow this advice, as time and the Prophets did not stand still. Now they were advocating also the abolition of property and law, as militating against the reign of the Spirit. They proclaimed that the millennium would shortly be established, through the imminent extermination of the ungodly—either by the Turks or at the hands of the elect, i.e. themselves. There were people who did not like it at all, there were people who were getting rather frightened.

"I cannot tell you how deeply I am agitated," Melanchthon via Spalatin besought the Elector to make Luther come down for a conference with the Prophets. "Nobody but Martin can judge them. They wish to meet with him. The gospel is at stake; I would not be writing to you if the matter were not so important."

So infectious was the Prophets' vaunted certitude. The town was seething with the prospects of new ordinances, as it were to make lawlessness legal. There were people who were growing much alarmed, and wavering in their new faith.

"Really," Luther wrote again to Melanchthon, "I cannot understand your indecision. All you have to do is discover [the Prophets'] private state of mind, enquire whether they have experienced those spiritual pangs by which God is wont to call men to his service. If they talk of sweetness and transportation to the third heaven, don't believe them. God is a consuming fire, and the dreams and visions of the saints are terrible, not bland and soothing. . . . Prove their spirits, and if you are unable to do so, then take the advice of Gamaliel and wait."

By this time Melanchthon had in fact made up his mind. Klaus Storch was letting it be known that an angel had announced to him he, Storch, was to become God's vice-regent on earth. Stübner, having preached early and late that there is no purgatory, one day excitedly confided to Melanchthon that he had just seen St. Chrysostom roasting in that very place. Melanchthon, who had not smiled for many days, recorded that he laughed.

There was not much to laugh at, for a certainty. Melanchthon's decision came too late to discredit the Prophets in Wittenberg: they had too good a start. With Karlstadt and Zwilling their indigenous allies, they had got practically the whole town behind them. They could no longer be preached down. They would have to be physically stopped, by the civil power, by the temporal sword. The Elector must step in.

"Surely," Luther wrote, "we can restrain the firebrands without such measures. I trust our Prince will not stain his hands with their blood."

Would he never comprehend? Melanchthon seriously contemplated throwing in his hand and going away, far away.

The Elector did intervene.

It was and always would be too easy to forget that he had other things to do than dithering about the reformation of which Wittenberg, though screaming, was yet only in an early stage of labour. His kinsman Duke George, too, had perhaps forgotten that next to the Emperor, who like Luther was not there, the dean of German princes was the most respected statesman in the Empire. The vice-regency, though no longer his by title, was still largely controlled by Uncle Fred, insofar as one could speak of control at all; perhaps it had slipped his own mind in all the to-do at home, that at the imperial assembly where Duke George sought to blacken and bait him the Elector of Saxony was bound to cut a great figure. Moreover, with that volatility which affects groups and institutions no less than it sways individual men, the Diet had got its chief attention on another quarter that year. The unceasing rise in prices and currency inflation within the Empire were being charged to the merchant class for a change, and it was hoped to devise curative measures. The German Gravamina looked like being in good hands, since upon Leo X's sudden death just before

Christmas Adrian VI had been elected Pope—none other than the Emperor's former preceptor, viceroy and Grand Inquisitor of Spain, and trusted friend, Adrian of Utrecht. Adrian was as different from the Medici Pope as chalk from cheese, and had declared that he bowed his neck to the yoke of Peter for the sole purpose of restoring Christ's disfigured bride, the Church, to purity. (Luther, said Adrian, was God's punishment for the sins of the curial prelates.)

From the vantage point of Nuremberg, the Elector of Saxony saw the affairs of Wittenberg diminished in perspective. He called a halt to reformation from below and decreed a return to the status quo— in very mild and reasonable terms under the circumstances, and not without a hint that sometime in the future the matter might be reconsidered.

Mild or no, it was a decree, and the town of Wittenberg would not have it. The seal of Wittenberg and its rights and liberties were being trodden underfoot, by the Catholic tyrant. Down with him! down with the town council which, though sorely affronted, hesitated to declare outright war on the sovereign! down, down with all restrictions and restraints.

The town council and parish elders sent an urgent message to the Wartburg, imploring Luther's aid against the "Enthusiastes," the possessed fanatics who were threatening to take over. "The dam has broken, and I cannot stem the waters," ran Melanchthon's postscript. "You must come."

＊

4. The Book

Luther had been writing the New Testament in German. That was
what it amounted to.

"Translating is not something anyone can do. It is not just a matter
of languages. A man may have perfect knowledge of the languages
involved without being able to render the living sense of the one into
the other. That needs a special grace and gift from God. It requires
a true, pious, honest, sedulous, reverent, knowledgeable, workmanlike
heart. You go by grammar and vocabulary alone at your peril. The
LXX Greek translators who put the Hebrew Bible into Greek were
unversed in the particular character and usages of the original language, and so their rendering turned out insipid and inconsistent. The
very letters of a language have their own individual looks and airs,
which have to be respected. If Moses and the prophets were to rise
again, they themselves would not be able to make sense of what they
are supposed to have said. . . .

"I try to write German, not Latin or Greek couched in German.
You don't get your German from the Latin, as those asses [previous
translators] did, you get it from the mother in the home, the child in
the street, the man in the market place."

You also get it from some unknown chemistry inside you, that art
of tongues.

As to this, even his worst enemy Duke George said of Luther, "One
thing about that absconding monk is you can learn the use of German
from him right well." It was true. In Luther's hands, the language
revealed unsuspected life and richness. Words came to him as animals

do to some people, idiom and imagery blossomed for him as plants will for green fingers, fresh springs leapt from the old rock to his diviner's plume: clear, flexible, strong, and thrilling.

That happened naturally when he wrote from himself. When it came to recreating in virtually another medium pre-formed effects of thought, mood, harmony, rhythm, and associations, the process was not so easy as it was meant to look, and did. The extensive practice Luther had put in on bilingual writing was of small advantage there. His German and Latin versions of the same treatises had not been translations but equivalents composed straight off, each in its own right, to the same purport, but by no means identical.

"This translation work is good for me: without it I might have gone to my grave in the fond belief that I was learned! Sometimes it takes a fortnight to find just the right expression for one single word," to convey exactly what should be conveyed. For, "A revelation should reveal!" as Luther made bold to disparage the Apocalypse, which to his mind did not help anybody to understand anything. To bring home understanding was the whole point of the Word, communication being after all the point of words.

To effect this purpose, to resurrect the message from the toils of esoteric rigmarole, it needs had to be brought up to date and to be naturalized, as it were, making "Moses so German that no one would think he was a Jew." But, oh, "What an immense, laborious task it is to force the Hebrew writers to talk German! How they struggle against being compelled to forsake their native manner and follow the crude German style! It is like trying to make a nightingale to give up its own sweet melody and imitate the song of the cuckoo."

The Hebrew language in his view was, "perhaps simple compared with some, but majestic and splendid, spare and yet full of meat. It is the purest of languages and richest in vocabulary, it neither begs, borrows, nor steals as do the Greek, Latin and German languages. It has no composite words nor single words with many meanings, but one precise word for every shade of meaning. To be sure, the Greeks have beautiful and piercing words, but their thought-vocabulary is inferior. For the wisdom of the Greeks, compared with the wisdom of the Jews (the truly pious, ancient Jews), is animal: the be-all and end-all of it are human virtue and probity, whereas the Jewish wisdom centres on righteousness in God."

After this it comes as a slight jolt to read, in the course of the self-same causerie, that Luther did not in fact know Hebrew at all well. "If I were younger, I would take up this language. Without it one can never truly comprehend the Scriptures. Even the New Testament though written in Greek is full of Hebraic thought and Hebrewisms. Rightly is it said that the Hebrews drank straight from the fount, the Greeks from the jet that flows out, and the Latins from the puddle. But though I am no master of either Greek or Hebrew, yet I'll take on any who are. Languages don't make a theologian, they are only aides when all is said."

To Luther, all his writing was theology. He breathed and felt and thought and lived religion. He was sure of himself as a theologian. "St. Jerome spoke nine languages yet had not half the insight of St. Augustine with only one." Equipped with the true recognitions, one did not need perfect command of the original languages to penetrate through the silt of past translations, back to the pure source. It needed conscientious digging, right enough, and languages were the tools: but the most consummate spadework would be nothing without the informed guidance of the archaeologist, who knows what he is looking for.

"I hold that no false Christian or other sectary can translate Scripture correctly. The Worms edition of the Prophets is a perfect example. Great labour was employed, and my German was closely imitated: but the translators were Jews, with little loyalty to Christ, and so their art and industry were all in vain."

It was so obvious to him, it seemed so elementary. The Jews just could not see the pre-Christian prophets as witnesses of Christ, even as the orthodox Catholics would not see the textual evidence throughout the Scriptures that salvation is by faith alone, and as later dissidents put on *their* distorting spectacles to see what they wanted. As shown, he realized full well that there is no absolute reading, much less translation, of a text; approximation to the spirit of the thing would come the closest to it—and there he would trust himself against anyone so long as he had the corroboration of St. Paul.

Translations might be likened to different dramatic productions based on one script. Luther's production was in modern dress, and transposed from a nebulous oriental setting to a graphically familiar one. Did not painters illustrating Biblical scenes do exactly the same? How else was the live reality of such scenes to be recreated? A turban here, a palm tree there did not make the universal Jerusalem any less a Flemish,

Italian, or German town. The people only knew that which they knew and pictured the rest of the world in the image of what reference they possessed.

Luther's powers of visual and sympathetic imagination were exceptionally strong, and he not only could readily place himself inside the given characters and situations, it did his heart a world of good to do so. His job was to transmit the same vivid experience to others. Being an artist, he succeeded. But he himself still had no conception of talent in any terms but those of theology and learning. He encouraged all his friends in other parts of the country who had the right theological and character qualifications plus the necessary time for such work, to make Bible translations of their own, tailored for the localities in question. If despite ample leisure and right-mindedness there proved to be something lacking in the result, Luther put it down to insufficient practice or instruction. Although being as susceptible to poetry as to music, he did not understand that making it is not in everybody's power.

He loved the work and thought that it was good: "I don't want to boast—but I think you will find it better and more useful than all the Greek and Latin versions and commentaries put together, for the stumps and stones are cleared out of the way so that everyone will be able to read it without stumbling-blocks."

But he set no over-great store by it: "This version won't last forever, either. In time the world will need something new again, and throw it away."

It was good enough to go on with, and the work went with such a swing that he could hardly wait to get down to the Old Testament after the New; but he was never satisfied with it. He enrolled Melanchthon for the task of meticulous revision before the Wartburg manuscript went to press, and he continued to revise every new edition of his whole Bible, to the day of his death—there were proof-sheets he had been marking among his luggage when he died, from home—always with a view to greater accuracy and clarity, according to his lights.

Compared with his burning of the canon law, his stand at Worms left a great deal to be desired; compared with his Catechism, his Bible was inadequate. That was his opinion.

The Bible by Martin Luther, however, was the version that struck root everywhere in Germany (incidentally inspiring the seminal English translation of Tyndale who worked in Wittenberg for a time as a refugee from Henry VIII's régime) and exceeded by centuries the author's estimate of its durability. He did not think it would outlive him.

Purists—guardians of pure scholarship and guardians of pure Catholic orthodoxy—would attack it, until such time at all events as Luther's Bible became itself archaic holy writ glazed with the invulnerable patina of traditional authority. The fact remained that it was read, unceasingly, and shaped an entire nation's consciousness of religious actuality. Thus, and only thus, spoke Moses and the patriarchs, the prophets, the Psalmist, Jesus, and the Almighty himself. Any variants seemed travesties, with the disturbing effect of faulty portraiture—like and yet not like, unconvincing, irritating: other, *wrong*.

So the style that Luther wrought became identified with the Word of God, which was unthinkable thereafter in any other cadence.

"I have no particular, peculiar, special language in German," he insisted, belligerently. "I just use the common-German, so that North and South may both understand me. I speak according to the Saxon chancery, which has set the pattern for all the governments in Germany —so that this is the most commonly written and spoken language in German lands."

It was true that the practice of publishing edicts and other government transactions in German rather than exclusively in Latin as had used to be the case, had originated at the Saxon court which therefore set a certain norm of orthography for such documents. But that norm was already antiquated, and it never had become binding upon dialects, which had a high degree of variability as regards both consonants and vowels, quite apart from variations in regional vocabulary. Sometimes it might be possible to tell where an author—or his printer!— came from, by the spelling. What Luther proudly called "common-German" was very much unfixed, fluid, and divers—till he got hold of it and fixed it.

Fortunately the New Testament was complete in first draft when the final summons came that he could not disobey—for it came from the flock, not from the shepherd as hitherto. He had done it in about eight weeks, before Easter as he had hoped.

It had already dawned on him that his deficiency in the original languages, Hebrew especially, made it impossible for him to tackle the Old Testament without assistance; and that he would have to come down from the Wartburg for that. What if he were to go and live privately somewhere outside Wittenberg, without causing embarrassment to the university and the Elector—only near enough to consult with scholars and linguists? He had sounded Spalatin on the idea some little time ago, with no very enthusiastic response at the time.

But enthusiasm—that was a bad word now, a new bad word that caused Luther to see red; worse than Antichrist. With their "enthusiasm" and "enthusiasts" they had now forced his hand and spoilt his project.

He never forgave them.

"God wills it," he said, like the crusaders of old, and like them girded himself with wrath and resolution.

‏✻

5. "I Will Protect You More Than You Will Protect Me"

Luther did not ask his sovereign employer's permission, but he did at least inform Elector Frederick that he was coming back to Wittenberg, which was more than the town council had done.

While Luther's resurrection, copiously attested by the writings from the Wartburg, was credited in most of Germany, knowledge of his hide-out and alias remained confined to a small handful of people. So long as nobody else knew where he was, the internal evidence of his literary style was conclusive only to the literary expert; the great majority had no proof that he lived: forgeries had been put about in his name before now. But also, so long as Elector Frederick "did not know," so long even Duke George could not accuse him of harbouring a heretic in flagrant contravention of an imperial edict which had ratified the ecclesiastical ban with the ban of the state; nor could the Catholic Church excommunicate him on the same score. And so long as Luther "did not know" who had been his host these ten months he was not bound by either etiquette or gratitude to await termination of hospitality.

As soon as Luther re-materialized from his state of official non-existence, however, the outlaw's overlord would be forced to declare himself. If Frederick let the outlaw freely walk about in his dominions, he broke the law and stood to have his lands placed under interdict, invaded, and "pacified" over his head. If he refused to protect the outlaw, he was warned that his subjects would take it as an invitation to revolt. He could have no wish to share in his old age the fate of the Duke of Württemberg, a poor vagrant, God knew where, by reason of his having got between those same upper and nether millstones.

The Elector asked Luther not to come. He asked, he did not really command. It was an order, but hedged in queries and quasi-apologies. That cross, on the acquisition of which Luther had congratulated him —he would be happy to bear it, if only he could be quite sure that was God's will. He did not have a pipeline to the Deity like the Zwickau Prophets, he had no doctor's degree like Martin, he had no certificate of infallibility like the Pope. Personally he would be very glad to see Martin—but not yet awhile, not just yet. The Elector would hate to find himself unable to protect him. Now it was Luther who was told to wait. Wait; suffer time to work on his side. Wait, the Diet might rescind the Edict of Worms one of these days, wait for Duke George to cool down a little before tempting providence by a jaunt right through his territory. . . .

Wait! Ridiculous. The Elector evidently still did not appreciate what was at stake. The souls of his subjects, once more torn between true Christianity and false, that's what was at stake. Wait? When Luther had made up his mind? Not likely.

On receipt of the Elector's message Luther started straight for Wittenberg. Wait, indeed. He would not even wait to indite his answer to the sovereign; *that* could wait till he was well on his way.

On the second day of his ride, in the effective camouflage of Squire George, he wrote:

"Your Electoral Grace knows, or if you don't know I herewith let you know, that I received the command of the gospel not from any man but from heaven alone. That I offered to be heard and judged was not because I was in any doubt, but entirely from excessive humility and in the hope of winning others. But now, perceiving that further humility can only result in bringing contempt upon the gospel and in the Devil's taking possession of the whole shoot if I let him have so much as a hand's breadth of leeway, I am compelled to change my tactic. I have done enough for Your Electoral Grace, in yielding to you all this year. The Devil knows I did not hold back from timidity, he knows it very well!

"I write thus that you may know I come to Wittenberg under the protection of a far higher power than the Elector, and I have no mind to crave shelter from Your Grace. If I thought you could or would protect me, then I would not come. I can protect you more than you can protect me.

"Since I suspect Your Electoral Grace is still weak in faith, I cannot regard you as the man who can guard or rescue me. God will have nothing of your effort, or mine. He will have everything left to him and no one else. If Your Grace will come to believe this, you will be happy and at peace. If you don't, well, I do and must leave you to sorrow in your unbelief, as it becomes all unbelievers to suffer.

"Since I will not obey Your Grace, you are excused in the sight of God if I am imprisoned or killed. Before men Your Grace should conduct yourself as follows. An an Elector you should be obedient to superior power and permit His Imperial Majesty to rule body and goods in your cities and lands in accordance with the law of the Empire, and you should offer no opposition and interpose no hindrance if he tries to arrest or slay me. For no one ought to withstand the lawful authorities save he who has instituted them. Else it is uproar and against God. I hope, however, that they will have the good sense to understand that Your Grace was born in too lofty a cradle to be yourself my executioner. If you leave the door open and see that they are unmolested if they come for me themselves, you will have been obedient enough. But should they be so lacking in intelligence as to ask Your Electoral Grace to lay hands on me yourself, I will then tell Your Grace what to do.

"I will keep Your Grace safe from harm and danger to body, goods, and soul on my account, whether Your Grace believes it or not.

"I write in haste that Your Grace shall not be distressed by the surprise of my arrival, for I must comfort everybody and hurt nobody, if I would be a true Christian. It is another enemy I face than Duke George (with whom I am not in the least concerned)—an enemy that knows me well, and I have some acquaintance with him too!

"If Your Electoral Grace but had faith, you would see the glory of God; but as you do not believe, you have as yet seen nothing. Love and honour to God forever. Amen. Given at Borna, by the side of my guide, this Ash Wednesday, 1522. Your Grace's humble servant, Martin Luther."

He rode into Wittenberg on the Friday, 4 March—having not exactly hurried on the journey itself, this time. It was his first taste, and was to be his last, of liberty; and he got some enjoyment out of his incognito.

One would hardly recognize the writer of that letter to the Elector in the benign, playful gentleman who stood drinks and a meal to two Swiss students who encountered him at an inn, the Black Bear, in Jena: "A knight who sat reading in the taproom, with a red beret, and a sword which he held by the hilt with his right hand while he held the book down with the left. . . ." For these students dined out on the ensuing little stock comedy of mistaken identity which had its due, merry denouement when they met him again at Wittenberg, their Mecca; one of them eventually wrote up and published their adventure syllable by syllable. "And when we came in—" this was at the house of Jerome Schurpff, now resident in Wittenberg together with his brother Augustine, to whom the Swiss pair had a letter of introduction—"there was he, looking exactly the same as at Jena, and with him Philip Melanchthon, Justus Jonas, Nicholas Amsdorf, and Dr. Jerome and Dr. Augustine Schurpff, who were all telling him what had been happening in Wittenberg. He greeted us with a laugh, and we all had a good laugh. . . ."

Luther pen in hand and Luther in personal intercourse were different creatures. He could never resist a joke and a good laugh—on his short list of best antidotes against the Devil—nor yet the temptation to be friendly: for, nearly always yielding to the impulse of friendliness face to face, he believed this to be one of his character faults.

That he could take time off to laugh with the Swiss students at Wittenberg was a high feat of human friendliness. He was extremely upset by what the reception committee were then telling him: it was Saturday, he had only got in the night before. Whether or not anybody said, "I told you so," Luther's state of mind could not have been improved by the reflection that he had been making light of their written reports, or by the common human urge to vent one's rage at oneself upon somebody else.

"My worst enemies, close as they have often struck, have never dealt me so hard a blow as I have now received from my own people. I can just see Satan grinning."

In his name, priests had been dragged by the hair (poor souls, perhaps they had been already letting their tonsures grow!), sanctuaries had been defaced, the holy oil thrown out and set alight, by jeering rabble. In his name, which as yet they did not disdain to use, the Zwickau Prophets with Karlstadt's and Zwilling's concurrence were fomenting war on law and order, peace and property, as like other heretics before them they preached the primitive communism of the Apostles. How they would rejoice, indeed, the enemies of the gospel, to see their predictions coming true, of chaos following at Luther's heels!

The Swiss caught him only just, "looking exactly as at Jena." Directly he had heard all, Squire George became a heap of empty clothes and gear and hair clippings, and Doctor Martin re-emerged in the black gown of St. Augustine with a beardless face and gleaming tonsure. Thus the next morning, Sunday, he mounted the pulpit of the town church after a year's absence from it as if he had never been away—except that he had noticeably put on weight, and not only as regards avoirdupois.

The brethren at the Black Cloister had expressed doubts of his wisdom to go to the people in full dress, there being so much hostility to monks. But of course, said Luther, there being so much hostility to monks—now if ever was the time to be a monk and stay a monk! Of course.

But who would have defied, hissed, manhandled their hero, the holy doctor? They wept for joy to have him back, risen from the grave in answer to the people's prayers, their saviour. He preached, "like a true prophet and a nightingale," they said. What he said was right; it had to be.

"God granted you a great blessing, in giving you the Word pure and undefiled. Yet I see none the more charity in you. You extend no helping hand to those who have never heard the Word. You take no thought for our brothers and sisters of Meissen, of Leipzig, and countless other places, whom we are bound to save in common with ourselves. You have rushed into your present proceedings, eyes shut, head down, like a bull, looking neither left nor right. . . .

"You are directing your energies against the mass, images, and other unimportant matters, and in doing so are laying aside that faith and charity of which you have so much need. You have offended by your outrageous conduct many pious people—people perhaps better than yourselves. You have forgotten what is due to the weak. If the strong run at the utmost of their speed, regardless of their feebler brethren who come more slowly after them, the latter, left helpless behind, must needs fall by the way. . . .

"It is by the aid of the Word alone we must fight; by the Word alone shall we overcome; by the Word alone we shall demolish what our opponents have raised up by force and oppression. I condemn only by the Word. Let him who believes, believe and follow me; let him who believes not, believe not and go his own way. No one must be compelled to the faith or to the things of the faith against his will; he must be prevailed upon by faith alone. I also condemn images, but I would have them assailed by the Word, and not by blows and fire. I would deal with them so that people should no longer have the faith in them that they used to have. Be assured, the images will fall of themselves, when the people shall have understood that they are as nothing in the eyes of God. By the Word and by the power of the Word alone would I efface from the minds of men all these devices of the Pope as confession, mass, vows, fasting and the rest. . . ."

In this vein, with for him extraordinary moderation considering his feelings, he preached on eight consecutive days—naming no names, detailing no specific misdeeds, stressing the spiritual not the social aspects of the disorders here. "Christianity consists neither in desisting from nor engaging in outward ceremonies, only in faith," was the refrain: precipitate reform was no better than papal coercion, to proscribe distasteful modes of worship was no less wrong than to enforce them. Consideration, patience, love—those were the only true stepping stones to the kingdom of righteousness.

He was the Doctor. The Zwickau Prophets might claim that they spoke for God, but they could no longer claim they spoke for Martin Luther.

He made short work of them. He told them to get out, and they left town. Such was his power. The mood of Wittenberg had changed as though miraculously by his return; all was peace, contrition, sweet reasonableness, obedience. The town council hastened to submit its ordinances to his judgment. Zwilling was made to see the error of his ways; Karlstadt was silenced. Luther—not the university, not the Elector, but Luther had the power to do so, though without any official civic standing.

"Karlstadt is annoyed with me because I have withdrawn his licence to preach! But with his foolish teaching, he has been leading the people to imagine that if they *don't* go to confession and *do* break images this immediately makes them perfect Christians. So he calls me persecutor. Behold—I, barely escaped from martyrdom myself, am now a maker of martyrs!" Annoyed was hardly the word. Karlstadt refused to be confined to his university chair and left Wittenberg without permission.

The Elector knew what he was doing when he swallowed Luther's letter and did nothing to prevent him taking up his ordinary duties again in the most ordinary way. Distance, as with Luther, had lent haziness to the view. He had now learned that the Enthusiasts had caused numbers of Wittenberg students to leave the university so as to acquire manual trades, among their other incitements to transgression. It was represented to the Diet that without Luther Luther's imitators would run wild elsewhere even as they "might have done" in Saxony. Meanwhile all he asked of Luther was a written statement absolving his sovereign from all responsibility for his return to Wittenberg, which the Elector would be able to show at the Diet in case of need.

The Elector realized what he was doing, did he? that herewith he acknowledged an excommunicate outlaw subject as a force above him—? The magistrates of Wittenberg, who had thrown off the tyranny of Rome—did they appreciate that they had herewith thrown themselves upon the superior guidance of another spiritual authority? And Luther, did he see it?

The Zwickau Prophets saw it, but they were crazy. Karlstadt saw it, but he was a disgruntled little man with the complexion of a kippered herring and an unattractive Bohemian accent. They called Luther the Pope of Wittenberg, they called him lackey of the princes and watch-dog of the city moneybags. "Doctor Pussyfoot," "Doctor Easychair," "Doctor Sit-on-fence," "Doctor Slime" were some of their names for him. The general flock, no doubt somewhat out of breath from running so fast, once they stopped, displayed the "universal gladness and rejoicing at his coming and his words," of relief; and, now that it could be told how he had lived through the past ten months, they called him their knight in armour.

Luther, the sane man and conquering hero, he did not see it, but he sensed the change which occurred the moment he came down from the mountain top like Moses to take charge in an entirely different capacity from any he might have held heretofore. His single-track mind chugged past political implications, but his practical instincts did not fail to take them in. If church and community were to become one whole, they must together work out the modus vivendi, from scratch. He was sanguine that that could be done.

Consciously he saw only that the people could not be left to dip into the Scriptures for themselves—not yet, at any rate, not till they had been thoroughly imbued with the correct interpretation: that otherwise the unity of Christian dogma would shiver into smithereens. Unity, continuity, gradualness: these formed his main theme for the present; disseminating pastoral instruction and providing workable administrative foundations for this were the main tasks.

Having staked his life for Christian freedom on the basis of the open Bible, Luther responded to a practical emergency by disallowing unrestricted, untutored Bible interpretation and unlicensed acts of conscience. He distinguished between acts and thoughts: "Thoughts are duty-free." Let people think what they liked and if they did not like to conform outwardly, go away. Thoughts should never be punishable; nor should expressed religious dissidence be punishable in life and limb: "To banish is enough," except for deeds of criminal violence.

Luther had gone out an ideologist and he came back a law-giver and organizer. Neither of the latter was his natural part, and he never would feel happy in them. But they were forced on him and he could not get out, until there might be others coming forward to take over. It exasperated him increasingly, that nobody would. The everlasting son manqué was made into a father figure, in the stance of the angry middle-aged man befitting such a one.

Up to this point, Martin Luther invariably had suited action only to carefully matured thought. Returning from the Wartburg, to plangent alarm signals, he acted first and suited thought to action. There were those who said it was a Procrustean fit.

Wittenberg had made the break away from Catholic tradition which he had shown to be false and evil, they said, and Luther came and cobbled up the breach again. "From the region of birds and air," "From the wilderness," "From Patmos," they said, he had approved the reforms of Karlstadt, and now he reversed them.

While one may doubt whether Luther, had he never been away from Wittenberg, would have even gone so far with practical reforms as to reach the middle position on which he took his stand in 1522, that accusation was not merited.

He did not "restore the whole Catholic rite in all its forms," as he was accused. Private masses, compulsory confession, compulsory fasting were not restored. The sacrificial canon of the mass—that central mystery of abhorrent *magic* of the central rite in the orthodox form—was not restored. Celibacy was not restored. The disbanded monasteries were not re-established, nor was ordination. The municipal laws against mendicancy and prostitution were not repealed. (Finding new jobs and places in secular life for the thousands of monks who had thrown themselves into it overnight was one of countless related social problems. A great many got a livelihood out of vending Luther's books on a commission basis, thanking God there were so many publishers, so well supplied.)

Communion in both kinds did not cease: but for the time being it was to be administered only at private celebrations on request of the congregation, not at the standard public services. Except on congregational request, too, liturgy and the rest of ceremonial went back to the old patterns until a suitable synthesis might be evolved as Luther pledged himself he would see that it did—at leisure and with care. Random distribution of foundation moneys ceased, images were restored, matrimony was not to be compulsory on priests, fasting and confession were optional, infants should continue to be baptized (as a kind of spiritual initiation), and private property was declared inviolate. The community was to assume responsibility for the upkeep of churches and ministers, and to be sure no ecclesiastical innovations were to be instituted without the consent or against the decision of the appropriate secular authorities. There were no more Peter's pence, clerical immunity to civil law, legally absolute subservience to Rome.

It was not so very little to go on with. It went along with much of the substance of the German Gravamina: except in that these reforms came from a territorial nucleus and not as formerly taken for granted from the central executive of the paramount institution. It was a reformation although not a revolution; it was a definite and positive beginning although a very great deal remained to be done.

Moreover, seeing that the Wittenberg experiment no longer seemed to threaten anarchy, a succession of towns and other sovereign units in the Empire began to try "the New Religion" for themselves—only that Luther hated to have it called that as much as he hated hearing it called Lutheran: it was not "new," it was fifteen hundred years old, he pointed out.

At the next Imperial Diet, when the flouted Edict of Worms came up once again under the head of priority business, the Estates declined to enforce it at last and so to annihilate Martin Luther, that proven bulwark against lawless upheaval. "I will protect you more than you will protect me." He had not been far wrong. The Enthusiasts were not far wrong.

In fact, regarding the event like this, the wonder would seem to be that the Reformed Religion was not adopted everywhere at once, in Germany.

Well now. First the knights, then the peasants, and the Enthusiasts, and finally the Great Man, the reluctant Father and unwilling party oracle of the evangelical movement—between them they helped mightily, to put paid to that.

III

THE WORD MADE FLESH

1. Sensation, 1525

On 27 June 1525, a Tuesday, shortly before ten o'clock in the morning, bells began to ring in Wittenberg. A small procession formed up before the Black Cloister—which continued to be known by that name although now a private dwelling—and headed by a pair of pipers marched along to the town church. The streets were lined with onlookers, every space in front of the church was packed, to witness the ceremony in the open porch.

There, then, the city pastor Bugenhagen performed the public consecration of a marriage which in civil law had been quietly contracted a fortnight earlier. That done, the young couple and their train, which increased appreciably on the way, returned to the old monastery for the wedding feast.

The invited guests included the parents of the groom though no relations of the bride, three university professors respectively of Wittenberg, Erfurt, and Magdeburg, three Saxon Electoral councillors, the secretary of the late Elector Frederick III, with his newly wed wife, the town apothecary of Wittenberg and a merchant of Torgau, also with their ladies. Many more came to the merry banquet, to which most of them had contributed in kind according to their means, and yet more to a dinner dance in the evening at the town hall, which closed down by order of the magistrate one hour before midnight.

Bride and groom were then seen to bed with customary pleasantries by the hard core of their witnesses and well-wishers.

Everything went according to plan—except that in the middle of the wedding night there came a very untoward knocking at the gates.

But it was only a fugitive craving asylum, who had to be let in and comforted though in every way unwelcome.

The celebrations of that day served as the general announcement of the marriage of Dr. Martin Luther, apostate friar, and Katharina von Bora, a runaway nun. Apart from the fact that he was under standing sentence of death, with death sentences hanging over several of the wedding guests as accessories to the crime of abducting a nun, the marriage was itself a capital offence in law.

The marriage was a world-wide scandal, and it was a noble deed; it was the crowning blasphemy, and it was a crowning act of faith; it was a piece of typical fecklessness and a typically practical solution to an acute social problem.

As Christ had suffered himself to be crucified, so Martin Luther married—with shame and opprobrium cast upon him by one side, doubts, grief, and nervous or defiant support on the other. In all honesty, so far as he was aware, he entered matrimony in a spirit of exalted necessity—characteristically resolved, however, to play down the sacrificial aspect once he had determined on the plunge, and also to make the best of it.

The same honesty compelled him, when he found out that he liked it, to proclaim with wonted forthrightness the excellencies of the married state in his considered experience. He took to marriage like a duck to water; and whatever else it did, the marriage cemented his position and the path of the Reformation.

2. Shooting War

The man who got Doctor Martin out of bed on his wedding night was Karlstadt.

Karlstadt, who had ceased to answer to that name since leaving Wittenberg and insisted on being addressed as Neighbour Andreas only, who wore peasant rags with a grey smock and "white" felt hat from choice and not for camouflage, was on the run for his life. He had made his way through the battle zones of Franconia, between the enemy lines, both of whom were out for his blood. There was a very bloody civil war on in Germany when Luther married.

Tritely, everybody blamed it on everyone else. Luther blamed Karlstadt not a little. A great many people blamed Luther.

"We have triumphed over the papal tyranny which weighed down kings and princes: it will be still easier to demolish the kings and princes themselves," Luther had written in the summer of 1522, for publication, when Duke George and like-minded suzerains in surrounding territories prohibited the sale of Luther's New Testament translation—even offering to return their money to those who had already purchased copies. "I fear if anyone continues to heed what that blockhead Duke George says, there will break out throughout Germany such disturbances as shall bring about the ruin of all princes and magistrates and drag down the whole body of the clergy with them. All round the people are in seething excitement; they have opened their eyes, so long closed, and they will not, they cannot, be oppressed any longer. I see before me Germany swimming in blood! The Lord himself is blinding the eyes of the great to the sword of civil war, suspended over their heads. They are exerting all their efforts to destroy Luther, while Luther is doing his utmost to save them. It is not for Luther, but for them, that perdition approaches; and they, instead of seeking to avert, advance it. . . . I write this fasting, quite early in the morning, my heart filled with pious confidence. My Christ lives and reigns, and I too shall live and reign."

He was aggrieved when some described his fatherly warning as incendiary.

He was greatly out of humour with kings and princes altogether at that season, when, also, Henry VIII's polemic against *The Babylonian Captivity* had made its appearance in Wittenberg.

"Herr Henry, by the disgrace of God King of England, has written in Latin against my treatise. Some say it is not his own work, but whether Henry wrote it, or Hal, or Old Harry, is beside the point. He who lies is a liar, and I fear him not, whoever he may be. If a king of England spits his shameless lies in my face, I have a right to vomit them back down his very throat. If he blasphemes my sacred doctrines, if he casts his filth at the throne of my monarch, my Christ, he cannot be surprised at my doing the same by his royal diadem and proclaiming him a liar, a rascal, and an imbecile. . . . His book is a kind of misguided penance, for his conscience is ever smiting him for having stolen the crown of England, murdering the last scion of the true royal line, and corrupting the blood of the kings of England. He trembles in his skin . . . and this makes him clutch at the Pope to keep him on his throne, makes him pay court now to the Emperor, now to the King of France: precisely what one would expect of a conscience-haunted tyrant. Hal and the Pope have exactly the same legitimacy: the Pope stole his tiara as the King did his crown; so naturally they are as thick together as two mules in harness."

And so forth, at prodigal length and with prodigious marksmanship: Henry who was but the second Tudor never forgave; though Luther, persuaded by Elector Frederick that the English King was himself contemplating church reform, published a handsome apology explaining how his pen had run away with him. No one had ever so addressed a king for all the world to read.

No one had ever discoursed on kings in general as Luther in his exuberant peroration:

"Since the world began, a wise and prudent prince has been a *rara avis,* and an *avis* still more *rara* has been a prince who was at the same time an honest man. . . . God being a great and mighty king, it was necessary that the hangmen and lictors he employed should be noble, rich, illustrious persons. It has pleased his divine will that we should address his hangmen and lictors as 'most gracious lord,' 'most exalted prince,' and so forth. . . . If we meet, in history or experience, with a prudent, honest, Christian prince, we cry, 'A miracle! a miracle!' for generally it happens to us as to the Jews, whom God threatened thus: 'I will give them a king in my anger.'

"Ay, princes, your just reward is at hand; you are estimated at what you really are, rogues and rascals; you are weighed in a just balance and found wanting; the people know you through and through, and terrible chastisement is hemming you round about, closer and closer, and will not be turned aside. The people, utterly wearied of you, will no longer endure your tyranny and iniquity, nor will God. The world now is not the world as it used to be, wherein at your pleasure you hunted men as though they were beasts. . . ."

Coming from him the great holy doctor, this sort of thing was not calculated to uphold respect and awe before crowned heads nor to inhibit those rebellious forces which were what he saw gathering by way of "terrible chastisement."

First, disappointed in their hopes of the new imperial reign ("Spanish Charles Go Home!") and a united heave by the Estates for political reform behind the spearhead of independent religious reformation, the radical knighthood of Germany made their final bid for power. For once burying all private feuds in genuine agreement to pool their resources and accept the leadership of Franz von Sickingen, the petty nobility throughout the Empire rallied to support the enterprise which, launched in the central and southern parts, aimed at destroying the power of the princes in all its mingled arbitrariness and inefficiency. With the means thus coming all at once to hand, the Franconian leadership was enabled to organize and stock up war materials on a far greater scale than at any time before, able, too, to hire mercenary reinforcements in far greater numbers, including those of the highest quality, from Switzerland, the Western world's best pool of professional fighting men. This, combined with the anti-Roman, pro-evangelical sentiments so strongly represented by Sickingen and Hutten, facilitated alliances with certain townships and city federations. Escalation of terrorism by raid and ambush, plus the impetus of initial successes, did the rest, to make the onslaught a veritable, full-dress campaign against the Empire from within: indeed at the outset there was, strange to say, some secret support emanating from such assorted quarters as the Archbishop-Elector of Mainz, the imperial regency, and the inner circle of the now distant Emperor's court.

However, that same resulting initial impetus was too devastating. The magnates of the Empire followed the example of the knighthood and in their turn buried jealousy and mutual predatoriness, not to mention present differences in religious outlook; so that under the leadership of the pugnacious Archbishop-Elector of Trier a mighty coalition formed—Trier, Hesse, the Palatinate, and the principal constituents of the Swabian League which had Württemberg, Brandenburg-Ansbach, Bayreuth and Baden, Augsburg, and some twenty other free cities among its subscribers. The tide was turned.

Till then, the mailed hand of knighthood had been on offer to Luther undeterred by rebuff. It is a question whether, as events turned out, Luther was proved wise to have rebuffed these champions, or whether they would have succeeded in the end had Luther made common cause with them. However that might be, defeat followed defeat, and after their false dawn of fire and blood the knights were crushed at last, forever, like the feudal chivalry of other countries long before them, upon the death of Sickingen in May 1523.

The Armageddon of the knights against the Empire marked the final ascendancy of firearms over the ancient, conventional weapons of man—even as Agincourt marked the triumph of the flexible archer over that lumbering human tank, the heavy-armoured horseman.

The explosive properties of saltpetre had been known in the West for some time, since the Crusades if not before; although the honour of harnessing these properties to effective warlike utility is commonly shared out between Roger Bacon (1214–94), who communicated the formula of gunpowder, and Berthold Schwarz (c.1300), who invented a prototypal gun—both of them Franciscan friars. The honour of first demonstrating the power of mobile field artillery belongs to Johann Ziska (1360–1424), formidable captain of the Hussites. One ponders the accident which linked lethal proficiency with the progress of a highly ethical religion.

Ordnance had come into use increasingly among the European nations since, but mainly as an auxiliary and by no means indispensable weapon. Great strides had been made particularly at Nuremberg—that flourishing centre of peaceful craftsmanship—in the further development of both light guns and cannon; and the loot from Sickingen's castle included a magnificent showpiece of Nuremberg manufacture, named The Nightingale—13½ feet long, weighing 7 cwt., and adorned with relief portraits of Sickingen, his wife, several ancestors, and his pre-Lutheran patron saint, St. Francis. Well—The Nightingale had remained in the nest; Sickingen had left it at home. The roads, of course, were bad, and scant. Always the roads. One ponders the indebtedness of civilization to the march of warfare—demanding always more and better roads, along which learning, trade, and even finally democracy, could also travel faster, as it happened.

However, the imperial loyalists come to hunt Sickingen down brought their artillery in strength. ("Never," Sickingen swore, "have I known such unchristian shooting!") His redoubt of Landstuhl, newly fortified and believed impenetrable, was shot to pieces: one piece, a great, splintered beam, penetrated Sickingen's side. The winning high command came in a body as he lay dying, to receive his signed capitulation, and briefly—perforce briefly—moralized about his crimes. When he had breathed his last, the three princes knelt down in the debris-strewn cellar where he had been carried, and recited the Lord's Prayer, for the comfort of his soul.

Hutten, indefatigably ambidextrous with sword and pen, outlived Sickingen by a bare four months. After the rout, there was no place of safety for him in the Empire, and he fled—very ill—to Switzerland, where, at Basel, Erasmus refused to harbour him for even one night. He died on an island in Lake Zürich, under the roof of a clerical physician versed in the treatment of venereal disease; thirty-five years old, unrepentant and unbowed to the end.

The wounds were hardly healed, the graves were scarcely overgrown; innumerable burned villages were not yet rebuilt, towns barely patched up, fortresses and whole districts just beginning to scrape together tribute and compensation levied on them by the victors—as was the Reformed Religion beginning to recover somewhat from the taint of Sickingen's championship—when a still more baneful association was foisted on the evangelical movement. The *Bundschuh* peasantry rose in emulation of the knighthood.

This amalgamation of secret societies of the lower orders, which foreshadowed the trade unions as well as the revolutionist cadres of future centuries, had spread a network of disaffection over the whole middle west and south of Germany. As well as the agrarian population the peasant class comprised all manual workers below master level, so that it covered a considerable urban section, and *Bundschuh* membership cut across the system of craft guilds as well as the land-bound frontiers of serfdom. In past decades, attempts at peaceable negotiation had mostly failed as peasant delegations were too often turned away and sent packing by their betters; attempted uprisings had mostly been betrayed, before ever reaching their utmost momentum—betrayed, mostly, via the confessional.

Ah yes, that had been before Luther became the hero of the German nation, before in his discursive fertility he scattered directions for social reforms inherent in his criticism of the Church; before Karlstadt, Münzer and kindred Enthusiasts, expelled from the centre, established a growing evangelical left wing outside. Under their common if unco-ordinate influence, the complaints of the peasantry became informed with Scriptural warrants, its physical necessity with a moral hunger for equity, and its plain, dumb, human desperation acquired the boost of articulate, spiritual fervour. This time the *Bundschuh* had its placards, too, its reasoned, printed manifesto; and in the regions where the biggest insurrection Germany had ever known began—in Thuringia, Württemberg, and along the Upper Rhine—all those who were privy to it had forsworn the confessional on religious principle. There were no betrayals—before they were ready, and struck.

These were the Twelve Articles of "Complaints and amicable demands of the united body of peasantry, with their Christian prayers," on which the Peasant War of 1524/5 was fought:

"1. Firstly, it is our humble prayer and desire that we should henceforth have the right and power for the parish as a whole to elect and choose its own pastor (I Timothy 3) and also to depose him should he misconduct himself (Titus 1). The same elected pastor shall preach to us the holy gospel as it stands, clear and pure, without human additions (Apostles 14). [Elaboration follows, with three quotations from the Pentateuch and two more from the New Testament.]

"2. Since tithe is established as lawful by the Old Testament, which the New Testament confirms in all things, we are willing to pay our legal tithe of corn, in a fair and legal manner. . . ." This was the "great tithe" on produce, out of which it was proposed to support the elected pastor, any possible surplus to be divided between the poor and a savings fund for emergency war taxation. The "little tithe" on all livestock, however, should go, since the Lord God had created the beasts for the free use of man. Article 2 had nine Biblical quotations.

"3. Thirdly, since Christ with his precious blood redeemed all men without exception (Isaiah 53:1, I Peter 1, II Corinthians 7, Romans 13), the lowliest along with the all-highest," they the undersigned wished to be free, "free but not licentious," and demanded the abolition of serfdom.

4. The common man should have the right to hunt, fish, and protect his land against game (whereas under the existing poaching laws "those animals which most harm the farmer we are forbidden to hurt, and to disobey is to have one's eyes put out").

5. The common man should have the right to take wood for firing and building from what used to be common forest land but had been appropriated by the nobles and ecclesiastical foundations—"by equitable arrangement," certainly not at random and unchecked.

6. was a request for reduction of the statutory labour services—which at present left the farmers no time for their own fields except on holidays or in bad weather "sometimes not even then"—to a "merciful amount such as our ancestors were bound to." 7. added that the lords should not to be allowed to pile on further gratuitous services. (The spark of this outbreak of the *Bundschuh*, as reported by a contemporary chronicler, was supplied by the Countess of Lupfen who sent out her villagers to collect snail shells on which they were then set to wind thread. But doubtless a freak hailstorm which caused the harvest to fail in that part of the country had also something to do with it.)

8. Rents should be revised by arbitration.

9. Justice should be administered impartially, and the constant additions of new pains and penalties should be halted.

10. Fields and grass lands which had been severed from the commons should be restored.

11. The ruinous death tax—by which the best of everything the deceased possessed, sometimes amounting to half his entire worldly

goods, went to the lord—should be done away with. "For widows
and orphans are left destitute, and God will not have it so."

"12. Twelfth, it is our decision and sincere intent that, should it
be found upon examination that one or more of the preceding articles
are falsely based on and opposed to the Holy Scriptures, we shall at
once renounce them so soon as this be proved to us. If, however, the
Scriptures should on further examination entitle us to additional protests against oppression, we equally reserve the right to make such
protests. The peace of Christ be with us all."

Such were the seditious, greedy requisitions—as they were then regarded by those in authority—of a class representing four fifths of
the population without counting the small artisans no longer working
on the land.

The document was noticeably modelled on the style of Luther,
more especially in the long preamble, as witness some extracts. "There
are at this time many Antichristians who take the occasion of the union
of the peasantry to blaspheme the gospel, saying: these are the
fruits of the new gospel, under which nobody is to obey but rise up
against their superiors insolently and with violence, in the intention of
abrogating all civil and ecclesiastical authority. . . . The gospel is not
a cause of insurrection and disorder . . . the word and the life which
it teaches us are not hatred and violence but love, peace and patience.
. . . It clearly results, hence, that the peasantry who in their articles
demand such a gospel for their doctrine and for their life, cannot be
justly called disobedient or rebellious. . . ." Different editions varied
slightly, sometimes citing Luther outright, for support.

Luther could not well remain silent. "In this document, what I
most approve of is the twelfth article. . . . If indeed they really mean
it, there is still ground for hope. . . . Being addressed by name, I
shall relieve myself before God and man from any reproach of having
contributed by my silence to the evil. . . ." For by then "the spirit
of rapine and murder manifested by the insurgent peasants in some
parts of the country" was beyond ignoring.

Luther's *Exhortation to Peace* was written in two parts, one addressed to the nobles and the second to the peasants. He told the
nobles they had only themselves to blame, that they had been robbing
and skinning the common people time out of mind and should
now listen to the people's fair complaints. He told the peasants Christians might never take the law into their own hands under no matter

what provocation, that there was absolutely no excuse for violence under any circumstances, that in demanding the abolition of serfdom they showed a deplorably materialistic spirit, since though serfs in the flesh they were free in Christ, and that refusal to pay tithe was tantamount to highway robbery. He advocated a settlement by mutual agreement.

Impartiality was not what was wanted, still less as he told neither party what it wanted to hear. Probably it was an error of judgment to write at both together; the tract was prosy, one feels, without inspiration. Impartiality was not really his line, either. But he was no longer accustomed to having any word of his entirely disregarded.

It was the old story of popular revolt. "Amicable demands and Christian prayers" cut no ice. On the contrary, last straws were laid on the petitioners' backs here and there, and so they armed themselves with their murderous everyday tools: scythes, pitchforks, axes, mallets, knives, flails, and anything that might be improvised from stone and timber—to which were added presently the more professional contents ot the armouries they stormed, with mounting success, mounting imitators, mounting atrocities.

It was the old story: a hundred parochial interests and idiosyncrasies ran through the uprising, which spread like a rash rather than a controlled inoculation once the toxin became well absorbed. Communications were as bad as ever, there was no synchronization as there was no ultimate unity of programme. There were as many different leaders, and different kinds of leader, as there were regional groups—ranging from vengeful victims of oppression and neo-primitive religious visionaries to odd remnants of the radical knighthood like Götz von Berlichingen and forcibly converted magistrates becoming genuinely indoctrinated. (Duke Ulrich of Württemberg hurried home from foreign parts, signed himself "Ulrich the Peasant," and fought to retrieve his heritage at the head of his district *Bundschuh*.) Nor, in spite of all the fine Lutheran ring and thickly sown Biblical footnotes of the Twelve Articles, was the evangelical element always clear-cut.

Castles fell, communities were sacked and taken over, cloisters were plundered and burned to the ground; and it was the old story: force and terror as they conquered fed upon themselves beyond purpose and satiety. Men became monsters.

All the same, the town of Würzburg went over to the rebels, dozens

of smaller towns between the Danube and the Rhine joined, also
five of the lesser imperial cities, while great ones like Mainz, Trier,
Frankfurt, Strassburg, Ulm and even lordly Nuremberg lent various
support. The Bishop of Speyer, the Bishop of Bamberg, the Elector
Palatine, not a few abbots and counts yielded the desired concessions;
in Austria the Emperor's brother Ferdinand granted evangelical decrees; the miners of Tyrol and Thuringia staged alarming demonstrations. The idea of a total political reformation such as had been the
aim of the knights, now under peasant auspices, began to gain ground
and win sympathizers among all classes, repeat all.

But at Mühlhausen in Alsace Thomas Münzer reigned as a new
theocrat, developing more and more bloodthirsty and megalomaniacal
tendencies, receiving near-divine honours, and sending his Enthusiast
agitators into Saxony.

Elector Frederick the Wise was dying. "That's nice," he said to
Spalatin when the latter overcame his hesitation to intrude on the old
man's sickbed. "One should visit the sick." He had no closer friend
and no relations near him, although in now constant correspondence
with his brother and heir, Johann. The uprising in Saxony was making
strides, with discernibly Enthusiastic rhythms.

"Perhaps the peasants have been given just cause, through the
impeding of the Word of God. In many ways the common people
have been wronged by the rulers, and now God is visiting his wrath
upon us. If it be his will, the common man will come to rule; and if
it be not his will, he won't," Frederick wrote to his brother who, forced
to accede to the peasants' demands in respect of tithes, wrote back,
"As princes we are finished."

No such spirit of defeat could work in Luther. He would not have
conceded that he had in any way brought this upon his princes; what
enraged him more and more was the responsibility falsely thrown on
him by the rebels who went all against his preaching in his name. Let
princes flinch from the rabble; he who had not flinched before the
princes would deal with the people once again. He would go out into
Thuringia where his own roots were and speak to "the unruly mad-
men" of his race.

No one could stop him; he went, preaching Christian resignation
with all the power of his lungs: "Suffering! Suffering! Cross! Cross!"
His message of Jesus Christ's example was reduced to that slogan, as

he was met with yells and insults and pelted with mud; and he was at length persuaded to retreat before worse befell.

Elector Frederick the Wise died in the Lord on 5 May 1525, having taken communion in both kinds and asked forgiveness of his servants, "in case I have ever offended any of you: we princes one way or another do a lot of things that are no good."

"He was a child of peace," said his physician, as he closed the old man's eyes, "and he departeth in peace."

Peace, forsooth! On that same day Martin Luther did a deed of murder—knowing not what he was doing, to be sure. They never do, that crucify.

The pen ran away with him again, but once too often. In the past when it had done so, he had been able to say, "Sorry," afterwards, to explain that he had not really meant it, that his unhappier turns of phrase were metaphorical, rhetorical, or mere allusions to the Psalmist in darker mood; and no bones broken. Not this time.

What did he do? He wrote another tract, *Against the Murderous and Thieving Hordes of Peasants,* inciting the nobles to "stab, smite, throttle, slay these rabid mad dogs without mercy, with a good conscience to the last ounce of strength, for nothing can be more poisonous, hurtful, or devilish than a rebel. He that shall be slain on the side of law and order is a true martyr before God, earning eternal bliss; he that perishes on the side of rebellion is doomed eternally to hell. Such times are these that a prince shall win heaven by bloodshed sooner than others by prayer. . . ." The passionate inspiration of the elixir of anger was not lacking this time.

The nobles did not need to be told twice. Not that they needed to be told in the first place: by the time the pamphlet came off the press, a number of princes had rallied to give battle, shamed and heartened by the example of the young Landgrave of Hesse—the impetuous youth who had shaken Luther by the hand at Worms and wished to prattle about sexual matters, and who had already fought with outstanding distinction against Sickingen: a young man right after Luther's heart, who had not waited to see how the revolt would get on in his lands but got in first at the earliest stirring. Now that Elector Frederick was gone, his successor Johann swiftly fell in with Philip of Hesse, and Duke George of Saxony, and Duke Heinrich of Wolfenbüttel whose territory adjoined theirs, with everything they could raise and hire of troops: 3400 horse and 8400 foot, mostly trained professionals, and excellently well equipped with artillery.

Münzer had intelligence of their approach; and the voice of God "that he thought he carried by him in his pocket," as Luther put it, told him that, being a new Daniel and new Moses, he was now to wield the sword of Gideon and smite the godless "pitilessly"—yes, he too—like Samson. Knowing nothing of war save what he had watched his own headsmen do at his bidding in Mühlhausen, Münzer issued a challenge to the princely coalition and commanded the whole peasantry within his orbit to leave house and home and come asoldiering for the Lord. By dint of prophetic predictions and immediate promises —of booty on the one hand and punitive raids against laggards on the other—Münzer raised an army of some 35,000 in a few days. But it was an army in name only. He had got together 35,000 *people,* not all of them men, not many of them with greater fighting experience than was gained in village brawls.

With this force, the Peasant Prophet marched to his tryst with the princes, choosing for his position a low rise in the valley of Frankenhausen, and there awaited the enemy. They had not long to wait, his motley conscripts. They did not know what they were waiting for, they only knew what their Prophet had told them, how it was going to be.

There were not enough halberds to go round, and precious few good swords; a handful of arquebusiers manned the flimsy wagon-fort which was Münzer's citadel. He had some cannon, but he had no gunpowder. He announced that a miracle was going to take place. The peasants intoned hymns as the guns of the allied princes opened fire on them; but as Luther had long told the world, the day of such a miracle as they trusted in, was past. In frightful carnage, the battle ended almost as soon as it had begun. There were not many prisoners taken, and not many of the fleeing got away; Münzer and others were tortured to death.

The terror was reversed. Although Münzer had not until that day figured as a military leader of the revolt, the manner of his defeat shook the morale of the seasoned peasant armies, and simultaneously recruited fresh forces against them. At every hand their allies fell away, the treaties they had secured were torn up, the mercenaries who had aided them as they had Sickingen, transferred to the enemy; the ranks of their own veterans thinned, crumbled, melted away—and where they stood fast and fought, they were beaten, again and again and again.

The cruelties which had been perpetrated by the rebels were as nothing to the horrors that requited them. With virtually the entire higher nobility now eager to wipe out an initial display of weakness, and able to claim Doctor Martin's sanction, nay orders, for doing it with blood, the massacres and sadistic inventiveness now enacted stopped short only of exterminating the class on which the country's food depended.

Oh, Luther had not meant it like that. Not like that. But he could not undo it by explaining that now. He could not disown his guilt— not without another twist of treachery, by passing off his guilt on to others. He had to show an impenitent front, or undermine his authority which was all for the good of the gospel. But he never lived it down, and never threw it off. Satan, the Devil Doubt, the projected scapegoat of intolerable inner burdens, Evil isolated, personified, and thus at once recognized and disowned, was his constant companion thereafter, with whom he had to wrestle nearly every day, and every lonely night.

Did the Devil ever tell him in those bouts, by any chance, that Luther had scurried to fall back on the princes since the knighthood was no more? Although he had not availed himself of the knights' assistance—the knights had been there, always in the background, on his side, should he change his mind or have it changed for him. If the Devil did not jeer at him for this, there were men who did; but then, ordinary human onslaught, from outside, Luther could stand up to.

True, true; it was not Luther who defeated the peasants, and it was not he who carried out the executions of them in their thousands. He had only passed the word and signified approval. Perhaps it would have happened without him. He could always try and tell his Devil that.

Before men, his defence was that "in open rebellion the peasants have placed themselves outside the law of God, for rebellion is not simply murder, but it is like a great fire which lays waste the whole land. If you don't extinguish it, it will extinguish you and the whole land with you." Authority, he taught, must be respected and obeyed absolutely—except when it must be absolutely disobeyed, for pro-hibiting the gospel of Luther.

Rebellion was worse than murder, for which the only penalty was death. In this spirit, when it came to the point and he was asked, Luther would declare in favour of the death penalty for witchcraft ("You shall not suffer a witch to live," it said succinctly in the Old Testament) because, as defined by himself, it was *crimen laesae Mai-estatis diuinae,* rebellion in the realm of the spirit. He remained con-sistent to the end in abrogating corporal punishment of any kind for heresy and dissidence as such. His hatred of Enthusiasm grew almost to outdistance what he felt for the papacy—naturally, since the former had sprung from his own camp—but he never would permit torture and killing for ideological reasons, even in his moments of blindest fury. We can say that for him.

It does not alter and cannot excuse his moral responsibility for the slaughter of the vanquished peasantry; one can explain it, that is all. Luther was no politician, and, his practicality notwithstanding, he was never a man of the world. His world was all religion, which, however, has no such demarkation line separating it from mundane affairs as wishfully he postulated. His real tragedy was that from the hour the concrete Reformation began, he became its slave. He was forced over the line, and forced to work for the Reformation in ways that were not his. The inventor was made planner, administrator, public relations officer, judge, party organizer and oracle, builder—brick by brick and without much straw—and withal sweeper and general dogsbody, to the going concern; when all the time he knew writing and praying to be his sole métier. He did what he was forced to do, to the best of his ability; and he too was only human.

His promise to the people of Wittenberg, when he called the mora-torium of reforms in 1522, was honoured. The Reformation afterwards went forward again, along the lines he had then sketched out. The liturgy was put all into the vernacular, the German mass was fully instituted, the structure of an evangelical church as a territorial body and community-amenity was methodically erected and furnished, com-mensurate education was provided for and public welfare services were put on a regular basis. On the basis of dogged gradualness, along what was at all events a fair approximation to that figment, the middle way, the Reformed Religion was extended to other towns and other regions until Elector Frederick's preferred scheme, of established reformation country by country, became realized. And the spirit of enquiry, together with the idea of human perfectibility and progress, was released and flew abroad—albeit possibly from a Pandora's box, as it is a fashion of the moment to say.

On the other hand, had Luther gone with the peasants, he would undoubtedly have lent the revolution that central focus, cohesion, and leadership which it so badly wanted; as his position then was, he could have put down excesses. At that brief moment when the peasant movement had the sympathies of cities, bishops, and other influential quarters, favouring an internal transformation of the Empire along the lines of the French Revolution which changed the socio-political patterns of all Europe two and a half centuries later—with Luther's approval, such a change might have been accomplished then. Lacking his approval, it was deferred until, under a more complex form of society, the cost in human suffering would be infinitely higher. It might have been—but then, it might not.

The resolute aggressiveness of the young and full-blooded Philip of Hesse, when the revolt menaced his dominion, would have been held in check by Luther's disapproval. At that time Philip of Hesse believed in Luther as his lodestar: even in victory over the peasants he granted some of the improvements laid down in the Twelve Articles —those improvements which Luther's earlier Peace Tract had supported. Had Luther endorsed the Twelve Articles in toto, had he lent his entire moral support to the peasantry, then Philip the acting leader of the counter-revolution might well have lacked that happy sense of righteousness which made him act where others guiltily hesitated. . . .

And so on. Speculation is a necessary part of assessment; but the thing we have to live with is what actually happened, and what came of it.

What had happened to Karlstadt was this. Having made himself into a peasant-priest or priest-peasant according to the logic of his beliefs, he had become trapped between both sides in the Peasant War. Like Luther and unlike Münzer, Karlstadt condemned violence. He was employed by the moderate left of the movement to try and reason with the extremists-terrorists. When the peasant movement collapsed the finer party-distinctions collapsed with it, and Karlstadt was hunted by the Margrave of Ansbach as a rebel and by the rebel rearguard as a traitor.

Thus he arrived at Luther's door, and Luther the butcher, Luther the coward, Luther who blamed everything that the papacy could not be blamed for on Enthusiasts like Karlstadt, took him in. As he would have taken in the Pope and King Henry VIII and the Jews, had they come to his door and smiled and said they were sorry for opposing the gospel and would not do it again. As the blameless Erasmus, who never physically hurt a fly, and who in Basel was out of reach of Pope and Emperor, did not take in *his* estranged comrade, Ulrich von Hutten (nor could it be argued that Erasmus feared bacterial infection rather than the displeasure of the Emperor and the Pope: he had syphilis himself).

Luther made many mistakes. More were to come. But his marriage was not one of them.

*

3. Katharina

The bride, who not only started married life traditionally in the public eye but remained under glaring observation all her days, was twenty-six years old, to her husband's rising forty-two. At a time when the Biblical span of three score and ten was seldom completed and when the majority of women married in their early teens and died in child-birth, a man of forty-two was commonly considered past middle age and a maiden of twenty-six to say the least mature.

There were virgins but no unmarried women in the class to which she had been born. Those for whom by reason of physical or financial deficiency no husbands could be found, wedded Christ. Although the heavenly bridegroom, too, required a dowry, this could become reduced or even waived through the right sort of connections with a given nunnery. Katharina von Bora had a cousin who was abbess at the Cistercian convent of Nimbschen in Saxony and an aunt who was a nun there. Her father was a nobleman of modest means, her mother died when she was in the cradle. The father remarried and the daughter was put into the cloister school when still an infant. She was formally designated for the religious life at age nine, and took the veil at sixteen; to throw it off would be adultery.

Like Charles V, in ignorance of the implications of a deprived child-hood, Katharina grew up strong of character. Her native intelligence and energies were not unduly fretted, but neither were they adequately taxed, at the convent. It did not belong to a reformed Order; routine and discipline were easy on the whole. The nuns led a fairly com-fortable and contented life. The rule of enclosure was not taken over-seriously; they could venture outside the cloister walls now and then, and the current news of the world would penetrate without too much delay or mutilation. The nuns' chaplains came from neighbouring monasteries. Nimbschen lay a short distance outside the little town of Grimma, where there was an Augustinian monastery headed by a male Bora relation; and Magdalena von Staupitz, a sister of the Augustinian Vicar-general, was a sister nun of Katharina's. What with one thing and another, Nimbschen thus was right in the firing line of the religious battle and received its fall of shrapnel, hot.

In 1522 Katharina's kinsman the prior of Grimma renounced his vows and with a number of his brethren joined the secularized, Lutheran priesthood. The nuns of Nimbschen were profoundly affected; there was turmoil within the placid walls, activated by those independent spirits among them which had been confined here hitherto without any prospect of positive occupation. We are not told that Katharina was a ringleader; but everything we are told of her from the moment she stepped over the convent threshold makes it hard to believe she was not.

Impassioned messages went out to the nuns' families, rudely shattering the illusion that one had done what one could and need trouble no more about them: and here, now, they asked to be got out. The harassed families to a man ignored the SOS—for that, in sober truth, was what the holy virgins' distress signals amounted to: they wished to save their souls.

"Our consciences, enlightened by the gospel, do not permit us to live as nuns any longer," so they finally wrote in a joint letter going straight to the top—to Doctor Martinus himself.

We are not told who framed the letter and who penned it. At least its straight shooting is suggestive. Luther in honour and decency and faith could not do as the poor ladies' kinsfolk in the flesh had done by them: if the ladies put it that way, he had to help.

A string of nuns could not just walk out of their convent into the blue, on pain of death. How were they to escape? To the late Squire George dare-devil stratagems presented no alien problem. A merchant whom he knew, of friendly, evangelical persuasion, happened to be in town: Leonard Koppe of Torgau, a robust sixty-year-old, who traded among other wares in fish and had a wagon. It was towards the end of the Lenten season, Master Koppe's herring barrels were nearly empty, and Nimbschen was on his round. With alacrity he grasped the new lease of life and adventure in, moreover, a sacred cause; and he rattled away to the rescue.

On Easter Eve, 1523, Leonard Koppe made off with eleven nuns, concealed under drawn covers and labelled herring, which he delivered in good condition at the Augustinian monastery of Wittenberg the Tuesday after Easter.

Honi soit qui mal y pense, the monastery was empty but for Dr. Martin and Prior Brisger; there was room and to spare for fitting segregation. What was lacking were clothes and money to feed the nuns.

"Their names are: Magdalena von Staupitz, Elsa von Kanitz, Eva Grossin, Eva Schönfeldt and her sister Margarethe Schönfeldt, Laneta von Golis, Margarethe von Zeschau, and Katharina von Bora, also Barba Rockenberg, Katherina Taubenheim, and Margarethe Hirstorf. The manner of their escape was perfectly astonishing. . . . Pray beg some money for me, to enable me to keep these poor girls for a week or a fortnight, until I can send them to their relations or if these reject them find friends who will receive them."

Two were placed at once, but nine remained. Not unnaturally the temporary arrangement caused some sardonic comment even among those most faithfully disposed towards the poor girls' host.

"I have no other news," a student of Wittenberg closed his letter to a friend, "except that a few days ago a wagonload of vestal virgins came to town, more eager for wedlock than for life. God grant them husbands before they fare worse!"

All Luther's colleagues were mobilized to assist these social anomalies. "They are beautiful and ladylike," Amsdorf advertised them persuasively, "all of noble birth and under fifty. The oldest of them, sister of my gracious lord and uncle Dr. Staupitz, would I suggest suit you well; then you might boast of your brother-in-law as I boast of my uncle! But if you would prefer a younger one, you can take your pick. Or if you desire to give something to the poor, give to them, for they are destitute and friendless, and they have no shoes. Do please if you can beg something for them from the court, any scrap of food or clothing will be appreciated, only hurry, for they are in great distress, but very patient. I pity the creatures; I wonder they can be so brave and merry as they are."

Before very long relatives and friends of a further six nuns relented and sent for them, leaving a mere three at Wittenberg. The two

Schönfeldt sisters got a berth with the Cranachs, and the third, Katharina von Bora, went to live with the family of a lawyer named Reichenbach.

Katharina was marking time. She was in love, with a former student of Melanchthon's, Hieronymus Baumgärtner of Nuremberg, who was on a visit to Wittenberg at the time of her arrival and who returned her affection, but whose well-to-do parents would have to be brought round to his espousing a portionless ex-nun.

How she got on at the Reichenbachs' one can only guess, from such internal evidence as that they were not named among her wedding guests, eventually. Meanwhile she stayed with them for two years, during which time the question of getting her finally settled was canvassed with increasing urgency; the Baumgärtners having contrived to detach their son from his undesirable entanglement directly they had him back in Nuremberg.

A home-help like Katharina, proud, headstrong, and unversed in domestic work which was done by lowly lay-sisters in the genteel nunneries, cannot have been an unmixed blessing. She looked down on Melanchthon's wife as the daughter of a rural burgomaster, and refused an eligible suitor, the parson Kaspar Glatz of Orlamünde, for no better reason than that she found him unprepossessing. And she was no beauty.

Or so Luther protested. Katharina's portraits show well-spaced features in a heart-shaped face which, whilst departing from the coeval feminine ideal oval, might have been attractive enough in animation, particularly in conjunction with the slender figure and spirited air which were hers. Erasmus, whom she detested, spoke of her as wonderfully charming; Hieronymus Baumgärtner clung wistfully to the acquaintance, Parson Glatz continued to importune, and the King of Denmark when he called on Lucas Cranach and had the three escaped nuns presented to him, dubbed her "Katharina of Siena" and gave her a gold ring for a keepsake.

Obviously she learned a lot in those two years; for she was to prove an outstanding household manager against crushing odds. But again and again the busy leaders of the Reformation were asked to have another word with this stubborn girl and break her resistance to poor Glatz. Probably the truth was that she would not give up hope of getting her Hieronymus if she held out; Luther wrote to the young man as late as the beginning of 1525, "If you don't wish to lose your Käthe von

Bora, bestir yourself before she is given to another who wants her. She has not yet conquered her love for you, and I should certainly be glad to see you joined together."

No doubt. For shortly after, when Amsdorf once more took his turn at urging her, Käthe said she would not have Kaspar Glatz at any price: but if they were so keen to dispose of her, she would take him, Amsdorf, or Luther if he asked her.

"Good God! not me," said Luther when the message was passed on.

"For heaven's sake, not that one!" echoed all his friends (according to Luther), when he changed his mind about Katharina's proposal— though for all we know in the heat of the moment she may have named the two old bachelors Amsdorf and Luther as who should say, the Emperor of China. The very fact that she knew her own mind so well and could not be brought to budge was sufficiently extraordinary to render her quite unsuitable for the honour—even aside from the blow to his fair fame, if he married at all, which some of his supporters anxiously foresaw.

But the thought had quickly taken root in Luther's mind: so quickly, putting forth exploratory shoots so soon after Amsdorf's report of the preposterous suggestion, that one might suspect the ground on which it fell was not altogether stony. While for years he had written and spoken against the celibacy of priests and applauded those who were taking wives, he had continued to hold himself bound by his personal, solemn vow of chastity until death. ("Carnal temptation? that's nothing," he was wont to squash enquirers after his famous Afflictions. Yet now, a week or two after Käthe had shot her bolt, Luther wrote waggishly to Spalatin, "Why don't you get on with it and get married? For my part, I have been urging on others with so many arguments, I have almost persuaded myself."

Many a true word is spoken in jest—as it were experimentally. In jest, too, he mentioned the matter to his parents. It was no joke at all to Hans Luther who leapt like a trout to the flash of his unforgotten hope of descendants "to carry on the name"—though heaven knew there were now Luthers aplenty, with enough grandchildren of his own to have satisfied the old man's desire for biological immortality. No, the old man was never satisfied. Käthe was not good enough for him. A fig for her noble blood; seeing she had "neither wealth nor position," could not Martin find a more creditable mate? Perhaps that was all Luther needed, to harden his intentions.

After that, rumours evidently got about. A few days later Luther had occasion to write to Spalatin again:

"As for what you write about my marrying, don't be surprised at my staying single, even if I am so famous a lover. You should rather be surprised that I who write so much about marriage and in this context am having so much to do with women have not turned into a woman myself by now. However, if you wish to have me for example, take it so: here I have had three wives at once and loved them so hard as to lose two to other husbands, while the third is perhaps about to be snatched from me as well. [This witticism, which his enemies would one day construe as an admission of multiple concubinage, referred of course to Kate and the two other girls from Nimbschen.] Indeed you are a timid lover, that dare not be the husband of even one wife. Take care! God has a way of doing what one least expects. Joking aside," he recovered himself in a hasty afterthought, "I only say this to give you encouragement."

This was in April, Kate having thrown her bombshell in the month of March. On 4 May, in a letter to Councillor Rühel dealing with the wicked peasants, there was the astonishing parenthesis, "To spite the Devil, I will yet marry my Käthe before I die, if I hear that the peasants go on as they are doing. They shall not take from me my courage and my joy!"

On 2 June he wrote an open letter to the Archbishop of Mainz, enjoining him to marry and secularize his see, with the following note attached to the copy sent to Rühel, "If His Grace should ask again, as I hear he has, why I do not take a wife when I am inciting everybody else to marry, tell him I am still afraid I haven't got what it takes. But if my marrying would strengthen him I am ready . . . even if it should be only a betrothal like St. Joseph's. . . . For I regard the married state as commanded by God."

And on 13 June he and Katharina were married privately in the Black Cloister.

Luther let it be known that he took this step for three reasons: 1. to fulfil the dearest wish of his aged father; 2. to bear witness; and 3. to infuriate the papists and spite the Devil. Fair enough; but one regrets that he was moved to add, "and taking pity on the deserted

woman." Equally one must regret the absence of any letters written by
her during this period. Her confidantes, such as she had, were too close
at hand for correspondence.

No matter how strong one's inner certitude, it is hard to behave
wholly beautifully when one is ill at ease vis-à-vis the outside. Luther
knew what to expect. Even his best friends were not happy about his
being so consistent as all that. There was a flurry of correspondence.
Justus Jonas, himself one of the first priests of Wittenberg to have
married, frankly described his mixed emotions to Spalatin: it was to
be feared, alas, that the sainted leader's motives would be mis-
understood and reflect on the entire cause. Town Pastor Bugenhagen,
in like case, defensively announced the event, "Malicious talk has
brought it to pass that Doctor Martin has unexpectedly become a
husband—" i.e. by circumstances outside his control. As for Melanchthon the beloved disciple, Gentle Philip, he really let himself go.
"Luther had married the woman Bora, without letting one who is
his friend know of his intention. He only invited Bugenhagen, Cranach,
and Dr. Apel to a supper in the evening and went through the
usual forms. You may perhaps wonder that at a time like this, when
the good are suffering at every hand, he does not suffer with them
but rather, it seems, devotes himself to revelry and compromises his
good name, at the very moment when Germany is in especial need
of all his mind and authority. I think the explanation is this: the man
is extraordinarily easily influenced [sic], and so the nuns, who chased
him in every way, ensnared him. Perhaps having so much to do with
the nuns softened him up, although he is a noble and upright man,
and caused the fire to flare up in him. . . . The talk that he had
already slept with the woman Bora is however a lie. Well, now that
it is done, we must put a good face on it. Even if this way of life—
matrimony—is low, it is yet holy and more pleasing to God than
celibacy. And since I see Luther somewhat troubled and perplexed over
this change in his life, I employ all my thought and strength to
reassure him, seeing that he has done nothing which could be made
a reproach to him or which he cannot justify. . . . On the other
hand I must say I have always wanted him to experience some
humiliation rather than nothing but elevation and exaltation all
the time. The latter is dangerous not only to priests but to every
human being. . . . Also I dare hope that matrimony will make him

more dignified, so that he may now give up that buffoonery which we have so often tried to get him out of. . . . I write at such length that you may not be too discomposed by the unexpected event. I know you have Luther's reputation at heart, and it would grieve you if it were to suffer any slur. I exhort you to bear the news with equanimity, remembering that Holy Scripture says marriage is an honourable estate. It is through the mistakes of the saints of old that God showed us we must use his Word as our only touchstone, and not form our opinions by outward appearances in a man but going by his words. Neither, on the other hand, may we condemn the teaching because of the mistakes of the teacher. . . ."

Undoubtedly the beloved Philip was discomposed. What had become of his celebrated clear thinking? Matrimony was an inferior way of life, yet it was more pleasing to God than celibacy; Luther had committed an error, yet he had done nothing wrong; he was noble and upright and at the same time easily seduced; his reputation must be protected, so let the writer hasten to purvey the current slander; Luther was wallowing in repugnant self-indulgence, which however would place a welcome curb on his indiscipline. He had not even thrown a proper party, yet he was giving himself up to revelry at a time like this. In other words, he had not had his soul-mate Melanchthon at the party; Melanchthon would no longer come first with him.

One does not know which to be the more surprised at, Melanchthon's spite and venom, or the fact that it was possible in tiny Wittenberg to do anything without everybody knowing about it.

When the time was come to make the matter public in due form, Luther wrote most of the wedding invitations himself (Melanchthon, having thought things over, decided to join whom he could not beat, and sent out some invitations off his own bat)—each and every one containing a disguised apology.

"I am not infatuated. . . ."

"I have determined at my death to be found in the state ordained of God, and so far as I can rid myself of every last trace of my former popish life." (He had rid himself of the monk's cowl the preceding October, and had a good head of hair for his nuptials.) "So, at my dear father's desire, I have now married, and have done the thing quickly, that I might not be put off by the scandal-mongers. . . ."

"I have brought myself into such contumely by my marriage that I trust the angels are laughing and all the demons weeping. . . ."

But here and there that unrepentant buffoonery broke through: "Doubtless you have heard the news of my venture upon the sea of matrimony. I can hardly believe it myself, but my witnesses are so positive I am in honour bound to take their word for it. . . . If convenient, I beg you will kindly support me with venison and come yourself to help seal the affair with joy."

"Suddenly and unexpectedly God has taken me captive in the bonds of holy matrimony, which is to be confirmed with a banquet on Tuesday. That my father and mother and all my good friends may be the merrier, my lord Katharina and I beg you will send us as soon as possible, at my expense, a keg of the best Torgau beer you can find. If it is not good, I shall punish you by making you drink it all yourself. . . ."

It wasn't me, he seemed to say: it was God, it was my dear old father, it was the Pope, it was the peasants hastening on the end of the world, it was the tittle-tattlers; it was to strengthen other people and show that the just man does what is right unafraid of giving offence. Perish the thought of a love match: he harped on this as men marrying for money have been known to protest the reverse. But yet, as he often said, he never felt so sure that his conduct was correct as when it was denounced, and clearly was enjoying himself in his novel situation.

"In truth there is a lot to get used to in marriage. One wakes up in the morning and finds a pair of pigtails on the pillow which were not there before."

Considering the religious climate in which the couple had been reared and the particular taboos on a union such as theirs, every bit as potent as the taboo upon incest, they evidently conquered their inhibitions in a commendably relaxed manner.

"My lord Katharina, my Käthe, my *Kette* (chain), my rib, Doctor Kate, my lady of the orchards and princess of the pig market," to quote some of her husband's playful addresses, was pregnant by September, and Luther could not wait longer than October to announce the marvel.

"My Katie is fulfilling Genesis 1:28!"

"There is to be born a child of a monk and a nun. It is clear such a child will have to have a great personage for godfather: so of course I am asking you! I cannot guarantee the time."

"My dear Katie brought into the world yesterday (7 June) by God's grace at two o'clock a little son, Hans Luther. I must stop. Sick Katie is calling."

"Hans is cutting his teeth and beginning to make a joyous nuisance of himself. These are the joys of marriage of which the Pope is not worthy."

"What if the neighbours laugh to see the master of the house hanging out the diapers: the angels in heaven are smiling."

"Child, what have you done that I should love you so? You are driving the whole household mad with your bawling. This is the sort of thing that caused the Church Fathers to vilify marriage!"

"My Katie is in all things so obliging and pleasing to me that I would not exchange my poverty for the riches of Croesus."

"I would not exchange Katie for all France or Venice, because God has given her to me—and other women have worse faults."

"All my life is patience. I have to have patience with the Pope, with the Enthusiasts, my family, and Katie."

"Think of all the squabbles Adam and Eve must have had in their nine hundred years of marriage! Eve would say, 'You ate the apple,' and Adam would retort, 'You gave it to me.'"

"I wish that women would recite the Lord's Prayer every time before opening their mouths."

"Christ said we must become as little children to enter the kingdom of heaven. Dear God, this is too much! Do we have to become such idiots?"

It was all very normal.

Katharina bore six living children in eight years, and kept her end up. From the first she had no light task. So far from taking it amiss, as people had predicted, that Luther celebrated his marriage only a month after Elector Frederick's death, the new Elector made him a wedding present of the Augustinian monastery. Practically deserted and uncared-for as it had now been for years—with Luther's bed "unmade from one end of the year to the other, so that finally the bed clothes and straw decayed with the sweat. I never noticed, I was working so hard I simply used to fall down on it at night and know no more till morning"—it was left to the new mistress to put in order.

The master's incurably bohemian habits did not make it any easier. He took no care of his clothes (except when once he cut up his small son's jerkin to mend his own leather breeches; apropos "The Elector Frederick always mended his breeches himself, though he was not very good at it."). He everlastingly littered the whole place with papers; he would not have his little dog ejected to live in the courtyard, any more than he would part with the painted Madonna on the wall which in some circles caused as much displeasure as his wife. He was incurably hospitable, too, and had absolutely no head for figures. He filled the house with students, orphans, refugees, and poor relations, and while Kate struggled to make ends meet was so openhanded that his good friend Lucas Cranach declined to stand surety for their debts.

"I don't worry about the debts," Luther explained. "As soon as Katie pays one, another comes along." He accepted this state of affairs as a law of nature, her preserve. "She plants our fields, pastures and sells our cows, et cetera. . . ."

For *et cetera* read: a market orchard she took on, some little distance outside the town (where also she leased the said fields and pasture), growing apples, pears, grapes, peaches, and nuts; a fish pond with trout, carp, pike, and perch; for domestic use she kept hens, ducks, and pigs; to say nothing of her services to family and neighbours as an unpaid physician, herbalist, masseuse, and brewer. She was generally regarded as stuck up, but everyone esteemed her skills; her son Paul (No. 5) who adopted the medical profession always said his mother was half a doctor, and her beer was noted as a healthful soporific and antidote to kidney stone. In times of epidemic the Luther household became Wittenberg's hospital, besides having its standing complement of boarders and being open to woman friends for their lying-in. And all the time the formidable woman had to keep a watchful eye on her great man—whom she never addressed other than as "Herr Doctor" and by the formal pronoun—lest he refuse useful gifts sent by admirers, or give away what he had got.

Sometimes she resorted to desperate expedients, so that Luther found himself writing to Agricola, "I am sending you a beaker for a wedding present. P.S. Sorry, Katie's hid it." Wedding presents were something of a sore point; Katie did not forget that she had had to go behind his back to accept her wedding present from the Archbishop of Mainz (of all unlooked-for well-wishers), an extremely welcome twenty-five gulden, which her high-minded lord had been determined to return.

He was the lord and master, high and mighty in the home even as he loomed high and holy over all the world; she was proud of him, proud to be his groaning helpmeet, proud of his faults of buffoonery, coarseness, unreasonableness, and his demanding ailments, proud to bow to his tenets of God-given authority. But she was not minded to be put down, passed by, overlooked, for all that; she deserved her share of attention, and of conversation. It maddened her as it would any housewife, to see the food she had provided get cold the while a cluster of intellectual parasites sat around prompting Luther to bring forth pearls of table-talk for them to write down (rightly, she predicted they were going to make fortunes out of these notes: they ought to be charged a regular fee), and ignoring the wife whom he was "too tired" to talk to at the end of his day's work.

He was never too tired to talk. There was nothing on which he had not an opinion, no association he would not be prompted by, no opening he could resist. If the pious leeches ran out of questions at all, they could always fall back on his encounters with Satan: that subject never failed. Katie would show them. One day, instead of putting in the usual futile requests to cease and eat, she stopped the performance by swooning clean away and afterwards reporting in fluent Latin on an attack of sore affliction by the Devil—just like Papa.

"If I were to marry again," Luther vowed, "I would hew me a meek wife out of stone: for I doubt whether any other kind be meek."

How would he have fared with a meek wife?

Under the Roman Church all the pleasures of the flesh had come to be classed as evil; yet so many of its functionaries notoriously indulged their carnal appetites to the full, and that in breach of those very vows which were designed to set the priesthood apart from the unhallowed laity. Luther when he abrogated vows freed earthly joys from the stigma of sin. Despite his infinite capacity for guilt he drew from his equal capacity for enjoyment the conclusion that these pleasures were gifts of God which it were impious to spurn.

"Who loves not wine, woman and song/Remains a fool his whole life long." If Luther was not the author of this jingle, long attributed to him, both form and sentiment bear his stamp.

But as regards woman, love—entailing a mutual relationship—was more complicated than could be the case with a passive object. To eat and drink and play the lute, no contract under God and law was necessary; to have the benefit of copulation, however, a man and a woman must be married. For both being equally creatures with immortal souls, they must become one spirit as well as one flesh.

Before Luther had himself cast off celibacy, he had condemned it merely as a source of continual temptation and distraction to those who were not equal to perpetual chastity—in other words, his attitude then was still basically orthodox, accounting chastity as the higher state. Upon his own experience of marriage, however, that attitude changed dramatically to one more positive. Perpetual chastity was *bad*. Only in marriage were human beings able to acquire the spiritual health which they had used to seek in the cloister. So the strange thing was that before he had ever experienced sexual release himself, Luther saw marriage as a primarily physical affair, and afterwards saw its benefits as primarily spiritual—evidently not for want of physical communion.

As a result, where to begin with priests of the Reformed Church were to be permitted marriage if they wished it, presently they would have to be married or tell the visiting inspectors the reason why. (A Saxon clergyman still only living with his housekeeper gave it as his excuse that he had hoped she might die before the visitation, so that he could have married someone younger.) An ordinary member of the congregation had more latitude, theoretically at least, since in practice few were rich enough to get along single.

In respect of fornication, adultery, and homosexuality, the Lutheran attitude remained unchanged from that of the Catholic Church and the Old Testament code which it had followed. Luther never took a step without the Bible—even if he somewhat reconstrued the Pauline view of marriage and fiddled a little with the Patriarchs. Illicit love and sodomy were unequivocally forbidden in the Bible, and Luther's well-nursed memories of clerical immorality in the Rome of 1510 made him relentless in his loathing especially of homosexuality.

Writing in the present day, one may not leave out of account the psychologist's equation of a rampant anti-homosexual animus with suppressed homosexual leanings; but then, on the same authority we all have those, and none more so than our Don Juans and Messalinas. It had not dawned on the Reformers that there might be espied any dubious tinge about the friendship of David and Jonathan, which, rather, set an admirable pattern for, say, the premarital effusions between Luther and Melanchthon.

At all events, Luther's expressed uxoriousness was not overdone. His "Marriage is the most blessed state when it turns out well; but when it turns out ill it is hell," sums up what one must surely call a balanced view.

Withal he paid his wife the greatest compliments which he had it in him to give. He called St. Paul's Epistle to the Galatians "my Katharina von Bora," to illustrate how utterly he was wedded to it; and he had to pull himself up on becoming aware of a bad habit he got into: "I give more credit to Katharina than to Christ who has done so much more for me!"

A friend hung up a cherry bough as a reminder of God's bounty. "But you need only look round at the faces of your children!" said Luther, in whom the wonder never ceased, at that loveliest of miracles, procreation.

Oh, he beat them, too, lovely miracle or no: it said to do so in the Bible, did it not. But he thought this should not be overdone either—as he deemed it had been overdone with him, when he was a young child.

4. The Tardy Millennium

"Satan rages!" How well Kate Luther knew that watchword. In the lonely nights of the monk the Devil had been wont to do his worst; but a married man was blessed with additional resources and could advise others, "If you can't make the fiend give over, even with scorn which he loathes more than anything—wake up your wife and talk to her."

What ground he lost in the nights Satan made up for at other times, however, in a hundred cunning ways. At the rambling Black Cloister, he took to making noises and knocking invisible objects about, occasionally, when the busy doctor had contrived to seclude himself for peaceful study. He got behind Erasmus and prodded him into a fierce pen duel with Luther (Luther for his part being ardently egged on by Kate) on the subject of free will. He got into faithful Agricola and induced him to desert to the murky colours of mysticism; other comrades followed. He had given strength to the arm of Antichrist in Flanders, where the first Lutheran martyrs opened a procession over the years, to the stake; and he used this very effectively indeed against Luther whose conscience might be tortured but whose body remained hale.

Hale, but not so free from torments as all that: at the same time as Luther was plunged right back into the pit he thought he had climbed out of long ago and forever, where God's loving kindness faded out of recognition, he fell prey to bodily afflictions also. Toothache, earache, rheumatism, colds, piles, vertigo, tinnitus, renewed accesses of sleeplessness, the first attacks of stone, and something like a cataleptic fit—Luther knew very well whence came all these visitations. "My maladies are decidedly not natural. No remedies have the slightest effect, though I obey all the physician's directions." But they should not get him down: "I have a hard, durable body." Yet sometimes a piteous cry from the heart would escape.

"You complain of the itch? I should be very glad to change with you and give you ten gulden into the bargain. You don't know what a horrible thing this dizziness of mine is. All day I haven't been able to read a letter through, nor even two or three lines of the Psalms consecutively. I get as far as three or four words, when buzz, buzz! the noise in my ears begins again, and I am near falling off my chair with the pain. The itch, that's nothing! on the contrary, you might call it a sort of stimulating complaint."

The Devil did not flag. Not content with his attacks on Luther's writhing soul and too-resistant body, Satan next led with fresh, massed assaults on the faith of the people. Karlstadt relapsed, and drew yet others with him to swell the ranks of the Enthusiasts. The Enthusiasts were showing much increase and profit on the devilish side of the ledger: they too had now split into a left wing and a right, steadily more divergent even to turning one against the other; but that did not make either of them less wrong or less dangerous in Luther's eyes.

The left were now called Anabaptists, Re-baptizers: rejecting infant baptism was the most readily identifiable common feature of their several sub-sects. They had something else in common with the right, causing Luther infinite worry, pain, and expenditure of effort. Both sides rejected transubstantiation; they denied that the eucharist became the body and blood of Christ which, they said, were only represented symbolically in the Lord's Supper. Luther denied that the sacrifice of Jesus was re-enacted but maintained the real presence of the Saviour in the sacrament.

Satan had fostered a rival Reformation in the South; its seat was Zürich and its prophet was a Swiss divine named Ulrich Zwingli—of peasant stock like Luther, but humanist-trained, reared in the republican atmosphere of the Swiss Confederation, and so at once more politically and more democratically minded. He was also more militant, true son of a land whose one export was soldiers for the wars of Europe: while banning images, music, and in fact all decorative ceremonial from his churches, he did not eschew the sword as a means of evangelical defence (indeed, he was himself to fall on the field of battle). Neither did he eschew the headsman's axe against the Anabaptist heretics, whom he abhorred as much as did Luther and very little more than Luther came to abhor him.

The emphasis on civic self-government of the Zwinglian reforms in Switzerland made a potent appeal to the cities of southern Germany. Thus, simultaneously with the general advance of secession from Rome, the movement itself was becoming divided, its strength sapped at a crucial stage of growth. At the same time, too, the Counter-Reformation—in both its senses of Catholic spiritual regeneration and systematic combat—had been launched. The term, Counter-Reformation, was yet uncoined, but the term "Protestant" had made its appearance.

The Edict of Worms, categorically prohibiting any alterations in the orthodox ecclesiastical system, not only had never been implemented: in the course of the years 1522–28 it had been more and more positively contravened. In Electoral Saxony, in Hesse, Ansbach, Anhalt, in parts of Brandenburg and the Palatinate and a collection of city units headed by Strassburg, Ulm, Augsburg, and Nuremberg, the outlawed reforms were being steadily promoted. In need of help against the Turks, the Emperor's brother King Ferdinand of Bohemia had had his hands tied, so that the same process had gone unchecked in his territory where the Hussite doctrine had long paved the way.

Acting as the Emperor's deputy at the Diet of Speyer of 1529, Ferdinand made a determined effort to stop the rot in Germany "as far as possible," to quote the edict of an earlier Diet concerned with enforcement of the Edict of Worms. The mirage of a General Council of the Church once more bloomed on the horizon: till it were convened, the Lutheran territories were to be left unmolested provided that they did not molest their remaining loyal Catholics. For the territories that had remained officially Catholic, the Edict of Worms was reaffirmed, so that in these there should be no corresponding toleration for Lutherans.

At this for the first time the reformist group declared themselves by name. Elector Johann of Saxony, Landgrave Philip of Hesse, Margrave George of Brandenburg, Prince Wolfgang of Anhalt, the ambassador of the Dukes Ernst and Franz of Lüneburg, and the representatives of sixteen towns signed a "Protestation" with the operative clause, "In matters concerning God's honour and the salvation of our souls, each man has the right to stand for himself and present his true account before God. For on the last day no man will be able to take shelter behind the power of another, be it small or great," i.e. they repudiated Ferdinand's measure and demanded absolute freedom of conscience for all. Ferdinand refused to accept the Protestation, and the *Protestantes,* as they were derisively dubbed by the Catholic majority, walked out.

Being a minority, however sturdy, the Protestantes were in serious danger. Nobody was to know that the Habsburg wars abroad would take a turn for the worse, in time to save the Lutheran bloc from imperial military intervention. They published their appeal, and formed a defensive league of the following members: the Elector of Saxony, the Margrave of Brandenburg, the Dukes of Lüneburg, the Landgrave of Hesse, the Prince of Anhalt, and the free cities of Strassburg, Nuremberg, Ulm, Kostnitz, Lindau, Memmingen, Kempten, Nördlingen, Heilbronn, Reutlingen, Isny, St. Gall, Weissenburg, and Windsheim.

A number of these lay in the south; St. Gall indeed was an imperial city only in name (a name which it would shortly discard) and the native canton of Zwingli himself. It became of the utmost urgency to reconcile the northern and southern reform movements, against the impending Catholic-imperial offensive.

Philip of Hesse, more than ever the life and soul of the Lutheran party, worked like a slave to bring about a conference of all the leading Reform-theologians, and finally succeeded. On 1 October 1529 there met together at his castle of Marburg, in order of their subsequent signatures, Ioannes Oecolampadius (formerly Hausschein)—one-time chaplain to Sickingen and now Zwingli's lieutenant, Huldrychus Zwinglius, Martinus Bucerius—the young Dominican converted by Luther at Heidelberg, now the reformer of Alsace; Caspar Hedio (Hédion of Basel), Martinus Luther, Justus Jonas, Philippus Melanchthon, Andreas Osiander (né Hosemann), reformer of Nuremberg; Stephanus Agricola (temporarily back in the fold), and Joannes Brencius (Brentz), Swabian reformer.

The Colloquy of Marburg went on for four days of discussions— which Landgrave Philip avowed fatigued him more than a week in the saddle—and reached agreement on fourteen points. On the fundamental point of transubstantiation, however, unity was frustrated.

Luther stood by the Latin *Hoc est corpus,* "Here is my body," Zwingli stood by Jesus' native Aramaic, in which the phrase had no verb, so that "signifies" was a likelier interpretation than "is." Luther having begun by apologizing to Zwingli for such insults as might have slipped off his pen in their preceding duel of pamphlets, at one stage came close to considering a compromise. But here it was Melanchthon who pointed out to him that by yielding, any future rapprochement with the Catholics would be rendered impossible. So late in the day, Luther and the Lutherans still thought of themselves literally as reformers within the Universal Church.

Zwingli was more realistic; but that did not help him either. The Zwinglians were the first to suffer by the movement's being cut in half; although without a doubt the consolidation of the Reformation as a whole was delayed by something of the order of a hundred years. Perhaps several wars, one of them among the most calamitous in history, could have been avoided by an amalgamation at Marburg— but then, when has the world, when had Europe been at peace for any length of time? Satan rages, and if one casus belli is removed, sure enough he will find another.

Always, it was two steps forward and one step back, when it was not one step forward and back again the same distance. For Luther, standstill too was regression—as, in a dynamic universe, of course it is.

He had thought implicitly that once everything was explained and the true teaching was completely available, the kingdom of righteousness would ipso facto be established, of itself. He had never thought that there could be any people so wrongheaded as to resist and go on resisting without any ground to stand on. He had known that Antichrist would put up a virulent struggle, but he had expected a little more help from the side of the angels. Nothing had led him to expect that the enemy would pop up, nightmare-like, all over his own camp. He knew that God had all eternity to move around in, but men had not, he knew that also. There was an unknown time limit for mankind to work out its salvation. If God was not giving more assistance than he did, the hardened sinfulness of men would be the reason for that. The slowness and setbacks all round might be an indication that the divine patience was at long last coming to an end—like Luther's.

"They keep on at me with questions and requests and foolish arguments as if I had never written a line," when the day of judgment could be tomorrow. He wished it would be; like the early Christians, he began to speak of "the *precious* Last Day." He was worn out. He was old. He was wretched.

From 1530, when his father died, to his great sorrow, Luther considered himself an old man. His health grew worse. Two little daughters died, and his grief for them was so terrible that he was quite amazed—seeing that he knew perfectly well they had gone to a happier place and were better off with God; also, "I had not realized that one could love even one's own children as boundlessly as this."

The translation of the Old Testament, continually interrupted by extraneous work and moreover carried on with the aid of a whole syndicate of linguists, theologians, and lawyers, took twelve years; and like all things else in this world required perpetual furbishing, no matter how many editions it went into.

Of course there were good things that happened, and Luther had his pleasures. If not just exactly as he could have wished nor as fast as he had hoped, the Reformation did progress: *we* know that, even though we too have our cavils. Luther himself could not but be well satisfied with the Confession of Augsburg which, at the Diet held at that town and three weeks after the death of Hans Luther, was presented to Charles V in person. This document, drafted after some vicissitudes by Melanchthon, constituted the first comprehensive statement of Protestant belief, and with that a platform sufficiently broad and firm to serve as a base to all future "Protestantism."

Luther saw an immense amount of practical achievement, especially in Saxony. He saw universal education introduced, he saw the Reformed Church taken for granted. He saw the papacy, firmed by the integrity of Adrian VI, totter and sink back again under another Medici pope, after a pontificate of only a year and a half. He saw the Anabaptists persecuted. He witnessed from afar the downfall of "those wild beasts and serpents," Zwingli and his crew. He would even live to hear credible reports, on Karlstadt's death, how the Devil had come personally to collect the fellow. He had unending and unalloyed delight in his living children. He enjoyed his garden, where he grew pumpkins and other vegetables for the family; he dug a well, and was very proud of that; he dabbled in woodwrithy and "made considerable progress in clock-making," at one time. One way and another, he still got quite a lot more writing done, as well: the bulk of his collected works, in fact.*

But he had passed that point which comes in every life, before which events show only their most grateful side, while after it they will tend to protrude the blacker aspects.

He himself slipped, though never again quite so badly as in the Peasant War. He was induced to give way on the question of the death penalty for "blasphemy and sedition," that is to say, open propagation of heresy and conscientious objection to military and other state service. And then there was the most unpleasant scandal of the Hesse bigamy case.

With this Luther got himself into really rather nasty trouble.

In 1523, some two years after he had made theoretical enquiries about grounds for annulment of marriage in chatting with Luther at Worms, Philip of Hesse had been married to Christina, daughter of Duke George of Saxony. He never liked her. He did not like her breath, he did not like her odour, he did not like her face, he did not like anything about her. He therefore sinned with others. That was all right while he could get regular absolution for adultery; but once he had become a convinced Lutheran that would no longer do. In spite of his conspicuous bravery in the wars against the knights and the peasants—so he confessed in 1539—he had always trembled lest he meet his death in such a state of iniquity, and dared not take holy communion. Now he had met a young lady, Margarethe von der Saal, on whom his affections were passionately fixed and so would cease to stray, if only he could make her his wife: for Margarethe had a mother who would not let her live with Philip as his mistress.

There was no divorce in Catholic law, but there was annulment on any number of flexible grounds. Luther recognized neither divorce nor annulment; but he recognized polygamy—since the Old Testament patriarchs had practised it and nowhere in the Bible was there any prohibition of it. Melanchthon, Zwingli, all of them took the same view: they had already expressed it when Henry VIII asked their advice on his marital problem. Since Philip meanwhile had developed certain leanings towards Zwinglian reform, and since he also hinted

---

* Eighty volumes, excluding his correspondence and recorded table-talk, in the Weimar Edition, which was begun in 1883 and the completion of which is not yet in sight.

that he might be compelled to seek an annulment from the Pope, Luther told him to marry the girl but to keep it a secret since bigamy was against the law of the land. A secret marriage, however, did not at all serve the purpose of Margarethe's mother; and so the marriage was made public. Luther's part in it would have been unfortunate enough had he merely licensed the unlawful union; that he had counselled the pair to lie about it (he recognized "necessity-lies" which also had been practised by the patriarchs) did untold harm to his reputation.

On top of that, Landgrave Philip was lost to the Protestant cause after all by the transaction. He had to seek pardon for his crime from the Emperor, and pay for it by withdrawing his military support from the Protestant League—till he broke his agreement with the Emperor, to be sure; but that was not to be for a year or so, by which time the Emperor's further, strategic preparations against the League were much advanced. Luther did not live to see the full consequences; but there was enough, for his Devil to rub in.

Then there were the Jews. The Jews were a most unholy disappointment to him. They were his concentrate of disillusion.

It has been said that today the only Jew it is permissible to abuse is Jesus Christ. While this is hardly a universal axiom, there is some justice for the epigram—and quite right too, as some of us may think: up to a point. A historic injustice is not repaired by turning it inside out. It would be sad if now the star of David were to be made a badge of sacrosanct immunity, and if it became obligatory to condemn out of hand any person who had ever slung mud at it in the past.

To some extent the latter has already happened. With Martin Luther it is becoming the custom either to skate over or apologize for the dreadful antisemitic pamphlets he produced at the end of his life; alternatively, either to ignore them or ignore him—unless indeed one wishes to make capital out of them in one or the other direction.

It is true, events have made it difficult to be fair; and it is true that Luther did his share in the ancient campaign of persecution against Jewry. Yet we have not seen the papacy exterminated, we have not seen Calvinism—descendant in the direct line of Zwingli—operating as an automatic licence for discrimination, and countless Christian sects descended from what Luther vituperated under the head of "Enthusiasm" flourish unburdened by intrinsic disabilities. Hitler cannot claim Luther for a guide: for Luther's plan and ambition was the conversion of the Jews to the true faith, which had first risen from their midst. The full title of his blast of 1543, usually quoted as *Against the Jews* reads *Against the Jews and Their Lies,* with the emphasis resting in fact on the second half.

He had cherished the firm conviction, with regard to the Jews as to everybody else, that once the Christian faith was cleansed of the Roman perversions, they would all come over to it in a body.

In a tract of 1523, entitled *Jesus Christ was born a Jew,* Luther wrote, "The papists have so discredited themselves that a good Christian would rather be a Jew than one of them, and a Jew would rather be a pig than a Christian. I therefore beg my dear papists, when they get tired of abusing me as a heretic, to abuse me rather as a Jew." And, "What good can we do the Jews by restricting them, maligning them, and treating them like dogs? by denying them honest work and forcing them to usury? How can that help? We should use towards the Jews not the Pope's law of hate but Christ's law of love. If some are stiff-necked, so what? We are not all good Christians."

He offered personally to instruct a group of rabbis and convert them, to which they replied, by all means, yes, and they would undertake to make a Jew of him; which did not please Luther.

The papists published a circumstantial account of how Luther had gone to visit Rome in 1510 on purpose there to take lessons from a Jew named Jakob, with whom he devised his plot for the downfall of the papacy.

And then around 1540 genuine reports came in of an outbreak of Christian defections to Judaism in Moravia, where a taint of Enthusiasm evidently was persuading converts to the Reformed Religion that this must be the logical conclusion to evangelical fundamentalism. Meanwhile in twenty years of Lutheran propaganda very few Jews had come to be baptized, and few that had done so continued in the Christian faith for long. Luther seeing the faith beset on all sides was not only furious but worried.

". . . What now shall we Christians do with this unregenerate, damned people?" [For as witness their own Prophets the sufferings of this people were in any case God's punishment for their recalcitrance.] "To suffer them in our midst means laying ourselves open to indoctrination by their lies, curses, and blasphemies [in denying the divinity of Christ and casting aspersions on the virginity of Mary]. It seems we can neither extinguish the inextinguishable wrath of God against them nor convert them. We must indeed with prayer and with the fear of God before our eyes exercise a sharp compassion towards them and seek to save at least some of them from the flames of hell. Avenge ourselves we dare not. . . ." But in Christian self-protection as well as sharp compassion he went on to propose that the Jewish schools and synagogues, where their doctrines were disseminated, be burnt down; that their books should be taken away and their rabbis forbidden to teach (shades of Pfefferkorn); that they should be made to work on the land and debarred from practising usury (he was continually advocating total abolition of "usury," by which he understood capitalism in general), prevented from moving about, dispossessed so as to live all together "in one barn like Gypsies," in the hope that thus they might at last learn their lesson. But as he wrote on Luther became doubtful even of this method, and concluded with a fiery exhortation to drive out the Jews altogether—shipping them to Palestine lock, stock and barrel was one suggestion—unless they would desist from calumny and usury "and become Christians."

Bucer, Bugenhagen and others protested against Luther's anti-Jewish writings—there were three in all, two such vitriolic ones with a scholarly dissertation on the Jewish doctrinal errors in the middle.

While during the same years, 1543–46, Luther's writings against the Pope, against the Anabaptists, and incidentally against the women of Wittenberg whose newfangled costumes shamelessly exposed their bosoms, were calculated to make any fishwife blench, it is a sorry fact that he preached thus, too, against the Jews once more in the last sermon of his life.

In the main that sermon was concerned with the truths of the gospel; but before he had got very far he lost the thread and felt faint. For the first time in his life he had to break off, and, saying, "This and much more is to be said about the gospel, but I am too weak and will close here," left the pulpit.

That was on 15 February 1546. Three days later he was dead.

*

5. Obituary, 1546

On 23 January 1546 Dr. Martin Luther departed from Wittenberg
for the last time. He was in his sixty-third year, "a bag of rotting
flesh," grossly distended and tormented by a complex syndrome of
protracted bodily decline. He still had all his hair, coarse, grey, and
stubborn, and the coarse, strong, prominent facial bones beneath the
deeply marked grooves of strain and wrath maintained the appearance
of vigour and vitality; but that was as far as it went. He was counting
the days to the end of the world, and was praying for death.

"Though overwhelmed with age and weariness—old, cold, and half-
blind as the saying goes—I am allowed no rest, besieged by circumstances which compel me to write on, on, on, and talk myself
hoarse. I know more than you about the destiny of the world: that
destiny is destruction. According to my calculations we are getting
very near. It is inevitably so, seeing how triumphantly the Devil
struts about and how mankind grows daily worse and worse. The Word
of God has become a wearisome thing to man, a thing viewed with
distaste. . . . Germany is finished. All her vigour is in the past. . . .
Nothing remains but to pray, Thy will be done. . . . What, live forty
years more? You are kind, but I would rather give up my chance of
paradise. . . . If I get back to Wittenberg I will take to good eating
and drinking, so that the worms may have a fine fat doctor to feast
on."

The errand on which he left for Mansfeld in the worst winter
weather was a dispute between the heirs of the late Count of Mansfeld
about their inheritance. What was the good of having Martin Luther

for their vassal under law, if they could not call on him to adjudicate? ("Truly I am very much occupied with other affairs. But I feel I shall lie down on my deathbed with joy when I have seen my dear lords friends once more," he wrote them.) This was the third attempt. The first time Melanchthon had tried by himself, the second time he and Luther had gone together; now he was ill and could not leave his bed. Luther was always ill these days but hated taking to his bed so long as he could manage to stay upright. No doubt, in spite of all his expressed death wish, a part of him knew that once you stop, from weariness, weariness is liable to become master.

Luther's three sons went with their father, to take the opportunity to meet relations; also his learned factotum Aurifaber/Goldschmidt (popular with Kate as he had always been very good with the children, and popular with posterity for his version of Luther's table-talk, later on, when he also traded lucratively in Luther-relics), and Dr. Jonas. Kate had tried everything to keep Luther at home. She wrote, and he replied, almost daily.

"Grace and peace in Christ," he wrote to her from Eisleben, "and my poor old love, impotent as I know it is, my Käthe. I had an attack of vertigo just before reaching Eisleben, but it was my own fault—" for having walked beyond his strength until his clothes were soaked with sweat, and then sat, wet through, in the wagon for the remainder of that day's journey. "You no doubt would have blamed the Jews, for we had to pass through a village where many Jews live. Perhaps they blew on me! True it is that near that village such a cold wind blew on my head, through my cap, that my skull was almost turned to ice. . . . But now, thank God, I feel fine—only that the seductiveness of the beautiful women here is such that I do not fear unchastity!"

Still she fretted.

"Grace and peace in Christ, most holy Doctoress! We thank you most cordially for your great anxiety which keeps you from sleeping. For no sooner did you get rightly into your stride of worrying, than a fire in our lodging, just outside my door, almost consumed us. And only yesterday, without a doubt because of your care, a stone fell straight upon my crown—and was crushed as if in a mousetrap! This was intended to repay your saintly efforts, but the dear holy angels prevented. I fear, unless you stop worrying, the earth will finally swallow us up and all the elements persecute us. Is this how well

you have learned the catechism and creed? Pray, and let God attend
to the watching."

He had made the error, however, of telling her about "a huge
she-Anabaptist, threatening us with re-baptism," at a river crossing
delayed by boiling torrents and ice floes.

"Dear Katherine, you upset yourself as though God were not all-
powerful and able to raise up new Doctor Martins by the dozen,
if the old Doctor Martin were to be drowned in the Saale. . . . I
had intended this very day to start home again, but the troubles here
in my native place still detain me. Would you believe it, I am become
a lawyer! It doesn't look as if I'll do much good in that line; they had
much better let me exercise my proper profession. If would be a great
blessing for these people [his two Counts] if I could succeed in
humbling their stubborn arrogance. They speak and act as if they were
gods, but I fear they will become devils if they go on like this."

At last he was able to inform her, "We hope to be with you again
this week, if it please God. The Almighty has manifested the power of
his grace in this affair. The lords have come to an agreement on all
the points in dispute, except two or three [sic]. . . . I am to dine
with them today and will endeavour to unite them as brothers again.
They have written against each other with great bitterness, and during
all the conferences have not as yet exchanged a single word. . . .
Our young nobles are all gaiety now; they take the ladies out in
sledges and make the horses' bells jingle to a pretty tune. . . . I
send you some trout that Countess Albrecht has given me. . . . There
is a rumour that the Emperor is advancing towards Westphalia and
that the French are now stepping up enlistments as well as the Landgrave, et cetera, et cetera. True or false, it matters little: we await
God's will in patience."

The next she heard was about his last days, from Jonas.

The day after his letter, Valentine's Sunday, was the one when he
had had to break off in mid-sermon. He felt better next day and
prepared to leave the day after, the 17th, but again postponed departure to the morrow. He complained of spasms in the chest, submitted to massage with hot cloths, and accepted a sleeping draught.
Soon after midnight he woke up in great pain.

"I feel very ill. I believe I shall remain here in Eisleben, here where
I was born and baptized."

The apothecary and two physicians were hurriedly summoned to the burgomaster's house where the company was staying. Luther was taken into the sitting room, made to walk up and down, then laid on a leather-covered settle and heaped with clothes and cushions to induce perspiration. The room became more and more crowded; Count and Countess Albrecht joined in the ministrations. Luther began to pray aloud and thrice repeated at the end the dying words of Jesus as he had first learned them, in Latin. He became unconscious, they succeeded in rousing him again, Dr. Jonas asked, "Reverend father, do you die firm in the faith you have taught?" and Luther with an effort fixed his half-shut eyes on him and answered, "Yes." Then coma supervened; his breathing stopped at a quarter to three in the morning.

The senior physician examined the body and pronounced a stroke of apoplexy the immediate cause of death. The second physician quickly objected: impossible. An apoplectic stroke was known to be a divine judgment, and Luther had been a holy man. So the official cause of death was a heart attack.

Even so rumours were not slow to start, of Luther's having hanged himself from a bedpost, of his having been carried off by devils in a cloud of sulphur and brimstone. Other rumours countered with his visible ascent to heaven in the fiery chariot of the Lord.

The news went out, church bells began to ring wherever it was received, and rang on while Eisleben and Wittenberg contended for the corpse. Though Luther had lately declared himself completely disgusted with Wittenberg and had actually made plans to leave and turn himself into a wandering preacher, Wittenberg won. In a lead coffin, he was taken there along the hard-frozen roads, thickly lined with mourners, across two flooded rivers, bells ringing all the way, by a great cavalcade with the Counts of Mansfeld at the head.

They were prominent again in the funeral procession, which emptied every house in Wittenberg but for such as could neither walk nor be carried. Funerals are for the living, and they had as fine a one of it as was to be expected. Yet there were no princes in attendance, only "the officers of the Elector: all on horseback," proudly mentioned, like the black velvet pall and horse-drawn hearse, the orations and brass plate, with which the dead man was honoured.

Great affairs were brewing: the Council of Trent which, sitting off and on for eight years, cemented the Catholic Counter-Reformation but also thereby affirmed the final schism of the Western Church, had got started a few months before the death of Luther, and war between the Emperor and the Protestants broke out a few months after. He was well out of it; for the end of what he had begun was not then, and is not yet.

His will left everything to "my Katharina, because she has always been a gentle, pious, and faithful wife to me, has loved me tenderly and has by the blessing of God given me and brought up for me five children still living besides others now dead . . . and more especially because I would not have her dependent on her children, but rather that her children should be dependent on her, honouring and submissive to her. . . . For whatever may happen to her after my death, I know that she will ever conduct herself as a good mother. . . . And here I beg all my friends to testify the truth, and defend my dear Katharina, should it happen as is very possible that evil tongues should charge her with misdealings [when it comes to settling the estate]. I hereby depose that we have no hoard of ready money of any description. Nor should this surprise anyone if he will consider that I have had no income beyond my [university] salary and a few presents now and then, and that yet with these limited means we have done a fair amount of building and kept a large establishment. I consider it therefore a special favour of God, and I thank him daily, that our debts are not greater than they are. . . ."

Indited in the midst of life, this had he known it was corroborated by a confidential warning to the Prince of Anhalt:

"The home of Luther is occupied by a motley crowd of boys, students, girls, widows, old women, and children. For this reason there is much disturbance in the place, and many deplore it for the sake of the good man, the venerable father. If but the spirit of Doctor Luther lived in all these people under his roof, his house would afford you an agreeable, friendly opportunity of enjoying for a few days the society of that man. But as things are and under the existing conditions in the Luther household, I would not advise that Your Grace stop there."

Whose spirit, then, did the candid friend suppose, prevailed in the house of Luther? It grew quiet enough when he was gone.

"Who would not be sorrowful and mourn for so noble a man as was my dear lord?" Kate wrote to her sister two months after she had lost him. "I cannot tell the sorrow of my heart to anybody and I hardly know what I think or feel. I cannot eat or drink nor can I sleep, now that our Lord God has taken from me this dear and precious man. God knows that for grief and weeping I can speak no more even to dictate this letter."

The property he had left her included a farm, a second house "purchased under the name of Wolff," and valuables such as silver goblets, gold medals, and some jewellery, against debts he had estimated at the time at 450 gulden. At the time of his death there was not enough to keep her from want, when the professorial salary and presents ceased.

Luther, who when he had nothing else would give away even his children's christening mugs to the needy, and who had said, "If I wanted to be rich, I need only give up work and show myself at fairs: infinitely more people would pay money to see me there than will listen to me even free of charge,"—all the same he had left her much.

Moving about, without home of her own, to live with charitable relations—yet wherever she went, there was the evidence of him. In the everyday language of the living, she heard his tones; she heard his very words, his liturgy, his catechism, his robust, palpitating Bible text, in every church she entered, every town or village school she passed. She heard the hymns that he had written and composed, the first of their kind in the German mode and tongue—like marching songs of faith and trust, that inspired as they presaged the music of Johann Sebastian Bach—wherever people congregated or whistled at their work, she heard them. Wherever she looked, she might see a new world taking form, of which he was as much the progenitor as is any father of a child. All men grow old, and the rapture of generation cannot linger; but it can be recalled.

Kate, who died six years after him, at Torgau, had contributed her share to the larger legacy of Luther.

A celibate monk could not have led the Reformation, as its father figure; he could not have become plumped out into the image of that "healthy philistinism"—as some have called it—without which the rising middle classes of the sixteenth century would scarcely have given the evangelical movement their decisive support.

The bourgeois virtues—prudence, tidiness, conformity, willing sub-servience to dull routine—were notably missing from Luther's own life. Those who can't, teach; he proved in some ways perhaps too good a teacher.

"Healthy," the dictionary tells us, is what makes for soundness of body, morals, and social progress; "a philistine" is *an uncultured person, one whose interests are material, commonplace, prosaic,* and the origin of the term in that sense is tentatively traced to Germany about 1600, when it first appeared in print, which commonly lags behind colloquial usage.

"Culture" is a two-edged word and was so then as now—depending whether it be used in a complacent or a hostile mood. Certainly Luther denigrated culture insofar as it smelled of Romanism, Human-ism, or Rationalism—covering, indeed, a sizable area of humane ac-complishment; that he possessed an artist's imagination perhaps would not make him less a philistine, seeing that on the whole his artistic appreciation was tied up with content and subject matter. But his severest opponents could hardly charge him with predominantly *ma-terial, commonplace, prosaic* interests—save insofar as he strove with all his powers to render his transcendent spiritual interest so, to all. Perhaps nothing can be spread a long way without being spread thin, and flattened.

Exemplifying independent thought, freedom of conscience, and the right of individual action, he extolled authority and obedience to authority, disallowed reason and will, demanded herd-submissiveness: little recollecting that what goes for ideal sheep goes equally for Gadarene swine.

Devoting his life to the disestablishment of material values, he raised things material to new honour. So anxious had he been to show that in the heavenly valuation all earthly occupations are equal, that he fetched up at the inference that the practical, industrial occupations are superior to the spiritual and intellectual. His followers took him at his word, when and as this suited them.

For as soon as he was dead and there were no more fresh words to come from him, what had been work in progress without end was treated as a finished oeuvre. As he had himself quarried the Bible, so others quarried him. He had never anticipated questions until they arose, but when they did had never answered, "I don't know." Now that he could not answer any more, his disciples sought guidance through extended application of past rulings. It was necessary for the founding father to have provided a whole, fundamental code: his disciples were but his interpreters. And lo and behold, forthwith there were almost as many different interpreters of Luther as there were leading disciples, and each of them had the only correct key to his thought. So in addition to a new authoritarianism, bigotry, and intolerance, a new scholasticism reared its head. But it was not he who had claimed infallibility for himself, any more than he had considered himself indispensable.

Revolutions like men have to die young, to keep their beauty, and revolutionaries have to die martyrs if they are to end unsullied. Nothing mars the aesthetic integrity of a Hus or Savonarola. Had Martin Luther been seized as they, on the road back from Worms, had be too been burned at the stake—

If Luther had perished in what came to be enshrined as his finest hour—there would not have been such an imperishable shrine to the freedom and indomitability of the human spirit in its transient, vulnerable shell. If he had perished then, what would have remained but ashes, pure and weightless, just like those of other martyrs? Then we might believe that the inevitable fate of integrity is defeat and destruction. We might never have learned that it is possible for a man to stand on his own feet, alone, supported by nothing but an absolute belief in truth and right, and stay unfelled. If we have not learned, or understandably forget sometimes, that to be human, fallible and expendable, can yet be a thing to be proud of, now and then: we have our few, towering examples, if we will only look at them.

Postscript

Those who cannot remember the past
are condemned to repeat it.
George Santayana

The value of periodical reassessments of history was never more succinctly stated than in the above epigraph, which highlights the practical utility of studying the past. Today nothing is "good" that cannot
show utilitarian credentials: kindness, justice, charity bear the tacit
onus of proof that in the long run they are more advantageous to
society than cruelty, injustice, ruthlessness. Love is a four-letter word
that had best hide under a bushel of scientific euphemisms untainted
by emotional associations, lest it discredit both motive and object with
a flavour of either subconscious dishonesty or, worse still, corniness.

Although this is a development of our present century, the germ
of it can be traced back to Martin Luther, whose one driving desire
was to restore what he believed to be literally divine utterance to
the immediate use of man. The irony is that once again the concept of
"righteousness" has come to roost in the ledger of profit and loss. So
be it—as long as we remain clever enough to keep truth and honour
out of the red.

History does not in fact repeat itself. Show me one single pair of
interchangeable events in the annals of even one single country.
Parallels there are: but it is the distinguishing feature of parallels
that they never meet. Reflections there are: but a mirror image is
not identical with what it shows. Events are merely reminiscent of
each other, very often, affording mankind that store of cumulative
comparisons which in the individual human being is called "experience"
—a thing, again, by which one is expected to be able to profit.

The element of irony, however, is a constant figure in the pattern of the past, always especially prominent at those moments when events are in the balance, as yet capable of turning either way; and never more so than during that crucial period which determined whether or not the event known to us as the Reformation would go forward. In my view that moment came during Luther's stay at the Wartburg. Therefore this book has its beginning and its focus in the intersecting point of that particular crossroads.

In this way, too, the circumstances leading up to it reveal their significance from the outset, so that one does not have to go over them again in detail afterwards to relate them to the upshot, nor so to relate them in advance (e.g. "Little the future reformer knew . . .") and thereby destroy the storyteller's most vital assets: suspense and apparent freshness of impact. One of the most difficult things in historical appraisal is to cancel out the effect of a foreknowledge which yet cannot be denied (save by fictional treatment, anathema), and to keep that foreknowledge of ours from retrospectively informing the actors in a given drama, whose very *lack* of such clairvoyance, on the contrary, played an important part in their actions. One of the most fascinating things in the story of Luther's leading part in the Reformation is the progression of small things uniting and enlarging into a huge mass.

For all that innumerable factors unknown to himself came to the aid of Luther, and for all that individual character as a factor in history is at present rather out of fashion, the influence of this man's personal make-up and experience on the event as a whole is constantly in evidence; and it has been my endeavour to do equal justice to the personal and impersonal causes and effects.

Or to as many of them as can be picked out without negating the pattern and form, and bursting the manageable bounds, which are what makes a book, one book. Inevitably, much has been omitted, although I have tried to mitigate selection by, as it were, implicit coverage of aspects which had to be passed over. I mean that what is missing in the lines can yet be found between them; it is not ruled out or blocked up. This applies to persons as well as circumstances— and of course to anecdotes.

Thus the only two incidents in his childhood, which Luther mentioned, of excessive beatings by his parents—one at the hands of his mother, for "stealing" a nut, the other at the hands of his father "whom thereafter I bore such a grudge that he had to spend a long time winning me back to his presence,"—are contained in the general outline of his upbringing, his ambivalence in respect of authority, and his proposals of milder discipline for the young that were the context in which he instanced these memories. They are cited in every biography of Luther, without fail, and there was no necessity and no room for them in my text.

On the other hand, "Here I stand, I cannot do otherwise. God help me, Amen," though universally associated with Luther, could not be taken as read. It had to be there—the more as doubt has been cast on the accuracy of the reported words. This opens up another field of discussion. At a time when there were no mechanical means of recording speech and when but a very small minority practised a form of shorthand which at that was nothing more than a system of abbreviations, *all* reports we have, of sermons, conversations, and the rest, were done chiefly from memory. Why then boggle at that ringing phrase, and not at others: why be, like Elector Frederick's councillors in Aleander's estimate, more Lutheran than Luther? Luther himself not only did not disown the words, which fast made the rounds in popular publications, but adopted them in his own subsequent accounts of the occasion. Again, if here and there one of the words got changed or transposed, sometimes, that is nothing to make a song about: whose memory is infallible, of what he has said or written that he said? The gist and general impression of it are what matter. Even had he phrased that concluding chord entirely differently, "Here I stand" would still legitimately represent it. No one worries whether, "I guzzle like a Bohemian and swill like a German," or, "Philip has both matter and words, Erasmus has words without matter, I have matter without words, Karlstadt has neither matter nor words," were exact renderings of Luther's more hyperbolic remarks. Let us not fear to accept the smooth along with the rough.

Regarding Luther's statements that he was flogged fifteen times in one day at school and produced fifteen arguments why he should not be forced to acquire the doctorate, the same figure occurs in other connections, in his table-talk. Clearly, the number fifteen does not represent an accurate count but stands for "many," as we are apt to say "dozens" or "hundreds" when we mean "a few."

Regarding my translations from contemporary writings and reported dialogue, I subscribe heart and soul to Luther's marvellous analysis of translation work [Chapter 4, Part II], placing the spirit before the letter, and the sound and the feel of idiom before its now archaic dress, every time. In some cases, with particularly well-known passages, I have used renderings in standard currency, because long usage has lent them a monumental quality.

As regards nomenclature, I have followed German practice in now giving, now dispensing with the prefix "von" (prerogative of the nobility), according as its inclusion is informative or merely pedantic. The use of first names in their German forms (Hans, Andreas, Ludwig, etc.), side by side with English-version Frederick, Charles, Jerome and so forth, seemed to me an economical and blameless way of imparting local colour, without rendering certain universal, historic figures unrecognizable, for the sake of absolute consistency.

No liberties have been taken with the thoughts and feelings of the persons described, none being attributed to them that they did not themselves attest, although of course I claim the right to question their honesty or penetration in this respect when they seem dubious to me —but then, it will be found, I always say so. My opinions, inferences and deductions are my own, and naturally I believe in them; but again, these too are always clearly set out as distinct from hard-and-fast data. I hope that my reconstruction deserves to be called imaginative, but nothing in it is imaginary. The poetry comes all of the events themselves; there is no poetic licence.

While, as stated, the subject of this study is the turning point of the schism of the Western Church, one could not end it there any more than it could be approached without the organic build-up. What happened afterwards, too, had its seeds in the same juncture, and, curiosity apart, wants indicating. To take leave of Luther in a blaze of glory and unsullied virtue would defeat the very purpose of "proving" the man's humanity as well as the ironies, fortuities, and poignancy inherent in all human affairs. It would falsify and sentimentalize the picture: here omission would be tantamount to lie. For a balanced portrait, it was indispensable to look also on the seamy side; yet the balance of the book permitted but a sketch. Except insofar as the rounding-off of Luther's life as a family man had a lineal bearing on the growth of Protestantism, the meandering and very unsmooth path of its consolidatory period is here merely roughed out. For that is quite another story.

E. S.

Short Bibliography

Altensteig, Joh.: *Lexicon Theologicum, editio Veneta,* 1563

Andreas, Willy: Deutschland vor der Reformation, 1948

Aurifaber, Johannes: Colloquia oder Tischreden D. Martin Luthers, 1567

Bainton, Roland H.: Here I Stand, 1950

Barge, Hermann: Andreas Bodenstein von Karlstadt, 1905

Bartels, Adolf: Der Bauer in der Deutschen Vergangenheit, 1900

Bloch, Marc: Feudal Society, 1961

Boehmer, Heinrich: Martin Luther, Road to Reformation, 1957
Luther im Lichte der neueren Forschung, 1918
Luther's Journey to Rome, 1914

Bouquet, A. C.: Comparative Religion, 1953

Bouyer, Louis: The Spirit and the Forms of Protestantism, 1956

Brandi, Karl: The Emperor Charles V, 1939

Brandt, Otto H.: Die Fugger, 1928
Der grosse Bauernkrieg, 1925

Burgdorf, Martin: Luther und die Wiedertäufer, 1928

Butterfield, H.: Christianity and History, 1958

Chadwick, Owen: The Reformation, 1964

Clough, Shepard B. and Charles W. Cole: Economic History of Europe, 1946

Coulton, G. G.: Ten Mediaeval Studies, 1906

Daniel-Rops, H.: The Church of Apostles and Martyrs, 1960

Dietz, Philipp: Wörterbuch zu Dr. Martin Luthers Deutschen Schriften, 1961

Dürer, Albrecht: Dürers Briefe, Tagebücher und Reime (ed. Thausing), 1872

Eels, H.: Bucer, 1931

Fischer, L.: Dr. Martin Luther von den Jüden und ihren Lügen, 1838

Geiger, L.: Johann Reuchlin, 1891

Geisberg, Max: Die Reformation im Einblatt Holzschnitt, 1929

Grabinski, B.: Wie ist Luther gestorben?, 1910

Habler, Konrad: Die Stellung der Fugger zum Kirchenstreite des 16. Jahrhunderts, 1898

Hartfelder, K.: Philipp Melanchthon als Praeceptor Germaniae, 1889

Hessen, J.: Luther in Katholischer Sicht, 1949

Hofmann, F. G.: Katharina von Bora, oder Dr. M. Luther als Gatte und Vater, 1845

Holborn, Hajo: Ulrich von Hutten and the German Reformation, 1937

Hughes, P.: A History of the Church, 1948
    The Church in Crisis: A History of the General Councils, 1961

Huizinga, J.: Erasmus and the Age of Reformation, 1957

Huizinga, M.: The Waning of the Middle Ages, 1949

Hutten, Ulrich von: Opera (ed. Böcking), 1862

Kalkoff, Paul: Briefe, Depeschen und Berichte über Luther vom Wormser Reichstage 1521 (Schriften des Vereins für Reformationsgeschichte, XV), 1898

Kawerau, Gustav: Chronological list of Luther's writings, in Schriften des Vereins für Reformationsgeschichte, No. 129, 1917

Klingner, Erich: Luther und der Deutsche Volksaberglaube, 1912
Luther und die Entscheidungsjahre der Reformation von den Ablassthesen bis zum Wormser Edikt, 1917

Köstlin, Julius: Luthers Theologie in ihrer geschichtlichen Entwicklung, 1901

Kroker, E.: Katherina von Bora, 1906

Küchenmeister, Fr.: Luthers Krankengeschichte

Latourete, K. S.: A History of Christianity, 1954

Löhr, Joseph: Methodisch-kritische Beiträge zur Geschichte der Sittlichkeit des Klerus (Ref. gesch. Studien und Text, No. 17)

Lortz, Joseph: Die Reformation in Deutschland, 1949

Luther, Martin: Werke (Weimar Edition), 1883–
Geistliche Lieder, 1845
Luther's Bible, 1534: facsimile 1934

MacKinnon, James: Luther and the Reformation, 1930

Manschreck, Clyde Leonard: Melanchthon the Quiet Reformer, 1958

Meissinger, K. A.: Luthers Exegese in der Frühzeit, 1911

Müller, A. V.: Luthers Werdegang bis zum Turmerlebnis, 1920

Müntzer, Thomas: Politische Schriften (ed. Hinrichs), 1950

Murray, R. H.: Erasmus and Luther, 1920

Paulsen, F.: The German Universities and University Study, 1906

Phillips, Margaret M.: Erasmus and the Northern Renaissance, 1950

Posse, Hans: Lucas Cranach der Ältere, 1942

Prat, F.: The Theology of St. Paul, 1957

Ranke, Leopold von: Deutsche Geschichte im Zeitalter der Reformation, 1925

Rupp, Gordon: The Righteousness of God, 1953

Schlaginhaufen, Johann: Tischreden Luthers aus den Jahren 1531–1532 (ed. Preger), 1888

Sell, K.: Melanchthon und die Deutsche Reformation bis 1531, 1897

Smith, Preserved, and C. M. Jacobs (trans. and ed.): Luther's correspondence and Other Contemporary Letters, 1913

Spalatin, Georg: *Annales Reformationis* (ed. Cyprian), 1718

Steinberg, S. H.: Five Hundred Years of Printing, 1962

Stokes, F. F. (trans.): *Epistolae Obscurorum Virorum,* 1925

Tawney, R. H.: Religion and the Rise of Capitalism, 1942
The Agrarian Problem in the 16th Century, 1961

Taylor, H. O.: Thought and Expression in the 16th Century, 1959

Ulmann, H.: Franz von Sickingen, 1872

Volbeding, J. E.: Philipp Melanchthon, wie er leibte und lebte, 1860

Wappler, P.: Thomas Münzer und die Zwickauer Propheten, 1908

Wolf, Ernst: Staupitz und Luther, 1927

Wright, Thomas: History of Caricature, 1864

Wulf, Maurice de: Histoire de la Philosophie Médiévale, 1905

INDEX

as teacher, 53, 55–56, 66, 85–87, 95, 132
visit to Rome of, 53–54, 116–17, 124–25
will of, 353
Luther, Paul (son), 335

Machiavelli, Niccolò, 98
Magdeburg, Archbishop of (Albrecht von Hohenzollern), see Mainz, Archbishop of
Mainz, Archbishop of (Albrecht von Hohenzollern), 25, 127, 129–39, 140, 158, 179, 213, 249, 278, 336
in election of Charles V, 199–200
Luther's letters to, 133, 136, 270–71, 330
Mansfeld, Count of, 349
Marburg, Colloquy of, 342–43
Marburg, Inquisitor of (Konrad), 265
Margaret (Archduchess of Austria), 228, 230
Marriage
Luther on, 223, 224
of Luther, 307–8, 329–39, 350–51
polygamy, 345–46
of priests, 274–75, 303
Mass, 303
for dead, 275–76
first German, 279–80
Maximilian I (Emperor), 63, 97–99, 102, 103, 108, 164, 174, 197, 198, 228
death of, 178
at Diet of Augsburg, 154, 157–58, 159, 160–61
Medici, Giulio Cardinal de, 143, 172
Melanchthon, Philippus (Schwarzerd), 154, 165, 246, 266–67, 270, 275, 282, 283, 285–88, 292, 342, 343, 344, 345, 350, 359
intellectual brilliance of, 181–84
in Karlstadt-Eckius debate, 186, 189, 192
on Luther's marriage, 331–32
work on Lutheran system of, 205–6, 218, 272
Merseburg, Bishop of, 137
Michelangelo, 125, 126
Miltitz, Karl von, 254–55
as nuncio, 172–79, 200, 209, 226, 234, 236–37, 239
Modernism, 75, 79, 80
More, Sir Thomas, 76, 113, 137
Mosellanus, Professor, on Luther, Karlstadt, and Eckius, 190–91

Münzer, Thomas, 285
in Peasant War, 318, 320
Mutianic Poets' Circle, 104, 105, 115
Mutianus (Muth) Rufus, Konrad, 104–6
Mysticism, 80, 81, 162

Neighbour Andreas, see Karlstadt
Nero (Emperor), 260
Ninety-five Theses Concerning the Power and Efficacy of Indulgences (Luther), 132–41, 151, 187
Nominalism, 75, 79, 80

Occamism, 75, 79, 80
Oecolampadius, Ioannes (Hausschein), 342
Offer and Protest (Luther), 242, 243
On Double Righteousness (Luther), 188
On Monastic Vows ("Ten Day Book") (Luther), 276
On the Abolition of Private Masses (Luther), 278
On the Contemplation of the Blessed Passion of Christ (Luther), 188
On the Holiness of Popes (Karlstadt), 273
On the Marriage Estate (Luther), 188
Open Letter to the Christian Nobility of the German Nation concerning the Reform of Christianity (Luther), 221–23, 232
Ordination, Luther on, 223–24
Osiander, Andreas (né Hosemann), 342

Palatine, Elector, 10, 25, 146
Papacy, 61, 71–75
Luther on, 222
See also specific popes
Paris, University of, 50–51
Paul II, Pope, 119
Paul III, Pope, 126
Peasant Prophet, see Münzer, Thomas
Peasant War (1524–25), 314–23
Penance, Luther on, 223, 224
Peutinger, Konrad, 164, 167
Pfefferkorn, Johannes, in Reuchlin scandal, 109–10
Pfeffinger, Degenhard, 175, 176
Philip (Landgrave of Hesse), 13–14, 341, 342
bigamy case of, 345–46
in Peasant War, 319, 323
Pius II, Pope, 212, 213–14